THE HISTORY OF AL-ṬABARĪ

AN ANNOTATED TRANSLATION

VOLUME XX

*The Collapse of Sufyānid Authority
and the Coming of the Marwānids*

THE CALIPHATES OF MuꜤĀWIYAH II AND
MARWĀN I AND THE BEGINNING OF
THE CALIPHATE OF ꜤABD AL-MALIK

A.D. 683–685/A.H. 64–66

The History of Al-Ṭabarī

Editorial Board

Ihsan Abbas, University of Jordan, Amman

C. E. Bosworth, The University of Manchester

Jacob Lassner, Wayne State University, Detroit

Franz Rosenthal, Yale University

Ehsan Yar-Shater, Columbia University (*General Editor*)

*The preparation of this volume was made possible in part
by a grant from the National Endowment for the
Humanities, an independent federal agency.*

Bibliotheca Persica
Edited by Ehsan Yar-Shater

The History of al-Ṭabarī

(Ta'rīkh al-rusul wa'l mulūk)

VOLUME XX

The Collapse of Sufyānid Authority and the Coming of the Marwānids

translated and annotated
by

G.R. Hawting

School of Oriental and African Studies,
University of London

State University of New York Press

Published by
State University of New York Press, Albany

For information, address State University of New York
Press, State University Plaza, Albany, N.Y., 12246

Library of Congress Cataloging-in-Publication Data

Ṭabarī, 838?–923.
  The collapse of Sufyānid authority and the coming
of the Marwānids.
  (The history of al-Ṭabarī = Ta'rīkh al-rusul
wa'l mulūk ; v. 20) (SUNY series in Near Eastern
studies) (Bibliotheca Persica)
  Translation of extracts from: Ta'rīkh al-rusul
wa-al-mulūk.
  Bibliography: p.
  Includes index.
  1. Islamic Empire—History—661–750. I. Hawting,
G. R. (Gerald R.), 1944–   . II. Title. III. Series:
Ṭabarī, 838?–923. Ta'rīkh al-rusul wa-al-mulūk.
English ; v. 20. IV. Series: SUNY series in Near
Eastern studies. V. Series: Bibliotheca Persica
(Albany, N.Y.)
DS38.2.T313 vol.20   [DS38.5]   909'.1s 88-24983
ISBN 0-88706-855-3   [909'.097671]
ISBN 0-88706-857-X (pbk.)
10 9 8 7 6 5 4 3 2 1

Preface

THE HISTORY OF PROPHETS AND KINGS *(Ta'rīkh al-rusul wa'l-mulūk)* by Abū Jaᶜfar Muḥammad b. Jarīr al-Ṭabarī (839–923), here rendered as the *History of al-Ṭabarī*, is by common consent the most important universal history produced in the world of Islam. It has been translated here in its entirety for the first time for the benefit of non-Arabists, with historical and philological notes for those interested in the particulars of the text.

Ṭabarī's monumental work explores the history of the ancient nations, with special emphasis on biblical peoples and prophets, the legendary and factual history of ancient Iran, and, in great detail, the rise of Islam, the life of the Prophet Muḥammad, and the history of the Islamic world down to the year 915. The first volume of this translation will contain a biography of al-Ṭabarī and a discussion of the method, scope, and value of his work. It will also provide information on some of the technical considerations that have guided the work of the translators.

The *History* has been divided here into 38 volumes, each of which covers about two hundred pages of the original Arabic text in the Leiden edition. An attempt has been made to draw the dividing lines between the individual volumes in such a way that each is to some degree independent and can be read as such. The page numbers of the original in the Leiden edition appear on the margins of the translated volumes.

Al-Ṭabarī very often quotes his sources verbatim and traces the chain of transmission *(isnād)* to an original source. The chains of transmitters are, for the sake of brevity, rendered by only a dash (—) between the individual links in the chain. Thus, according to Ibn Ḥumayd—Salamah—Ibn Isḥāq means that al-Ṭabarī received the report from Ibn Ḥumayd who said that he was told by Salamah, who said that he was told by Ibn Isḥāq, and so on. The numerous subtle and important differences in the original Arabic wording have been disregarded.

The table of contents at the beginning of each volume gives a brief survey of the topics dealt with in that particular volume. It also includes the headings and subheadings as they appear in al-Ṭabarī's text, as well as those occasionally introduced by the translator.

Well-known place names, such as, for instance, Mecca, Baghdad, Jerusalem, Damascus, and the Yemen, are given in their English spellings. Less common place names, which are the vast majority, are transliterated. Biblical figures appear in the accepted English spelling. Iranian names are usually transcribed according to their Arabic forms, and the presumed Iranian forms are often discussed in the footnotes.

Technical terms have been translated wherever possible, but some, such as dirham and imām, have been retained in Arabic forms. Others that cannot be translated with sufficient precision have been retained and italicized as well as footnoted.

The annotation aims chiefly at clarifying difficult passages, identifying individuals and place names, and discussing textual difficulties. Much leeway has been left to the translators to include in the footnotes whatever they consider necessary and helpful.

The bibliographies list all the sources mentioned in the annotation.

The index in each volume contains all the names of persons and places referred to in the text, as well as those mentioned in the notes as far as they refer to the medieval period. It does not include the names of modern scholars. A general index, it is hoped, will appear after all the volumes have been published.

For further details concerning the series and acknowledgments, see Preface to Volume I.

Ehsan Yar-Shater

Contents

Preface / v

Abbreviations / ix

Translator's Foreword / xi

The Events of the Year 64 (cont'd) (683/684) / 1

The Caliphate of Muᶜāwiyah b. Yazīd / 1

ᶜUbaydallāh b. Ziyād and the People of al-Baṣrah Following
the Death of Yazīd / 6

The Deposition of ᶜAmr b. Ḥurayth by the People of al-
Kūfah and Their Appointment of ᶜĀmir b. Masᶜūd as
Governor over Them / 38

The Rendering of Allegiance to Marwān b. al-Ḥakam in
Syria / 47

The Battle at Marj Rāhiṭ between al-Ḍaḥḥāk b. Qays and
Marwān b. al-Ḥakam and Its Immediate
Consequences / 56

The Disturbances in Khurāsān Associated with ᶜAbdallāh b.
Khāzim / 70

The Beginnings of the Movement of the Penitents *(al-
Tawwābūn)* in al-Kūfah / 80

The End of the Khārijites' Support for ᶜAbdallāh b. al-
Zubayr in Mecca and the Dissensions among Them / 97

viii   Contents

The Arrival of al-Mukhtār in al-Kūfah / 105
Ibn al-Zubayr's Demolition of the Kaᶜbah / 122

The Events of the Year 65 (684/685) / 124

The Departure of the Penitents from al-Kūfah and Their
   Destruction by the Syrian Army at the Battle of
   ᶜAyn al-Wardah / 124
Marwān's Designation of His Two Sons ᶜAbd al-Malik and
   ᶜAbd al-ᶜAzīz as His Heirs Apparent / 160
The Death of Marwān / 160
The Failure of the Syrian Expedition against
   Medina / 162
The Plague of al-Jārif in al-Baṣrah / 163
The Threat to al-Baṣrah from Nāfiᶜ b. al-Azraq and the
   Khārijites and al-Muhallab b. Abī Ṣufrah's Victory over
   Them / 164
Ibn al-Zubayr's Dismissal and Appointment of Governors in
   al-Kūfah and Medina / 175
Ibn al-Zubayr's Rebuilding of the Kaᶜbah / 176
The Continuation of Tribal Warfare in Khurāsān under
   ᶜAbdallāh b. Khāzim / 177

The Events of the Year 66 (685/686) / 182

Al-Mukhtār's Revolutionary Movement in al-Kūfah and His
   Appeal to the Shīᶜah There / 182

Bibliography of Cited Works / 227

Index / 231

Abbreviations

Add. et emend.: List of *addenda et emendanda* included in the final
  volume of the Leiden edition of the text of al-Ṭabarī's *Ta'rīkh*.
Ar.: Arabic.
Cairo: The edition of al-Ṭabarī's *Ta'rīkh* by Muḥammad Abū al-
  Faḍl Ibrāhīm, 10 vols., Cairo, 1960–1969.
EI¹: The Encyclopaedia of Islam, first edition.
EI²: The Encyclopaedia of Islam, second edition.
GAS: F. Sezgin, *Geschichte des arabischen Schrifttums,* Leiden, 1967.
Gloss.: Glossary included in the final volume of the Leiden edition
  of the text of al-Ṭabarī's *Ta'rīkh*.
JAOS: Journal of the American Oriental Society.
JNES: Journal of Near Eastern Studies.
LA: Ibn Manẓūr, *Lisān al-ᶜarab,* 15 vols., Beirut, 1955–.
RSO: Rivista degli studi orientali.
TA: Al-Zabīdī, *Tāj al-ᶜarūs,* 10 vols., Benghazi, n.d.
Ṭabarī: When followed by a reference, the Leiden edition of the
  Arabic text of the *Ta'rīkh*.
tr.: Translation.
ZA: Zeitschrift für Assyriologie.
ZDMG: Zeitschrift der Deutschen Morgenländischen Gesellschaft.

In citations from the Qur'ān the numbering is that of Flügel's text.

Translator's Foreword

I. The context of events described in this volume

This volume of the translation of al-Ṭabarī's *History* covers the early years of what has come to be called the second civil war or the second *fitnah*. The background to the events described is the almost total collapse of Umayyad authority, even in the dynasty's heartland of Syria, following the death of Yazīd I and the short reign of his son Muʿāwiyah II, in 64 (683–84). In the vacuum which ensued, various political and religious groups attempted to seize leadership of the still emerging Arab-Muslim empire before, somewhat less than a decade later, the Umayyads were able to reimpose their caliphate over all the territories the Arabs had conquered. In addition to describing the events whereby the Umayyads, in the person of Marwān b. al-Ḥakam, managed to restore their position in Syria and Egypt, this volume is chiefly concerned with three of the movements which contested power with the Umayyads during the second civil war.

ʿAbdallāh b. al-Zubayr, associating himself closely with the sanctuary at Mecca, was recognized as caliph by many throughout the lands ruled by the Arabs. It is the gradual elimination by the Umayyads of his support and, finally, of Ibn al-Zubayr himself, which provides the main theme in the accounts of the second civil war. By the end of this volume, the Umayyads have, in effect, brought to an end Zubayrid ambitions in Syria and Egypt: in Syria as a consequence of the victory, in 64 (684) at the battle of Marj Rāhiṭ, of the pro-Umayyad Quḍāʿī tribal confederation over the pro-Zubayrid Qaysīs, and in Egypt as a result of expeditions sent there by the Umayyad

Marwān once his position in Syria was secured. In Iraq, Mesopotamia and the east, however, the Zubayrids remain dominant.

In Iraq, the Zubayrid dominance was threatened more by the emergence of movements claiming that religious and political leadership belonged by right to the Prophet Muḥammad's descendants through his cousin and son-in-law ᶜAlī, than by any Umayyad revival. Generally, these movements are referred to as Shīᶜite. In the present volume the history of two of these movements is described. First, there is that of the Penitents (the Tawwābūn), so called, it is said, because of the need they felt to repent their failure to help ᶜAlī's son al-Ḥusayn when he made a bid for power in 61 (680) at the battle of Karbalāʾ. The rise of this group in the Iraqi garrison town of al-Kūfah until its virtual annihilation at the hands of an Umayyad army in Mesopotamia is described here in some detail. Second, there is the development of the movement, again in al-Kūfah, led by Mukhtār, claiming to act on behalf of another son of ᶜAlī, Muḥammad b. al-Ḥanafiyyah. This volume of translation ends with the account of how Mukhtār and his followers seized the town and drove out the Zubayrid governor.

The third movement challenging the Umayyads and the other parties involved in the civil war is given the general name of Khārijite. At this period the movement, which is characterized by its stress on righteousness, rather than genealogy, as the only necessary precondition for the leader of the community, was strong among certain of the Arab tribes in Mesopotamia and Iraq. In the volume here we are told that the Khārijites at first united with Ibn al-Zubayr in his defense of the sanctuary against the Umayyads but then, as a result of religious and ideological divisions, broke with him and split into a number of subgroups. One of these, the Azāriqah, then raised a revolt in Iraq, and we are given a description of its vicissitudes before suppression by al-Muhallab on behalf of the Zubayrids.

Together with the accounts of these rival movements for power, the volume contains detailed accounts of the confused situation in two important provinces as a result of the power vacuum which followed the temporary collapse of Umayyad authority, sc. Iraq and Khurāsān. For Iraq, there is an account of the unsuccessful attempt to maintain his position by the former governor on behalf of the Umayyads, ᶜUbaydallāh b. Ziyād, of the effect this had on tribal divisions, and then of the recognition of Zubayrid authority in the province. For Khurāsān, there is an account of the troubles there associated with ᶜAbdallāh b. Khāzim's imposition of his own authority over the province. Again, we are told, these troubles had important consequences for the development of tribal factionalism among the Arabs.

The volume opens in the middle of an attack by an Umayyad army on Ibn al-Zubayr in Mecca. The army had been sent by the caliph Yazīd I b. Muᶜāwiyah with the double objective of subduing Medina, where a number of leading men had declared their rejection of Yazīd as caliph, and putting an end to the refusal of Ibn al-Zubayr in Mecca to accept Yazīd's caliphate. Previously, we have been informed that Ibn al-Zubayr's refusal to accept Yazīd went back even to the lifetime of Muᶜāwiyah I, who had attempted to secure the succession of his son while he himself was still alive. On the death of Muᶜāwiyah I, Ibn al-Zubayr had fled from Medina to Mecca to escape the attempts of Yazīd's governor to force him to declare his acceptance of Yazīd's caliphate. At first, Ibn al-Zubayr had not put himself forward as a candidate for the caliphate, but merely refused to recognize Yazīd.

Yazīd had then raised an army in Syria and sent it to the Ḥijāz under the command of Muslim b. ᶜUqbah al-Murrī. After capturing Medina following the battle on the Ḥarrah, Muslim had set out for Mecca, but died en route, and his position as leader of the army was taken by al-Ḥuṣayn b. Numayr al-Sakūnī. The latter had laid siege to Mecca and begun a bombardment with catapults, and in the course of the siege the sanctuary in Mecca, the Kaᶜbah, had been damaged by fire. Before the siege could be brought to a successful conclusion, however, news arrived of the death of the caliph in Syria, whereupon the besiegers entered into negotiations with Ibn al-Zubayr. The first section of this volume tells us of the outcome of these negotiations and of subsequent developments.

II. Tribes, clans, families, etc.

Prominent in many of the episodes recounted here are tribal divisions among the Arabs. During the second civil war these divisions really became important for the first time—in Syria in the events associated with the battle of Marj Rāhiṭ, in Iraq in connection with ᶜUbaydallāh b. Ziyād's attempt to maintain his authority, and in Khurāsān with Ibn Khāzim's *fitnah*. The emergence of large-scale and widespread tribal alliances and feuds among the Arabs in lands they had conquered is undoubtedly to be explained by reference to events in the period before the second civil war: migrations and tribal settlements which led to competition for land and resources, and the tendency of caliphs and governors to form links with particular groups among the Arabs thereby fueling the resentment of others. With the breakdown of Umayyad authority and the emergence of different contenders for power in the second civil war, the tensions and pressures which had been created now came to the surface.

The multiplicity and diversity of tribal names, and the relationship between them, can pose a problem for non-specialists. In the notes to the translation I have generally tried to identify the family or tribal affiliations of individuals and have frequently referred to Caskel and Strenziok's systematization of the work on the genealogy of the Arabs by the Muslim scholar Hishām b. Muḥammad al-Kalbī (d. 206(821)). But the nonspecialist may still find the names puzzling, and it may be useful, therefore, to attempt here a simplified account of the genealogy of the Arabs as elaborated by Muslim scholars, in the hope that the reader will be able to relate the more detailed information in the text and notes to this simplified scheme.

It is important to remember that complete agreement was never reached among the genealogists and that doubts and differences of opinion about the position in the scheme of this or that group persisted. Furthermore, the scheme as we know it was elaborated in Islamic times by Muslim scholars, and we cannot be sure how far it reflects the ideas of the Arab nomads themselves or how relevant it is to the situation of the Arabs before Islam. Finally, the scheme is presented as a genealogy, but it seems likely that this was a fiction which embodied the reality of alliances for political and other reasons, and there is clear evidence that at the time of the second civil war the genealogical position of important groups, notably the Quḍāᶜah in Syria, was changed in order to accommodate political and military realities.

The genealogists, then, distinguished two main descent groups among the Arab peoples, that is, the peoples who first developed the Arabic language in the Arabian peninsula and its geographical extension northward into the Syrian Desert. One group, regarded as the original inhabitants of Arabia, is said to be descended from a certain Qaḥṭān, perhaps to be identified with the Biblical Joktan (Gen. 10: 25–26). These may be conveniently referred to as "southerners" since they are said to have come from the southern regions of Arabia. Sometimes they are called Yemenīs. The other main group, the "northerners," is said to be descended from Ismāᶜīl (biblical Ishmael), the son of Ibrāhīm (Abraham), who, according to Muslim tradition, came to live in Arabia at a time when the "southerners" were already established there. These "northerners" are commonly called Nizār, after one of their ancestors, sometimes Maᶜadd, after another.

In this volume, several groups among the "southerners" are particularly prominent. In al-Baṣrah and Khurāsān, the Azd play an increasingly important role. They were relative latecomers to al-Baṣrah, whence many migrated to Khurāsān. Their rise in Khurāsān was closely associated with the career of al-Muhallab, himself an Azdī, and his family. In al-Kūfah, especially in connection with Mukhtār's revolt, Hamdān and Kindah seem to be the two most frequently mentioned southern tribal groups. In Syria, the Quḍāᶜah, under the leadership of the tribe of Kalb, were the chief supporters of the Umayyads following the death of Muᶜāwiyah II, the Umayyads having established marriage ties with the Kalb in the time of Muᶜāwiyah I and Yazīd I.

The "northerners" present a rather more complicated picture. They are subdivided into the two main groups of Muḍar and Rabīᶜah. In Iraq and the east Tamīm is the most prominent group among the Muḍar, while in Syria it is Qays.

The tribe of Quraysh, to which the Prophet Muḥammad belonged, was also part of Muḍar. Quraysh also numbered among its members the Hāshimid, Umayyad and Zubayrid families, as well as several other prominent families and individuals. The main group of Rabīʿah about whom we read in this volume is Bakr b. Wāʾil, established in Iraq and Khurāsān. Despite their common Nizārī descent, Tamīm and Bakr came to be hostile to each other and the Bakr (and other parts of Rabīʿah) formed an alliance with the Yemenī Azd against Tamīm (and other Muḍarī groups).

When a man's tribal origin is indicated by his *nisbah* (the part of his name which usually end in a long -*ī*), it is sometimes easy to place because it refers to one of the main groups already mentioned (al-Bakrī, al-Tamīmī, al-Qurashī, etc.), but more usually the *nisbah* refers to a family or clan within the wider group. For example, a man of Bakr might more commonly be called al-Sadūsī or al-Yashkurī or by a name derived from any of the many smaller groups which went to make up the Banū (i.e., the tribe of) Bakr, rather than simply al-Bakrī. In such cases, it is obviously important to relate the sub-group to the larger group of which it is a part, and it is hoped that the information provided in the footnotes here facilitates that task.

III. Al-Ṭabarī's sources in this volume

Al-Ṭabarī composed his work by selecting from and piecing together the reports of a number of earlier authorities. Indeed, much of his importance lies in the number of authorities which he quoted and which would now largely be lost to us if it were not for al-Ṭabarī's works: not only his *History* but also his voluminous Qurʾān commentary and other works. In the present volume, he draws upon a number of different sources, depending upon the area with which his work is concerned at any particular point. The bulk of his information is derived from two intermediaries, sc. ʿUmar b. Shabbah and Hishām b. Muḥammad al-Kalbī. The former, whose information mainly relates to events in al-Baṣrah and its dependency Khurāsān, transmits extracts from a variety of earlier sources, notably Abū al-Ḥasan ᶜAlī b. Muḥammad al-Madāʾinī. Ibn al-Kalbī, relevant mainly for events in al-Kūfah and to some extent those in Syria, transmits materials from two important earlier authorities, ᶜAwānah b. al-Ḥakam al-Kalbī and Abū Mikhnaf. In addition, al-Ṭabarī has material from Abū ᶜUbaydah, al-Wāqidī, al-Haytham b. ᶜAdī and other important earlier collectors and systematizers of historical tradition whose works have not come down to us.

The way in which the chain of transmitters (the *isnād*) for a particular report is set out is not always consistent: sometimes it is given complete; sometimes only parts of it are given, it being assumed that the reader understands this. I have sometimes, in the interests of clarity, inserted information in the *isnād*, usually signaled by parentheses. Ultimately, the material is usually traced back to eyewitnesses and participators in the events, many of whom cannot be otherwise identified. Brief information about the more important transmitters, together with references to works giving more information, is usually given in the note accompanying the first reference to the authority concerned.

The question of the authenticity of the reports given by al-Ṭabarī, of their value for reconstructing the events of which they purport to be a record, is too complicated to go into here. Suffice it to say that modern scholarship has drawn attention to the bias which inevitably affects the Muslim tradition at all stages of its collection and systematization, and to the literary stereotypes and topoi which it contains. Among many important analyses of the sources and methods of Muslim historians like al-Ṭabarī, his predecessors and contemporaries, particularly worthy of mention seem to me to be those by J. Wellhausen in his "Prolegomena zur ältesten Geschichte des Islams," in the introduction to his *Arab Kingdom*, and in his *Religio-Political Factions* (see the Bibliography at the end of this volume for full details); by Albrecht Noth in his *Quellenkritische Studien*; and more radically and succinctly, by Patricia Crone in the "Historiographical Introduction" to her *Slaves on Horses*.

IV. Principles of translation and acknowledgments

In general, I have attempted to translate on the basis of the printed Leiden text except where a comparison with other texts shows that the Leiden text needs to be modified. In such cases I have drawn attention to the alteration in a footnote. It has not proved possible for me to take into account any new manuscript material, but, even using the printed material which has become available since the Leiden edition was made, notably volumes IVb and V of al-Balādhurī's *Ansāb al-ashrāf*, I have been able to make what I think are a significant number of improvements to the Leiden text.

It should be noted, however, that appended to the Leiden text was a substantial list of *Addenda et emendanda*, which are frequently overlooked. Most of them were incorporated in the Cairo edition of al-Ṭabarī's *History*, and, at least for the part of the work translated here, virtually all of the occasions where the Cairo text differs from the Leiden can be explained by referring to the Leiden *Add. et emend.* It has seemed a good idea, therefore, to refer the reader to the *Add. et emend.* wherever my translation is based on it and consequently seems to depart from the printed text.

I have tried to translate Arabic technical terms as far as possible, but sometimes have judged it preferable to leave words or phrases in Arabic, with a footnote accompanying their first occurrence. Sometimes I have offered a simple translation but have alerted the reader to a possible problem by supplying the Arabic in parentheses.

I have become increasingly aware of the problems involved in translating a text which is relatively distant from us in time and culture; even apparently simple sentences acquire new complexities the more one looks at them. I have been helped considerably by a number of people who may not always have been aware of what they were doing when responding off the cuff to apparently random questions. In particular, I am grateful to my colleague at SOAS, Dr. A.A.M. Shereef, who has read the whole translation and offered innumerable valuable comments, and to Dr. Albert Arazi of the Hebrew University of Jerusalem, whose expertise in classical Arabic poetry saved me from several crass errors.

G. R. Hawting

The

Events of the Year

64 (cont'd)

(AUGUST 30, 683—AUGUST 17, 684)

The Caliphate of Muᶜāwiyah b. Yazīd

In this year, the oath of allegiance as caliph was given to Muᶜāwiyah b. Yazīd b. Muᶜāwiyah b. Abī Sufyān in Syria, and to ᶜAbdallāh b. al-Zubayr in the Ḥijāz.[1]

When Yazīd b. Muᶜāwiyah died, al-Ḥusayn b. Numayr and the Syrians continued fighting against Ibn al-Zubayr and his companions in Mecca—according to Hishām's report from ᶜAwānah[2]—for forty days. The Syrians had strenuously besieged Ibn al-Zubayr and his men and blockaded them. Then news of Yazīd's death reached Ibn al-Zubayr and his companions, but not al-Ḥusayn b. Numayr and his.

[430]

---

1. For background to the following section see p. xiii of the Introduction. For more details on ᶜAbdallāh b. al-Zubayr and al-Ḥusayn b. Numayr, see the articles s.vv. in *EI*². For parallels and other accounts, see Balādhurī, *Ansāb*, IVb, 51–2; Masᶜūdī, *Murūj*, V, 190–1; Yaᶜqūbī, *Ta'rīkh*, II, 301–2; Ibn al-Athīr, IV, 107–8; J. Wellhausen, *Arab Kingdom*, 165–7; G. Rotter, *Die Umayyaden und der zweite Bürgerkrieg*, 53–9, 134ff. (with other references to sources and secondary literature).

2. For Hishām b. Muḥammad al-Kalbī, important Kūfan scholar, d. *ca.* 206/ 821, see *EI*², s.v. Kalbī, and *GAS*, I, 268–71; for ᶜAwānah b. al-Ḥakam al-Kalbī, Kūfan collector of historical tradition, d. *ca.* 153/770, see *EI*², s.v., and *GAS*, I, 307–8.

According to Isḥāq b. Abī Isrā'īl—ʿAbd al-ʿAzīz b. Khālid b. Rustam al-Ṣanʿānī Abū Muḥammad—Ziyād b. Jiyal:[3] While Ḥusayn b. Numayr was fighting against Ibn al-Zubayr, news of Yazīd's death arrived unexpectedly. Ibn al-Zubayr then shouted to the Syrians saying, "Your tyrant[4] is dead. Whoever of you wishes to enter what the people have entered into, let him do so; but whoever is unwilling, let him take himself to his Syria!" Consequently, they left off fighting him.

Ibn al-Zubayr said to al-Ḥusayn b. Numayr, "Draw close to me and I will speak with you." He did so and Ibn al-Zubayr spoke with him. The horse of one of them began to drop dung (yajfilu; a gloss in the text explains that the word jafl here refers to dung, rawth) and the pigeons of the sanctuary area[5] started to scavenge in the droppings. Al-Ḥusayn reined back his horse from them and Ibn al-Zubayr said, "What is the matter with you?" He replied, "I am afraid lest my horse kill the pigeons of the sanctuary area." Ibn al-Zubayr said, "You would refrain from this sin[6] and yet you wish to kill the Muslims!" Al-Ḥusayn answered, "I will not fight you; allow us to perform the ritual circumambulation of the sanctuary[7] and then we will leave you." He did so, and they departed.

ʿAwānah b. al-Ḥakam said, according to the report of Hishām from him: When news of the death of Yazīd reached Ibn al-Zubayr, whom the Syrians, unaware of it, had strenuously

---

3. Isḥāq b. Abī Isrā'īl, d. 245/859 (Ṭabarī, III, 1121, 1440); the Leiden text gives the source of the report as Ziyād b. Jiyal, citing the reference in Dhahabī, *Mushtabih*, Leiden 1881, 88, to Ziyād b. Jiyal al-Abnawī as a Kūfan transmitter; the Cairo text has Ziyād b. Jabal.

4. Ar. *ṭāghiyah:* the word seems to be connected with an Aramaic or possibly Abyssinian root with the connotation of "great wickedness" and an association with idols (see A. Jeffery, *Foreign Vocabulary*, s.v. *ṭāghūt*); *ṭāghiyah* is often a designation of the Byzantine ruler.

5. Ar. *al-ḥaram*, here apparently the area surrounding the sanctuary (the Kaʿbah or *al-bayt*); in a general sense, any sacred area (such as those at Medina or Jerusalem) may be referred to as a *ḥaram*.

6. Following the reading of the Cairo text *a-tataḥarraju;* Leiden has *ataḥarraju*, "should I refrain. . . ?"

7. The sanctuary, *al-bayt*, is usually in this context a reference to the Kaʿbah (see *EI²*, s.v. Kaʿba); the ritual of *ṭawāf*, walking seven times around the outside of the Kaʿbah, is performed in connection with pilgrimage to Mecca (see *EI²*, s.v. Ḥadjdj).

besieged and blockaded, he and the Meccans began to shout out to them, "Why are you fighting? Your tyrant is dead!" At first they would not believe them, until Thābit b. Qays b. al-Munqaᶜ al-Nakhaᶜī[8] of the Kūfans arrived among the leaders of the Iraqis and passed by al-Ḥusayn b. Numayr. He was a confidant of his, there were marriage ties between them, and he had used to see him at Muᶜāwiyah's court. Ibn Numayr recognized the excellence of his character, the strength of his Islam, and the nobility of his descent, and he asked about the news. Thābit told him about Yazīd's death and thereupon al-Ḥusayn b. Numayr sent to ᶜAbdallāh b. al-Zubayr, saying, "Let us meet tonight in al-Abṭaḥ[9] to discuss what concerns us." [431] When they met, al-Ḥusayn said to Ibn al-Zubayr, "If it be that this man is dead, then you, of the people, have the most right in this matter. Come, and we will give you the oath of allegiance, and then leave with me for Syria. This army which is with me consists of the foremost of the Syrians and their champions. By God, there are not two of them who will disagree about you if you will grant the men security and indemnity for the blood spilled between us and you and between us and the people of the Ḥarrah."[10]

Saᶜīd b. ᶜAmr[11] used to say that the only thing which prevented Ibn al-Zubayr's accepting the oath of allegiance from them and leaving for Syria was a foreboding [taṭayyur], because it was at Mecca where God protected him—that was from the army of Marwān[12]—and, by God, if ᶜAbdallāh had gone

---

8. One of the ashrāf (tribal notables) of al-Kūfah exiled to Syria, where Muᶜāwiyah was governor, by the caliph ᶜUthmān; see Ṭabarī, I, 2917, 2921 and, on his name, Ansāb, IVb, 51.

9. Literally, "the hollow," a name applied to several places in and around Mecca, especially its central part; see Yāqūt, Buldān, I, 92–3, EI², s.v. Makka.

10. A reference to those killed at the battle outside al-Madīnah in Dhū al-Ḥijjah, 63 (August, 683) by the army of which Ibn Numayr subsequently assumed command (see EI², s.v. Ḥarra).

11. A leading Umayyad, his father had been governor of Medina for a time; elsewhere Ibn al-Kalbī cites information from him through his son Khālid.

12. The sense here seems rather elusive. Marwān at this time has not yet been chosen as caliph, and, even as caliph, he never sent an army against Ibn al-Zubayr in Mecca. It may be that we are to understand that Ibn al-Zubayr foresaw Marwān's being chosen as caliph [taṭayyur = "omen," "augury"], but that he would be inhibited in sending an army against him so long as he remained in Mecca, a sacred territory [ḥaram].

with them to Syria, no two of them would have disagreed about him. Some of Quraysh claimed that Ibn al-Zubayr said, "Shall I grant indemnity for this shed blood! Indeed, by God, I would not be satisfied if I killed ten for every man of those killed!"[13]

Al-Ḥusayn began to speak with him in private, but he answered publicly, saying, "No, by God, I will not do so." Al-Ḥusayn b. Numayr said to him, "May God shame whoever, henceforth, counts you as a subtle or intelligent[14] man! I thought you had perception, but do I not address you privately while you address me publicly, and I call you to the caliphate, but you threaten me with death and destruction."

Al-Ḥusayn arose and left, called out to his men, and set out with them toward Medina. Ibn al-Zubayr, however, repented of what he had done and sent a message to him, "As for going to Syria, I will not do it, for I do not like to leave Mecca; but give me the oath of allegiance here and I will grant you security and act justly among you." Al-Ḥusayn answered, "What do you think I am to do if you will not come yourself while I have found there (in Medina and/or Syria) many mem-
[432]   bers of this family[15] who are seeking it and to whom the men will respond?" So he continued with his men and those with him in the direction of Medina.

ᶜAlī b. al-Ḥusayn b. ᶜAlī b. Abī Ṭālib[16] met him. With him he had dates of fodder quality and barley, and he was riding a camel of his. He greeted al-Ḥusayn, but the latter scarcely paid any attention to him. Al-Ḥusayn b. Numayr had a well-bred mare of his own, but his own dates and barley for the mounts had run out and he was worried. He was reviling his serving lad, saying, "Where will we find here fodder for our mounts?" ᶜAlī b. al-Ḥusayn said to him, "We have fodder with us, so feed your mounts from it." Thereupon he gave

---

13. The text seems slightly ambiguous as to whether Ibn al-Zubayr agreed to give indemnity or not; Wellhausen, *Arab Kingdom*, 167, seems to draw the conclusion that he was willing to do so; Ibn al-Athīr, IV, 107, has a *lā*, clearly understanding that he was not.

14. Read *arīb* for *adīb* (*Add. et emend.*).

15. I.e., the Umayyads.

16. I.e., ᶜAlī Zayn al-ᶜĀbidīn, regarded as the third Imām by the majority of the Shīᶜah.

his attention to ᶜAlī, and the latter ordered that the fodder
he had with him be offered to him.

The people of Medina and the Ḥijāz became emboldened
against the Syrians, who were humiliated so much that no
man of them could go out alone without the bridle of his
mount being seized and he pushed off it. Consequently, they
gathered in their army camp and kept together. The members
of the Umayyad family said to them, "Do not leave without
taking us with you to Syria." So they did that and the army
continued until it reached Syria. There, Yazīd b. Muᶜāwiyah
had willed that the oath of allegiance be given to his son
Muᶜāwiyah b. Yazīd, but the latter survived for only three
months. According to ᶜAwānah, Yazīd b. Muᶜāwiyah designated
his son Muᶜāwiyah b. Yazīd as caliph, but the latter only
survived forty days.

ᶜUmar told me on the authority of ᶜAlī b. Muḥammad:[17]
When Muᶜāwiyah b. Yazīd had been designated caliph, gathered
together the officials of his father and the oath of allegiance
given to him in Damascus, he perished there after forty days
of his rule. His *kunyah* was Abū ᶜAbd al-Raḥmān and also
Abū Laylā.[18] His mother was Umm Hāshim bint Abī Hāshim
b. ᶜUtbah b. Rabīᶜah, and when he died he was thirteen years
and eighteen days old.

In this year also, the Baṣrans gave the oath of allegiance to
ᶜUbaydallāh b. Ziyād[19] on the understanding that he would   [433]
remain in control of their affairs until the people settled on
an *imām*[20] satisfactory to themselves. Then ᶜUbaydallāh sent
a messenger to al-Kūfah summoning the Kūfans to do the

---

17. For ᶜUmar b. Shabbah, a Baṣran scholar, d. 264/877, see *GAS*, I, 345;
for ᶜAlī b. Muḥammad, i.e., al-Madāʾinī, d. *ca.* 235/850, see *EI*[1], s.v. Madāʾinī;
GAS, I, 314–5; Rotter, "Zur Überlieferung einiger historische Werke Madāʾinīs
in Ṭabarīs Annalen," *Oriens*, XXIII–XXIV (1974), 103ff.

18. The *kunyah* is the part of the name describing a man as "father of so-
and-so" or "father of such-and-such," sometimes indicating real paternity,
sometimes used as a sort of nickname (see *EI*[2], s.v. Ism); for discussion of
the *kunyah*s of Muᶜāwiyah b. Yazīd, see H. Lammens, "Moᶜâwia II," 12–3,
17.

19. Son of Ziyād b. Abīhi, ᶜUbaydallāh had been made governor of Iraq by
Yazīd (see *EI*[1], s.v.).

20. Here, as generally in this volume, indicating the supreme leader of the
Muslims (see *EI*[2], s.v. Imāma).

same as the Baṣrans, but they refused and threw stones at the
prefect who was over them. Next the Baṣrans, too, came out
in opposition to ᶜUbaydallāh, civil commotion[21] sprang up in
al-Baṣrah and ᶜUbaydallāh b. Ziyād betook himself to Syria.

ᶜUbaydallāh b. Ziyād and the People of al-Baṣrah Following the Death of Yazīd[22]

According to ᶜUmar b. Shabbah—Mūsā b. Ismāᶜīl—Hammād
b. Salamah—ᶜAlī b. Zayd—al-Ḥasan:[23] Al-Ḍaḥḥāk b. Qays[24]
wrote to Qays b. al-Haytham[25] after the death of Yazīd b.
Muᶜāwiyah: "Greetings! Yazīd b. Muᶜāwiyah is dead. You are
our brethren, so do not anticipate anything we might do before
we have made a choice for ourselves."

According to ᶜUmar—Zuhayr b. Ḥarb—Wahb b. Ḥammād—
Muḥammad b. Abī ᶜUyaynah—Shahrak:[26] Following the death
of Yazīd b. Muᶜāwiyah I saw ᶜUbaydallāh b. Ziyād stand to
deliver an official address. He praised God and extolled Him
and then said:[27]

> Men of al-Baṣrah! Examine my origins and, by God,
> you will surely find that my father was an Emigrant

---

21. Ar. *fitnah:* of frequent occurrence in this volume, the word generally
indicates a time of trouble and distress, sometimes with apocalyptic overtones;
it is often applied to periods of conflict within the Muslim community (see
EI², s.v.).

22. For parallel and variant accounts of the following, see *Ansāb*, IVb,
97–123; *Naqā'iḍ Jarīr wa'l-Farazdaq*, 112–7, 721–44; Khalīfah b. Khayyāṭ,
Ta'rīkh, I, 324–5; Ibn al-Athīr, IV, 108–18; Wellhausen, *Arab Kingdom*,
209–10, 401–11; Rotter, *Bürgerkrieg*, 68–78 (with further references).

23. I.e., al-Ḥasan al-Baṣrī (d. *ca.* 110/728; see *EI²*, s.v.).

24. Of the clan of Fihr (of Quraysh), drawing support mainly from the
"northern" tribal grouping of Qays in Syria, he had control of Damascus
following the death of Muᶜāwiyah II, and he frequently appears in the following pages in connection with events in Syria (see *EI²*, s.v.).

25. Of the tribe of Sulaym (Qays), a previous governor of Khurāsān, he was
now one of the *ashrāf* of Muḍar in al-Baṣrah.

26. On the *isnād*, see Rotter, *Bürgerkrieg*, 70, n. 462.

27. For parallel versions of Ibn Ziyād's speech, see *Ansāb*, IVb, 115f.;
Naqā'iḍ Farazdaq, 722; *Murūj*, V, 194 ff.; Jāḥiẓ, *Bayān*, II, 130; for translations
or summaries, Wellhausen, *Arab Kingdom*, 402; Lammens, *L'avènement des
Marwānides*, 9f./49f.; and Rotter, *Bürgerkrieg*, 70–2.

and that my birthplace and abode are among you.[28]
When I became governor over you, the register of your
fighting men was reckoned at only 70,000, but today
it is counted at 80,000; and the register of your dependents[29] was only reckoned at 90,000, but today it
is counted at 140,000. I have not left alone any suspicious person whom I feared on your behalf but he
is in this prison of yours. The Commander of the　　　[434]
Faithful, Yazīd b. Muᶜāwiyah, has died and the Syrians
have fallen into dispute among themselves. Today you
are the biggest group of the people in numbers, the
most spacious of them as to your courts, the least
needful of them for others, and the most extensive of
them as to territory.[30] Choose for yourselves a man
whom you find pleasing for your religion and your
community and I shall be the first to accept and follow
him with whom you are pleased. Then, if the Syrians
agree on a man whom you find acceptable, you will
enter into that which the Muslims have entered. But,
if you dislike that, you will act independently until
you are given what you require. You need nothing
from any of the men of the provinces, but the people
cannot do without you.

The orators of the Baṣrans then arose and said, "We have
given ear to what you have said, Oh *amīr*, and we do not
know of anyone with more aptitude for it than you. Come,
therefore, and let us give you the oath of allegiance."
ᶜUbaydallāh replied, "I have no need for that. Choose somebody for yourselves." They insisted and he insisted until, when
they had repeated it to him thrice and insisted again, he held
out his hand and they gave him the oath of allegiance. After

---

28. Following the reading *la-tajidunna muhājir abī* (or *wālidī*) *wa-mawlidī
wa-darī fīkum*, as in *Ansāb* and the Cairo text of Ṭabarī; the Leiden text has
la-tajidunī a-hājara (uhājiruɬ) wālidī. "Emigrant" would refer to his father's
having left Arabia to settle in Iraq.

29. Following, with Rotter, the text of *Ansāb* (ᶜiyālatukum); the text of
Ṭabarī here has ᶜummāl, translated by Lammens as *employés*; Wellhausen has
mawālī.

30. I.e., with respect to the conquered land dependent upon it.

the oath of allegiance, however, they went away saying, "Surely the son of Marjānah[31] does not imagine that we will be led by him in both unity and dissension! He is wrong, by God!" Then they arose against him.

According to ʿUmar—Zuhayr—Wahb—al-Aswad b. Shaybān—Khālid b. Sumayr: Shaqīq b. Thawr,[32] Mālik b. Mismaʿ,[33] and Ḥuḍayn b. al-Mundhir[34] came to ʿUbaydallāh by night while he was in the government house,[35] and a man of the quarter of the Banū Sadūs[36] heard about that. This man said: I came and stuck close to the government house and they remained with him until the night had passed. Then they left with a mule heavily laden with treasures. I went up to Ḥu-

[435] ḍayn and said, "Tell them to give me something from these treasures," but he said, "Go and ask your cousin."[37] So then I went up to Shaqīq and said, "Tell them to give me something from these treasures." In charge of the treasures was a mawlā[38] of Shaqīq called Ayyūb. Shaqīq said to him, "Ayyūb, give him a hundred dirhams!" but I said, "A hundred dirhams! By God, I will not accept that." He did not speak to me for a time but continued on his way for a while. Then I went up to him

---

31. A scornful name for ʿUbaydallāh b. Ziyād, referring to his Persian mother Marjānah.

32. Of the Banū Sadūs, he was one of the *ashrāf* of Bakr b. Wāʾil (Rabīʿah) in al-Baṣrah and a contender for the leadership of Bakr there (see below, pp. 19, 25f.; P. Crone, *Slaves on Horses*, 120).

33. Of the Banū Shaybān, he was a rival of Shaqīq for the leadership of Bakr b. Wāʾil in al-Baṣrah; he later negotiated the alliance between Bakr and Azd (see below, pp. 25f., 28; and see Crone, *Slaves*, 116).

34. Of the Banū Shaybān, he was another *sharīf* of Bakr b. Wāʾil in al-Baṣrah (see Crone, *Slaves*, 113).

35. Ar. *dār al-imārah*; often, it seems to be synonymous with the governor's residence, but not always (e.g., pp. 40, 129 below, where there is mention of *al-qaṣr*, and 36, for Qaṣr al-Bayḍāʾ, which seems to have been Ibn Ziyād's residence).

36. For the genealogy of the Banū Sadūs b. Shaybān, a fraction of Bakr b. Wāʾil, see Caskel/Ibn Kalbī, I, table 153.

37. The text has "cousins" in the plural, but farther down the page the term reappears in the singular, and Ḥuḍayn seems to be referring to the relationship between the anonymous Sadūsī and Shaqīq b. Thawr.

38. A word which frequently indicates a client (an intermediate status between a slave and a free man) of a prominent Arab and/or a non-Arab adherent of Islam; however, the word does not necessarily tell us anything about the ethnic or religious derivation or status of the individual to which it is applied (see Crone, *Slaves*, 49 ff.).

again and said, "Tell him to give me something from these treasures." Shaqīq said, "Ayyūb, give him two hundred dirhams," but I said, "By God, I will not accept two hundred." Then he told him to give me three hundred, and then four hundred. When we reached al-Ṭufāwah,[39] I said, "Tell him to give me something," but he said, "If I do not, what do you think you will do?" I answered, "By God, I will go into the midst of the houses of our quarter, stick my fingers into my ears and then I will shout out at the top of my voice, 'Oh group of Bakr b. Wā'il,[40] here are Shaqīq b. Thawr, Ḥudayn b. al-Mundhir and Mālik b. al-Mismaᶜ, who have gone to Ibn Ziyād and made a pact about[41] your blood.'" Shaqīq said, "What is wrong with this man? May God do with him what He will! Woe to you! Give him five hundred dirhams." So I took it and went quickly on to Mālik. (Wahb said that he could not remember what Mālik ordered for the man.) Then I saw Ḥudayn and went in to him. He asked me what my cousin had done, and I told him and said, "Give me something from these treasures." But he said, "It was we who took this wealth and carried it to safety. We will have nothing to fear from the people." And he gave me nothing.

Abū Jaᶜfar (al-Ṭabarī) said: According to Abū ᶜUbaydah Maᶜmar b. al-Muthannā—Yūnus b. Ḥabīb al-Jarmī:[42] When ᶜUbaydallāh b. Ziyād killed al-Ḥusayn b. ᶜAlī (peace be upon him!) and his kin,[43] he sent their heads to Yazīd b. Muᶜāwiyah. At first, Yazīd was pleased about their killing and ᶜUbaydallāh's standing with him improved as a result of it. It was not long, [436] however, before Yazīd began to repent of the killing of al-Ḥusayn, saying, "What would it have been to me if I had borne the injury and lodged him with me, allowing him to

---

39. There is no entry for al-Ṭufāwah in Yāqūt's *Buldān*; Ṭabarī has two further references to this place in connection with events in al-Baṣrah, III, 290, 1855, neither of which helps to identify it.

40. For this tribal confederation, of which Sadūs was a part, see *EI*², s.v.

41. Ar. *iḥtalafū fī*; Cairo ed. has *ikhtalafū fī*, "they have disputed about."

42. For Abū ᶜUbaydah Maᶜmar al-Muthannā, Baṣran scholar d. 209/824–25, see *EI*², s.v.; Yūnus b. Ḥabīb al-Jarmī was a Baṣran philologist and teacher of Abū ᶜUbaydah.

43. A reference to the battle of Karbalā' in 680 when the Prophet's grandson, attempting a revolt against the caliph Yazīd, was killed by forces sent by the governor of Iraq, ᶜUbaydallāh b. Ziyād (see *EI*², s.v. Karbalā').

decide about what he wanted, even if it had been for me a loss and weakening of my authority, out of respect for the memory of the Prophet and regard for al-Ḥusayn's rights and kinship with him? God's curse on the son of Marjānah! It was he who drove him out and oppressed him. Al-Ḥusayn asked him to allow him to go back, but he would not, or to put his hand in mine, or to go to one of the frontiers of the Muslims where God might take him unto Himself, but he would not. He refused it, flung it back at him and killed him. He has made me hateful to the Muslims by killing him, and he has cultivated enmity for me in their hearts. Both the pious and the profligate hate me because of the gravity with which the people view my killing of al-Ḥusayn. What have I to do with the son of Marjānah, God's curse and hatred be upon him?"

Then ᶜUbaydallāh sent a mawlā of his called Ayyūb b. Ḥumrān to Syria to bring him news of Yazīd. One day, ᶜUbaydallāh was out riding and when he was in the Square of the Butchers he came unexpectedly on Ayyūb b. Ḥumrān, who had arrived back. Ayyūb came over to him and confided to him the news about the death of Yazīd b. Muᶜāwiyah. ᶜUbaydallāh, therefore, abandoned that trip of his and went to his abode where he gave orders to ᶜAbdallāh b. Ḥiṣn, one of the Banū Thaᶜlabah b. Yarbūᶜ,[44] who gave the call for an assembly for prayer.

According to Abū ᶜUbaydah—ᶜUmayr b. Maᶜn al-Kātib: The man ᶜUbaydallāh sent to Yazīd was his mawlā Ḥumrān. ᶜUbaydallāh paid a visit to ᶜAbdallāh, son of Nāfiᶜ the uterine brother of Ziyād,[45] and he left on foot by an opening which led from the house of Nāfiᶜ to the mosque. When he was in the courtyard of the mosque, suddenly there was Ḥumrān, his mawlā, as dusk was falling at evening. Ḥumrān had been the [437] messenger of ᶜUbaydallāh b. Ziyād to Muᶜāwiyah during his lifetime and to Yazīd. When ᶜUbaydallāh saw him, and he had

---

44. Part of the Banū Ḥanẓalah of Tamīm (Caskel/Ibn Kalbī, I, table 69).

45. Read *akhī* for *akhā* (see *Add. et amend.*); in other words, it is Nāfiᶜ who is the uterine brother of Ziyād (the father of Nāfiᶜ was allegedly the famous "doctor of the Arabs," al-Ḥārith b. Kaladah, who is said to have been the master of the slave girl Sumayyah, the mother of Ziyād; see *EI²* Suppl., s.v.).

only just arrived,[46] he said, "How goes it?"[47] and he replied, "Good." ᶜUbaydallāh asked, "How are things where you have come from?" and Ḥumrān replied, "May I draw near you?" ᶜUbaydallāh gave him permission and he confided to him about the death of Yazīd and the disputes concerning the affairs of the people of Syria. Yazīd had died on a Thursday in the middle of the month of Rabīᶜ I of the year 64 (November 683). ᶜUbaydallāh immediately hastened to give the order for someone to call an assembly for prayer.

When the people had gathered, ᶜUbaydallāh mounted the *minbar*[48] and announced the death of Yazīd. He set about criticizing him on account of what Yazīd had intended for him before he died, as a result of which ᶜUbaydallāh had come to fear him. Al-Aḥnaf[49] then said to ᶜUbaydallāh, "There was an oath of allegiance to Yazīd on our necks, and it used to be said, 'Avoid (speaking evil of) the dead,' so avoid it."[50] Then ᶜUbaydallāh arose, telling them of the divisions among the Syrians. He said, "When I became govenor over you . . . ," and Abū ᶜUbaydah reported it as did ᶜUmar b. Shabbah from Zuhayr b. Ḥarb as far as: "And they gave him the oath of allegiance of their good pleasure and as a result of consultation." Then Abū ᶜUbaydah continued (ᶜUmayr's account?): But when they left him, they began to wipe their hands on the door and walls of the house, saying, "The son of Marjānah imagines we have given him authority over our affairs in this discord!" He continued: ᶜUbaydallāh did not remain as governor long before his authority began to weaken. He gave us orders which were not carried out, he expressed opinions which

---

46. See *Add. et amend.*

47. Ar. *mahyam:* a word said to be of Yemeni origin (see R. Dozy, *Suppl.*, s.v.).

48. Often translated as "pulpit," it may better be envisaged as a podium, or even "throne," from which the caliph or his official delivered an important speech (a *khuṭbah*); it was a symbol of authority. On its origin and character, see C.H. Becker, "Die Kanzel im Kultus des alten Islam," in *idem, Islamstudien*, I, 450ff.; J. Sauvaget, *La mosquée omeyyade de Médine*, 138ff.; *EI²*, s.vv. Khaṭīb, Khuṭba.

49. Al-Aḥnaf b. Qays al-Tamīmī, a leader of the Tamīm in al-Baṣrah, proverbial for his tact and diplomacy (see *EI²*, s.v.).

50. See *Gloss*, s.v. *f-n-n* for the suggestion that *fanan* should here be read *qabr* and the subsequent translation; *Naqāʾiḍ Farazdaq*, 722, also reads *qabr*.

were rejected, and he ordered the wrongdoer to be imprisoned, but the governor's assistants were prevented from reaching him.

According to Abū ᶜUbaydah—Ghaylān b. Muḥammad—ᶜUthmān al-Battī: ᶜAbd al-Raḥmān b. Jawshan said:[51] I was walking in a funeral procession and when it reached the Camel Market suddenly there appeared a man on a grey mare, covered with weapons and with a banner in his hand. He was saying, "People, gather around me, for I am calling you to support that which nobody else does. I am summoning you to support 'He who takes refuge in the sanctuary area'[52] (meaning ᶜAbdallāh b. al-Zubayr)."

[438]   A few men rallied to him and began clasping his hand.[53] We went on our way until we had performed the prayers over the bier, and when we came back we found that he had been joined by more than those we had seen previously. Then he made his way between the dwelling place of Qays b. al-Haytham b. Asmā' b. al-Ṣalt al-Sulamī and that of the Ḥarithiyyūn[54] toward the Banū Tamīm on the road which leads to them, and he said, "If anyone wants me, I am Salamah b. Dhu'ayb." (He was Salamah b. Dhu'ayb b. ᶜAbdallāh b. Muḥakkim b. Zayd b. Riyāḥ b. Yarbūᶜ b. Ḥanzalah.)[55]

ᶜAbd al-Raḥmān b. Abī Bakrah[56] met me at the Square and I told him the news about Salamah after I had got back. He

---

51. ᶜUthmān al-Battī, d. 143/760, is well known as the recipient of a letter attributed to Abū Ḥanīfah; according to the version of this *isnād* in *Naqā'iḍ Farazdaq*, 722–3, Abū ᶜUbaydah heard Ghaylān giving the report to ᶜUthmān al-Battī, but, given the latter's death date, this seems unlikely; for the reading Jawshan instead of Ḥawshab, see *Add. et emend.*

52. More commonly given as *al-ᶜā'idh bi 'l-bayt*, "he who seeks refuge in the sanctuary," the title is said to have been used by Ibn al-Zubayr after his flight to Mecca and before he began to take the oath of allegiance to himself.

53. Sc. in giving him the oath of allegiance.

54. For Qays b. al-Haytham, see above p. 6, n. 25; the Ḥarithiyyūn are possibly the descendants of al-Ḥārith b. Wā'il of Rabīᶜah (see Rotter, *Bürgerkrieg*, 73, n. 486).

55. A Tamīmī who elsewhere is called al-Faqīh. For his descent, see Caskel/Ibn Kalbī, II, 504; *Naqā'iḍ Farazdaq*, 723, has Malḥam for Muḥakkim.

56. Both Leiden and Cairo have ᶜAbd al-Raḥmān b. Bakr, but the reading in *Ansāb*, IVb, 102, and *Naqā'iḍ Farazdaq*, 723, is to be preferred. ᶜAbd al-Raḥmān b. Abī Bakrah, Abū al-Ḥurr(?), was the brother of ᶜUthmān and ᶜUbaydallāh b. Abī Bakrah of Thaqīf and an associate of ᶜUbaydallāh's father, Ziyād; his family, with links to the Umayyads, was important in al-Baṣrah (see below, p. 36).

went to ᶜUbaydallāh and told him what he had heard from me. ᶜUbaydallāh sent for me, and when I went to him he said, "What is this which Abū al-Ḥurr⁵⁷ has reported to me from you?" So I told him the story to its end and then he gave the order and an assembly for prayer was proclaimed on the spot.

The men gathered and ᶜUbaydallāh began recounting the start of their joint concern—how he had appealed to them to choose whoever was pleasing to them and how he would give him the oath of allegiance together with them. "You refused to choose anybody but me, but now I have heard that you wiped your hands on the walls and door of the house and said what you said. I give orders which are not executed, my opinions are rejected, and the tribes obstruct my assistants from seizing those I seek. Now this Salamah b. Dhu'ayb is calling down discord upon you, desiring to split your community and that you will use the sword to smite each other's forehead."

Responding, al-Aḥnaf Ṣakhr b. Qays b. Muᶜāwiyah b. Ḥu-ṣayn b. ᶜUbādah b. al-Nazzāl b. Murrah b. ᶜAbīd b. al-Ḥārith b. ᶜAmr b. Kaᶜb b. Saᶜd b. Zayd Manāt b. Tamīm said while the men were gathered together, "We will bring you Salamah." They went off to get Salamah, but were surprised to find that his party had swollen and the division had widened beyond repair, and he refused to go with them. When they saw that, they held aloof from ᶜUbaydallāh b. Ziyād and did not go back to him. [439]

According to Abū ᶜUbaydah—several transmitters—Sabrah b. al-Jārūd al-Hudhalī—his father, al-Jārūd: In his address ᶜUbaydallāh said, "Baṣrans! By God, we have been wearing clothes of silk, (fine) Yemeni material and smooth stuff so much that we have come to loathe it and our skins have become disgusted with it. Now we have to follow it with iron. Men of al-Baṣrah! By God, even if you united against the tail of a wild ass to break it, you could not do it." Al-Jārūd continued: By God, not even a practice arrow was fired

---

57. The text has Abū al-Baḥr but, given the likely corruption of his name (see previous note), it seems likely we should read the *kunyah* as Abū al-Ḥurr with *Ansāb*.

before ᶜUbaydallāh fled and took refuge with Masᶜūd.[58] When Masᶜūd was killed, he betook himself to Syria.

(According to Abū ᶜUbaydah)—Yūnus (b. Ḥabīb al-Jarmī) said: In ᶜUbaydallāh's treasury on the day he addressed the people before the revolt of Salamah there were eight million dirhams or just under (ᶜAlī b. Muḥammad [al-Madā'inī] said nineteen million), and he said to the people, "These are your spoils,[59] so take your wages and the sustenance for your dependents out of them." He ordered the secretaries to count the men and set forth the names and he made them be quick about it, even appointing somebody to keep them there at night in the revenue office, and they lit the candles. When they had finished their task and withdrawn, and then there happened Salamah's opposition to him, he refrained from dividing the money and took it with him when he fled. To this day it is still circulating in the family of Ziyād. If there is a marriage or funeral among them, the like of them is never seen among Quraysh, and among Quraysh there is no one more affluent or better dressed than they.

ᶜUbaydallāh summoned the heads of the government detachment of the Bukhāriyyah[60] and desired them to fight for him, but they refused; he summoned the Bukhāriyyah themselves and desired of them similarly but they said, "If our [440] commanders tell us to, we will fight for you." And the brothers of ᶜUbaydallāh said to him, "By God, there is no caliph for whom you can fight, to whom you can go back if you are defeated, and who can send you help if you ask him for it. You know that war is a matter of fortune, and we do not know but that perhaps fortune will be against you. We have amassed wealth among these people (of al-Baṣrah), and if they

---

58. Masᶜūd b. ᶜAmr, the leader of Azd in al-Baṣrah (see below).

59. Ar. *fay'*: technically the immovable booty (i.e., land) conquered in the wars of conquest, and the property of the Muslim state as whole rather than of the particular warriors who conquered it; here the word may be intended in an untechnical and general way or it may refer specifically to income raised from the conquered land (see *EI²*, s.vv. Fay', Ghanīma).

60. A force, originally of two thousand men, which Ibn Ziyād had raised in Khurāsān when he was governor there (see Ṭabarī, II, 170; Narshakhī, *History of Bukhara*, tr. R.N. Frye, 37). For the reading of the text, which seems to have gone astray here, see *Add. et amend.*

are victorious they will destroy both us and it, and no remnant will be left for you." His brother ᶜAbdallāh, a full brother by his father and his mother Marjānah, said to him, "By God, if you fight this people I will lean on the tip of the sword until it comes out of my back."

When ᶜUbaydallāh heard that, he sent to al-Ḥārith b. Qays b. Ṣuhbān b. ᶜAwn b. ᶜIlāj b. Māzin b. Aswad b. Jahḍam b. Jadhīmah b. Mālik b. Fahm,[61] saying, "Oh Ḥār,[62] my father advised me that, if I ever had need of flight one day, I should choose you, and my soul rejects any other." Al-Ḥārith replied, "They have deserved well of you[63] for the help which they gave your father as you know, and they deserved well of him, but they found neither with him nor with you any recompense. If you choose to flee to us there will be no place of refuge for you, but I do not know how I should get you to a safe place[64] if I took you out by day. I am afraid that I would not reach my tribe with you before we would both be killed. However, I will stay with you until, when the darkness of night brings obscurity[65] and the footfall (of the traveler) is quieted,[66] you will ride on my mount behind me so as not to be recognized. Then I will take you to my maternal relatives of the Banū Nājiyah."[67] ᶜUbaydallāh answered, "All right; whatever you think."

---

61. The Banū Jahḍam b. Jadhīmah (the Jahādim) were a section of Azd (see Caskel/Ibn Kalbī, I, table 211); al-Ḥārith was a uterine brother of al-Muhallab b. Abī Ṣufrah.

62. Shortening the name in the vocative in this way is called *tarkhīm* (see Wright, *Grammar*, II, 88).

63. See *Gloss*, s.v. *b–l–w* (the reference to ᶜUbaydallāh's father and his lack of gratitude refers to the time when he was governor of al-Baṣrah for ᶜAlī in the first civil war and Muᶜāwiyah tried to stir up trouble in al-Baṣrah; at that time, Ziyād received help from the Azd Sarāt in the town).

64. See *Gloss*. s.v. *b–w–'*. However, the sense still seems problematic. The Cairo text has *wa-mā adrī kayfa ata'attā(?) laka in akhrajtuka naharan*. See also *Add. et amend.*

65. See *LA* s.v. d–m–s (VI, 88).

66. See E.W. Lane, *Lexicon*, s.v. *h–d–'*.

67. The Banū Nājiyah b. Jarm; for discussion of the genealogy of this group, for whom some canvassed a Qurashī descent, see I. Goldziher, *Muhammedanische Studien*, I, 188–9 (Eng. tr., I, 173–4), Caskel/Ibn Kalbī, II, 4–5, 75; see too L. Massignon, "Explication du plan de Baṣra," 158.

So he waited until, when one says, "Your brother or the wolf?"[68] al-Ḥārith carried him on his mount behind him. He had already removed those treasures and set a guard on them. Then he set off with him, passing with him by the men, who were keeping watch out of fear of the Ḥarūriyyah.[69] ᶜUbaydallāh was asking, "Where are we?" and al-Ḥārith kept telling him. When they were among the Banū Sulaym[70] ᶜUbaydallāh said, "Where are we?" and he answered, "We are among the Banū Sulaym," to which he responded, "God willing, we are safe."[71] Then when he reached the Banū Nājiyah he asked, "Where are we?" and al-Ḥārith said, "Among the Banū Nājiyah," to which ᶜUbaydallāh said, "God willing, we have got away."[72] The Banū Nājiyah, however, asked, "Who are you?" and he answered, "Al-Ḥārith b. Qays." "Your nephew," they said.[73] One of them, however, recognized ᶜUbaydallāh, said, "The son of Marjānah!" and fired an arrow which stuck in his turban. But al-Ḥārith continued on his way with him and lodged him in a house of his own among the descendants of Jahḍam b. Jadhīmah. Next, he went on to Masᶜūd b. ᶜAmr b. ᶜAdī b. Muḥārib b. Ṣunaym b. Mulayḫ b. Sharṭān b. Maᶜn b. Mālik b. Fahm.

The narrators of the Azd, Abū Mikhnaf and Muḥammad b. Abī ᶜUyaynah, said:[74] When Masᶜūd saw him he said, "Oh Ḥār, he has been granted refuge from the evils of the roads at night but we seek refuge with God against the evil which you have brought to us by night with him." But al-Ḥārith said, "I have only brought good to you by night. You know that your people saved Ziyād and fulfilled their obligations to

---

68. See *LA* s.v. *d–m–s* (VI, 88).

69. I.e., the Khawārij; the name is said to derive from that of the village near al-Kūfah, where the Khawārij established their camp at the time of their secession from ᶜAlī in the first civil war (see *EI*², s.v. Ḥarūrā').

70. Of Qays.

71. Ar. *salimnā*, a pun on the name of the Banū Sulaym.

72. Ar. *najawnā*, a pun on the name of the Banū Nājiyah.

73. Read *ibn ukhtikum* for *ibn akhikum* (see *Add. et amend.*), i.e., al-Ḥārith b. Qays is the son of a woman of the Banū Nājiyah.

74. The rather laconic note in *Add. et emend.* seems to suggest the *isnād* should be understood in this way (the text has "The Azd and Muḥammad b. ᶜUyaynah said:"); the latter was a nephew of al-Muhallab, and flourished in the late Umayyad period.

him, and this became among the Arabs a noble deed for them, which they could boast about over the others. Now you have willingly given the oath of allegiance to ᶜUbaydallāh, willingly after consultation,⁷⁵ and another oath of allegiance which was incumbent upon you before this one (meaning the oath of allegiance of the community)." Masᶜūd replied, "Oh Ḥār, do you think that we would fall out with our garrison comrades for the sake of ᶜUbaydallāh after the good we deserved on account of his father but then received no reward or thanks for it! I never considered that this would be your opinion." Al-Ḥārith answered, "Nobody would fall out with you on account of your fulfilling your oath of allegiance to the extent of bringing him to a place of safety."

Abū Jaᶜfar (al-Ṭabarī) said: According to ᶜUmar (b. Shabbah)—Zuhayr b. Ḥarb—Wahb b. Jarīr—his father—al-Zubayr b. al-Khirrīt—Abū Labīd al-Jahḍamī—al-Ḥārith b. Qays:⁷⁶ He, [442] that is ᶜUbaydallāh b. Ziyād, placed himself before me and said, "Truly by God, I realize the antipathy to me which has existed among your people." So I took pity on him and put him up behind me on my mule. It was nighttime and I took the direction of the Banū Sulaym. He asked me, "Who are these?" and when I told him, "The Banū Sulaym," he said, "God willing, we are safe." Then we continued on our way to the Banū Nājiyah who were sitting in assembly with their weapons by them, for at that time the people were sitting in their assemblies on watch. They said, "Who goes there?" I answered, "Al-Ḥārith b. Qays," and they said, "Pass, friend!" But when we passed on, one of them said, "By God, this is the son of Marjānah behind him!" and he fired an arrow and embedded it in the roll of his turban. ᶜUbaydallāh said to me, "Who are these, Oh Abū Muḥammad?" I replied, "Those who you claimed belonged to Quraysh⁷⁷—these are the Banū Nājiyah," and he said, "God willing, we have got away."

---

75. Read *riḍan ᶜan* for *riḍan min* (see *Add. et emend.*).

76. Wahb b. Jarīr was a Baṣran traditionist, d. 208/821; his father, Jarīr, d. 170/786, is the author of a book on the Azāriqah Khārijites (see below, p. 164, for Ṭabarī's citations, and see *GAS*, I, 310–1); note that Abū Labīd belongs to the Jahāḍimah, the clan of al-Ḥārith b. Qays.

77. See above, n. 67.

Then ᶜUbaydallāh said, "Oh Ḥārith, you have done well and acted excellently. Will you now do what I suggest? You know the standing of Masᶜūd b. ᶜAmr among his people, his noble descent, his seniority, and the obedience which his people show to him? Well, how about taking me to him, and then I will be in his dwelling place which is in the midst of Azd? If you do not, your people's affair will be shattered over you." I agreed and took him there. Masᶜūd knew nothing about it until we went in to him, and on that night he was sitting kindling a piece of wood on a brick and struggling with his shoes, one of which he had removed while the other stayed on. When he looked into our faces, he recognized us and said, "He has been given refuge from the evils of the roads." I said, "Would you send him away after he has entered your house?" So he told him what to do, and ᶜUbaydallāh entered the house of ᶜAbd al-Ghāfir b. Masᶜūd,[78] whose wife at that time was Khayrah bint Khufāf b. ᶜAmr.

[443]   On the same night, Masᶜūd, together with al-Ḥārith and a group of his people, saddled up and went around among Azd and their assemblies, saying, "Ibn Ziyād's absence has been noted and we fear that you will be held responsible for it, so come armed!" And the people did miss Ibn Ziyād, and said, "Where has he headed?" The answer was, "Nowhere but among the Azd."

(ᶜUmar b. Shabbah—Zuhayr b. Ḥarb)—Wahb—Abū Bakr b. al-Faḍl—Qabīṣah b. Marwān: They began to say, "Where do you think he has headed?" and an old woman of the Banū ᶜUqayl[79] said, "Where do you think he has headed! By God, he has thrust himself into the same thicket as his father did." When news of Yazīd's death reach Ibn Ziyād, there were sixteen million dirhams in the treasuries of al-Baṣrah, and he divided part of it among his father's descendants and carried off the rest with him. He had summoned the Bukhāriyyah to

---

78. I.e., Masᶜūd's son.

79. The Leiden edition is vocalized ᶜAqīl; the Banū ᶜUqayl (of Qays) seems more obvious; the Cairo text and *Ansāb*, IVb, 118[14] are unvocalized; Levi Della Vida preferred ᶜUqayl (see the note *ad. loc.* in the Jerusalem ed. of the *Ansāb*).

fight with him and also the descendants of Ziyād, but they refused.

According to ᶜUmar—Zuhayr b. Ḥarb—al-Aswad b. Shaybān—ᶜAbdallāh b. Jarīr al-Māzinī: Shaqīq b. Thawr sent to me, saying, "I have heard that this Ibn Manjūf[80] and Ibn Mismaᶜ have gone under cover of night to the dwelling of Masᶜūd to fetch Ibn Ziyād back to the government house[81] so they might unite these two forces[82] together, shed your blood and make themselves mighty. I had planned to send to Ibn Manjūf, put him in chains and send him away from me. So go to Masᶜūd, deliver my greetings to him and tell him that Ibn Manjūf and Ibn Mismaᶜ are doing such-and-such and he should send these two away from him." With Masᶜūd were ᶜUbaydallāh and ᶜAbdallāh the two sons of Ziyād. So I went to Masᶜūd and the two sons of Ziyād were with him, one on his right and the other on his left. I said, "Peace be upon you, Abū Qays,"[83] and he replied, "And upon you." Then I said, "Shaqīq b. Thawr sent me to you to deliver his greetings to you and to say that he has heard . . . ." (He repeated the words exactly down to: "So send those two away from you.") Masᶜūd said, "By God, I will do that."[84] ᶜUbaydallāh then said, "How so, Oh Abū Thawr?" He forgot his *kunyah*, for he was only called Abū al-Faḍl.[85] And his brother ᶜAbdallāh said, "By God, we will not separate from you. You have given us shelter and promised us protection and we will not leave unless we are killed in your midst, which would be a disgrace against you until the Day of Resurrection."

[444]

---

80. Suwayd b. Manjūf b. Thawr al-Sadūsī, i.e., Shaqīq's nephew. For the rivalries within the family of Thawr, see *Ansāb*, IVb, 92.

81. Ar. *al-dār*.

82. Ar. *hādhayn al-ghārayn*; the word *ghār* has the double meaning of "army" and "pit" (see Lane, *Lexicon*, s.v.).

83. Presumably Masᶜūd's *kunyah*?

84. Literally, "I have done that" (i.e., "done!") following the reading of the Cairo ed. and Bevan's proposal in the *Add. et. emend. (faᶜaltu dhāka)*; the Leiden text has *qultu dhāka*, which is difficult to make sense of.

85. Ibn Ziyād seems to be addressing Masᶜūd, using a *kunyah*, although Masᶜūd has already been addressed by his *kunyah* as Abū Qays; then we are told that, presumably in his agitation, Ibn Ziyād had made a mistake in the *kunyah*; it should have been Abū al-Faḍl. It seems possible that the text is disordered; note how Shaqīq, sent to bring back Ibn Manjūf and Ibn Mismaᶜ, now seems concerned with the two sons of Ziyād.

(ᶜUmar b. Shabbah—Zuhayr)—Wahb—al-Zubayr b. al-Khir-rīt[86]—Abū Labīd: The Baṣrans gathered and delegated their affairs to al-Nuᶜmān b. Ṣuhbān al-Rāsibī[87] and a man of the Muḍar[88] so those two could choose somebody for them and give him authority over them. They said, "Whomever you two are satisfied with for us, we will be satisfied with him." (According to other than Abū Labīd, the man of Muḍar was Qays b. al-Haytham al-Sulamī.) The man of Muḍar thought that a candidate should be chosen from among the Banū Umayyah, while al-Nuᶜmān's view was that he should be from the Banū Hāshim.[89] However, al-Nuᶜmān said he did not think anyone had more right to authority than so-and-so, indeed a man from the Banū Umayyah. The Muḍarī said, "Is that what you think?" and al-Nuᶜmān answered, "Yes." The Muḍarī, therefore, said, "I have invested my authority in you and I will be satisfied with whomever you are satisfied with." Then they both went out to the people and the Muḍarī announced, "I will be satisfied with whomever al-Nuᶜmān is satisfied with. Whomever he names for you, I will be pleased with him." Then they said to al-Nuᶜmān, "What do you say?" He replied, "I do not consider fitting for it anybody other than ᶜAbdallāh b. al-Ḥārith, Babbah."[90] Thereupon the Muḍarī said, "This is not the one you named to me," but al-Nuᶜmān said, "Yes indeed, by my life, it was he!" And the people were pleased with ᶜAbdallāh and gave him the oath of allegiance.

According to my companions,[91] Muḍar called for support for al-ᶜAbbās b. al-Aswad b. al-ᶜAwf[92] while Yemen[93] called

---

86. Cf. p. 17 above, where Jarīr is cited in the *isnād* between Wahb and Ibn al-Khirrīt.

87. Of Quḍāᶜah; see p. 446 below, but cf. Rotter, *Bürgerkrieg*, 76, n. 512, and Caskel/Ibn Kalbī, II, 453, 485.

88. According to the genealogists, this is the "northern" descent group which includes Qays and Tamīm, but not Rabīᶜah.

89. Two families of Quraysh, the former that from which the three previous caliphs had come, the latter that of the Prophet, ᶜAlī and the future ᶜAbbāsid caliphs.

90. A Qurashī of the Banū Hāshim (on him, see W. Madelung, "ᶜAbd Allāh b. al-Zubayr and the Mahdī," *JNES*, XL [1981], esp. 297 ff.).

91. Presumably it is Wahb b. Jarīr who is speaking?

92. Of Quraysh, he would be a nephew of ᶜAbd al-Raḥmān b. ᶜAwf and brother of Jābir b. al-Aswad, Ibn al-Zubayr's governor over Medina.

for support for ᶜAbdallāh b. al-Ḥārith b. Nawfal. So the people agreed to appoint Qays b. al-Haytham and al-Nuᶜmān b. Ṣuhbān al-Rāsibī as arbitrators to look into the question of the two candidates. Both the arbitrators agreed that they should confer authority on the man of Muḍar belonging to the Banū Hāshim[94] until there should be general agreement on an *imām*. About that it was said: [445]

> We have effected a deposition and appointed a governor
> while Bakr b. Wā'il
> dallies[95] seeking someone with whom to make an
> alliance.

And when they gave Babbah authority over al-Baṣrah, he appointed Himyān b. ᶜAdī al-Sadūsī[96] over his police force.[97]

Abū Jaᶜfar (al-Ṭabarī) said: As for Abū ᶜUbaydah (according to the report of Muḥammad b. ᶜAlī from Abū Saᶜdān from him), he told the story about Masᶜūd and ᶜUbaydallāh b. Ziyād and his brother differently from the way in which Wahb b. Jarīr told it on the authority of those from whom he transmitted it. Abū ᶜUbaydah said: Maslamah b. Muḥārib b. Salm b. Ziyād[98] and others of Ziyād's family, reporting from those of them and their mawlās who were alive at the time (the family knows best its own story), told me that al-Ḥārith b. Qays never spoke to Masᶜūd but granted protection to

---

Muṣᶜab al-Zubayrī, *Nasab Quraysh*, 273, lists an ᶜAyyāsh among the offspring of al-Aswad but no ᶜAbbās. Rotter, *Bürgerkrieg*, 77, n. 514, argues that ᶜAyyāsh is the correct form and should be read here. Other reports give the name of the candidate as ᶜAbdallāh b. al-Aswad (see below). Rotter thinks that this is the brother of ᶜAyyāsh, while Madelung, *loc. cit.*, 301, seems to regard ᶜAbdallāh and ᶜAbbās as variant names for the same man (Zubayrī does not list an ᶜAbdallāh b. al-Aswad).

93. A name for the "southern" descent group according to the genealogists.

94. As a Qurashī, Babbah belongs to the wider group of Muḍar (see above, n. 88).

95. Literally "draw out its testicles" (see *Gloss.*, with reference to Freytag, *Proverbia* II, 480, n. 263, and Lane, *Lexicon*, s.v. khaṣā). See below, p. 26, n. 128, for parallels.

96. Of Bakr b. Wā'il.

97. Ar. shurṭah, a small force controlled by the governor and distinct from the tribally based army.

98. Maslamah was the grandson of the brother of ᶜUbaydallāh b. Ziyād; see Rotter, "Madā'inī," 117 (for Salm b. Ziyād, see below, pp. 70f.).

ᶜUbaydallāh, took 100,000 dirhams with him, and came with it to Umm Bisṭām, the wife of Masᶜūd and his own paternal cousin. With him were ᶜUbaydallāh and ᶜAbdallāh, the two sons of Ziyād. He asked permission to go in to her and when she granted it, al-Ḥārith said to her, "I have come to you about a matter in which you would become the leader of your women and secure the nobility of your people, and you would be paid on the spot wealth and riches. In particular, there is this 100,000 dirhams for you. Take it, it is yours, if you will take in ᶜUbaydallāh." But she replied, "I am afraid that Masᶜūd will not like it and will not accept him." Al-Ḥārith then said, "Clothe him in one of your garments, take him in to your house and leave Masᶜūd to us." So she took the money and did that. But, when Masᶜūd came, she told him about it and he seized her by the head, whereupon ᶜUbaydallāh and al-Ḥārith came out of her chamber and the former said, "Your cousin has granted me protection in respect of you. This is your garment I am wearing, your food in my belly, and your house around me." Al-Ḥārith testified to the truth of that for him and they both mollified Masᶜūd until he agreed. Abū ᶜUbaydah said: ᶜUbaydallāh gave al-Ḥārith about 50,000 dirhams and he remained in Masᶜūd's house until Masᶜūd was killed.

[446]

Abū ᶜUbaydah—Yazīd b. Sumayr al-Jarmī—Suwwār b. ᶜAbd Allāh b. Saᶜīd al-Jarmī:[99] When ᶜUbaydallāh fled, the Baṣrans were for some time without an *amīr* and they differed as to whom they should give authority over them. Then they agreed on two men who would make a choice for them, and they would accept the choice if those two could agree on it. They agreed that Qays b. al-Haytham al-Sulamī and Nuᶜmān b. Ṣuhbān[100] al-Rāsibī (Rāsib b. Jarm b. Rabbān b. Ḥulwān b. ᶜImrān b. al-Ḥāf b. Quḍāᶜah) would choose someone they found acceptable. Those two mentioned two possibilities: ᶜAbdallāh b. al-Ḥārith b. Nawfal b. al-Ḥārith b. ᶜAbd al-Muṭṭalib (his

---

99. Abū ᶜUbaydah's sources seem to be Quḍāᶜī kinsmen of al-Nuᶜmān b. Ṣuhbān (see n. 87 above).
100. The text has al-Nuᶜmān b. Sufyān.

mother was Hind bint Abī Sufyān b. Ḥarb b. Umayyah,[101] he was nicknamed Babbah and he was the grandfather of Sulaymān b. ᶜAbdallāh b. al-Ḥārith[102]) and, alternatively, ᶜAbdallāh b. al-Aswad al-Zuhrī.[103] When they had both agreed on those two, they decided on the public square[104] as the place for the selection and they arranged for the people to meet there so that they might come to an agreement on one of these two. So the people were gathered there and I was with them in the "brow"[105] of the square (its top part). Qays b. al-Haytham came forward, and then al-Nuᶜmān afterwards, and they were preoccupied one with another. Al-Nuᶜmān gave Qays to believe that he favored Ibn al-Aswad, but then said, "We cannot speak both together," and desired that he would make him the spokesman. Qays did so and they contracted one with another. And al-Nuᶜmān imposed a promise on the people that they would accept whatever he thought best.

Then al-Nuᶜmān went up to ᶜAbdallāh b. al-Aswad, took his hand and began to lay conditions upon him so that the people thought he was about to give him the oath of allegiance. But he left and took the hand of ᶜAbdallāh b. al-Ḥārith and started imposing conditions on him in the same way. Next he praised God and extolled Him, mentioned the Prophet and the rights of his family and relatives, and said, "Oh people, what do you have against a man descended from the paternal uncle of your Prophet and whose mother was Hind bint Abī Sufyān? He is a man of the Banū Hāshim and also son of a woman of those who possess the kingship."[106] Then he clasped him

[447]

---

101. Descended on his father's side from the Prophet's grandfather, ᶜAbd al-Muṭṭalib, Babbah's mother was the sister of the first Umayyad caliph, Muᶜāwiyah.

102. Sulaymān b. ᶜAbdallāh al-Nawfalī, a prominent Hāshimī of the early ᶜAbbāsid period and transmitter of some historical material relating to al-Saffāḥ and al-Manṣūr.

103. See n. 92 above.

104. Ar. *mirbad*; for a tentative sketch map of al-Baṣrah at this period, see Massignon, "Baṣra," 157; see also M. Morony, *Iraq after the Muslim Conquest*, 246.

105. Ar. *qāriᶜah* (the gloss is in the text).

106. It is difficult to make sense of Ṭabarī's text here ("if he is one of them, he is the son of your sister"); Ibn al-Athīr has: *qad kāna 'l-amru fīhim fa-huwa 'bnu ukhtihim* ("authority belonged to them [the Umayyads] and he [Babbah] is the son of one of their women"); *Ansāb*, IVb, 104[22] (the same report as Ṭabarī from Abū ᶜUbaydah) has: *huwa Hāshimī wa-'bnu ukhti 'l-qawmi 'lladhīna 'l-mulku fīhim*, the reading translated here.

by the hand, saying, "Indeed I approve of you for it," and they cried out, "We accept!" They brought ᶜAbdallāh b. al-Ḥārith to the government house and he dwelled there. That was at the beginning of the month of Jumādā II, 64 (January, 684). He appointed Himyān b. ᶜAdī al-Sadūsī over his police force and summoned the people to come to give the oath of allegiance. They came and gave him it.

When he gave him the oath of allegiance, al-Farazdaq[107] said:

I have given the oath of allegiance to many people and
I have fulfilled the pledge to them;
but to Babbah I have given the oath of allegiance
without repenting.[108]

Abū ᶜUbaydah—Zuhayr b. Hunayd[109]—ᶜAmr b. ᶜĪsā: The dwelling place of Mālik b. Mismaᶜ al-Jaḥdarī was in al-Bāṭinah[110] by the gate of ᶜAbdallāh al-Iṣbahānī in the quarter of the Banū Jaḥdar[111] near the great mosque. Mālik used to frequent the mosque. While he was sitting in it shortly after the affair of Babbah,[112] there was a man of the family of ᶜAbdallāh b. ᶜĀmir b. Kurayz al-Qurashī[113] in the group in the mosque in which he was sitting, and news came of ᶜAbdallāh b. Khāzim's attack on Rabīᶜah in Herat.[114] A quarrel broke out and the Qurashī spoke rudely to Mālik, whereupon a man of Bakr b. Wā'il struck the Qurashī and those there of Muḍar and Rabīᶜah became incensed one with another.[115] The members of Rabīᶜah who were in the group were in the

---

107. I.e., the poet Hammām b. Ghālib, d. 110/728 or 112/730 (see EI², s.v. al-Farazdaḳ.).

108. Variants cited by Madelung, "ᶜAbd Allāh b. al-Zubayr and the Mahdī," 302.

109. For the form of the name, see *Add. et emend.*

110. See Massignon, "Baṣra," 157.

111. The Banū Jaḥdar was Mālik's clan within the Banū Qays b. Thaᶜlabah (Shaybān); for its descent, see Caskel/Ibn Kalbī, I, table 155.

112. The Leiden text is corrupt here; see *Add. et emend.* for the text translated here, and cf. *Ansāb*, IVb, 105²¹¹.

113. A former governor of al-Baṣrah and Khurāsān, related by marriage to the Umayyads (see, Zubayrī, *Nasab Quraysh*, 147–9).

114. See pp. 73ff. below.

115. ᶜAbdallāh b. Khāzim al-Sulamī (of Qays/Muḍar) had originally been given authority in Khurāsān by ᶜAbdallāh b. ᶜAmir; Mālik belonged to Bakr b. Wā'il of Rabīᶜah, the object of Ibn Khāzim's attack.

majority, but someone shouted out, "Come on Tamīm!" and
a group of Ḍabbah b. Udd[116] who were with the judge heard   [448]
the shout, seized the spears and shields of the guards from
the mosque,[117] bore down on the members of Rabīᶜah and
routed them. Ashyam b. Shaqīq b. Thawr al-Sadūsī,[118] who at
that time was head of Bakr b. Wā'il, heard about that and
came to the mosque. He said, "Indeed, you shall not come
upon anyone of Muḍar but you will kill him!" When Mālik
b. Mismaᶜ heard about it, he came in his indoor clothes[119] to
pacify the people and they refrained from fighting one another.
They remained like that for a month or less and then a man
of the Banū Yashkur[120] was sitting in the mosque with a man
of the Banū Ḍabbah, and they talked about the Bakrī's striking
the Qurashī, and the Yashkurī boasted about it.

The Yashkurī then said that the blow had been received
without retaliation[121] and thus annoyed the Ḍabbī, who struck
him on the neck. The people in the mosque gave him a fatal
blow, and he—I mean the Yashkurī—was carried dead to his
people. Bakr then flew to their chief Ashyam b. Shaqīq and
said, "Come along with us." But he answered, "No, rather I
will send a messenger to them and if they give us our rights,[122]
well and good, but if not, then we will go to them." Bakr,
however, rejected that and went to Mālik b. Mismaᶜ.

(Previously, Mālik b. Mismaᶜ had had authority over them
before Ashyam, but the latter had obtained the headship when
he went to Yazīd b. Muᶜāwiyah and Yazīd had written to
ᶜUbaydallāh b. Ziyād on his behalf, telling them to restore the
leadership to Ashyam. The Lahāzim[123] (that is, the Banū Qays

---

116. Allies of Tamīm (see *EI²*, s.v.; Caskel/Ibn Kalbī, II, 240).

117. The *min* seems slightly odd; *Ansāb*, IVb, 106², omits it: *(wathaba ᶜalā)
rimāḥi ḥarasi 'l-masjidi wa-tirasatihim*.

118. The text reads Shaqīq b. Thawr, but cf. the next paragraph and the
parallel in *Ansāb*, IVb, 106.

119. Ar. *mutafaḍḍilan* (see Lane, *Lexicon*, s.v. *mifḍal*).

120. Subtribe of Bakr b. Wā'il.

121. See *Add. et emend.* for the reading *ẓalafan*; perhaps Wellhausen's
paraphrase (*Kingdom*, 405), based on the printed *ṭilqan*, indicating that the
Yashkurī claimed the Qurashī had taken the blow without retaliating and was
therefore dishonored, gives the intended sense?

122. Read *shani'ū* for *sayyabū* (see *Add. et emend.*).

123. For the following see Caskel/Ibn Kalbī, II, 26–7, *EI¹*, s.v. Taimallāh
b. Thaᶜlaba, and *EI²*, s.v. Bakr b. Wā'il, 963b, at the bottom.

b. Thaᶜlabah with their allies ᶜAnazah, and Taym al-Lāt[124] with their allies ᶜIjl) had refused unless they and the family of Dhuhl b. Shaybān with their allies Yashkur, and Dhuhl b. Thaᶜlabah with their allies Ḍubayᶜah b. Rabīᶜah b. Nizār, all agreed—the four tribes balanced with the other four. This alliance had existed among the nomads of the Banū Bakr in the Time of Ignorance before Islam,[125] but Ḥanīfah had re-

[449]   mained apart from the other tribes of Bakr and had not joined this alliance in the Time of Ignorance because they were settled. Then they had entered Islam with their brothers ᶜIjl and become Lihzimah.[126] Afterwards, they had accepted the decision of ᶜImrān b. ᶜIṣām al-ᶜAnazī, one of the Banū Humaym, and restored the headship to Ashyam.)

Now, when this civil commotion broke out, Bakr considered Mālik b. Mismaᶜ as of little account, for he lacked weight. He, therefore, gathered his men and made ready and sought of the Azd that they would renew the alliance which had existed between them previously in unity concerning Yazīd b. Muᶜāwiyah.

Concerning that, Ḥārithah b. Badr[127] said:

> We have effected a deposition and appointed a governor while Bakr b. Wā'il
> dallies seeking someone with whom to make an alliance
> And no Bakrī passes a night out of time,
> and comes to morning without recognizing the disgrace.[128]

Abū ᶜUbaydah continued: While ᶜUbaydallāh was in the abode of Masᶜūd, he heard the news of the falling out of Bakr and Tamīm. He, therefore, said to Masᶜūd, "Go and meet Mālik and renew the previous alliance between you." Consequently, Masᶜūd met Mālik and the two of them began to

---

124. Text has Shayᶜ al-Lāt.
125. Ar. *jāhiliyyah* (see *EI²*, s.v. Djāhiliyya).
126. I.e., the angle of the lower jaw (see Lane, *Lexicon*, s.v., in supplement).
127. Ḥārithah b. Badr al-Ghuḍānī of Tamīm.
128. See above, p. 21; *Ansāb*, IVb, 106; *Naqā'iḍ Farazdaq*, 112, 729; see too Mubarrad, *Kāmil*, 435.

discuss that pact.[129] However, a party on each side rejected their joint decision, and ᶜUbaydallāh, therefore, sent his brother ᶜAbdallāh together with Masᶜūd with plenty of money (so much that he spent more than 200,000 dirhams in that business) to ensure that the dissidents would give the two of them the pledge of allegiance.[130] ᶜUbaydallāh said to his brother, "Make sure of the feelings of the people (of Bakr) toward the people of Yemen." They renewed the alliance and wrote two documents between them, like the two documents they had written[131] between them in unity, and they deposited a document with Masᶜūd b. ᶜAmr.

Abū ᶜUbaydah: One of Masᶜūd's descendants told me that the first of those named in the document was al-Ṣalt b. Ḥurayth b. Jābir al-Ḥanafī.[132] And they also deposited a document with al-Ṣalt b. Ḥurayth in which the first of those named was Ibn Rajā' al-ᶜAwdhī[133] of ᶜAwdh b. Sūd. Previously, there had been an alliance between them.

Abū ᶜUbaydah: Muḥammad b. Ḥafṣ, Yūnus b. Ḥabīb, Hu-[450]
bayrah b. Ḥudayr,[134] and Zuhayr b. Hunayd claimed that Muḍar outnumbered Rabīᶜah in al-Baṣrah and that the group of the Azd was the last to settle there; they were where the garrison town of al-Baṣrah was founded and ᶜUmar b. al-Khaṭṭāb moved into it those Muslims who adopted a fixed abode,[135] while the group of the Azd remained where they were and did not move. But they had come to al-Baṣrah subsequently at the end of the caliphate of Muᶜāwiyah and the beginning of that of Yazīd b. Muᶜāwiyah. When they came there, the Banū Tamīm said to al-Aḥnaf, "Make an approach to these newcomers before Rabīᶜah anticipate us in it." But

---

129. Read *tarāssā* (see *Add. et emend.*, and *Gloss.*, s.v. *rassa*).

130. Read *yubāyiᶜuhumā* (see *Add. et emend.*).

131. Read active for passive (see *Add. et emend.*).

132. For the suggestion that Ḥanafī be read Juᶜfī, see *Add. et emend.*

133. *Naqā'iḍ Farazdaq* has him as Abū Rajā', and, at p. 126, refers to his tomb at al-Baṣrah. ᶜAwdh b. Sūd is a tribe of Azd (for its descent, see Caskel/Ibn Kalbī, I, table 206).

134. See *Add. et emend.*

135. The printed text with its reference to the tribe of Tanūkh must be corrupt (see *Add. et emend.* which suggests the reading *man tanakha* with the interpretation adopted here; the reading is adopted in *Naqā'iḍ Farazdaq*, 729).

al-Aḥnaf answered, "If they come to you, then accept them, but otherwise do not go to them because, if you do, you will become followers of theirs." So Mālik b. Mismaᶜ went to them, and at that time the chief of Azd was Masᶜūd b. ᶜAmr al-Maᶜnī.[136] Mālik said to him, "Let us renew the pact which existed between us and Kindah in the Time of Ignorance and the pact of the Banū Dhuhl b. Thaᶜlabah with Thuᶜal of Ṭayyi' b. Udad."[137] Al-Aḥnaf said, "Indeed, since they went to them they will always be to them as following tails!"

Abū ᶜUbaydah—Hubayrah b. Ḥudayr—Isḥāq b. Suwayd: When the Bakr were led[138] to seek the help of Azd against Muḍar and renewed their previous alliance and desired that they should set out, the Azd said, "We will not go with you unless the chief is one of us." So they made Masᶜūd chief over them all.

Abū ᶜUbaydah—Maslamah b. Muḥārib: Masᶜūd said to ᶜUbaydallāh, "Come with us so that we can restore you to the government house," but he answered, "I cannot do that, you go." So Masᶜūd ordered his mounts, they fastened their equipment and saddles[139] on them, and he was engrossed in the preparations for the journey. They brought out a chair for [451] ᶜUbaydallāh which was placed at Masᶜūd's door and he sat in it. Masᶜūd set off, and ᶜUbaydallāh sent with him in charge of the horses some slaves of his to whom he said, "I do not know what is going to happen, so I am telling you that, if such-and-such happens, one of you is to bring me the news, but, whatever happens, make sure that one of you comes to me with news of it." What happened was the Masᶜūd never came to a lane or passed by a tribe without one of those slaves bringing ᶜUbaydallāh news of it.

---

136. The Banū Maᶜn b. Mālik b. Fihr of Azd (*Ansāb*, IVb, 98²⁻³); elsewhere he sometimes has the *nisbah* al-ᶜAtakī.

137. "Us" refers to Mālik's own tribe of Qays b. Thaᶜlabah (of Shaybān/Bakr b. Wā'il); Kindah is the important tribal group counted as "southerners" by the genealogists (*EI²*, s.v.; Caskel/Ibn Kalbī, I, tables 176, 233, II, 371); Dhuhl b. Thaᶜlabah also belongs to Shaybān/Bakr b. Wā'il; Thuᶜal is Thuᶜal b. ᶜAmr, a subtribe of Ṭayyi' b. Udad, the important tribal group of the north Arabia-Mesopotamia area, counted as "southerners" by the genealogists (Caskel/Ibn Kalbī, I, tables 176, 249, 252, II, 555).

138. Read *ujī'at* (see *Add. et emend.*).

139. Read *wa-shawāraḥā* (see *Add. et emend.*).

Mas{c}ūd came to Rabī{c}ah[140] under Mālik b. Misma{c} and together they took the lane to the public square, where Mas{c}ūd
continued until he entered the mosque and ascended the *minbar*. {c}Abdallāh b. al-Ḥārith was in the government house, and
he was told that Mas{c}ūd had come with the people of Yemen
and Rabī{c}ah and that trouble was going to be stirred up among
the people. "So why do you not make peace between them
or ride against them with the Banū Tamīm?" he was asked.
He replied, "God damn them! By God, I will not corrupt
myself by conciliating them." One of Mas{c}ūd's men began to
say:

Indeed, I will marry Babbah
    to a maiden in a tent
    who combs the head of her doll.[141]

This is what the Azd and Rabī{c}ah say, but as for Muḍar, they
say that it is what his mother, Hind bint Abī Sufyān, used to
say rocking him in his cradle.

When nobody prevented Mas{c}ūd's ascending the *minbar*,
Mālik b. Misma{c} went out with his troop of armed men until
he overlooked al-Jabbān[142] from the road to the public square
[*sikkat al-mirbad*]. Then he began passing several of the dwellings of the Banū Tamīm and entered the lane of the Banū al-
{c}Adawiyyah[143] opposite al-Jabbān and started to set fire to their
dwellings because of the hatred which was in their hearts as
a result of the Ḍabbī's killing the Yashkurī and Ibn Khāzim's
slaughter of Rabī{c}ah in Herat. But while he was engaged in
that, suddenly they came to him and said, "They have killed
Mas{c}ūd," and they said, "The Banū Tamīm have attacked
Mas{c}ūd." So he set off, but when he was near the mosque of
the Banū Qays in the road to the public square, he came to
a halt, hearing the news of the killing of Mas{c}ūd.

[452]

---

140. *Ansāb*, IVb, 107[4], suggests that *qadima* should be read *qaddama*, i.e.,
Mas{c}ūd sent Rabī{c}ah ahead.
141. See the note to *Ansāb*, IVb, 107[9], and Madelung, *op. cit.*, 297, for
other citations and variants.
142. Al-Jabbān was one of the six cemeteries of al-Baṣrah (see Massignon,
"Baṣra," 157, 161).
143. A subgroup of the Banū Ḥanẓalah of Tamīm (see Caskel/Ibn Kalbī, I,
table 59, II, 136).

Abū ᶜUbaydah—Zuhayr b. Hunayd—al-Ḍaḥḥāk or al-Waḍ-dāḥ b. Khaythamah, one of B. ᶜAbdallāh b. Dārim—Mālik b. Dīnār:[144] I was one of the youths who went to al-Aḥnaf, waiting to see what would happen. I came to him and then the Banū Tamīm came and said, "Masᶜūd has entered the govenor's residence, and you are our *sayyid*," but he answered, "I am not your *sayyid*, your *sayyid* is only Satan."

Abū ᶜUbaydah—Hubayrah b. Ḥudayr—Isḥāq b. Suwayd al-ᶜAdawī: I came with the onlookers to the place where al-Aḥnaf was staying. They came to him and said, "Oh Abū Baḥr, Rabīᶜah and Azd have entered the square," but he replied, "You do not have any more right to the mosque than they." Next, they came to him and said, "They have entered the government house," but he answered, "You do not have any more right to the house than they." Salamah b. Dhu'ayb al-Riyāḥī[145] then rushed up, saying, "Gather round me, Oh band of youths! This one is merely a coward[146] who is no good for you!" He summoned[147] the "wolves"[148] of the Banū Tamīm, and five hundred who were with Māh Afrīdhūn[149] stood ready with him. Salamah asked them, "Where do you want to go?" and they answered, "We want whatever you want." He said, "Forward, then!"

Abū ᶜUbaydah—Zuhayr b. Hunayd—Abū Niᶜāmah—Nāshib
[453] b. al-Ḥashḥās and Ḥumayd b. Hilāl: We two came to the place where al-Aḥnaf was staying near the mosque. We were among

---

144. This Mālik b. Dīnār is perhaps the well-known ascetic who died shortly before 131/748–9; however, the biographies of Mālik do not mention his involvement in these events, and it is difficult to see why he, a non-Tamīmī, should have participated (on him see Ibn Saᶜd, VII/2, 11).

145. See above, n. 55.

146. Read *jibs* (see *Add. et emend.* which, together with the parallel in *Ansāb*, IVb, 107[16], suggests the full text should read: "a coward who trails his ears").

147. Read *fa-nadaba* for *fa-badarat* (see *Add. et emend.*).

148. The Banū Kaᶜb b. Mālik b. Ḥanẓalah of Tamīm are called figuratively "wolves of *ghaḍā*" (see W. Robertson Smith, *Kinship and Marriage*, 230, n. 2; Lane, *Lexicon*, s.v. *ghaḍā*); it may be that they, closely related to the clan of Salamah b. Dhu'ayb, are referred to here.

149. The Persian leader of the Asāwirah, former Sasanian troops who had gone over to the Arabs during the conquest of Iraq and become incorporated into Tamīm; for the reading of his name, cf. *Add. et emend.* It seems that the 500 who stood ready were Asāwirah.

those waiting to see what would happen. A woman came up to him carrying an incense burner[150] and she said, "What have you got to do with the leadership? Look after the incense burner, for you are just a woman!" He replied, "A woman's arse is more suitable for the incense burner." Then they came to him and said that the anklets of ʿUlayyah[151] bint Nājiyah al-Riyāḥī, the sister of Maṭar, had been seized from her very legs (others said ʿUzzah bint al-Ḥurr al-Riyāḥiyya).[152] Her dwelling place was on the street in the square of the Banū Tamīm overlooking the public washing place. And they told him, "They have killed the dyer on your road and the cripple who was at the gate of the mosque." And they told him, "Mālik b. Mismaʿ has gone into the lane of the Banū al-ʿAdawiyyah opposite al-Jabbān and set fire to some houses." But al-Aḥnaf answered, "Establish some proof of this, for without it it is illicit to fight them." So they bore witness to all that in front of him.

Then al-Aḥnaf said, "Has ʿAbbād come?" (He was ʿAbbād b. Ḥuṣayn b. Yazīd b. ʿAmr b. Aws b. Sayf b. ʿAzm b. Ḥillizzah b. Bayān b. Saʿd b. al-Ḥārith al-Ḥabiṭah b. ʿAmr b. Tamīm.) They replied, "No," and he waited for a short time and then repeated, "Has ʿAbbād come?" Again they said, "No." Al-Aḥnaf said, "Is ʿAbs b. Ṭalq b. Rabīʿah b. ʿĀmir b. Bisṭām b. al-Ḥakam b. Ẓālim b. Ṣarīm b. al-Ḥārith b. ʿAmr b. Kaʿb b. Saʿd[153] here?" and they answered, "Yes." So he summoned him, drew forth a ribbon from his head, got down on his knees, and fastened it on a lance which he gave to him. Then he said, "Go!" When he turned around he said, "O God, do not shame it today, for you never shamed it in the past." And the people cried out, "Zabrā'[154] is aroused!" Zabrā' was a slave girl of al-Aḥnaf and by her they were alluding to him.

[454]

---

150. Cf. the note to *Ansāb*, IVb, 99[5], referring to the custom of the bedouin women of perfuming themselves with incense before cohabitation.

151. Or ʿAliyyah or ʿAblah (cf. *Add. et emend.* and *Ansāb*, IVb, 107[21]); note that she belongs to the same Tamīmī family as Salamah b. Dhu'ayb.

152. See *Add. et emend.* and *Ansāb*, IVb, 107[22], both of which suggest that Ṭabarī's text is inadequate here.

153. Of the Banū Saʿd of Tamīm.

154. The printed text has Zayrā', but see *Add. et. emend.* and the reference to Maydānī.

When ᶜAbs had set off, ᶜAbbād came with sixty horsemen. He asked what the people had done, and they told him that they had gone. "Who is in command?" he asked, and they told him, "ᶜAbs b. Ṭalq al-Ṣarīmī." ᶜAbbād said, "Shall I go under the banner of ᶜAbs!" and he and the horsemen went back to his people.

Abū ᶜUbaydah—Zuhayr—Abū Rayḥānah al-ᶜUraynī: On the day Masᶜūd was killed I was beneath the belly of al-Zard b. ᶜAbdallāh al-Saᶜdī's horse, rushing headlong until we reached the street of al-Qadīm.

Abū ᶜUbaydah—Hubayrah b. Ḥudayr—Isḥāq b. Suwayd: They advanced and when they reached the openings of the lanes they halted. Māh Afrīdhūn said to them in Persian, "What is the matter, Oh band of youths?" They replied, "They have met us with the points of their lances." He said to them in Persian, "Strike them with the *fanjaqān*"[155] (that is, Persian for "five arrows in a shot"). There were four hundred of the Asāwirah and they hit them with 2,000 arrows in one burst so that they retreated from the gates of the lanes and took up position by the gates[156] of the mosque. The Tamīmiyyah slowly advanced toward them, but when they reached the gates they halted. Māh Afrīdhūn asked them, "What is the matter?" They answered, "They have pointed the tips of their lances at us." He replied, "Fire at them too!" So they fired 2,000 arrows at them and pushed them back from the gates so that they entered the mosque and moved forward. Masᶜūd was on the *minbar* delivering a speech and inciting his men.

Ghaṭafān b. Unayf b. Yazīd b. Fahdah, one of the Banū Kaᶜb b. ᶜAmr b. Tamīm (Yazid b. Fahdah was a hero of the Time of Ignorance before Islam), began to fight and to urge on his own people, declaiming in the meter of *rajaz:*

Come on Tamim! It will be remembered.
[455]   If Masᶜūd escapes it will be notorious.
So hold to the side of the *maqṣūrah*.[157]

(That is, he shall not flee and escape.)

---

155. See *Gloss.*, s.v. *banjakān*.
156. Read *abwāb* as later in the line and as in *Ansāb*, IVb, 108[17].
157. The enclosed area in mosque reserved for the caliph or governor.

Isḥāq b. Suwayd[158] (continuing his account): They came on
Masᶜūd while he was on the *minbar* urging on his men, and
they dragged him down and killed him. That was at the
beginning of Shawwāl, 64 (end of May, 684).[159] His people
were useless and were routed. Ashyam b. Shaqīq rushed ahead
of them, fleeing to the door of the *maqṣūrah*. One of them
stabbed him, but he survived and escaped.

Al-Farazdaq said about that:

If Ashyam had not outstripped the points of our lances,
　　and had missed the door when our fires ignited,
Then he would have accompanied Masᶜūd and his companion,
　　and the guts and the innards would have spilled out.[160]

Abū ᶜUbaydah: Sallām b. Abī Khayrah reported to me, and
I also heard it from Abū al-Khansā' Kusayb al-ᶜAnbarī, who
was transmitting reports in the circle of Yūnus in the mosque.
Those two said: We heard al-Ḥasan b. Abī al-Ḥasan[161] saying
to his group in the mosque of the governor: Masᶜūd came
from over here (he indicated with his hand the dwellings of
the Azd) looking like a bird, wearing a *qabā'* of yellow brocade
figured with black "eyes,"[162] ordering the people to abide by
the accepted conventions[163] and avoid civil commotion: "Indeed, it is an accepted convention that you restrain yourselves."[164] And they were saying, "The moon, the moon!"[165]
By God, it was only an hour before their moon became a
small one and they came to him and dragged him down from
the *minbar* where he was—God knows—and killed him. (In
his report, Sallām said that al-Ḥasan had said, "The people
came from over here" and that he had indicated with his hand
the dwellings of the Banū Tamīm.)

---

158. Not Isḥāq b. Yazīd as printed.
159. Cf. the parallel passage in *Ansāb*, IVb, 108, which has Shaᶜbān.
160. Reading *tamā'at lahu* (see *Add. et emend.*).
161. I.e., al-Ḥasan al-Baṣrī (see n. 23 above).
162. Reading *muᶜayyan* (see *Add. et emend.*); for the *qabā'*, usually a long
outer garment, see Dozy, *Vêtements*, s.v.; *EI²*, s.v. Libās, 733b.
163. Ar. *sunnah*.
164. See *Gloss.*, s.v. *akhadha*.
165. Nickname for Masᶜūd, allegedly referring to his good looks (*Ansāb*,
IVb, 98³); short for *qamar al-ᶜIrāq* (Caskel/Ibn Kalbī, II, 402).

Abū ᶜUbaydah—Maslamah[166] b. Muḥārib: They came to
ᶜUbaydallāh and said, "Masᶜūd has gone up on to the *minbar*
and no arrow[167] has been fired against him outside the government house." While things were like that, he conceived
the idea of going there. But then they came and said, "Masᶜūd
has been killed!" and he set his foot in the stirrup and betook
himself to Syria. That was in Shawwāl, 64 (May-June, 684).[168]

Abū ᶜUbaydah—Rawwād al-Kaᶜbī: Some men of Muḍar came
to Mālik b. Mismaᶜ and besieged him in his residence, which
they set on fire. Concerning that, Ghaṭafān b. Unayf al-Kaᶜbī
recited in the meter of *rajaz:*

Ibn Mismaᶜ finds himself besieged,
    and wishes for other mansions and abodes,
    But we have set the blaze around him.[169]

When ᶜUbaydallāh b. Ziyād fled, they pursued him. But he
outstripped the pursuers,[170] so they plundered what they found
of his. Wāfid[171] b. Khalīfah b. Asmā', one of the Banū Ṣakhr
b. Minqar b. ᶜUbayd b. al-Ḥārith b. ᶜAmr b. Kaᶜb b. Saᶜd, said
about that:

How many a brutal and violent tyrant we have killed,
    we have seized his crown and pillaged his goods.
ᶜUbaydallāh was one of them when we plundered him,
    and despoiled him of his horses and clothes,
On the day when our horsemen and his met.
    If only Ibn Ziyād's flight had not saved him!

And ᶜArham[172] b. ᶜAbdallāh b. Qays, one of the Banū al-
ᶜAdawiyyah, said concerning the killing of Masᶜūd, in a long
poem:

---

166. Text reads Salamah b. Muḥārib, but cf. n. 98 above.

167. Read *kuththāb:* it can mean a practice arrow without head or feathers
(see Lane, *Lexicon,* s.v., and cf. p. 13 above, *jummāḥ*).

168. *Ansāb,* IVb, 108,[22] has Shaᶜbān (again) with a note (by Balādhurī?) that
some put ᶜUbaydallāh's departure and Masᶜūd's death in Shawwāl, but that
Shaᶜbān is more correct (*aṣaḥḥ*).

169. Cf. *Ansāb,* IVb, 111[3].

170. Read *ṭalaba* (see *Add. et emend.*).

171. *Ansāb,* IVb, 111[4], and *Naqā'iḍ Farazdaq,* 735, prefer the reading Wāqid.

172. See *Add. et emend.*

And when Mas^cūd b. ^cAmr came against us,
    all we offered him to drink was a blade
    whetted and honed.
Mas^cūd hoped to be made *amīr*, but he was[173]
    killed. We have invested him with death.

Abū Ja^cfar Muḥammad b. Jarīr (al-Ṭabarī) said: As for ^cUmar
(b. Shabbah), he reported to me concerning ^cUbaydallāh's departure for Syria, from Zuhayr—Wahb b. Jarīr b. Ḥāzim—al-
Zubayr b. Khirrīt: Mas^cūd sent with Ibn Ziyād a hundred men
of Azd led by Qurrah b. ^cAmr b. Qays, and they brought him
to Syria.

^cUmar: Abū ^cĀṣim al-Nabīl reported to me—^cAmr b. al-   [457]
Zubayr: and Khallād b. Yazīd al-Bāhilī, and al-Walīd b. Hi-
shām—his paternal uncle—his father—^cAmr b. Hubayrah—
Yasāf b. Shurayḥ al-Yashkurī; and (^cUmar b. Shabbah said) ^cAlī
b. Muḥammad (al-Madā'inī) reported it to me too; they differed
in their narratives and some of them added to the others'
accounts: Ibn Ziyād left al-Baṣrah. One night he said: "Riding
a camel has become burdensome to me; make me something
soft on a beast with hoofs." So a rug was thrown over a
donkey for him, and he rode on it with his feet almost making
furrows in the ground.

The Yashkurī said: He was riding in front of me and he
had been silent for a long time. So I said to myself, "This is
^cUbaydallāh, governor of Iraq yesterday, now sleeping on a
donkey. If he fell off it, he would treat it harshly." Then I
said, "By God, if he is sleeping, I will certainly spoil his sleep
for him." So I went up to him and said, "Are you sleeping?"
"No," he answered. "Then what has made you so quiet?" I
asked. He replied, "I was communing with myself." I said,
"Shall I tell you what you were saying to yourself?" He said,
"Go on then. I do not think you will be clever enough to get
it." I said to him, "You were saying, 'Would that I had not
killed al-Ḥusayn.' " "Not that," he said. I said, "You were
saying, 'Would that I had not killed those whom I did.' "[174]

---

173. Cf. *Ansāb*, IVb, 111², where this hemistich is part of the verse of
Ghaṭafān b. Unayf.
174. I.e., the Khawārij.

"Not that," he said. "You were saying, 'Would that I had not built al-Bayḍā'.' "[175] "Not that," he said. I said, "You were saying, 'Would that I had not appointed the dihqāns[176] to financial authority.' " "Not that," he said. I said, "You were saying, 'Would that I had been more generous than I was.' "

He answered, "By God, you have not spoken right or avoided mistakes by keeping quiet. As for al-Ḥusayn, he came wanting to kill me, but I preferred killing him to his killing me. As for al-Bayḍā', I bought it from ʿAbdallāh b. ʿUthmān al-Tha-qafī[177] and Yazīd sent me a million which I spent on it. If I survive, it will be for my family; if I perish, I will not grieve over something in which I did not act harshly. As for giving authority over the finances to the dihqāns, ʿAbd al-Raḥmān b. Abī Bakrah[178] and Zādhān Farrūkh[179] disparaged me before Muʿāwiyah, going as far as taking even the husks of rice into account and making the total of the tax[180] of Iraq come to a hundred million, so that Muʿāwiyah made me choose between taking responsibility for raising that amount or being deposed from office. I had no desire to be deposed, but, whenever I appointed one of the Arabs and the tax was insufficient[181] and I investigated him or imposed a fine on the leaders of his people or upon his clan, I caused them offense. But if I left them alone, then I abandoned God's property; and I know where it properly belongs. So I found the dihqāns more punctilious in collecting taxes, more trustworthy, and less de-

[458]

---

175. Qaṣr al-Bayḍā', ʿUbaydallāh's residence in al-Baṣrah (see Yāqūt, *Buldān*, I, 793⁴).

176. Local gentry of the Sasanids in Iraq, who remained as a distinct group for some time after the Arab conquest (see *EI²*, s.v. Dihḳān).

177. A Baṣran related to the Umayyads by marriage and a member of the tribe of Thaqīf from al-Ṭā'if, to which ʿUbaydallāh's own grandmother, Sumayyah, belonged.

178. See above, n. 56.

179. This seems to be a common name for dihqāns in Arabic sources; the one in question here may be the same one who worked in the financial administration under al-Ḥajjāj and was connected with the change in the language of the administration from Persian to Arabic.

180. Ar. *kharāj*, presumably, inferring from the mention of the husks of rice, here a land tax estimated as a percentage of the produce (see *EI²*, s.v. Kharādj).

181. Or "he withheld the tax," *kasara/kusira 'l-kharāj* (see *Gloss.*, s.v. *kasara*).

manding than you Arabs. Even so, I made you responsible for them so that they would not oppress anyone. As for what you say about generosity, by God I never had any wealth but that I bestowed it generously on you. If I had wanted, I could have taken some of your wealth and favored some of you with it at the expense of others so that they would say, 'How generous he is!' but I treated you all the same. With me there were benefits for you all. As for what you say about 'Would that I had not killed those whom I did,' there is nothing which I have done, apart from my confession of God's unity,[182] which brings me nearer to God in my opinion than my killing of those of the Khawārij whom I killed.

"Now I will tell you what I really said to myself: I said, 'Would that I had fought the Baṣrans, for they took an oath of allegiance to obey me willingly.' I swear by God that that is what I wanted, but the family of Ziyād came to me and said, 'If you fight them and they defeat you, they would never allow anyone of us to remain; but, if you leave them alone, then any one of us could hide with his maternal relatives and his in-laws.' So I gave in to them and did not fight. And I was saying, 'Would that I had brought out the prisoners and cut off their heads.' But, since I have missed these two opportunities, would that I arrive in Syria before the Syrians have settled anything."

Some of them said: And he reached Syria and they had not decided on anything. Compared with him they were mere youths. But some of them said: And he reached Syria and they had settled matters. He, however, quashed what they had settled in favor of his own opinion.

In this year also the people of al-Kūfah drove ʿAmr b. Ḥurayth out,[183] removed him from authority over them, and agreed on the appointment of ʿĀmir b. Masʿūd.[184]

---

182. See Lane, *Lexicon*, s.v. *akhlaṣa*; Qur'ān, sūrah 112 *(Sūrat al-Ikhlāṣ)*, begins "Say: He is God, one!"

183. Of the Banū Makhzūm of Quraysh, he had governed al-Kūfah for Ziyād (see Zubayrī, *Nasab Quraysh*, 333).

184. Of the Banū Jumaḥ of Quraysh (Zubayrī, op. cit., 391).

The Deposition of ᶜAmr b. Ḥurayth by the People of al-Kūfah and Their Appointment of ᶜĀmir b. Masᶜūd as Governor over Them[185]

Abū Jaᶜfar (al-Ṭabarī) said: According to al-Haytham b. ᶜAdī—Ibn ᶜAyyāsh:[186] The first under whom the two garrison towns of al-Kūfah and al-Baṣrah were united as one governorate were Ziyād and his son. They killed 13,000 of the Khawārij and ᶜUbaydallāh put 4,000 of them in prison. When Yazīd died, ᶜUbaydallāh made an official address in which he said, "He for obedience to whom we fought is dead. If you give me authority over you, I will collect for you your spoils (fay') and fight your enemies." He sent Muqātil b. Mismaᶜ[187] and Saᶜīd b. Qarḥā,[188] one of the Banū Māzin, with that message to the Kūfans, and his deputy over al-Kūfah was ᶜAmr b. Ḥurayth. The two messengers announced their message, and then Yazīd b. al-Ḥārith b. Ruwaym al-Shaybānī[189] arose. He said, "Praise be to God who has given us respite from Ibn Sumayyah![190] No, nor anything else!"[191] Thereupon, ᶜAmr gave orders concerning him and he was seized by the collar and led off to prison, but Bakr hindered the arrest and Yazīd, fearing, escaped to his people. Muḥammad b. al-Ashᶜath[192] then sent to him saying, "Keep firm in your opinion," and messengers continually came to him bringing that message.

---

185. For parallel and variant accounts of the following events in al-Kūfah, see *Ansāb*, IVb, 97; Ibn al-Athīr, IV, 109; Rotter, *Bürgerkrieg*, 95–6; when the narrative reverts to events in al-Baṣrah, see n. 22 above.

186. For al-Haytham b. ᶜAdī, d. 206/821 or 207/822, see *GAS*, I, 272 and *EI²*, s.v.; for Ibn ᶜAyyāsh, d. 193/809, see Yāqūt, *Irshād*, II, 373–80.

187. Brother of Mālik b. Mismaᶜ (see above, p. 8).

188. In the report from ᶜAwānah, below and at *Ansāb*, IVb, 97¹³, he is called Saᶜd; whether Saᶜīd here is merely a slip or genuinely represents the tradition of Ibn ᶜAyyāsh is not ascertainable. The Banū Māzin b. Mālik are of Tamīm.

189. Of Bakr b. Wā'il, he was a member of a prominent family of al-Kūfah which provided governors and other high officials during the Umayyad period; he himself was to become governor of al-Rayy and al-Madā'in for the Zubayrids (see Crone, *Slaves*, 119).

190. I.e., Ziyād b. Abīhi, but perhaps here indicating Ziyād's son ᶜUbaydallāh.

191. Ar. *lā wa-lā karāmah*, literally, "No, and no jar cover!" (see Lane, *Lexicon*, s.vv. *ḥubb* and *karāmah*, the latter in the supplement).

192. The leader of the Banū Kindah in al-Kūfah.

When ᶜAmr ascended the *minbar*, they stoned him and he went inside his residence. The people gathered in the mosque and said, "Let us appoint somebody to authority until a caliph is agreed upon," and they resolved on ᶜUmar b. Saᶜd.[193] But the women of Hamdān[194] came, weeping for al-Ḥusayn, while their menfolk were girt with swords, and they encircled the *minbar*. Muḥammad b. al-Ashᶜath said, "Our situation has changed." Kindah had been supporting the authority of ᶜUmar [460] b. Saᶜd because his maternal uncle was one of them, but now they all agreed on ᶜĀmir b. Masᶜūd, wrote to Ibn al-Zubayr about it, and he confirmed him in office.

As for ᶜAwānah b. al-Ḥakam, according to the report of Hishām b. Muḥammad from him, he said: When the Baṣrans gave the oath of allegiance to ᶜUbaydallāh b. Ziyād, he sent ᶜAmr b. Mismaᶜ[195] and Saᶜd b. al-Qarḥā al-Tamīmī as envoys from himself to al-Kūfah to tell the Kūfans what the Baṣrans had done and to ask that they give the oath of allegiance to ᶜUbaydallāh b. Ziyād until the disputes among the people had been settled. ᶜAmr b. Ḥurayth called the people together, praised God and extolled Him, and then said, "These two men have come to you from your governor, summoning you to a course of action by means of which God will give you one voice and smooth out what divides you. Listen to them, then, and accept what they say, for they have brought you true guidance." Then ᶜAmr b. Mismaᶜ arose, praised God and extolled Him, and referred to the Baṣrans and how they had agreed to make ᶜUbaydallāh b. Ziyād governor until the people should concur as to whom they should give authority. "We have come to you so that we can work together and have a common governor, for al-Kūfah is part of al-Baṣrah and al-

---

193. ᶜUmar b. Saᶜd b. Abī Waqqāṣ (see *Add. et emend.*), of the Banū Zuhrah of Quraysh, a son of the important Companion of the Prophet; his mother was of Kindah (Zubayrī, *Nasab Quraysh*, 264[12-13]).

194. A "southern" tribe with substantial settlement in al-Kūfah (see *EI²*, s.v.; Caskel/Ibn Kalbī, II, 277); Hamdānīs of al-Kūfah had been prominent in support of al-Ḥusayn while ᶜUmar b. Saᶜd was one of the leading opponents of al-Ḥusayn.

195. Brother of Mālik and Muqātil b. Mismaᶜ (see n. 187, above; appears variantly as ᶜĀmir).

Baṣrah part of al-Kūfah." Ibn al-Qarḥā arose and spoke in the same manner as his companion.

However, Yazīd b. al-Ḥārith b. Yazīd al-Shaybānī (he was Ibn Ruwaym) stood up. He was the first of the people to stone the two envoys and he was followed by the others afterwards. He then said, "Are we to give the oath of allegiance to Ibn Marjānah? No, and nothing else!" That action increased Yazīd's status in the garrison town and elevated him. The delegation returned to al-Baṣrah and informed the people there of what had passed, and the Baṣrans said, "The Kūfans are casting him off while you are conferring authority on him and giving him the oath of allegiance!" Then they rose against him.

Whenever Ibn Ziyād was in difficulty, it led him to seek protection from the Azd,[196] and now, when the people rejected him, he sought the protection of Masʿūd b. ʿAmr al-Azdī. Masʿūd granted him protection and guarded him, and he stayed there for ninety days after the death of Yazīd and then left for Syria. The Azd and Bakr b. Wā'il sent some of their men with him and they brought him to Syria. When he set out he appointed Masʿūd b. ʿAmr as his deputy over al-Baṣrah, but the Banū Tamīm and Qays said, "We will not accept, we will not approve of, and we will not confer authority on anybody unless our community generally approves of him." Masʿūd said, "He has appointed me his deputy and I will never abandon it," and he went out with his clansmen to the governor's court (al-qaṣr) and entered it. Tamīm gathered around al-Aḥnaf b. Qays and said to him, "Azd have entered the mosque." He replied, "They have entered the mosque, so what? It is for you and them equally, and you enter it." They said, "And he has entered the governor's court and gone up to the minbar."

When ʿUbaydallāh b. Ziyād had departed for Syria, a group of the Khawārij had rebelled and established camp on the river of the Asāwirah,[197] and it was claimed that al-Aḥnaf sent to them, saying, "This man who has entered the governor's res-

[461]

---

196. Cf. *Ansāb*, IVb, 98[1], *istajāra fīhā*, which seems better.
197. At al-Baṣrah near the house of Fīl the mawlā of Ziyād (Yāqūt, *Buldān*, IV, 834).

idence is your enemy as well as ours, so what is stopping you
from making the first move against him?" A band of them,
therefore, came and penetrated into the mosque while Mascūd
b. cAmr was on the *minbar* taking the oath of allegiance from
those who came to him. A non-Arab called Muslim, who was
a Persian and had come to al-Baṣrah and accepted Islam and
then joined the Khawārij, shot at him, got him in the heart
and killed him. The timorous ones among the people there
then rushed out in a panic, saying, "Mascūd b. cAmr has been
killed! The Khawārij have killed him!" Thereupon Azd came
out to attack those Khawārij. They killed some of them,
wounded others, and drove them out of al-Baṣrah. After they
had buried Mascūd they were approached by some who told
them, "Do you know that the Banū Tamīm are claiming that
they killed Mascūd b. cAmr?" So the Azd sent to ask if that
was true and, indeed, some of them were saying it.

Consequently, Azd met together, made Ziyād b. cAmr al-
cAtakī[198] chief over them, and hurried off to the Banū Tamīm.   [462]
Qays came out with the Banū Tamīm, and Mālik b. Mismac
with Bakr b. Wā'il came out with Azd. Azd and its allies came
toward the Banū Tamīm, and the latter went to al-Aḥnaf,
saying, "Come out, for our people are here!" but he remained
there doing nothing, and a woman of his people brought an
incense burner and said, "Oh Aḥnaf, look after this!" meaning,
"You are only a woman" but he replied, "Your arse is better
suited for it." Never again did any one hear him use such a
coarse expression, for he was known for his subtlety *(ḥilm)*.
He called for his banner and said, "Oh God, grant it victory
and do not shame it. May its help mean that those fighting
with it will not be defeated because of it and will not lose it
by conquest.[199] Oh God, spare our blood and overcome our
divisions." He then set out, and so did his nephew Iyās b.
Qatādah[200] going ahead of him, and the people met and fought
a great battle. Many from each party were killed and the Banū

---

198. I.e., Mascūd's brother.
199. Cf. *Ansāb*, IVb, 99, which omits the troublesome middle phrase.
200. Text has ibn Mucāwiyah for ibn Qatādah; *Ansāb*, IVb, 99[7-8], has *ibn
ukhtihi* (for *akhīhi*) *Iyās b. Qatāda b. Awfā min B. cAbd Shams b. Sacd;* so
too Wellhausen, *Arab Kingdom*, 408.

Tamīm appealed to the others, saying, "For God's sake, Oh party of Azd, let the Qur'ān and whoever you desire of the people of Islam decide between us concerning our blood. If there is proof against us that we killed your fellow tribesman, then choose the best man among us and kill him in recompense for your fellow. But, if there is no proof, then we will swear by God that we did not kill and did not order or know of a killer for your man. If you do not want that, we will pay 100,000 dirhams in blood money for him. But make peace!"

Al-Aḥnaf b. Qays came with the leading men of Muḍar to Ziyād b. ʿAmr al-ʿAtakī and said, "Oh party of Azd, you are our neighbors in dwelling place and our brethren in warfare. We have come to you in your abode to dampen the fires of your hostility[201] and remove your hatred. The decision is entrusted to you, so decide[202] the fate of our mature men and our properties. The loss of anything we possess, if it would bring peace between us, would not seem too much to us." They answered, "Would you pay ten times the accepted blood money for our companion?" and he said, "It is yours." So the people left and they made peace.

Al-Haytham b. al-Aswad[203] said:

[463]   The crier loudly proclaimed the death of Masʿūd, and
                 I said to him,
                 "How much braver was the Yamanī than he who
                 proclaims his death!
           He fulfilled fourscore years, no one could defeat him,
                 a hero[204] whom the summoner called to head le-
                 gions of men.
           He led[205] Ibn Ḥarb[206] when his ways had been barred,
                 and he widened the escape passages, such widen-
                 ings

---

201. See *Gloss.*, s.v. *ḥashsh*; Ansāb, IVb, 99, reads *li-nuṭfi'a ḥasīkatakum*, "so that we may quench your rancor!"
202. Read ʿawwilū ʿalā (not quwlū ʿalā) "decide on," as in *Ansāb*, IVb, 99.
203. A notable of the Banū Nakhaʿ of Madhḥij (see *Ansāb*, IVb, 100[1-2]).
204. Ar. *fatan*; Ansāb reads *ḥattā*.
205. *Ansāb* reads *awā*, "he sheltered," for *addā*.
206. I.e., ʿUbaydallāh b. Ziyād counted as a descendant of Abū Sufyān b. Ḥarb.

That the earth and its inhabitants could disappear in
   them,
   and he was surrounded by his helpers and parti-
   sans.''

   And ᶜUbaydallāh b. al-Ḥurr[207] said:

I never ceased to hope for Azd until I saw
   that they fell short of their ancestral glory.
Has Masᶜūd been killed and they never sought
   vengeance for him,
   and have the swords of Azd become like
   sickles?
What is the good of blood money which has
   brought humiliation to Azd?
   Their living ones are reviled for it in the
   assemblies,
As gray-haired ones, as if their beards
   were (skins of) foxes with bells hung on
   their necks.[208]

The Baṣrans decided together to give authority to one of
themselves to lead the prayer until an *imām* should be agreed
upon. They appointed ᶜAbd al-Malik b. ᶜAbdallāh b. ᶜĀmir[209]
for a month and then they appointed Babbah, who was ᶜAbdallāh
b. al-Ḥarith b. ᶜAbd al-Muṭṭalib. He led them in prayer for
two months until ᶜUmar b. ᶜUbaydallāh b. Maᶜmar[210] came to   [464]
them from Ibn al-Zubayr. He stayed for a month until al-
Ḥārith b. ᶜAbdallāh b. Abī Rabīᶜah al-Makhzūmī came bringing
orders for his removal from office. Al-Ḥarith then became
prefect of al-Baṣrah, and he was (the one called) al-Qubāᶜ.[211]

---

207. ᶜUbaydallāh b. al-Ḥurr al-Juᶜfī of Madhḥij, as in *Ansāb*, IVb, 100⁶ (see
Add. et emend.; also see Rotter, *Bürgerkrieg*, 105 f., 219–21, Wellhausen,
Arab Kingdom, 190).
   208. The simile in the last two lines presumably indicates cowardice (the
fox) and stupidity (the bells are the sort which are hung on the necks of
livestock).
   209. Of the Banū ᶜAbd Shams of Quraysh (see Zubayrī, *Nasab Quraysh*,
149).
   210. Of the Banū Taym of Quraysh (*ibid.*, 189).
   211. See *Add. et emend.* for the missing Abī in al-Ḥārith's name; another
Qurashī (see Zubayrī, *Nasab Quraysh*, 318 and n. 3, for an offered derivation
of the name al-Qubāᶜ).

Abū Jaᶜfar (al-Ṭabarī) said: As for ᶜUmar b. Shabbah, he gave me a report about the tenure of authority by ᶜAbd al-Malik b. ᶜAbdallāh b. ᶜĀmir b. Kurayz and Babbah, the killing of Masᶜūd , and the holding of office by ᶜUmar b. ᶜUbaydallāh[212] which was different from Hishām's report from ᶜAwānah.

According to ᶜUmar b. Shabbah—ᶜAlī b. Muḥammad—Abū Muqarrin ᶜUbaydallāh al-Duhnī: When the people gave the oath of allegiance to Babbah, he appointed Himyān b. ᶜAdī over his police troops. One of the people of Medina came to Babbah and the latter ordered Himyān b. ᶜAdī to give the Medinese a lodging place close to himself. Himyān, therefore, went to a house which belonged to al-Fīl,[213] a mawlā of Ziyād, which was in the district of the Banū Sulaym,[214] thinking to turn everyone out of it so that he could lodge the Medinese there. But al-Fīl had fled and locked the doors, and the Banū Sulaym resisted Himyān and fought against him. They appealed for help to ᶜAbd al-Malik b. ᶜAbdallāh b. ᶜĀmir b. Kurayz, who sent his Bukhāriyyah and his mawlās with weapons. They drove Himyān out and prevented him from taking the house.

Next day, ᶜAbd al-Malik went to the government house to greet Babbah and a man of the Banū Qays b. Thaᶜlabah[215] met him at the door. This man said, "You are the one who helped them against us yesterday!" and raised his hand and hit him. Thereupon a crowd of the Bukhāriyyah struck off the hand of the Qaysī and sent it flying. (It is also reported that the Qaysī escaped without injury.) Ibn ᶜĀmir was enraged. He went back, and Muḍar were stirred up on his behalf. When they met, Bakr b. Wā'il went to Ashyam b. Shaqīq and appealed for his help and he came bringing Mālik b. Mismaᶜ with him. He went up on to the *minbar* and said, "Any Muḍarī whom you find, crucify him!" (The family of Mismaᶜ claim that Mālik came on that day wearing his indoor clothes[216] and without weapons in order to deflect Ashyam from what he intended.)

---

212. *Sic.*
213. See n. 197 above.
214. Of Qays.
215. Of Bakr b. Wā'il, the clan of Mālik b. Mismaᶜ.
216. Ar. *mutafaḍḍilan* (see Lane, *Lexicon*, s.v. *mifḍal*).

Then Bakr went back. Bakr and Muḍar had previously held off from one another, but now Azd seized the chance to make an alliance with Bakr[217] and they went with Masᶜūd to the communal mosque. [465]

Tamīm fled to al-Aḥnaf, who fastened his turban to a spear which he then gave to Salamah b. Dhu'ayb al-Riyāḥī. The Asāwirah went ahead of him, and he entered the mosque while Masᶜūd was addressing the gathering. They dragged him down and killed him. The Azd, however, claimed that it was the Azāriqah[218] who had killed him. Then there was civil tumult *(fitnah)* in al-Baṣrah. ᶜUmar b. ᶜUbaydallāh b. Maᶜmar and ᶜAbd al-Raḥmān b. al-Ḥārith b. Hishām[219] acted as mediators between them, and eventually Azd accepted ten times the blood money for Masᶜūd. Then ᶜAbdallāh b. al-Ḥārith remained in his house, professing his piety and saying, "I will not make righteous the people by corruption of myself."

According to ᶜUmar—Abū al-Ḥasan:[220] The Baṣrans wrote to Ibn al-Zubayr, who in turn wrote to Anas b. Mālik[221] asking him to lead the prayer for the people. He led the prayer for them for forty days.

According to ᶜUmar—ᶜAlī b. Muḥammad (al-Madā'inī): Ibn al-Zubayr wrote to ᶜUmar b. ᶜUbaydallāh b. Maᶜmar al-Taymī appointing him over al-Baṣrah. He sent the commission to ᶜUmar and he accepted it,[222] but as he was setting out, desiring to perform the minor pilgrimage,[223] ᶜUmar wrote to ᶜUbaydallāh[224] asking him to lead the people in prayer, and he did so until ᶜUmar came.

---

217. *Ansāb*, IVb, 105[16-17], seems to read better: *thumma inna 'l-qawma taḥājazu wa 'nṣarafat Bakru wa 'l-Muḍariyyatu wa-taḥālafat Bakru wa 'l-Azd.*

218. Extremist Khārijites, followers of Nāfiᶜ b. al-Azraq (see *EI¹*, s.v. Nāfiᶜ b. al-Azraḳ).

219. *Ansāb*, IVb, 106[16], has ᶜAmr b. ᶜAbd al-Raḥmān b. al-Ḥārith b. Hishām; *Naqā'iḍ Farazdaq*, 738[11], has ᶜUmar b. ᶜAbd al-Raḥmān; possibly a descendant of Hishām b. al-Mughīrah of the Banū Makhzūm of Quraysh?

220. Al-Madā'inī?

221. Medinese Companion of the Prophet (see *EI²*, s.v.).

222. Ar. *wāfaqahu*; *Ansāb*, IVb, 106[19], has *fa-wafāhu*, "it reached him," which seems better.

223. Ar. ᶜ*umrah*, a ritual which involves pilgrimage to Mecca but may be performed at any time of the year and does not include all of the ceremonies of the *ḥajj.*

224. ᶜUmar b. ᶜUbaydallāh's brother (see *Ansāb*, IVb, 106[19-20]).

According to ᶜUmar—Zuhayr b. Ḥarb—Wahb b. Jarīr—his father:[225] I heard Muḥammad b. al-Zubayr say: The people of al-Baṣrah agreed on a peace on condition that ᶜAbdallāh b. al-Ḥārith al-Hāshimī governed them. He directed their affairs for four months, but Nāfiᶜ b. al-Azraq went in revolt to Ahwāz[226] and it was said to ᶜAbdallāh, "The men have devoured one another and women are seized from the roads but no one prevents it, and the result is that you are put to shame." He answered, "What is it that you want?" and they said, "That you put on your sword and act firmly with the people." He said, "I will not make them righteous by my own corruption. Slave, bring me my sandals!" And he put on his sandals and betook himself to his family. The people appointed as governor ᶜUmar b. ᶜUbaydallāh b. Maᶜmar al-Taymī.

[466]

My father (Jarīr) said from al-Ṣaᶜb b. Zayd: The plague [al-jārif] broke out while ᶜAbdallāh was in authority over al-Baṣrah. His mother died in it. Nobody could be found who would carry her body for burial, so they had to hire four non-Arabs who carried her to her grave. And he was governor at that time!

According to ᶜUmar—ᶜAlī b. Muḥammad: While Babbah was in charge of al-Baṣrah, he had taken 40,000 dirhams from the treasury and deposited it with somebody. When ᶜUmar b. ᶜUbaydallāh came as governor, he took and imprisoned ᶜAbdallāh b. al-Ḥārith and tortured a mawlā of his to find out where that money was and compelled him to pay it back.

According to ᶜUmar—ᶜAlī b. Muḥammad—al-Qaflānī—Yazīd b. ᶜAbdallāh b. al-Shikhkhīr: I said to ᶜAbdallāh b. al-Ḥārith b. Nawfal, "When you had authority over us I saw that you acquired money but were wary about the shedding of blood." He replied, "The consequences of money are easier than those of blood."

In this year also, the Kūfans appointed ᶜĀmir b. Masᶜūd over their affairs. Hishām b. Muḥammad al-Kalbī reported from ᶜAwānah b. al-Ḥakam that when they rejected the two delegates from the Baṣrans, the Kūfan notables met and con-

---

225. See n. 76 above.
226. The province of southwestern Iran bordering Iraq.

cluded a peace on condition that ᶜĀmir b. Masᶜūd should lead them in prayer (he was ᶜĀmir b. Masᶜūd b. Khalaf al-Qurashī, the "ball made by dung beetles"[227] referred to by ᶜAbdallāh b. Hammām al-Salūlī:[228]

Cling fast to Zayd if you catch him,
    and cure the widows of the dung beetles' ball,[229]

for he was short of stature)[230] until the people should make   [467]
up their minds. He remained in office for three months after Yazīd b. Muᶜāwiyah perished and then ᶜAbdallāh b. Yazīd al-Anṣārī, al-Khaṭmi,[231] came to lead the prayer and Ibrāhīm b. Muḥammad b. Ṭalḥah b. ᶜUbaydallāh[232] to be in charge of taxes.[233] And the Kūfans, the Baṣrans, those Arabs in the region toward which prayer is performed,[234] the Syrians and the people of Mesopotamia all accepted Ibn al-Zubayr, except for the people of Jordan.

In this year also, the oath of allegiance as caliph was given to Marwān b. al-Ḥakam[235]in Syria.

The Rendering of Allegiance to Marwān b. al-Ḥakam in Syria

According to al-Ḥārith—Ibn Saᶜd—Muḥammad b. ᶜUmar:[236] When the oath of allegiance was given to ᶜAbdallāh b. al-

---

227. According to *Ansāb*, IVb, 101[1], he was called *duḥrūjat al-juᶜal* because of his shortness.

228. On him see *EI*[2], s.v.; *GAS*, II, 324.

229. *Cf. Ansāb*, IVb, 101[3], V, 191[15]; "Zayd" is sometimes identified as a mawlā of Ibn Masᶜūd; "cure the widows of" may refer to their amorous infatuation with the governor.

230. Ar. *wa-kāna qaṣīran ḥattā. . .*: all parallels indicate that this must refer to ᶜĀmir's short stature, not the passage of time.

231. Of the Anṣār, among whom Khaṭmah b. Jusham is a subgroup of the Aws (see Caskel/Ibn Kalbī, I, table 182).

232. Of the Banū Taym of Quraysh, known as al-Aᶜraj (the Lame; see Zubayrī, *Nasab Quraysh*, 283–4).

233. Ar. *kharāj*, i.e., the governorship was divided into its political/religious and financial components.

234. The *qiblah*, i.e. (here), the Ḥijāz in general.

235. A leading Umayyad of the family of Abū al-ᶜĀṣ (see further *EI*[2], s.v. Marwān b. al-Ḥakam). For parallel and variant accounts of the following two sections see *Ansāb*, V, 127–46, Ibn Saᶜd, V, 27–9, *Naqāʾiḍ Akhṭal*, 6ff., Wellhausen, *Arab Kingdom*, 170–83, Rotter, *Bürgerkrieg*, 107(esp. 133 ff.)–51 (with further references).

236. On Muḥammad b. ᶜUmar al-Wāqidī, d. 207/822–3, see *EI*[1], s.v. al-

Zubayr, he appointed ᶜUbaydah b. al-Zubayr[237] over Medina and ᶜAbd al-Raḥmān b. Jaḥdam al-Fihrī[238] over Egypt, and he expelled the Banū Umayyah and Marwān b. al-Ḥakam to Syria. At that time, ᶜAbd al-Malik[239] was twenty-eight years old. When Ḥuṣayn b. Numayr and those who were with him reached Syria, he told Marwān of the situation in which he had left Ibn al-Zubayr and that he had summoned Ibn al-Zubayr to accept the oath of allegiance but he had refused. Ḥuṣayn said to Marwān and to the Banū Umayyah, "We can see that you are in great confusion, so put your affairs in order before he moves into your Syria against you and indiscriminate civil discord breaks out."[240] It was Marwān's opinion that he should set out and hurry to Ibn al-Zubayr to give him the oath of allegiance. Then ᶜUbaydallāh b. Ziyād arrived, however, and the Banū Umayyah met with him. ᶜUbaydallāh had heard what Marwān wanted to do and he said to him, "I am ashamed at you for what you want! You are the senior man of Quraysh, and its *sayyid*. It will do what you do." And he said, "Nothing is yet lost." The Banū Umayyah and its mawlās supported him and the Yemenis[241] rallied to him, and he set out, saying, "Nothing is yet lost." He and those who

[468] were with him came to Damascus, the people of which had given the oath of allegiance to al-Ḍaḥḥāk b. Qays al-Fihrī on the understanding that he should lead them in prayer and manage their affairs until the question of authority over the community of Muḥammad had been settled.

As for ᶜAwānah, according to Hishām's report from him, he said: When Yazīd b. Muᶜāwiyah had died and his son Muᶜāwiyah after him (I heard that after his accession Muᶜā-wiyah b. Yazīd b. Muᶜāwiyah had given the command and a

---

Wāḳidī, *GAS*, I, 294–7; on Muḥammad b. Saᶜd, d. 230/845, see *EI²*, s.v., *GAS*, I, 300–1.

237. ᶜAbdallāh b. al-Zubayr's brother (of the Banū Asad of Quraysh).

238. Also called ᶜAbd al-Raḥmān b. ᶜUtbah, of the Banū Fihr of Quraysh (see Zubayrī, *Nasab Quraysh*, 445 and n. 1).

239. Marwān's son and successor; see *EI²*, s.v.

240. Literally, "a blind and deaf *fitnah*."

241. I.e., the "southern" Arab tribes in Syria which were regarded as descendants of Qaḥṭān, or allies of these tribes.

communal prayer was proclaimed in Damascus.[242] He praised
God and extolled Him and then said, "To come to the point,
I have considered the matter of authority among you and I
do not have the strength for it. I sought for you somebody
like ᶜUmar b. al-Khaṭṭāb [God's mercy be upon him] when
Abū Bakr had recourse to him, but I have not found such a
man. And I have sought for you six men to consult among
themselves like the six appointed by ᶜUmar, but I have not
found them. You are best fitted to decide your own affairs,
so choose for them somebody you love." Then he went into
his residence and did not again come out to the people,
remaining absent until he died. Some authorities say that he
was secretly given poison to drink, some that he was stabbed.
We now return to the report of ᶜAwānah], ᶜUbaydallāh b.
Ziyād came to Damascus.

Al-Ḍaḥḥāk b. Qays al-Fihrī was in authority there.[243] In
Qinnasrīn, Zufar b. al-Ḥārith al-Kilābī[244] revolted and gave the
oath of allegiance to ᶜAbdallāh b. al-Zubayr, and in Ḥimṣ, al-
Nuᶜmān b. Bashīr al-Anṣārī[245] also gave Ibn al-Zubayr his
allegiance. In Palestine, Ḥassān b. Mālik b. Baḥdal al-Kalbī[246]
was governing, first for Muᶜāwiyah b. Abī Sufyān and then
afterward for Yazīd b. Muᶜāwiyah. He was fervently for the
Banū Umayyah and he was the *sayyid* of the people of Palestine. Ḥassān b. Mālik b. Baḥdal al-Kalbī summoned Rawḥ
b. Zinbāᶜ al-Judhāmī[247] and said, "I am appointing you deputy
over Palestine. Include this clan of Lakhm with Judhām[248] and

---

242. Here al-Sha'm presumably means Damascus, although above and below
the town is called Dimashq.

243. The following paragraph summarizes the situation in each of the
military and administrative districts *(ajnād)* of Syria: Damascus, Qinnasrīn,
Ḥimṣ, Palestine and Jordan (see *EI²*, s.v. Djund).

244. Al-Ḥārith rather than ᶜAbdallāh (see *Add. et emend.*); on him, see
Crone, *Slaves*, 108–9; Rotter, *Bürgerkrieg*, 135–6; *Ansāb*, V, 132⁴, says that
Zufar b. al-Ḥārith *had* revolted, *wa-qad thāra Zufar*.

245. Son of a Medinese Companion (on him see *EI¹*, s.v.; Crone, *Slaves*,
155; Rotter, *Bürgerkrieg*, 137).

246. Related to the Sufyānids by marriage, leader of Quḍāᶜah (see *EI²*, s.v.;
Crone, *Slaves*, 93–4; Rotter, *Bürgerkrieg*, 128 ff.).

247. One of two rivals for the leadership of Judhām (see next note); on
him see Crone, *Slaves*, 99–100.

248. Tribes settled alongside each other in the Jordan/Palestine region and

[469]   you will not be short of men. Since you are the most eminent
of them, you will have the backing of those of your people
who are with you." Ḥassān b. Mālik then went to the district
of Jordan and left Rawḥ b. Zinbāᶜ as his deputy over Palestine.
Nātil b. Qays,[249] however, revolted against Rawḥ b. Zinbāᶜ,
expelled him, proclaimed himself in authority over Palestine
and gave the oath of allegiance to Ibn al-Zubayr.

ᶜAbdallāh b. al-Zubayr had written to his governor over
Medina telling him to expel the Banū Umayyah from the
town, and they were expelled with their dependents and women
to Syria. They reached Damascus, where Marwān b. al-Ḥakam
was.[250] The people were divided into two parties: Ḥassān b.
Mālik in Jordan was fervently for the Banū Umayyah and
propagandized on their behalf, while al-Ḍaḥḥāk b. Qays al-
Fihrī in Damascus was fervently for ᶜAbdallāh b. al-Zubayr
and propagandized for him.

Ḥassān b. Mālik remained in the Jordan district and said,
"Oh people of Jordan, what do you witness for Ibn al-Zubayr
and those who were killed of the people of the Ḥarrah?"[251]
They replied, "We bear witness that Ibn al-Zubayr is a hypocrite [munāfiq][252] and those of the people of the Ḥarrah who
were killed are in hell." "And what do you witness for Yazīd
b. Muᶜāwiyah and those of you who were killed at the Ḥarrah?"
he said. They answered, "We witness that Yazīd was in the
right and that those of us killed are in heaven." He said, "And
I witness that, if the religion [dīn] of Yazīd b. Muᶜāwiyah was
truth while he was alive at that time, it is still so today and
his party [shīᶜah] are in the right. And if Ibn al-Zubayr and
his party were at that time in falsehood, he is today still in
falsehood and so is his party." They told him, "You have
spoken right. We give you the oath of allegiance on condition

---

in alliance, with Judhām dominating; Lakhm seems already to have been
assigned to Yemen, while Judhām's descent was still an open question, some
claiming a Yemenī affiliation, others a "northern" (Maᶜadd) (see Caskel/Ibn
Kalbī, I, table 176, II, 264, 375–6; EI², s.vv. Djudhām, Lakhm).

249. Ibn Zinbāᶜ's rival for the leadership of Judhām.

250. Ansāb, V, 132¹⁰, reads wa-fīhim Marwān "and Marwān was among
them," which seems better.

251. See n. 10 above.

252. On this word, see Jeffery, Foreign Vocabulary, s.v.

that we fight those of the people who oppose you and obey
Ibn al-Zubayr, and on condition that we do not have either
of these two lads to rule over us for we find that abhorrent
(they meant the two sons of Yazīd b. Muᶜāwiyah, ᶜAbdallāh
and Khālid).[253] They are short in years and we dislike the idea
that the others should come to us with a shaykh while we
bring them a youngster."

Al-Ḍaḥḥāk b. Qays in Damascus was fervently for Ibn al-   [470]
Zubayr, but the fact that the Banū Umayyah were present
there prevented him from proclaiming it openly, so he worked
secretly in support of him. However, Ḥassān b. Mālik b.
Baḥdal heard of it and sent a letter to al-Ḍaḥḥāk in which he
stressed the legitimacy of the Banū Umayyah, reminded him
of the importance of obedience and communal unity, the favor
which the Banū Umayyah had shown him and the pains they
had taken for him, and he called upon him to obey them.
Further, he referred to Ibn al-Zubayr, disparaged him and
abused him, mentioned that he was a hypocrite who had
refused to accept two caliphs, and he told al-Ḍaḥḥāk to read
out the letter to the people. Ḥassān then called for a man of
Kalb, named Nāghiḍah,[254] and sent him off with the letter to
al-Ḍaḥḥāk b. Qays, but he also made a copy of the letter and
gave it to Nāghiḍah saying, "So long as al-Ḍaḥḥāk reads out
my letter to the people, that is all right, but if he does not,
then you are to get up and read this letter out to them." In
addition, he also wrote to the Banū Umayyah asking them to
be present when the letter was read.

Nāghiḍah came to al-Ḍaḥḥāk with the letter and gave it to
him. He also gave the Banū Umayyah their letter. On the
Friday, al-Ḍaḥḥāk went up on the *minbar* and Nāghiḍah stood
before him and said, "God save the governor! Call for the
letter of Ḥassān and read it out to the people," but al-Ḍaḥḥāk said, "Sit down!" He sat down but then stood up a second

---

253. The two surviving sons of Yazīd by different mothers; the former is
known as al-Uswār, the latter is famous as a (legendary?) alchemist (see
Zubayrī, *Nasab Quraysh*, 128–9 and on the latter, see *EI²*, s.v. Khālid b. Yazīd).
254. *Ansāb*, V, 133¹, has "Nāᶜiṣah, one of the descendants of Thaᶜlab b.
Wabarah, the brother of Kalb"; Ibn ᶜAsākir and Ibn al-Athīr read Bāghiḍah.
Goitein refers to *LA*, VIII, 368⁴, for the name Nāᶜiṣah.

time, and again al-Ḍaḥḥāk said, "Sit down!" The same happened on a third occasion and when Nāghiḍah saw that he was not going to do what he asked, he got out the letter which he had with him and read it out to the people. Al-Walīd b. ᶜUtbah b. Abī Sufyān[255] then arose and said that Ḥassān spoke the truth while Ibn al-Zubayr, whom he reviled, was a liar. Next Yazīd b. Abī al-Nims al-Ghassānī[256] got up, proclaimed the truth of what Ḥassān had said and of his letter, and he abused Ibn al-Zubayr. He was followed by Sufyān b. al-Abrad al-Kalbī,[257] who said exactly the same. But then ᶜAmr b. Yazīd al-Ḥakamī[258] arose and he reviled Ḥassān and heaped praise on Ibn al-Zubayr.

[471]

Consequently, the people were in a tumult. Al-Ḍaḥḥāk ordered that al-Walīd b. ᶜUtbah, Yazīd b. Abī al-Nims, and Sufyān b. al-Abrad, who had asserted the truth of what Ḥassān said and reviled Ibn al-Zubayr, be imprisoned, and they were. The people assailed one another and Kalb attacked ᶜAmr b. Yazīd al-Ḥakamī, setting him on fire and tearing his clothes. Khālid b. Yazīd b. Muᶜāwiyah arose and ascended two steps of the *minbar*. At that time he was still a boy. Al-Ḍaḥḥāk b. Qays was on the *minbar*, but Khālid b. Yazīd delivered a very succinct speech, the like of which had never been heard, and the people fell quiet. Al-Ḍaḥḥāk came down from the *minbar* and led the assembly in the Friday prayer, and then went to his residence. The Kalb came and released Sufyān b. al-Abrad while Ghassān did the same for Yazīd b. Abī al-Nims, so that al-Walīd b. ᶜUtbah complained, "If only I were of Kalb or Ghassān, I would have been released!" However, the two sons of Yazīd b. Muᶜāwiyah, Khālid and ᶜAbdallāh, came with their maternal relatives of Kalb and got him out of the prison.

---

255. Former governor of Medina, member of the family to which the first three Umayyad caliphs had belonged, had unsuccessfully attempted to obtain the oath of allegiance for Yazīd from Ibn al-Zubayr and al-Ḥusayn following the death of Muᶜāwiyah (Zubayrī, *Nasab Quraysh*, 132–3).

256. Leader (?) of the Ghassānī tribe, settled in Jordan before the Arab conquests (see Rotter, *Bürgerkrieg*, index s.v.).

257. Later prominent in fighting on behalf of the Umayyads under ᶜAbd al-Malik and al-Ḥajjāj (see Caskel/Ibn Kalbī, I, table 286, 515).

258. Wellhausen, *Arab Kingdom*, 172, makes him the son of the Umayyad Yazīd b. al-Ḥakam, but cf. Lammens, *Marwānides*, 29/69, n. 1, Rotter, *Bürgerkrieg*, 139, n. 207.

That was the day which the Syrians call "the first day of Jayrūn."[259] The people remained as they were in Damascus, and al-Ḍaḥḥāk came out to the mosque of the town and took his seat there. He referred to Yazīd b. Muʿāwiyah and disparaged him and then a young man of Kalb arose with a staff with which he struck him. The people were sitting in the groups girded with their swords and they attacked one another in the mosque and fought, the Qays appealing for support for Ibn al-Zubayr and assistance for al-Ḍaḥḥāk, while Kalb shouted for the Banū Umayyah, especially for Khālid b. Yazīd, since they felt family solidarity with Yazīd. Al-Ḍaḥḥāk retired into the government house.

Next day, he did not come out for the dawn prayer ritual. Some of the soldiers were fervently for the Banū Umayyah, some fervently for Ibn al-Zubayr. Al-Ḍaḥḥāk sent for the Banū Umayyah and they went to him on the morrow. He apologized to them and mentioned the pains they had taken in showing favor to his mawlās[260] and to himself and said that he desired nothing which they disliked. He said, "So let us both write to Ḥassān and he will come from Jordan and camp at al-Jābiyah[261] and we will all go and join him there. Then we will give the oath of allegiance to one of you." The Banū Umayyah accepted that, and they and al-Ḍaḥḥāk both wrote to Ḥassān. And then the Banū Umayyah and the people came out, the banners were put in front, and they set out aiming for al-Jābiyah.

[472]

Thawr b. Maʿn b. Yazīd b. al-Akhnas al-Sulamī[262] now came to al-Ḍaḥḥāk and said, "You summoned us to obedience to Ibn al-Zubayr and we gave you the oath of allegiance on that understanding. But now you are going to this Kalbī bedouin to make his nephew,[263] Khālid b. Yazīd, caliph." Al-Ḍaḥḥāk

---

259. See Wellhausen, *Arab Kingdom*, 172, n. 1, F. Buhl, "Zur Krisis der Umajjadenherrschaft im Jahre 684," *ZA*, XXVII (1912), 61; for a possible eschatological connection, see N. Wieder, *The Judaean Scrolls and Karaism*, London, 1962, 19.

260. See Crone, *Slaves*, 198; the parallel passage in *Ansāb*, V, 133[20-21], does not refer to the mawlās.

261. Former center of the Ghassānid "kings," about 50 miles south of Damascus (see *EI²*, s.v. Djābiya).

262. Of Qays, killed at Marj Rāhiṭ (see below).

263. Read *ibn ukhtihi*.

said to him, "So what do you think?" and he answered, "I think we should proclaim openly that which we were keeping secret, summon to obedience to Ibn al-Zubayr, and fight for it." And al-Ḍaḥḥāk turned aside with those of the people who were with him and won them over. Then he continued journeying as far as Marj Rāhiṭ,[264] where he pitched camp.

There are variant accounts of the battle which took place at Marj Rāhiṭ between al-Ḍaḥḥāk b. Qays and Marwān b. al-Ḥakam.

According to Muḥammad b. ᶜUmar al-Wāqidī: Marwān b. al-Ḥakam was given the oath of allegiance in Muḥarram, 65 (August–September 684). Marwān was in Syria and did not concern himself with the matter until ᶜUbaydallāh b. Ziyād encouraged him to do that when he came to him from Iraq. He said to him, "You are the senior man of Quraysh and its head, but al-Ḍaḥḥāk b. Qays has authority over you!" That led to what followed. Marwān went against al-Ḍaḥḥāk with an army and slew him and his supporters. At that time al-Ḍaḥḥāk was obedient to Ibn al-Zubayr. There was a slaughter [473] of the Banū Qays at Marj Rāhiṭ such as had never occurred on any field.

According to Muḥammad b. ᶜUmar—Ibn Abī al-Zinād—Hishām b. ᶜUrwah:[265] Al-Ḍaḥḥāk was killed at the day of Marj Rāhiṭ while calling on people to accept Ibn al-Zubayr. We were told of it in a letter sent to ᶜAbdallāh b. al-Zubayr, and al-Ḍaḥḥāk's obedience to him and the rectitude of his views were referred to.[266]

Several authorities say that the battle of Marj Rāhiṭ between al-Ḍaḥḥāk and Marwān was in the year 64 (August 683–August 684).

I was told on the authority of Ibn Saᶜd—Muḥammad b. ᶜUmar—Mūsā b. Yaᶜqūb—Abū al-Ḥuwayrith: The people of Jordan and others said to Marwān, "You are a great shaykh, while the son of Yazīd is a boy and Ibn al-Zubayr is in middle age. Only iron will strike iron, so do not challenge him with

---

264. On the site, see *EI*[2], s.v.
265. Hishām b. ᶜUrwah b. al-Zubayr, d. 146/763, Ibn al-Zubayr's nephew (on him, see *GAS*, I, 88–9).
266. The text seems to be corrupt (see *Add. et emend.*).

this boy. Meet him head on and we will give you the oath of allegiance. Hold out your hand!" So he held out his hand and they gave him the oath of allegiance at al-Jābiyah on Wednesday when three days had passed of Dhū al-Qaʿdah in the year 64 (June 22, 684).

According to Muḥammad b. ʿUmar—Muṣʿab b. Thābit—ʿĀmir b. ʿAbdallāh: When al-Ḍaḥḥāk heard that they had given Marwān the oath of allegiance as caliph, he took the oath of allegiance from his supporters on behalf of Ibn al-Zubayr. Then they marched against one another and fought a great battle. Al-Ḍaḥḥāk and his men were killed.

According to Muḥammad b. ʿUmar—Ibn Abī al-Zinād—his father: When ʿAbd al-Raḥmān b. al-Ḍaḥḥāk[267] was governor over Medina, he was just a young man. He said that al-Ḍaḥḥāk b. Qays had invited Qays and others to give the oath of allegiance to himself (al-Ḍaḥḥāk) and that he took the oath of allegiance from them as caliph. Zufar b. ʿAqīl al-Fihrī[268] said to ʿAbd al-Raḥmān, "That is how we understood and heard it, but the descendants of al-Zubayr say that al-Ḍaḥḥāk only gave ʿAbdallāh b. al-Zubayr the oath of allegiance and went out in obedience to him until he was killed. They lie, by God! What led to that (his taking the oath of allegiance for himself) was that Quraysh summoned him to it. He at first refused, only agreeing to it reluctantly."[269]

[474]

---

267. The son of al-Ḍaḥḥāk b. Qays governed al-Madīnah for Yazīd (II) b. ʿAbd al-Malik (regn. 101–5/720–4).

268. Of the same Qurashī family as al-Ḍaḥḥāk.

269. The sense of the text here is somewhat uncertain, particularly with regard to the meaning and function of al-bāṭila in the first line of p. 474. My translation results from a comparison with the parallel passage in Ibn ʿAsākir, Tahdhīb, VII, 6, which is virtually the same as far as wa-kharaja fī ṭāʿatihi, but then continues ḥattā qutila ʿalayhā qāla al-bāṭila wa'llāhi ya-qūlūna. This seems to show that ʿAbd al-Raḥmān b. al-Ḍaḥḥāk is denying what the descendants of al-Zubayr say regarding al-Ḍaḥḥāk's allegiance. That Quraysh summoned al-Ḍaḥḥāk to take the oath of allegiance to himself and not to Ibn al-Zubayr is indicated by a further addition in the text of Ibn ʿAsākir: wa-lākin kāna awwalu dhālik an Qurayshan daʿathu ilayhā wa-qālat inta kabīrunā wa 'l-qā'im bi-dami 'l-khalīfati 'l-maẓlūm. . . . All this may, however, be merely an attempt to make sense of a garbled text. See further, Wellhausen, Arab Kingdom, 176, 178; Buhl, "Krisis," 53–4, 59 (based on Ibn Saʿd, V, 27–9); Lammens, Marwānides, 40–1/80–1; EI², s.v. al-Ḍaḥḥāk b. Kays; Rotter, Bürgerkrieg, 141, 143.

The Battle at Marj Rāhiṭ between al-Ḍaḥḥāk b. Qays and Marwān b. al-Ḥakam and Its Immediate Consequences

Abū Jaʿfar (al-Ṭabarī) said: According to Nūḥ b. Ḥabīb—Hishām b. Muḥammad—ʿAwānah b. al-Ḥakam al-Kalbī: When he headed for al-Jābiyah to meet Ḥassān b. Mālik, al-Ḍaḥḥāk b. Qays turned aside with those who were with him and won them over.[270] Then he pressed on and pitched camp at Marj Rāhiṭ. There he publicly proclaimed the oath of allegiance to Ibn al-Zubayr and renounced the Banū Umayyah. The majority of the men of Damascus, both Yemenis and others, gave him the oath of allegiance on that basis. The Banū Umayyah and their followers traveled on until they reached Ḥassān at al-Jābiyah. Ḥassān led their ritual prayers for forty days while the men consulted among themselves. Al-Ḍaḥḥāk wrote to al-Nuʿmān b. Bashīr who was governor over Ḥimṣ, to Zufar b. al-Ḥārith who was over Qinnasrīn, and to Nātil b. Qays who was over Palestine, asking for help, for they were all in obedience to Ibn al-Zubayr. Al-Nuʿmān sent him Shuraḥbīl b. Dhī al-Kalāʿ [271] to help him, Zufar sent the men of Qinnasrīn, and Nātil sent the men of Palestine. The forces joined al-Ḍaḥḥāk at the "meadow."[272]

At al-Jābiyah, the people had various wishes. Mālik b. Hubayrah al-Sakūnī[273] was a fervent supporter of Yazīd b. Muʿāwiyah's sons and wanted the caliphate to be among them; al-Ḥusayn b. Numayr al-Sakūnī eagerly desired the caliphate for Marwān b. al-Ḥakam. Mālik b. Hubayrah said to al-Ḥusayn b. Numayr, "Come on, let us give the oath of allegiance to this lad whose father we begat. He is descended from one

[475]

---

270. This is the continuation of ʿAwānah's account which broke off at p. 54 above.

271. Member of one of the two chief Ḥimyarī families of Ḥimṣ; one is to understand he was sent as leader of a force of men from Ḥimṣ (see Crone, *Slaves*, 94–5; Rotter, *Bürgerkrieg*, 131, 151, 187, 191).

272. Ar. *al-marj*, i.e., presumably Marj Rāhiṭ, although Lammens postulated an earlier engagement at Marj al-Ṣuffar.

273. Like his fellow Sakūnī, al-Ḥusayn b. Numayr, he was a leader of Kindah in Syria (Rotter, *Bürgerkrieg*, 131 and index).

of our women[274] and you know that our present status derives from his father, and he will shortly place our yoke on the necks of the Arabs" (he meant Khālid b. Yazīd). But al-Ḥusayn said, "No, by God Eternal, the Arabs will not come to us with a shaykh while we go to them with a youth!" Mālik said, "You say this even though you (my female riding camel) have not reached Tihāmah and the girth has not yet reached the two teats!"[275] Those present said, "Gently, Oh Abū Sulaymān!" but Mālik said to al-Ḥusayn, "By God, if you give the caliphate to Marwān and his family, they will be jealous even of your whip, the lace of your sandal, and the shade of a tree where you seek shelter from the sun. Marwān is the father of a clan, the brother of a clan and the uncle of a clan, and if you give him the oath of allegiance you will be their slaves. Rather, accept the authority of Khālid, the descendant of a woman of your own blood." But al-Ḥusayn replied, "In a dream I saw a candlestick suspended from the heavens. Those who are now eager for the caliphate reached out for it but did not obtain it, but Marwān reached out for it and got it. By God, we will indeed appoint him as caliph." Mālik said to him, "Woe to you, Ḥusayn. Will you give the oath of allegiance to Marwān and the family of Marwān when you know they are a leading family of Qays?"

When they had made up their minds to give the oath of allegiance to Marwān b. al-Ḥakam, Rawḥ b. Zinbāᶜ al-Judhāmī arose, praised God and extolled Him, and then said, "Oh people, you talk about ᶜAbdallāh b. ᶜUmar b. al-Khaṭṭāb,[276] his companionship with the Prophet and his precedence in Islam. He is just as you say, but Ibn ᶜUmar is a weak man and no weak man can be master of the community of Muḥammad.

---

274. Khālid b. Yazīd's mother seems to have been a Qurashī, and Mālik's reference is to Khālid's grandmother, wife of Muᶜāwiyah, who was a woman of Kalb (see Zubayrī, *Nasab Quraysh*, 129).

275. See Freytag, *Proverbia*, II, 873, and I, 293 (Maydānī, *Amthāl*, under *hā'* and *jīm*). Two proverbs which seem together to mean "come on faint-heart, things have not yet become impossible." Cf. p. 69 below, where they are attributed to Mālik as a response to Marwān.

276. Son of the second caliph, sometimes mentioned as a possible candidate for the caliphate although he seems to have been unwilling to accept nomination (see *EI²*, s.v.).

As for what is said about ᶜAbdallāh b. al-Zubayr and what is
[476] claimed for him, by God it is just as they say as to his being
the son of al-Zubayr, who was the disciple of the Messenger
of God,[277] and of Asmā', who was the daughter of Abū Bakr
the Righteous One, and 'mistress of the two girdles.'[278] Furthermore, he is just as you say regarding his precedence in
Islam and his merit. But Ibn al-Zubayr is a hypocrite [*munāfiq*]
who has rejected two caliphs, Yazīd and his son Muᶜāwiyah
b. Yazīd, shed blood, and broken the staff of the Muslims.[279]
A hypocrite cannot be the master of the affairs of Muḥammad's
community. As for Marwān b. al-Ḥakam, by God, there has
never been a split in Islam but that Marwān was one of those
who repaired it. He fought for the Commander of the Faithful
ᶜUthmān b. al-ᶜAffān on the 'Day of the House,'[280] and he
fought against ᶜAlī b. Abī Ṭālib at the 'Day of the Camel.'[281]
We think the people should give the oath of allegiance to the
elder and consider the junior too immature." (By the "elder"
he meant Marwān b. al-Ḥakam, and by the "junior" Khālid
b. Yazīd b. Muᶜāwiyah.)

Agreement was reached on allegiance to Marwān, then to
Khālid b. Yazīd as his successor, and then to ᶜAmr b. Saᶜīd b.
al-ᶜĀṣ as successor to Khālid, on condition that the governorate
of Damascus should be for ᶜAmr b. Saᶜīd b. al-ᶜĀṣ and that
of Ḥimṣ for Khālid b. Yazīd b. Muᶜāwiyah. Ḥassān b. Mālik
b. Baḥdal, therefore, summoned Khālid b. Yazīd and said, "Oh
my nephew, the people have rejected you on account of your

---

277. Ar. *ḥawārī*, a word which is used in the Qur'ān in its plural form to
refer to the followers of Jesus and seems to be related to the Ethiopic word
for "apostle" (Jeffery, *Foreign Vocabulary*, s.v.). It is not clear why al-Zubayr,
among all the Companions of Muḥammad, should be designated as his *ḥawārī*.

278. Daughter of the first caliph Abū Bakr, Asmā' was married to al-Zubayr;
her sobriquet is attributed to her having torn her girdle or waistband (*ni-
ṭāq*) in two at the time of the *hijrah* in order to provide the Prophet with a
provision bag and a strap for his waterskin (see *EI²*, s.v.).

279. A common expression indicating disruption of the community.

280. The traditional name for the attack against the third caliph ᶜUthmān
in 656; he was killed in his "house" (*dār*) in Medina; Marwān is said to have
been ᶜUthmān's secretary.

281. Traditional name for the battle near al-Baṣrah between the fourth
caliph ᶜAlī and his opponents, among whom was Ibn al-Zubayr's father, at
the end of 656 (see *EI²*, s.v. Djamal).

lack of years. I myself do not want this matter to be entrusted
to anybody but you and your family, and I will only give
Marwān the oath of allegiance out of regard for you." Khālid
b. Yazīd said to him, "No, rather, you were not strong enough
for us." Ḥassān answered, "No by God, it was not that I was
not strong enough for you but what I think is considered best
for you." Then Ḥassān summoned Marwān and said, "Oh
Marwān, by God not everyone is satisfied with you." Marwān   [477]
replied, "If God wishes to give it to me, none of His creatures
can stop me getting it, but if He wishes to keep it away from
me, none of His creatures can give it to me." Ḥassān said to
him, "You have spoken the truth."

On the Monday, Ḥassān went up on the *minbar* and said,
"Oh people, we shall, God willing, appoint a caliph on Thursday." On the Thursday, he gave the oath of allegiance to
Marwān and so did the people. Marwān then journeyed with
the people toward al-Jābiyah and pitched camp at Marj Rāhiṭ among the men of Jordan of the Banū Kalb[282] over against
al-Ḍaḥḥāk. The Sakāsik, the Sakūn,[283] and the Ghassān joined
him while Ḥassān b. Mālik b. Baḥdal rode off to the Jordan
district.

In command of the forces of his right wing (I mean of
Marwān) was ᶜAmr b. Saᶜīd b. al-ᶜĀṣ,[284] and of his left wing
ᶜUbaydallāh b. Ziyād. Ziyād b. ᶜAmr b. Muᶜāwiyah al-ᶜUqaylī[285]
led the right wing of al-Ḍaḥḥāk, and somebody else whose
name I do not remember was over his left. Yazīd b. Abī al-
Nims al-Ghassānī was not present at al-Jābiyah, for he was
concealed in Damascus. When Marwān camped at Marj
Rāhiṭ, Yazīd b. Abī al-Nims led a rising of the people of
Damascus with its slaves,[286] got control there, and drove al-

---

282. I.e., the Kalb from the military district of Urdunn.

283. The Sakāsik (pl. of Saksak) and Sakūn were two tribes of Kindah (see
Caskel/Ibn Kalbī, I, table 233, II, 503).

284. A leading Umayyad of the family of al-ᶜĀṣ (see *EI²*, s.v. ᶜAmr b. Saᶜīd
al-Ashdaḳ).

285. Of the Banū Qays.

286. Ar. *bi-ahli Dimashq fī ᶜabīdihā;* the sense of this is unclear to me; the
parallel passage, *Ansāb*, V, 136, merely says that Yazīd "got control over
Damascus," Rotter, *Bürgerkrieg*, 149, n. 254, interprets Ṭabarī's text to mean
that Yazīd received help from the slaves living in Damascus; cf. Crone, *Slaves*,
264, n. 647, "with the help of the slaves of the Damascenes."

Ḍaḥḥāk's official out. He obtained possession of the store-houses and the treasury, proclaimed the oath of allegiance to Marwān and sent him help in the form of wealth, men and arms. That was the first success won for the Banū Umay-yah.

Marwān fought al-Ḍaḥḥāk for twenty days and then the people of the "meadow" were defeated and slain. Al-Ḍaḥḥāk was killed and with him on that day were killed eighty of the most notable of the Syrians who supported him, all of whom "took the rug"[287] (those who "took the rug" drew two thousand dirhams in pay). And there was a slaughter of the Syrians on that day such as had never occurred before, from all of the tribes. On that day there were killed with al-Ḍaḥḥāk a Kalbī of the Banū ᶜUlaym called Mālik b. Yazīd b. Mālik b. Kaᶜb[288] and also the standard bearer of Quḍāᶜah at the time when they had first entered Syria, the grandfather of Muddalij b. al-Miqdam b. Zaml b. ᶜAmr b. Rabīᶜa b. ᶜAmr al-Jurashī.[289] Killed, too, was Thawr b. Maᶜn b. Yazīd al-Sulamī, who had caused al-Ḍaḥḥāk to change his mind. A man of Kalb brought the head of al-Ḍaḥḥāk, and it is reported that when the head was brought to Marwān it troubled him and he said, "Now, when I am old and my bones are brittle and I have become thirsty like an ass,[290] I have started striking the detachments one with another."

It is reported that on that day, Marwān passed by one of the slain and said:

[478]

---

287. Ar. *akhadha 'l-qaṭīfah*, evidently an indication of status; the *qaṭīfah* here seems to be a riding rug; cf. p. 35 above, where it is reported that Ibn Ziyād had a *qaṭīfah* thrown over his mount while fleeing from Iraq.

288. For the Banū ᶜUlaym (of Kinānah/Kalb), see Caskel/Ibn Kalbī, I, tables 280, 283; *ibid.*, II, 396, says that Mālik b. Yazīd fell at Ṣiffīn fighting for Muᶜāwiyah.

289. This name seems to be corrupt: I suspect it refers to Mudlij b. al-Miqdād b. Ziml al-ᶜUdhrī (of Quḍāᶜah; see Caskel/Ibn Kalbī, I, table 331); according to Ibn Saᶜd, I/2, 67, the grandfather of Mudlij, Zamil *(sic)* b. ᶜAmr al-ᶜUdhrī, was given a banner for his people by the Prophet, subsequently was at Ṣiffīn with Muᶜāwiyah and then fought at al-Marj where he was killed.

290. Proverbial for "only a short life remaining"; the ass is reputedly the thirstiest of animals, and Marwān is saying that he only has left a time comparable to that between the two drinkings of an ass (see Lane, *Lexicon*, s.v. *ẓama'*).

It was only their mutual hatred which
   led them to harm,
   whichever of the two Qurashī commanders triumphed.[291]

And when he was given the oath of allegiance and called upon the people to support him, he said:

When I saw that the affair would be one
   of plunder,
   I made ready Ghassān and Kalb against
   them,
And the Saksakīs, men who would
   triumph,
   and Ṭayyi', who would insist on the
   striking of blows,
And the Qayn[292] who would come weighed
   down with arms,[293]
   and of Tanūkh a difficult lofty peak.[294]
(The enemy) will not seize the kingship
   unless by force,
   and if Qays approach, say, "Keep
   away!"[295]

According to Hishām b. Muḥammad—Abū Mikhnaf Lūṭ b.   [479]
Yaḥyā—one of the Banū ʿAbd Wadd[296] of the people of Syria—
someone who witnessed the killing of al-Ḍaḥḥāk b. Qays:
There passed by us a man of Kalb called Zuḥnah b. ʿAbdallāh.
It was as if he were simply bombarding the earth with men.
He never hit anybody without felling him and never struck
anybody without killing him. I was looking at him, astonished
at what he did and at his killing of men, when someone
attacked him. Zuḥnah, however, felled him and left him. I

---

291. See *Ansāb*, V, 137, n. *i*, for other citations.
292. Qayn are part of Quḍāʿah (see *EI²*, s.v. Ḳayn); all the tribal groups named as opponents of Qays are "southerners."
293. Ar. *nukb* (see *Add. et emend.*); i.e., like camels walking unevenly because weighed down on one side (see *Gloss.*, s.v.).
294. Ar. *mushmakhirr* (see *LA*, IV, 429; *TA*, III, 316).
295. *Ansāb*, V, 138, n. *m*, for other citations.
296. The Banū ʿAbd Wadd of Kinānah/Kalb (Caskel/Ibn Kalbī, I, tables 280, 294).

went up and examined the slain man and was surprised to find that it was al-Ḍaḥḥāk b. Qays. I took his head and brought it to Marwān who said, "Did you kill him?" "No," I said, "It was Zuḥnah b. ᶜAbdallāh al-Kalbī." It amazed him that I told the truth about it and did not claim it for myself, and he ordered that I be treated graciously and he rewarded Zuḥnah.

According to Abū Mikhnaf—ᶜAbd al-Malik b. Nawfal b. Masāḥiq—Ḥabīb b. Qurrah: By God, on that day Marwān's banner was with me. Pushing the "shoe" of the scabbard[297] of his sword into my back, he said, "Move forward with your banner, you bastard! If they do not feel the edge of the swords, these men will be separated like the head is separated (from the body) or like the sheep are separated from their shepherd." Marwān had a force of 6,000. ᶜUbaydallah b. Ziyād was in charge of his cavalry and Mālik b. Hubayrah of the foot soldiers.

ᶜAbd al-Malik b. Nawfal said: They reported that Bishr b. Marwān[298] had a banner with him on that day. He was fighting with it and saying:

On the leader there is indeed a duty,
    that his spear is dyed in blood or is broken
    to pieces.[299]

On that day also ᶜAbd al-ᶜAzīz b. Marwān was thrown to the ground. And on that day Marwān passed by a man of [480] Muḥārib[300] who was fighting for Marwān in a small group beneath a banner. Marwān said to him, "May God have mercy on you! If you and your companions drew tight together, then I would see how few in number you are." The man replied, "Oh Commander of the Faithful, there is a reinforcement of angels with us, many times the number of those with whom you tell us to draw together." Marwān was delighted at that

---

297. Ar. naᶜl, i.e., "the iron or silver thing (or shoe) at the lower end of the scabbard" (Lane, Lexicon, s.v.).

298. Marwān's son, future governor of al-Kūfah.

299. See Ansāb, V, 139, n. r; cf. Sīrah (Cairo), II, 74 = tr. Guillaume, 377.

300. The Banū Muḥārib b. Khaṣafah of Qays (?) (Caskel/Ibn Kalbī, I, table 92, II, 425).

and laughed and he reinforced the man with some of those who were around himself.

The men fled defeated from the "meadow" to their military districts. Those of Ḥimṣ came to Ḥimṣ, where al-Nuᶜmān b. Bashīr was in charge. When al-Nuᶜmān heard the news, he fled at night with his wife Nā'ilah bint ᶜUmārah al-Kalbiyyah together with his baggage and his children. All that night there was confusion, and next morning the people of Ḥimṣ looked for him. A man of the Banū al-Kalāᶜ[301] called ᶜAmr b. al-Khalī led the search for him. He killed al-Nuᶜmān and brought his head, together with Nā'ilah his wife and her children, and threw the head into the lap of Umm Abān, al-Nuᶜmān's daughter who was subsequently married to al-Ḥajjāj b. Yūsuf. But Nā'ilah said, "Throw the head to me for I have more right to it than she," and the head was thrown into her lap. Then they brought them along, together with the head, and reached Ḥimṣ with them, and the Kalbīs among the men of Ḥimṣ took charge of Nā'ilah and her children.

Zufar b. al-Ḥārith fled from Qinnasrīn and reached Qarqīsiyā. When he came there, ᶜIyāḍ al-Jurashī[302] was in charge and he prevented Zufar from entering. (ᶜIyāḍ was Ibn Aslam b. Kaᶜb b. Mālik b. Laghaz b. Aswad b. Kaᶜb b. Ḥadas b. Aslam, and Yazīd b. Muᶜāwiyah had appointed him prefect of Qarqīsiyā.) Zufar said to him, "I promise you on pain of having to divorce my wives and set free my slaves that once I have entered its bath I will leave the town." Once he had reached [481] the town and entered it, however, he never went into its bath but set himself up there and expelled ᶜIyāḍ. Zufar fortified the place and Qays gave him support.

Nātil b. Qays al-Judhāmī, the commander of Palestine, fled and joined Ibn al-Zubayr in Mecca.

The Syrians agreed on Marwān's ruling them and gave him their support, and he appointed his officials.

According to Abū Mikhnaf—one of the Banū ᶜAbd Wadd of the people of Syria (i.e., the eastern ᶜAbd Wadd): After

---

301. One of the two leading Ḥimyarī families of Ḥimṣ; on Shuraḥbīl b. Dhī al-Kalāᶜ, see n. 268 above.

302. According to *Ansāb*, V, 301⁵⁻⁶, he is ᶜIyāḍ b. ᶜAmr al-Ḥimyarī. Jurash was a tribe of Ḥimyar (Caskel/Ibn Kalbī, I, table 278).

authority over Syria had been vested in him, Marwān left and went to Egypt. When he reached it, ᶜAbd al-Raḥmān b. Jaḥdam al-Qurashī was in authority, summoning the people to obedience to Ibn al-Zubayr. He went out to meet Marwān with those of the Banū Fihr who were with him, but Marwān sent ᶜAmr b. Saᶜīd al-Ashdaq around behind. ᶜAmr entered Egypt[303] and stood on its *minbar*, where he delivered an official address to the people. Ibn Jaḥdam's supporters were told that ᶜAmr had entered Egypt and they turned back. The people recognized Marwān as *amīr* and gave him the oath of allegiance. Then he set out returning toward Damascus, but as he drew close to it he heard that Ibn al-Zubayr had sent his brother Muṣᶜab b. al-Zubayr toward Palestine.

Marwān despatched ᶜAmr b. Saᶜīd b. al-ᶜĀṣ with a force against him, and he confronted Muṣᶜab before he could enter Syria. ᶜAmr fought against him and Muṣᶜab's men were routed. With Muṣᶜab there was a man of the Banū ᶜUdhrah[304] called Muḥammad b. Ḥurayth b. Sulaym, one of whose female relatives had married into the family of al-Ashdaq.[305] This man said, "By God, I never saw anyone like Muṣᶜab b. al-Zubayr for the fierceness of his fighting on horseback or on foot. I saw him on the road going on foot and urging on his men, and he punished his own feet so much that I saw that both of them bled." Marwān went on and established his residence in Damascus, where ᶜAmr b. Saᶜīd returned to join him.

It is said that when ᶜUbaydallāh b. Ziyād came from Iraq to Syria, he found the Banū Umayyah at Palmyra. Ibn al-Zubayr had driven them out of Medina and Mecca and the Ḥijāz as a whole and they had settled in Palmyra, finding al-Ḍaḥḥāk b. Qays governing Syria for Ibn al-Zubayr. When Ibn Ziyād came, Marwān wanted to ride to Ibn al-Zubayr, give him the oath of allegiance as caliph, and obtain a pledge of security for the Banū Umayyah from him. But Ibn Ziyād said to him, "I implore you by God not to do so! It is not a good idea that you, the shaykh of Quraysh, should rush to Abū

[482]

---

303. Text has Miṣr; presumably Fusṭāṭ is meant, as indicated by the subsequent reference to "its *minbar*."

304. Of Quḍāᶜah (see Caskel/Ibn Kalbī, II, 565–6, *EI¹*, s.v.).

305. The family of the Umayyad ᶜAmr b. Saᶜīd al-Ashdaq (see n. 284, above).

Khubayb[306] to give him the caliphate. Rather, summon the people of Palmyra, take the oath of allegiance from them, and then go against al-Ḍaḥḥāk b. Qays with them and those of the Banū Umayyah who are with you and drive him out of Syria." ᶜAmr b. Saᶜīd b. al-ᶜĀṣ then said, "By God, ᶜUbaydallāh b. Ziyād has spoken right! I say again that you are the *sayyid* of Quraysh and its branch, and of all the people you have the most right to stand in this matter. Only the claims of this lad (he meant Khālid b. Yazīd b. Muᶜāwiyah) are under consideration, but you marry his mother and then you will be his guardian."

Marwān, therefore, did that and married the mother of Khālid b. Yazīd, Fākhitah,[307] the daughter of Abū Hāshim b. ᶜUtbah b. Rabīᶜah b. ᶜAbd Shams. Afterward, he gathered together the Banū Umayyah and they gave him the oath of allegiance as the one with authority over them, and the people of Palmyra also gave him the oath of allegiance. Then he set out with a great host against al-Ḍaḥḥāk b. Qays, who at that time was in Damascus. When al-Ḍaḥḥāk heard what the Banū Umayyah had done and of their coming against him, he set off with those of the people of Damascus and others who followed him, including Zufar b. al-Ḥārith. The forces met at Marj Rāhiṭ, where they fought a great battle. Al-Ḍaḥḥāk b. Qays al-Fihrī and most of his men were killed, while the survivors fled and scattered.

Zufar b. al-Ḥārith and two youths of the Banū Sulaym took part in this and Marwān's mounted soldiers came seeking them. When the two Sulamīs were afraid that Marwān's horsemen would catch up with them, they said to Zufar, "Save yourself, for we are slain!" So Zufar left them and carried on [483] until he reached Qarqīsiyā, where Qays rallied to him and made him their chief. That was when Zufar b. al-Ḥārith said:[308]

---

306. The *kunyah* of Ibn al-Zubayr (who also had the *kunyah* Abū Bakr); Khubayb was his eldest son; he died after a flogging he received in Medina during the governorate of ᶜUmar b. ᶜAbd al-ᶜAzīz there.
307. Zubayrī, *Nasab Quraysh*, 152, calls her Ḥayyah.
308. *Ansāb*, V, 141, note x, for other citations.

Show me my weapon you bastard[309] for I
    think the war will only increase in duration.
Secretly I heard that Marwān
    is seeking retaliation against my blood or cutting out
    my tongue.
But in the yellowy-white camels[310] there is salvation and
    in the land a refuge,
    when we have put upon them the reins.
Do not think me heedless if I am absent,
    and do not rejoice at meeting me if I come to you.
The pasture land might spring up on the ruins of the earth,
    but the souls' hatreds remain just as before.
Do Kalb depart and our spears not reach them,
    and are the slain ones of Rāhiṭ abandoned as they were?
By my life, the battle of Rāhiṭ has left
    for Ḥassān[311] a clear fissure ever-widening.
[484]   After Ibn ʿAmr and Ibn Maʿn,[312] one after the other,
    and the killing of Hammām,[313] do I still hope for
    anything?
Never was anything hateful seen of me before this
    flight of mine and my leaving my two companions
    behind me,
On the evening when I was running in al-Qirān[314] and
    only saw
    people who were against me and not for me.
Does one single day, if I have spoiled it, dispel
    the goodness of my days and the merit of my deeds?
There will be no peace until the horsemen come with spears,
    and my wives take vengeance from the women of Kalb.

---

309. See Lane, *Lexicon*, s.v. *abū*, for the statement that the exclamation is to be understood "may you have no father, for then you will need to exert yourself, relying on your own power!"

310. ʿĪṣ is the pl. of aʿyāṣ, according to Lane meaning a dingy or yellowy-white camel said to be of a good breed.

311. I.e., Ibn Baḥdal.

312. Ziyād b. ʿAmr al-ʿUqaylī and Thawr b. Maʿn (see pp. 59–60 above).

313. Hammām b. Qabīṣah al-Numayrī, a leader of the Qays in Damascus (see Crone, *Slaves*, 98; Rotter, *Bürgerkrieg*, 44).

314. The context seems to indicate that al-Qirān is a place name. Lammens, *Marwānides*, [71] 111, has: Le soir, où, dans la plaine, je courais. . .

I wish I knew, will my raiding
    Tanūkh and the tribe of Ṭayyi' achieve my cure?

Jawwās b. Qaᶜṭal[315] answered him:

By my life, the battle of Rāhiṭ has left   [485]
    for Zufar a malady which lingers
And persists. Its seat remains between the ribs
    and in the gut. It defies the doctor attempting a cure.
It (the battle) causes weeping for the slain of Sulaym, ᶜĀmir
    and Dhubyān[316] with reason and it makes the mourners
    weep and wail.
He calls for arms but then recoils when he sees
    the swords of Janāb[317] and the sleek and powerful horses.
On them are the young men of courage[318] like lions of the
    forest,
    when they advance toward the lofty spears.

ᶜAmr b. al-Mikhlāt al-Kalbī, of Taym Allāt b. Rufaydah, also
answered Zufar, saying:

Zufar the Qaysī wept for the destruction of his people
    with tearful eyes which will not cease to flow.
He orders mourning for those slain who were struck down
    at Rāhiṭ,
    and there answer him the small bird and the owl of the
    desert.
At Rāhiṭ we despoiled a protected area of the tribe of Qays
    which turned in fragments, and its women were made
    violable.
Hotly he mourns them while his tears flow,
    making Nizār wish that their nobility of spirit would   [486]
    return.
Die with grief or live humbled and oppressed
    with the sadness of a soul whose grief never sleeps.

---

315. Of the Banū Ḥiṣn b. Ḍamḍam b. Janāb al-Kalbī (see *Ansāb*, V, 142,
note y, for further citations).

316. All three Qaysī tribes.

317. I.e., the poet's clan.

318. Ar. *fityān najdah*, probably involving a play on the idea of "lion"
(*najīd*).

When Quḍāʿah brandish the spears around me,
   its noble steeds trample on the deeds of the unbroken
   mares.[319]
I have trampled with them on any tribe which has attacked
   me.
   Who, then, when misfortunes arise, desires to accept
   them?

Zufar b. al-Ḥārith also said:

Is it God's decree that, as for Baḥdal and Ibn Baḥdal,
   he should live, while, as for Ibn al-Zubayr, he should
   be killed?
No, by the House of God, you will not kill him!
   There was not yet a day glorious and triumphant
And not yet for the *mashrafiyyah*[320] sword above you
   rays like those of the rim of the sun when it begins
   to set.

ʿAbd al-Raḥmān b. al-Ḥakam, the brother of Marwān b. al-
Ḥakam, answered him and said:

Will Kalb vanish when their spears have protected
   them
   and will they leave unavenged the slain of Rāhiṭ
   which are unburied?
May God revile Qays, Qays ʿAylān, who
   neglected the borders of the Muslims and fled.
Be rivals of Qays in times of ease, but do not be
   their brother when the *mashrafiyyah* sword is
   drawn.

[487]   Abū Jaʿfar (al-Ṭabarī) said: Ḥusayn b. Numayr having given
the oath of allegiance to Marwān b. al-Ḥakam, and Mālik b.
Hubayrah having gone back on what he had made out he was
going to do as regards giving the oath of allegiance to Khālid
b. Yazīd b. Muʿāwiyah, the rule had become firmly established
with Marwān b. al-Ḥakam. Al-Ḥusayn b. Numayr had imposed

---

319. See Lane, *Lexicon*, s.v. muṣʿab.
320. A famous type of sword; the name is variously explained.

a condition on Marwān that he would settle those Kindīs who were in Syria in the Balqā' and make it a source of sustenance for them, and Marwān had agreed to that,[321] and the family of al-Ḥakam, when it became possible that the matter would be settled in Marwān's favor, had agreed to certain stipulations in favor of Khālid b. Yazīd b. Muʿāwiyah. Then one day as Marwān was in session with his council and Mālik b. Hubayrah was sitting with them, he said, "Among those who allege that conditions have been agreed to is one who is a bekohled and perfumed woman" (he meant Mālik b. Hubayrah, for he was a man who perfumed and bekohled himself). Mālik b. Hubayrah said, "You say this while you (my female riding camel) have not yet reached the Tihāmah and the girth has not yet reached the two teats!"[322] Marwān said, "Gently, Oh Abū Sulaymān! We are only joking with you." Mālik said, "So that is it!"

ʿUwayj al-Ṭā'ī said, praising Kalb and Ḥumayd b. Baḥdal:

The peoples have learned of the descent of Ibn Baḥdal
    and others upon them. If he lives he will do it again.
And they will lead the sons of the prominent man and
    those who join them
    from the fertile land for a month, he who leads them
    not flagging.
This because of this, and then I will scatter
    upon the people utterances many-edged.
If it were not for the Commander of the Faithful (re-
    straining us),
    Quḍāʿah would be lords and Qays their slaves.

In this year also, the army of Khurāsān gave the oath of allegiance to Salm b. Ziyād[323] following Yazīd b. Muʿāwiyah's death, on the understanding that he would remain in charge of their affairs until a caliph was agreed upon.   [488]

---

321. Cf. *Ansāb*, V, 149, where it is Mālik b. Hubayrah who imposes the condition on Marwān; the Balqā' is the region west of the Jordan south of Jerash, see *EI²*, s.v.
322. Cf. p. 57 above; here the proverb has a slightly different significance.
323. Brother of ʿUbaydallāh b. Ziyād.

And in it there occurred the troubles [*fitnah*] associated with ᶜAbdallāh b. Khāzim[324] in Khurāsān.

The Disturbances in Khurāsān Associated with ᶜAbdallāh b. Khāzim

According to ᶜUmar b. Shabbah—ᶜAlī b. Muḥammad—Maslamah b. Muḥārib:[325] Salm b. Ziyād sent ᶜAbdallāh b. Khāzim with the tribute he had received from Samarqand and Khwārazm to Yazīd b. Muᶜāwiyah. Salm remained as governor over Khurāsān until the death of Yazīd b. Muᶜāwiyah and Muᶜāwiyah b. Yazīd, whose death he heard about. News came to him too of the killing of Yazīd b. Ziyād in Sijistān and the capture of Abū ᶜUbaydah b. Ziyād,[326] but he kept the news secret.

Ibn ᶜArādah[327] said:

Oh you king who causes his door to be barred,
    matters have occurred recently of great importance!
Those slain at Junzah and those at Kabul,[328]
    and Yazīd whose hushed-up affair has been made known.
Oh Banū Umayyah, the end of your rule
    is a corpse at Huwwārīn,[329] there remaining.
His fate came upon him while by his pillow

---

324. Of the Banū Sulaym/Qays (see *EI²*, s.v.). For parallels and variants for the following section, see Balādhurī, *Futūḥ*, 413–4; Yaᶜqūbī, *Ta'rīkh*, II, 301; Ibn Aᶜtham, V, 309–11; Ibn al-Athīr, IV, 128–31; A.A. Dixon, *Umayyad Caliphate*, 105–9 (citing the ms. of *Ansāb*); C. E. Bosworth, *Sistan*, 48–9; Rotter, *Bürgerkrieg*, 88–93.

325. For the work of al-Madā'inī, which is Ṭabarī's source for events in Khurāsān, see Rotter, "Madā'inī," 122–8; for Maslamah b. Muḥārib, see n. 98 above.

326. For the events involving these two brothers of Salm in Sijistān and Afghanistan, see Bosworth, *Sistan*, 44; Rotter, *Bürgerkrieg*, 87–8.

327. Al-Saᶜdī (*Ansab*, IVb, 76); see Ibn Aᶜtham, V, 310, Ibn al-Athīr, IV, 128, for parallels.

328. A reference to the events in Sijistān and Afghanistan.

329. The place where the caliph Yazīd died, between Damascus and Palmyra, two stages from the latter (see Yāqūt, *Buldān*, II, 355; cf. Rotter, *Bürgerkrieg*, 1).

was a cup and a wineskin filled to the brim
and overflowing.
Many a plaintive singing girl weeps by his drunk-
en companions,
with a cymbal, now sitting and now standing.

Maslamah said: When the poem of Ibn ᶜArādah became
known, Salm made the death of Yazīd b. Muᶜāwiyah and
Muᶜāwiyah b. Yazīd public and called on the men to give him
the oath of allegiance, with general consent, until the affairs   [489]
of the people should be put in order with the choice of a
caliph. They gave him the oath, remained two months in that
situation, and then broke their agreement with him.

According to ᶜAlī b. Muḥammad—a shaykh of the people
of Khurāsān: The people of Khurāsān never loved a governor
as they loved Salm b. Ziyād. In those two years when Salm
was there, more than 20,000 children were named Salm because of their love for Salm.

According to ᶜAlī b. Muḥammad—Abū Ḥafṣ al-Azdī—his
paternal uncle: When the people of Khurāsān fell into disa-
greement and broke their oath of allegiance to Salm, he departed, leaving al-Muhallab b. Abī Ṣufrah[330] in his place. When
Salm reached Sarakhs,[331] Sulaymān b. Marthad, one of the
Banū Qays b. Thaᶜlabah,[332] met him. He asked him, "Who
have you left behind over Khurāsān?" and Salm answered,
"Al-Muhallab." Sulaymān said to him, "Was Nizār[333] so strait-
ened that you made one of the Yemen prefect!" Consequently,
Salm made Sulaymān prefect over Marw al-Rūdh, al-Fāryāb,
al-Ṭāliqān and al-Jūzjān,[334] and Aws b. Thaᶜlabah b. Zufar,[335]
the master of Qaṣr Aws in al-Baṣrah, prefect over Herat.[336]

---

330. Of Azd ᶜUman (Mazūn), founder of the fortunes of the Muhallabid
family and of the Azd in Khurāsān (see *EI²*, s.v.).

331. Between Ṭūs and Marw on the Tajand river (see G. Le Strange, *Eastern
caliphate*, 395–6).

332. I.e., of Bakr b. Wā'il/Rabīᶜah (see n. 111 above).

333. I.e., the "northern" Arabs (Muḍar and Rabīᶜah).

334. Jūzjān is the district east of Marw al-Rūdh, and Fāryāb and ṬTāliqān
were important towns in it (Le Strange, *Eastern Caliphate*, 423–5).

335. Another Bakrī (see *EI¹* s.v. Taimallāh b. Thaᶜlabah; Caskel/Ibn Kalbī,
II, 215).

336. At that time counted as part of Khurāsān (see Le Strange, *Eastern
Caliphate*, 407 ff.).

Then he continued on his way. When he reached Nīsābūr[337] ʿAbdallāh b. Khāzim met him. He asked Salm, "Who have you put in charge of Khurāsān?" When Salm told him, Ibn Khāzim said, "Could you not find a man among Muḍar[338] to appoint to office that you had to divide Khurāsān between Bakr b. Wā'il and Mazūn of ʿUmān?"[339] And he said to Salm, "Write me a commission over Khurāsān." Salm answered, "Am I the prefect of Khurāsān?" but Ibn Khāzim persisted, "Write a commission for me and you will be free of blame." So he wrote a commission over Khurāsān for him. Ibn Khāzim then said, "Now help me with 100,000 dirhams," and Salm ordered that it be given him. Ibn Khāzim came toward Marw, and when al-Muhallab b. Abī Ṣufrah heard the news he went off, leaving behind a man of the Banū Jusham b. Saʿd b. Zayd Manāt b. Tamīm.[340]

[490]   (According to ʿAlī b. Muḥammad)—al-Mufaḍḍal b. Muḥammad al-Ḍabbī—his father: When ʿAbdallāh b. Khāzim went to Marw with Salm b. Ziyād's commission, the Jushamī opposed him and there was skirmishing between them. A shot hit the Jushamī with a stone on his forehead and they broke off the engagement. The Jushamī opened the way to Marw al-Rūdh for Ibn Khāzim, who entered it. Two days later the Jushamī died.

According to ʿAlī b. Muḥammad al-Madā'inī—al-Ḥasan b. Rashīd al-Jūzajānī—his father: When Yazīd b. Muʿāwiyah and Muʿāwiyah b. Yazīd died, the people of Khurāsān rose against their officials and drove them out. Each tribal group seized control over a district and civil commotion broke out. Ibn Khāzim seized control of Khurāsān and war broke out.

Abū Jaʿfar (al-Ṭabarī) said:[341] According to Abū al-Dhayyāl Zuhayr b. Hunayd—Abū Naʿāmah: ʿAbdallāh b. Khāzim came and seized control over Marw. Then he went against Sulaymān

---

337. The garrison town of western Khurāsān (see Le Strange, *Eastern caliphate*, 383 ff.).

338. The division of Nizār (n. 329 above) with which Ibn Khāzim's own tribe, Qays, aligned itself, Bakr b. Wā'il belonging to Rabīʿah.

339. I.e., Sulaymān b. Marthad, Aws b. Thaʿlabah, and al-Muhallab.

340. Of Muḍar (see Caskel/Ibn Kalbī, I, tables 59, 75).

341. Still citing al-Madā'inī.

b. Marthad and met him at Marw al-Rūdh, where he fought him for some days and Sulaymān b. Marthad was killed. Then ᶜAbdallāh b. Khāzim went against ᶜAmr b. Marthad[342] who was at al-Ṭāliqān with 700 men. News of ᶜAbdallāh b. Khāzim's coming against him and of his killing his brother Sulaymān reached ᶜAmr, who headed out to face him. They met at a river before Ibn Khāzim's men had all arrived, so ᶜAbdallāh b. Khāzim gave the order to those who were with him and they pitched camp. He too encamped and asked about Zuhayr b. Dhu'ayb al-ᶜAdawī.[343] He was told that he had not come. But then, while he was in the same state, Zuhayr came. When he did, Ibn Khāzim was told, "Here, Zuhayr has come," and ᶜAbdallāh b. Khāzim gave the command, "Advance!" The forces met and fought together for a long time. ᶜAmr b. Marthad was killed and his men routed. They fled and joined Aws b. Thaᶜlabah in Herat while ᶜAbdallāh b. Khāzim returned to Marw.

The one who was in command when ᶜAmr b. Marthad was killed, according to what is narrated, was Zuhayr b. Ḥayyān al-ᶜAdawī. The poet said:

Do the days of war pass and you have not killed   [491]
    Zuhayr b. Ḥayyān in retaliation for ᶜAmr b. Marthad?

(According to al-Madā'inī): Abū al-Sarī al-Khurāsānī, one of the people of Herat, reported to us: ᶜAbdallāh b. Khāzim killed Sulaymān and ᶜAmr, the two sons of Marthad, the two Marthadīs of the Banū Qays b. Thaᶜlabah, and then returned to Marw. Those of Bakr b. Wā'il who were at Marw al-Rūdh fled to Herat. Those of Bakr b. Wā'il in the districts of Khurāsān crowded there, too, so that there was a large body of them there. Aws b. Thaᶜlabah was over them. They said to him, "Let us give you the oath of allegiance on the condition that you go against Ibn Khāzim and drive Muḍar out of Khurāsān completely." But he said to them, "That would be unjust, and those who participate in injustice are lost. Hold fast in this place of yours. If Ibn Khāzim leaves you alone,

---

342. Sulaymān's brother.
343. Of Tamīm.

which I do not think he will do, then be satisfied with this district and let him and his business be." The Banū Ṣuhayb, mawlās of the Banū Jaḥdar,[344] however, said, "No, by God, we will not accept that we and Muḍar should be in the same land while they have killed the two sons of Marthad. If you respond to our offer, it still stands; otherwise, we will make somebody else our commander." He replied, "I am only one of you, so do what seems good to you," and they gave him the oath of allegiance.

Ibn Khāzim came toward them, having left his son Mūsā behind as his deputy. He continued his advance and pitched his camp on a dry river bed between his army and Herat. The Bakrīs said to Aws, "Go out and dig a trench outside the town and give battle to them in it so the town will be behind us." Aws replied, "Stick to the town, for it is well fortified and let Ibn Khāzim be in the place where he is. If he stays there much longer he will get worried and give you something to satisfy you. If you are forced to fight, then you will fight." But they refused, went out of the town and dug a trench outside it. And Ibn Khāzim fought them for about a year.

[492]   Al-Aḥnaf b. al-Ashhab al-Ḍabbī claimed, and Abū al-Dhayyāl Zuhayr b. al-Hunayd told us: Ibn Khāzim went to Herat, where there was a large concentration of Bakr b. Wā'il who had fortified themselves with a trench and sworn together to drive out Muḍar if they won control of Khurāsān. He encamped facing them. Hilāl al-Ḍābbī,[345] one of the Banū Dhuhl of the Banū Aws, said to him, "You will only be fighting your brethren of your father's family.[346] By God, if you get what you want from them, then after them there will be no good left in life, you having killed at Marw al-Rūdh those of them whom you have killed. Why do you not give them something to satisfy them and settle this matter peacefully?" He replied, "By God, if I were to abandon Khurāsān to them, they would not be satisfied, and if they could drive you out of the world

----

344. See n. 111 above.

345. The Banū Ḍabbah b. Udd were allies of Tamīm (see Caskel/Ibn Kalbī, I, tables 59, 89, II, 240; *EI²*, s.v. Ḍabba).

346. Apparently a reference to the joint descent of Ibn Khāzim's tribe, Qays, and Bakr b. Wā'il from Nizār.

they would do so!" Hilāl said, "No, by God, I will not fire
an arrow with you and nor will any man of Khindif[347] who
obeys me until you send offering them conciliation."

Ibn Khāzim said, "Then you are my messenger to them.
Give them satisfaction!" So Hilāl went to Aws b. Thaᶜlabah
and implored him by God and by ties of kinship, saying, "In
God I ask you to remember Nizār,[348] that you avoid spilling
its blood or setting it against itself." Aws replied, "You have
encountered the Banū Ṣuhayb?" "No, by God," he said. "Well
then, go and meet them." So Hilāl went out and met Arqam
b. Muṭarrif al-Ḥanafī, Ḍamḍam b. Yazīd or ᶜAbdallāh b.
Ḍamḍam b. Yazīd and ᶜĀṣim b. al-Ṣalt b. al-Ḥārith, both of
them Ḥanafīs,[349] and a group of Bakr b. Wā'il. He addressed
them in the same way as he had done Aws, and they said,
"Have you encountered the Banū Ṣuhayb?" He answered, "God
has made the matter of the Banū Ṣuhayb very important among
you. No, I have never met them." They said, "Go and meet
them." So Hilāl went to the Banū Ṣuhayb and spoke to them.
They said, "If you were not a messenger, we would kill you."
He said, "Is there nothing which will satisfy you?" "One of
two things," they said. "Either you abandon Khurāsān and no   [493]
one calls for support for Muḍar in it, or else you remain but
renounce all your livestock, weapons, gold and silver to us."
Nothing but these two options?" he said. "No," they said.
"God is our sufficiency and the best protector," Hilāl responded.

He went back to Ibn Khāzim who asked him, "Well?" "I
have found our brethren actively rupturing the ties of kinship,"
he said. "I told you that Rabīᶜah would never cease raging
against its Lord since God sent the Prophet from among
Muḍar,"[350] Ibn Khāzim said.

---

347. Khindif is shown as an ancestor of Tamīm and others including Ḍabbah
(see Caskel/Ibn Kalbī, I, table 1, II, 347).

348. Rabīᶜah (here Bakr) and Muḍar (here Qays and Khindif) are counted
as descendants of Nizār.

349. The Banū Ḥanīfah were part of Bakr b. Wā'il; could this ᶜĀṣim b. al-
Ṣalt b. al-Ḥārith al-Ḥanafī be related to the al-Ṣalt b. Ḥurayth al-Ḥanafī named
in connection with the document of alliance between Rabīᶜah and Azd in al-
Baṣrah (p. 27 above)?

350. Quraysh, the tribe of the Prophet, were counted as a part of Muḍar.

Abū Jaᶜfar al-Ṭabarī said: According to Sulaymān b. Mujālid al-Ḍabbī:[351] While Ibn Khāzim was at Herat, the Turks raided Qaṣr Asfād[352] and besieged its garrison. Some men of Azd were in it—the majority of its garrison—and the Turks defeated them. They sent to those of Azd in the surrounding area and they came to help, but the Turks defeated them. Then they sent to Ibn Khāzim and he dispatched Zuhayr b. Ḥayyān[353] to them with a contingent of the Banū Tamīm. Ibn Khāzim told him, "Watch out for the Turks' attacks when you see them, and bear down on them." Zuhayr advanced and came upon them on a cold day. His force pressed hard against them. The Turks could not withstand them and were defeated. They gave chase to the Turks until, when much of the night had passed, they reached a castle in the desert. The body of the force remained there while Zuhayr pursued the Turks with some horsemen, for he was knowledgeable about the roads. In the middle of the night, he returned because his hand had frozen to his spear from the cold. He summoned his slave lad Kaᶜb, who went out to him and brought him in and began to warm up some fat for him which he put on his hand. They rubbed it in for him and lit him a fire, and eventually, his hand became soft and warm. Then he returned to Herat.

Concerning that, Kaᶜb b. Maᶜdān al-Ashqarī[354] said:

Help indeed came to you in a flash of lightning,
    armor and steel which Tamīm filled.
[494] They refused to add to their ranks the common folk
    which the villages gather,
      and the purity of their descent held them together
      on the day of the battle.

---

351. Wellhausen, *Arab Kingdom*, 418, n. 1, argues that this report about the Turkish attack is out of place and refers to a later period; cf., however, Rotter, *Bürgerkrieg*, 92; Sulaymān b. Mujālid was a contemporary of Abū Mikhnaf, often cited by him (Wellhausen, *loc. cit.*).

352. Evidently a fortified place, but to translate as "castle" might be misleading; possibly this place is to be associated with the district east of Nīshāpūr called variously Asfand, Ashbandh or Ashfand (Le Strange, *Eastern Caliphate*, 388); see Rotter, *Bürgerkrieg*, 92 for discussion.

353. See above, p. 73.

354. Poet of Azd (Iṣfahānī, *Aghānī*, XIII, 56–64; *GAS*, II, 377–8).

Their sustenance comes from the odors which
    female camels broad-girthed and high-humped give
    forth.

  And Thābit Quṭnah[355] said:

May my soul be a ransom for horsemen of Tamīm
    for what there was of close confinement
At the Bāhilī's castle.[356] I saw myself
    defending when the defenders there were few,
With my sword, after my spear had been shattered
    upon them,
    driving them back with a broad-bladed sword,
Assaulting them in the thick black smoke with an
    assault
    like that of those drinking from bowls of wine.
If it were not for God, who has no partner,
    and my striking the brow of the aspirant ruler,
Then the women of the Banū Dithār[357] would have
    given up their souls
    before the Turks, displaying their anklets.

Abū Jaᶜfar (al-Ṭabarī) said: According to Abū al-Ḥasan—al-
Khurāsānī—Abū Ḥammād al-Sulamī:[358] Ibn Khāzim remained
at Herat fighting Aws b. Thaᶜlabah for more than a year. One
day he said to his men, "Our position here confronting these
opponents has dragged on for too long." They called out to
them, therefore, "Oh band of Rabīᶜah, you have sought protection behind this trench of yours. Out of all Khurāsān, are
you satisfied with this ditch?" That caused them to remember
their situation and the people called each other to fight. Aws
b. Thaᶜlabah said to them, "Stick to your trench and fight
them as you have been doing. Do not go out to them in a
body." But they disregarded him and went out against them,

[495]

---

355. Poet of Azd (*Aghānī*, XIII, 49–56; *GAS*, II, 376–7).
356. I am unable to account for the designation *al-qaṣr al-bāhilī*.
357. I.e., the family of Shammās b. Dithār?
358. See *Add. et emend.* for the suggestion that there is a lacuna in this
isnād; Abū al-Ḥasan must be al-Madā'inī himself; for the identification of al-
Khurāsānī as Abū Sarī al-Khurāsānī (above, p. 73), see Rotter, *Bürgerkrieg*,
91, n. 603.

and the forces met. Ibn Khāzim said to his men, "Make the day yours. The rule will belong to whoever triumphs. If I am killed your commander will be Shammās b. Dithār al-ᶜUṭā-ridī,[359] and if he is killed your commander will be Bukayr b. Wishāḥ al-Thaqafī."[360]

According to ᶜAlī—Abū al-Dhayyāl Zuhayr b. Hunayd—Abū Naᶜāmah al-ᶜAdawī—ᶜAbīd b. Naqīd—Iyās b. Zuhayr b. Ḥayyān:[361] On the day when Aws b. Thaᶜlabah fled and Ibn Khāzim defeated Bakr b. Wā'il, the latter said to his men when they met, "I am not steady in the saddle. Fasten me on to my saddle and know that I have upon me such weapons that I will not be killed even by that which would slaughter two camels. If you are told that I have been killed, do not believe it!"

The banner of the Banū ᶜAdī was with my father and I was on an incompletely broken-in horse.[362] Ibn Khāzim had said to us, "When you encounter the horses, stab them in their nostrils, for no horse will be stabbed in its nostril without either turning tail or throwing its rider." When my horse heard the clanging of the weapons it leaped with me over a river bed which lay between me and the enemy, and a man of Bakr b. Wā'il confronted me. I stabbed his horse in its nostril and it threw him. My father carried the banner with the Banū ᶜAdī, and the Banū Tamīm followed him from every direction. The two sides fought for an hour, and the Bakr b. Wā'il were defeated and eventually retreated to their ditch. They were assailed from both right and left and some men fell into the ditch and suffered a quick death. Aws b. Thaᶜlabah [496] fled with his wounds, while Ibn Khāzim swore that he would kill every captive brought to him before sunset. The last one to be brought to him was a man of the Banū Ḥanīfah called Maḥmiyah. Ibn Khāzim was told, "The sun has set!" but he replied, "Finish the execution!" and Maḥmiyah was killed.

---

359. ᶜUṭārid b. ᶜAwf was a subgroup of the Banū Saᶜd/Tamīm (see Caskel/Ibn Kalbī, I, table 77).

360. The *nisbah* al-Thaqafī seems to be a mistake; he was of Tamīm (Wellhausen, *Arab Kingdom*, 418, n. 2).

361. I.e., the son of the hero referred to above, nn. 353, 343.

362. See *Add. et emend.* and *Gloss.*, s.v. ḥ-z-m.

A shaykh of the Banū Saᶜd b. Zayd Manāt told me that Aws b. Thaᶜlabah fled with his wounds to Sijistān, but when he got there or was near to it he died.

On the subject of the killing of Ibn Marthad and the affair of Aws b. Thaᶜlabah, al-Mughīrah b. Ḥabnā',363 one of the Banū Rabīᶜah b. Ḥanẓalah, said:

In the war you were in the whole of Khurāsān
    killed, imprisoned and restrained.
And one day Ibn Khāzim confined you in the ditch
    and you found the trench no more than a tomb.
And one day you left Ibn Marthad in the dust,
    and you left Aws where he came and camped.

Abū al-Dhayyāl Zuhayr b. Hunayd told me on the authority of his maternal grandfather: Eight thousand of Bakr b. Wā'il were killed on that day.

Al-Tamīmī, one of the people of Khurāsān, told me on the authority of a mawlā of Ibn Khāzim: Ibn Khāzim fought Aws b. Thaᶜlabah and Bakr b. Wā'il, and was victorious at Herat whence Aws fled. Ibn Khāzim seized Herat from him and appointed his son Muḥammad over it, attaching Shammās b. Dithār al-ᶜUṭāridī to him and placing Bukayr b. Wishāḥ over his police troop. He told them, "Show him the ropes, for he is the offspring of one of your women." (His mother was a woman of the Banū Saᶜd364 called Ṣafiyyah.) And he said to Muḥammad, "Do what they say." Then Ibn Khāzim returned to Marw.

Abū Jaᶜfar (al-Ṭabarī) said: In this year also, the Shīᶜah365 were stirred up in al-Kūfah and arranged to gather at al- [497]

---

363. Poet of Tamīm (Aghānī, XI, 162–71; GAS, II, 374–5).

364. The Banū Saᶜd of Tamīm were the clan of Bukayr and of Shammās.

365. Literally, "party." In our sources for early Islam we read of several different "parties" (see, e.g., p. 50 above). The party of ᶜAlī eventually came to be called al-shīᶜah without further specification and developed into the Shīᶜite tradition of Islam, distinct from the Sunnī form of the religion. It is questionable whether in the time of the second civil war the word shīᶜah was generally used with this distinct and specific meaning. In the following account I have sometimes kept the Arabic word with a capital S as is now customary, but sometimes it seems clear that the word has the general meaning "the

Nukhaylah[366] in the year 65 (684-5) to set out against the Syrians and to seek vengeance for the blood of al-Ḥusayn b. ᶜAlī.[367] They exchanged correspondence about that.

The Beginnings of the Movement of the Penitents [al-Tawwābūn] in al-Kūfah

According to Hishām b. Muḥammad—Abū Mikhnaf—Yūsuf b. Yazīd—ᶜAbdallāh b. ᶜAwf b. al-Aḥmar al-Azdī: After al-Ḥusayn b. ᶜAlī had been killed and Ibn Ziyād had returned from his army camp at al-Nukhaylah and entered al-Kūfah, the Shīᶜah gathered, full of self-reproach and repentance. They thought they had committed a grave offense in inviting al-Ḥusayn to receive their support then failing to respond to him, and in letting him be killed so near to them while they never gave him any help. They thought their ignominy and sin which had resulted from his slaying would only be washed away by killing those who killed him or by dying in the attempt. Therefore, they had recourse to five leaders of the Shīᶜah in al-Kūfah: Sulaymān b. Ṣurad al-Khuzāᶜī,[368] who had been a Companion of the Prophet; al-Musayyab b. Najabah al-Fazārī,[369] one of the best of the supporters of ᶜAlī; ᶜAbdallāh b. Saᶜd b. Nufayl al-Azdī; ᶜAbdallah b. Wāl al-Taymī;[370] and Rifāᶜah b. Shaddād al-Bajalī.[371] Those five men then met at the abode of Sulaymān b. Ṣurad, and they were among the

---

party" or "our party," and it has been translated using such phrases.

For parallel and variant accounts of the following, see *Ansāb*, V, 203-13; Ibn Aᶜtham, VI, 47-53, 58-87; Ibn al-Athīr, IV, 131-6, 144-56; Yaᶜqūbī, II, 306; Wellhausen, *Oppositionsparteien*, 71-4 (Eng. tr. 121-4); S.H.M. Jafri, *The Origins and Early Development of Shīᶜa Islam*, 222-34; Rotter, *Bürgerkrieg*, 96-8.

366. Probably to the northwest of al-Kūfah on the Syrian road (see Ṭabarī, I, 3345).

367. See n. 43 above.

368. For him, see *EI¹*, s.v. Sulaimān b. Ṣurad, and Caskel/Ibn Kalbī, I, table 197, II, 518; for Khuzāᶜah, *EI²*, s.v. Khuzāᶜa.

369. For him, see Caskel/Ibn Kalbī, II, 436; Fazārah b. Dhubyān are counted to Ghaṭafān/Qays (*ibid.*, I, table 92).

370. Taym of Bakr b. Wā'il (see below, p. 84).

371. For him, see Caskel/Ibn Kalbī, I, table 223, II, 487; for the Banū Bajīlah, ibid., table 221, II, 219, *EI²*, s.v. Badjīla.

best of the supporters of ʿAlī. With them were some of the
members of the Shīʿah, their pick and their leaders.

When they had gathered at Sulaymān b. Ṣurad's dwelling,
al-Musayyab b. Najabah began to address those assembled. He   [498]
praised God, extolled Him and prayed for His Prophet, and
then said:

> Now, we have been afflicted by the length of our lives
> and by exposure to all types of trials. We ask of our
> Lord that He does not make us one of those to whom
> He will one day say: "Did We not give you long life
> so that whoever would be admonished might be ad-
> monished therein? And the warner came to you."[372]
> Also, the Commander of the Faithful said, "The life
> in which God grants forgiveness to the son of Adam
> is sixty years,"[373] and there is not a man among us
> who has not reached that term. We were enamored of
> self-justification and praising our party until God put
> our best men to the test and found us sham on two
> of the battlefields[374] of the son of our Prophet's daugh-
> ter. Before that, we had received his letters and his
> messengers had come to us offering forgiveness, asking
> us to help him again in public and in private. But we
> withheld ourselves from him until he was killed so
> near to us. We did not help him with our hands, argue
> on his behalf with our tongues, strengthen him with
> our wealth or seek help for him from our clans. What
> will be our excuse for our Lord and at the meeting
> with our Prophet[375] when his descendant, his loved
> one, his offspring and his issue has been slain among
> us? No, by God, there is no excuse unless you kill his
> murderer and those who assisted him or unless you
> are killed while seeking that. Perhaps our Lord will be

---

372. Qur'ān, 35:34.

373. "The Commander of the Faithful" here is ʿAlī; for the ḥadīth in
conjunction with the Quranic verse, see Bukhārī, *Riqāq, bāb* 5.

374. Apparently a reference to Karbalā' and the rising of Ḥujr b. ʿAdī (see
*EI*², s.v. Ḥudjr b. ʿAdī).

375. At the Last Judgment, when the Prophet will intercede with God on
behalf of the Muslims.

satisfied with us in that, for I have no security against
His punishment after meeting Him. Oh people, appoint
over you a man from among you, for you cannot do
without a commander from whom you can seek help
and a banner round which you can assemble. This is
what I have to say. I ask God's forgiveness for me and
for you.

[499]

After al-Musayyab, Rifāᶜah b. Shaddād addressed the group.
He praised God, extolled Him and prayed for His Prophet,
and then he said:

God has led you to speak aright, and you have summoned us to matters in which we would be most rightly
guided. You have praised God and extolled Him, you
have offered prayers for His Prophet, and you have
called us to fight against [jihād] the iniquitous ones [al-
fāsiqīn] and to repent the great sin. We have listened
to you, responded to you and accepted what you have
said. You told us to appoint over us a man from among
us from whom we could seek help and gather around
his banner. That is a view in which we concur. If you
are that man, you will be acceptable within our band.
But if you and our companions are of the same opinion,
we will appoint over this business the shaykh of the
Shīᶜah and Companion of the Prophet who has precedence and seniority in Islam, Sulaymān b. Ṣurad, who
is praised for his fortitude and his religion and trusted
for his resoluteness. This is what I have to say and I
ask God's forgiveness for me and for you.

Next, ᶜAbdallāh b. Wāl and ᶜAbdallāh b. Saᶜd spoke. They
praised their Lord and extolled Him, and spoke in a similar
fashion to Rifāᶜah b. Shaddād. They referred to al-Musayyab
b. Najabah and his merits and to Sulaymān b. Ṣurad with his
precedence in Islam, and they mentioned that they would be
satisfied with his appointment. Al-Musayyab b. Najabah said,
"Indeed you are right. My opinion is like yours: put Sulaymān
b. Ṣurad in charge of your affairs."
Abū Mikhnaf said that he narrated this account to Sulaymān
b. Abī Rāshid, who said to him that Ḥumayd b. Muslim had

told him: By God, I was there on this day—the day they put Sulaymān b. Ṣurad in charge—and at that time there were more than a hundred of us, warriors and prominent members of the Shīʿah, in his dwelling place. Sulaymān b. Ṣurad spoke and made a forceful speech which he continued to repeat at every assembly until I learned it by heart. He began and said: [500]

I extol God for His goodness and I praise Him for His blessings and His tribulations. I bear witness that there is no god but God and that Muḥammad was His messenger. Now, by God I fear that this time in which life has become so miserable and calamity so great and injustice so prevalent is assigned to be our last. What good is it for the most virtuous of this Party that we were yearning for the family of our Prophet to come,[376] offering them help and urging them to come, but when they came we were weak and feeble and spineless, we delayed and waited to see what would happen, until the descendant of our Prophet, his offspring and his progeny, flesh of his flesh and blood of his blood, was killed in our very midst? He called for help but received none, he asked for justice but was not given any. The impious ones made him a target for arrows and a butt for spears until they had broken him, assaulted him and stripped him. Rise up indeed, for your Lord has been angered. Do not go back to your wives and children until God has been satisfied! By God, I do not think He will be satisfied unless you fight against those who killed him or perish.[377] Do not fear death! By God, no man ever feared it without debasing himself. Be like those Israelites when their prophet said to them, "You have done evil to yourselves by your adoption of the Calf. Turn in repentence to your Creator and kill yourselves. That will be best for you with your

---

376. See *Add. et emend.* and cf. *Ansāb*, V, 205, bottom.

377. Text has *tubīrū* (?), "you destroy," the *Ansāb* reads *tubīrūhu*, "you destroy him" (i.e., he who killed al-Ḥusayn); the translation "or perish" is based on my suggested reading *tabīdū*.

[501]

Creator."[378] And do what that people did. They fell on their knees and stretched out their necks and accepted the judgment, until they understood that nothing would save them from the magnitude of their offense except patient acceptance of the slaughter. How will it be with you, if you are summoned to something similar? Make sharp the swords, assemble the lances, and get ready against them what strength you can. Prepare for war [*ribāṭ al-khayl*] so you can be assembled when you are summoned to fight.[379]

Khālid b. Saʿd b. Nufayl then stood and spoke, "As for me, by God, if I knew that my killing of myself would release me from my sin and my Lord would be pleased with me, I would kill myself! But that is something which was ordered to a people who were before us while we have been prohibited from it. I bear witness before God and those of the Muslims here present that, except for the weapon with which I shall fight against my enemy, everything I possess I make over as alms for the Muslims. With it I strengthen them in their fight against the unrighteous [*al-qāṣiṭīn*]."

Abū al-Muʿtamir Ḥanash b. Rabīʿah al-Kinānī[380] next stood and said, "And I bear witness similarly."

Sulaymān b. Ṣurad said, "It is enough that anyone who wishes to give something should bring his property to ʿAbdallāh b. Wāl al-Taymī (Taym of Bakr b. Wā'il), and when everything which you wish to donate of your property is assembled with him, we will equip the poor and needy of your followers with it."

---

378. Qur'ān, 2:51. This verse contains the word *tawwāb*, the self-designation of Sulaymān b. Ṣurad and his followers. But in the Quranic verse it refers to God rather than human beings, hence it means something like "He who relents" rather than "the penitent." "Your selves" could equally be translated "your souls." According to traditional Muslim commentary on the verse, in response to the command of Moses, and in atonement for the sin of the Golden Calf, the Israelites began to kill one another until God allowed them to stop in response to Moses' intercession. A large number of the Israelites were killed.

379. See *Add. et emend.* for the dittography at p. 501, l. 3.

380. For Kinānah b. Khuzaymah (of Khindif), see Caskel/Ibn Kalbī, II, 371.

According to Abū Mikhnaf Lūṭ b. Yaḥyā—Sulaymān b. Abī Rāshid—Ḥumayd b. Muslim al-Azdī: When Khālid b. Saʿd b. Nufayl said to Sulaymān b. Ṣurad, "By God, if I knew that my killing of myself would release me from my sin and my Lord would be pleased with me, I would kill myself. But that is something which was ordered to another people who were before us while we have been prohibited from it," Sulaymān said to him, "This brother of yours tomorrow will be the prey of the first of the spear points." And when he donated his property as alms for the Muslims he said, "Rejoice at the great rewards of God for those who spread for themselves (a couch in Paradise)."[381]

According to Abū Mikhnaf—al-Ḥusayn b. Yazīd b. ʿAbdallāh   [502] b. Saʿd b. Nufayl: I obtained a letter which Sulaymān b. Ṣurad had written to Saʿd b. Hudhayfah b. al-Yamān[382] at al-Madāʾin and I read it at the time when Sulaymān was put in charge. The letter surprised me, and I took pains to learn it and have not forgotten it. He wrote to him:

> In the name of God, the Merciful, the Compassionate! From Sulaymān b. Ṣurad to Saʿd b. Hudhayfah and those of the Believers who are with him, greetings! Now, this world is an abode away from which turns that which is honorable and to which tends that which is dishonorable. It has become hateful to those with understanding. The best servants of God have determined to depart from it and they have exchanged a fleeting little of this world for a never-ending abundance with God.
>
> The friends of God among your brethren and the Party of your Prophet's family have reflected upon the way they were put to the test in the matter of the Prophet's grandson. He responded when he was invited but received no answer when he called, wanted to go back but was detained, asked for safe-conduct but was denied it. He refrained from attacking the people al-

---

381. An allusion to Qurʾān, 30:43.
382. Of Fazārah (ʿAbs/Ghaṭafān); on him, see Caskel/Ibn Kalbī, I, table 132, II, 495.

though they did not refrain from him, but attacked and killed him, then plundered and stripped him wrongfully and in enmity, heedless and ignorant of God. What they did offended God[383] and they will not return to Him. "Those who commit evil will know the reversal which they will endure."[384] When your brethren considered and thought about the end to which they were coming, they saw they had sinned greatly in betraying the pure and good one, in delivering him up and refraining from aiding and helping him. They saw there was no release for them and no repentance apart from killing his murderers or killing themselves so that their spirits would be consumed in it. Your brethren have thought seriously, and you should too and prepare. We have fixed for our brethren an appointed time for them to come to us and a place for them to meet us. Regarding the time, it is the first day of the month of Rabīᶜ II of the year 65 (November [503] 16, 684), and regarding the place where they will meet us, it is al-Nukhaylah.

You are they who have never ceased to be for us a party, brethren, and an alliance.[385] We have considered that we should appeal to you to join in this affair for which God desires your brethren, as they assert and proclaim to us, to repent. You are proper ones for seeking merit and soliciting reward and turning in repentance to your Lord from sin. Even if that involves your necks being cut, your offspring killed, your money spent and your clans destroyed, it did not harm those whose guilt was pardoned and who were killed that they are not "alive" today when they are with their Lord rewarded as martyrs. They met God patiently counting on His reward and He has given them the reward of the patient. (He was referring to Ḥujr [b. ᶜAdī] and his companions.) Nor did it harm your breth-

---

383. See *Add. et emend.*
384. Qur'ān, 26:228.
385. See *Add. et emend.*

ren who were slain patiently, crucified unjustly and maimed unlawfully that they are not "alive" and being put to the test by your sins. He let them choose, they met their Lord, and, please God, God has fully rewarded them.

So be patient and may God have mercy on you in the face of wretchedness, harm and the occasion of misfortune! Turn to God in penitence from what is near at hand! By God, it is surely fitting that none of your brethren should have patiently endured any tribulation, desiring its reward, unless you would patiently endure something like it seeking its reward. And it is surely fitting that none (of them) should have sought God's acceptance by means of anything, even slaughter, if you would not seek God's acceptance by it. Fear of God is the best provision in this world, and apart from that everything perishes and passes away. So turn yourselves away from this world and be desirous of the abode of your well-being and the fight [jihād] against the enemies of God, the enemies of yourselves and of the family of your Prophet, so that you may approach God penitently and desiring Him. May God grant us and you a good life, may He give us and you protection from the fires of Hell, and may He allot as our fate being killed in His path at the hands of the most hateful of His creatures and the bitterest in enmity toward Him! He has power over whatever He wants and achieves everything for His friends. Peace be upon you!

[504]

Ibn Ṣurad wrote the letter and sent ᶜAbdallāh b. Mālik al-Ṭā'ī[386] with it to Saᶜd b. Hudhayfah b. al-Yamān, and Saᶜd, after he had read his letter, sent it to those of the Shīᶜah in al-Madā'in. There were several groups of the people of al-Kūfah there who had found it pleasant and settled in it. Every time pay and provisions were distributed they came to al-Kūfah to collect what was due to them and then returned to

---

386. See p. 221 below, where he is appointed qāḍī by Mukhtār.

their settlements. Saʿd read Sulaymān b. Ṣurad's letter to them and then he praised God, extolled Him and said, "Now, you were united together intent on helping al-Ḥusayn and fighting his enemies. The beginning of his murder did not take you unawares and God will recompense you with the best of rewards for your good intentions and the support which you had decided upon for him. Now your brethren have sent to you asking you for help and assistance and calling you in the truth and to that in which you hope there will be for you the best reward and portion with God. What is your opinion, and what do you say?" The people as a whole answered, "We will respond to their call and fight together with them. Our opinion of that is the same as theirs."

ʿAbdallāh b. al-Ḥanẓal al-Ṭāʾī al-Ḥizmirī[387] arose. He praised God and extolled Him and then said, "Now, we have responded to that which our brethren call us to and we have formed an opinion which is as theirs. Send me to them with some horsemen!" But Saʿd said to him, "Gently, do not rush; get ready for the enemy and prepare to make war on him, and then we will set out together."

Saʿd b. Hudhayfah b. al-Yamān then wrote to Sulaymān b. Ṣurad and sent the letter with ʿAbdallāh b. Mālik al-Ṭāʾī:

[505]   In the name of God, the Merciful, the Compassionate! To Sulaymān b. Ṣurad from Saʿd b. Hudhayfah and those of the believers who are with him, greetings! We have read your letter and understood the matter to which you summon us and upon which the assembly [al-malaʾ] of your brethren concurs. You have been led to your destiny and the way made smooth for your right guidance. We are earnest and serious, getting ready and fixing the saddles and bridles. We are waiting for the affair to start and listening out for the summons. When the call comes we will proceed without delay, please God.

When Sulaymān b. Ṣurad had read the letter, he read it to his companions who rejoiced to hear it.

---

387. For Ḥizmir b. Akhzam, see Caskel/Ibn Kalbī, I, table 256.

(Our authorities) said: Sulaymān b. Ṣurad wrote a copy of the letter which he had written to Saᶜd b. Hudhayfah b. al-Yamān for al-Muthannā b. Mukharribah al-ᶜAbdī[388] and sent Ẓabyān b. ᶜUmāra al-Tamīmī[389] of the Banū Saᶜd with it. Al-Muthannā wrote back to him, "I have read your letter and had it read out to your brethren. They have praised your reasoning and responded to you. Please God, we will meet you at the time you have appointed and the place you have mentioned. Peace be with you!" And at the bottom of his letter he wrote:

Consider! It is as if I had come to you marked out
    on a long-necked charger, snorting hoarsely,
Long-backed, high-stepping, long-legged,
    urgent and champing at the bit,
With every youth whose gorge knows no fear,
    experiencing the sting of war without weariness,
A trustworthy brother whose rush has as its aim
    God,
    striking with the blade of the sword without sin.

According to Abū Mikhnaf Lūṭ b. Yaḥyā—al-Ḥārith b. Ḥa- [506]
ṣīrah—ᶜAbdallāh b. Saᶜd b. Nufayl: The start of their affair was in the year 61 (680-81) when al-Ḥusayn was killed. From that time, the people never ceased gathering the instruments of war, preparing for fighting and summoning in secret the people of the Shīᶜah and others to seek vengeance for the blood of al-Ḥusayn. Group after group and band after band responded to them. Things continued in that way until Yazīd b. Muᶜāwiyah died on Thursday, the fourteenth of Rabīᶜ I 64 (November 11, 683).[390] Between the killing of al-Ḥusayn and the death of Yazīd b. Muᶜāwiyah there were three years, two months and four days. When Yazīd perished, the governor of Iraq was ᶜUbaydallāh b. Ziyād who was in al-Baṣrah, while his deputy in al-Kūfah was ᶜAmr b. Ḥurayth al-Makhzūmī.

---

388. Of ᶜAbd al-Qays (Rabīᶜah) in al-Baṣrah; he subsequently worked there on behalf of al-Mukhtār.

389. A supporter of ᶜAlī at Ṣiffīn, where he is described as a "raw youth"; at I, 3263, he is named as Ẓabyān b. ᶜAmmār.

390. Thursday is a mistake for Tuesday; cf. p. 11 above.

Sulaymān came to his companions of the Shīʿah and they said, "This tyrant is dead and the situation is now unstable. If you wish, we will rise up against ʿAmr b. Ḥurayth, drive him out of the governor's residence, proclaim that we are seeking vengeance for the blood of al-Ḥusayn, track down his murderers, and call the people to support the members of this family who have been expropriated and barred from their rights." They spoke about that and talked extensively.

But Sulaymān b. Ṣurad said to them, "Gently! Do not rush! I have reflected on what you say, and my opinion is that the murderers of al-Ḥusayn are the notables of the people of al-Kūfah and the champions of the Arabs. It is they from whom vengeance for his blood is to be sought. But if they knew what you want and that they are the ones sought after, they would come down heavily on you. And I have thought about those of you who have followed me and I know that if they [507] revolted, they would not obtain their vengeance, not obtain satisfaction for themselves, and not injure their enemy but be merely a slaughter for them. Rather, send your propagandists (duʿāt) into the garrison town and summon this party of yours, and others not of it, to your affair. For I hope that today when the tyrant has perished the people will respond more quickly to your affair than before his death."

They did what he suggested and groups of them left as propagandists summoning the people. A large number responded to them after the death of Yazīd b. Muʿāwiyah, many more than responded to them before that.

According to Hishām, Abū Mikhnaf said—al-Ḥusayn b. Yazīd—a man of Muzaynah: I never saw anyone in this community more eloquent in speech or admonition than ʿUbaydallāh b. ʿAbdallāh al-Murrī.[391] He was one of the propagandists to the people of the garrison town in the time of Sulaymān b. Ṣurad. Whenever a group of people assembled to hear him preach, he began by praising God and extolling Him and praying for the Messenger of God, and then he would say:

---

391. It is not clear to which Banū Murrah (or Murr?) he belongs.

Now, God singled out Muḥammad from all His creatures by his prophethood and distinguished him with
every merit. He made you strong by following him,
honored you by belief in him, spared by him the blood
which you shed, and through him gave security to your
perilous roads. "You were on the brink of a pit of
hellfire but he rescued you from it. Thus God makes
clear to you His signs, perhaps you will be led aright."[392]
Has God created among the first and the last anyone
with a greater right to authority over this community
than its Prophet? And have the descendants of any one
of the prophets and messengers or anyone else a greater
right to rule over this community than those of its
Messenger? No, by God, there has not been and there
will not be. You belong to God. Have you not seen
and have you not heard what evil was done to the son
of your Prophet's daughter? Did you not regard how
the people violated his sanctity, considered as weakness   [508]
his solitariness, splattered him with blood, and pulled
him down to the ground? In it they did not respect
their Lord or al-Ḥusayn's kinship with the Prophet.
They made him a target for arrows and left him a
slaughter for the hyenas. Blessed are the eyes of him
who has seen the like of him, and blessed is Ḥusayn
the son of ʿAlī. What a man was he they betrayed! He
was true and patient, trustworthy, helpful and resolute;
he was the son of the first of the Muslims in Islam
and the son of the daughter of the Messenger of the
Lord of the Worlds. His defenders were few while his
foes flocked around him, and his enemy killed him
while his friend betrayed him. Woe to the killer and
shame on the traitor! God will accept no plea from
his killer and no excuse from his betrayer unless he
sincerely turns to God in repentance, struggles against
the murderers, and opposes the unrighteous [al-qāsi-
ṭīn]. Perhaps on those conditions God will accept the
repentance and disregard the offense. We call you to

---

392. Qur'ān, 3:99.

the Book of God, the Sunnah of His Prophet, the seeking of vengeance for the blood of his family, and the struggle [*jihād*] against the violaters of God's law and renegades [*al-muḥillīn al-māriqīn*]. If we are killed, that which God has prepared for us with Him is better for the godfearing; if we are victorious, then we will restore this authority to the family of our Prophet!

He used to repeat this speech to us every day until the mass of us had it by heart. When Yazīd b. Muʿāwiyah perished, the people rose against ʿAmr b. Ḥurayth, expelled him from the governor's residence and settled on ʿĀmir b. Masʿūd b. Umayyah b. Khalaf al-Jumaḥī. He was the "ball made by dung beetles,"[393] about whom Ibn Ḥammām al-Salūlī said:

Cling fast to Zayd if you catch him,
   and cure the widows of the "dung beetles'
   ball."

He was so short he was like a thumb, and Zayd was his mawlā and treasurer. He used to lead the people in prayer, and he took the oath of allegiance for Ibn al-Zubayr.

The companions of Sulaymān b. Ṣurad continued to summon their Shīʿah and others of their garrison town, and their following became numerous. After the death of Yazīd b. Muʿā-

[509] wiyah, the people joined them more quickly than they had done previously; and six months after the death of Yazīd b. Muʿāwiyah, al-Mukhtār b. Abī ʿUbayd[394] came to al-Kūfah. He arrived in the middle of Ramaḍān on a Friday.

ʿAbdallāh b. Yazīd al-Anṣārī, al-Khaṭmī, came, sent by ʿAbdallāh b. al-Zubayr with authority over the military affairs of al-Kūfah and the frontier regions controlled from it, and with him there also came Ibrāhīm b. Muḥammad b. Ṭalḥah b. ʿUbaydallāh al-Aʿraj, sent by Ibn al-Zubayr with authority over the tax [*kharāj*] of al-Kūfah. ʿAbdallāh b. Yazīd al-Anṣārī, al-Khaṭmī, arrived on Friday when eight days remained of Ramaḍān, 64 (May 15, 684). Al-Mukhtār arrived eight days

---

393. See p. 47 above; according to *Ansāb*, V, 191[20], Zayd was a mawlā of ʿAttāb b. Warqā'.

394. Of Thaqīf from al-Ṭā'if; on him see *EI*[1], s.v., and below, pp. 105ff.

before ʿAbdallāh b. Yazīd and Ibrāhīm b. Muḥammad. When he entered al-Kūfah, the leaders and prominent members of the Shīʿah had assembled with Sulaymān b. Ṣurad. They did not consider al-Mukhtār of equal status with him. When al-Mukhtār called upon them to support him and to seek vengeance for the blood of al-Ḥusayn, the Shīʿah said to him, "This Sulaymān b. Ṣurad is the shaykh of the Party; they have yielded to him and agreed upon him." But al-Mukhtār began saying to the Shīʿah, "I have come to you from the *mahdī*, Muḥammad b. ʿAlī, Ibn al-Ḥanafiyyah,[395] with his trust and confidence, chosen by him and as his *wazīr*.[396] And, by God, he kept on at them until a section broke away to join him, honoring him, responding to his call and expecting his success. Most of the Shīʿah, however, were with Sulaymān b. Ṣurad, and he was the firmest of God's creatures against al-Mukhtār. Al-Mukhtār used to say to his companions, "Do you know what this one (meaning Sulaymān b. Ṣurad) wants? He only wants to go out and kill himself and you. He has no under- [510] standing of warfare and no knowledge of it."

Yazīd b. al-Ḥārith b. Yazīd b. Ruwaym al-Shaybānī[397] went to ʿAbdallāh b. Yazīd al-Anṣārī and said, "The people are saying among themselves that this Shīʿah is going to rebel against you with Ibn Ṣurad and that there is another section of them with al-Mukhtār, the smaller of the two groups in number.

---

395. Muḥammad b. al-Ḥanafiyyah was a son of ʿAlī by a woman from the tribe of Ḥanīfah, unlike al-Ḥasan, a-lḤusayn and the Imāms of most Shīʿite groups, who were descended from ʿAlī through his wife Fāṭimah, the daughter of the Prophet (on Muḥammad b. al-Ḥanafiyyah, see *EI¹*, s.v.). It seems that it was in connection with the propaganda of Mukhtār and of the *Tawwābūn* that the term *mahdī* first became current. The term is used generally to refer to the Messiah figure of Islam, the Mahdī. Literally, the term may be translated as "the rightly guided one," and it is not certain how far, at the time of Mukhtār and the *Tawwābūn*, its eschatological associations had developed (see further *EI²*, s.v. Mahdī).

396. The word is used here, as at other times in early Islam, with a religious connotation, referring to an individual acting as the representative of a prophet or religious leader; only in ʿAbbāsid times, it seems, does the word come to be used only to mean a government official; see S. D. Goitein, "On the origin of the term vizier," *JAOS*, LXXXI (1961), 425–6 (= Goitein, *Studies in Islamic History and Institutions*, 194–6).

397. The leader of Bakr b. Wā'il in al-Kūfah (see Crone, *Slaves*, 119; Rotter, *Bürgerkrieg*, index).

According to what the people are saying, al-Mukhtār does not wish to revolt until he sees what becomes of the affair of Sulaymān b. Ṣurad. The latter's preparations have been made and he is ready to start his revolt at any time. If you think that you should get together the police force, the soldiers and the prominent ones among the people and then take the initiative in going against him, we will do so with you. Then, when you have pushed on to his dwelling place, you will appeal to him. If he responds, that is enough. But if he fights against you, you will fight him. You will have gathered your forces and got ready while he will be taken by surprise. I fear for you that, if he starts things against you and you leave him alone until he comes out against you, his power will have increased and his affair become grave."

ᶜAbdallāh b. Yazīd replied, "God prevents us from attacking them. If they attack us, we will fight them, but if they leave us alone, we will not seek to confront them. Tell me what they want." He replied, "They say that they seek vengeance for the blood of al-Ḥusayn b. ᶜAlī." Ibn Yazīd answered, "Did I kill al-Ḥusayn? The curse of God on al-Ḥusayn's killer!"

Sulaymān b. Ṣurad and his companions wished to revolt in al-Kūfah. ᶜAbdallāh b. Yazīd went out and mounted the *minbar*. He stood among the people, praised God and extolled Him, and then said:

> Now, I have heard that some of this garrison town wish to revolt against us. I have asked what it was which called them to that and I was told they assert that they are seeking vengeance for the blood of al-Ḥusayn b. ᶜAlī. May God have mercy on that people! Their haunts have been shown to me and I have been asked to seize them. I was told, "Move against them before they move against you," but I rejected that and said if they fight me I will fight them, but if they leave me alone I will not seek them out. Why should they fight against me? By God, I did not kill Ḥusayn and I am not one of those who fought against him. I was stricken by his death, may God have mercy on him. If these people have no hostile intention (toward us),

[511]

let them go out and openly reveal themselves so that they may move against he who fought against al-Ḥusayn, he who has come against them. I will help them against this murderer. This Ibn Ziyād, the one who slew al-Ḥusayn and slew your best men and your models, has set out against you. The latest information about him puts him at one night's journey from Jisr Manbij.[398] Fighting against him and being ready to face him is better and sounder than settling your grievances among yourselves, killing one another and shedding each other's blood. Then, when that enemy meets you afterwards, you are weak. By God, that is just what your enemy wants! He has come against you, the most aggressive of God's creatures toward you, he who, with his father, had authority over you for seven years, the two of them not refraining from killing the people of righteousness and religion. He, who killed you, by whom you were ruined, and who killed the one for whose blood you seek vengeance has come against you. So face him with your weapons and your strength. Use them against him, not against yourselves. I have not spared you good advice. May God join our forces together and preserve our *imāms* for us.

Ibrāhīm b. Muḥammad b. Ṭalḥah said:

Oh people! The words of this flattering pacifier will surely not conjure away from you the sword and repression. By God, if someone attacks us, we will fight him, and, if we are sure that a people wants to attack us, we will seize the father for his child, the descendant [512] for its begetter, the friend for the friend, and the ᶜarīf for his ᶜirāfah,[399] until they submit to the truth and humble themselves to obedience.

Al-Musayyab b. Najabah rose up and cut off his speech, and said, "Son of the faithless ones! You threaten us with your

---

398. See Le Strange, *Eastern Caliphate*, 107.
399. In the garrison towns the ᶜirāfah (or ᶜarāfah) was a unit of men grouped together mainly for distribution of pay (see F. M. Donner, *Early Islamic Conquests*, 237–8).

sword and your repression. By God, you are too debased for that. We do not blame you for hating us, for we killed your father and your grandfather.[400] By God, I hope that God does not drive you out of the midst of the people of this garrison town before they add you to your father and grandfather and make three! As for you, oh governor, you have spoken appositely. By God, I think that whoever wants success in this matter should seek your advice and accept what you say."

Ibrāhīm b. Muḥammad b. Ṭalḥah answered, "Yes by God, let him be killed. He started by dissimulating but then showed his true colors."[401] ᶜAbdallāh b. Wāl al-Taymī came up to him and said, "Oh brother of the Banū Taym b. Murrah,[402] what is your opposition to that which concerns us and our governor? By God, you are no governor over us and you have no authority over us. You are only the head of the fiscal administration [amīr al-jizyah], so go back to your taxes [kharāj]. By the Eternal God, if you are a corrupt one, it was your father and grandfather, the faithless ones, who corrupted the affairs of this community. It was through them that discord came about. The calamity was their responsibility."[403] Then Musayyab b. Najabah and ᶜAbdallāh b. Wāl went up to ᶜAbdallāh b. Yazīd and said, "Regarding your opinion, Oh Governor, we hope, by God, that you will be praised for it among the populace and that you will be welcomed for what you meant and intended."

[513] Some of the people who were officials of Ibrāhīm b. Muḥammad b. Ṭalḥah and a group of those who were with him were enraged and poured out abuse on everyone but him, while the people reviled them and argued against them. When ᶜAbdallāh b. Yazīd heard that, he came down from the minbar and entered his residence. Ibrāhīm b. Muḥammad left, saying, "ᶜAbdallāh b. Yazīd has duped the people of al-Kūfah. By God,

---

400. Ibrāhīm's father and grandfather were both killed fighting against ᶜAlī at the Battle of the Camel (see EI¹, s.v. Ṭalḥa b. ᶜUbayd Allāh).

401. It is not clear if the second sentence is a comment by Ibrāhīm on the behavior of ᶜAbdallāh b. Yazīd or a comment by the narrator on the behavior of Ibrāhīm.

402. According to p. 84, ᶜAbdallāh b. Wāl himself was not of the Banū Taym b. Murra (Quraysh) but of the Banū Taym of Bakr b. Wā'il.

403. See Gloss. s.v. yad, and Lane, Lexicon, s.vv. dā'ir and sū'.

I will write to ᶜAbdallāh b. al-Zubayr about that." Shabath b. Ribᶜī al-Tamīmī[404] came to ᶜAbdallāh b. Yazīd and told him about that, and ᶜAbdallāh b. Yazīd rode out together with him and Yazīd b. al-Ḥārith b. Ruwaym and entered in to Ibrāhīm b. Muḥammad b. Ṭalḥah. And he swore to him by God that in making the speech which Ibrāhīm b. Muḥammad had heard he only wanted to promote the welfare of the community and to pacify those who were at enmity. "Yazīd b. al-Ḥārith came to me telling me such-and-such, and I thought I should stand up among them to say what you heard, out of the desire that there should be no falling out, no breakdown of concord, and that this people's misfortune should not divide them." Ibrāhīm b. Muḥammad relented and accepted his explanation.

Then the companions of Sulaymān b. Ṣurad came into the open, displaying their weapons, and making public the preparations they undertook and which benefited them.

In this year also, the Khawārij who had come to Ibn al-Zubayr in Mecca, and fought alongside him against Ḥusayn b. Numayr al-Sakūnī, separated from him and went to al-Baṣrah, where they fell into dissension and developed into parties.[405]

The End of the Khārijites' Support for ᶜAbdallāh b. al-Zubayr in Mecca and the Dissensions among Them

I was told on the authority of Hishām b. Muḥammad al-Kalbī—Abū Mikhnaf Lūṭ b. Yaḥyā—Abū al-Mukhāriq al-Rāsibī: Ibn Ziyād, following Abū Bilāl's killing,[406] hunted down the Khawārij strenuously. Even before that he had not held back from them or spared them, but following the killing of Abū Bilāl he devoted himself to eradicating them and extir-   [514]

---

404. On Shabath b. Ribᶜī al-Riyāḥī, leader of the Tamīm in al-Kūfah, see Crone, *Slaves*, 118; Rotter, *Bürgerkrieg*, index.

405. For parallel and variant accounts of the following, see al-Mubarrad, *Kāmil*, 604-9; Ibn ᶜAbd Rabbihi, *ᶜIqd*, II, 391-5; Ibn al-Athīr, IV, 136-9; Wellhausen, *Oppositionsparteien*, 27-32 (= Eng. tr. 45-53).

406. For Abū Bilāl Mirdās b. Udayya al-Tamīmī, leader of the Baṣran Khawārij killed in 61/680-81, see Wellhausen, *Oppositionsparteien*, 25-7 (= Eng. tr. 39-43).

pating them. Thereupon, when Ibn al-Zubayr revolted in Mecca and the Syrians moved against him, the Khawārij gathered to consider what had happened to them.

Nāfiᶜ b. al-Azraq[407] said to them, "God sent down the Book to you and in it He imposed *jihād* as an obligation upon you and remonstrated with you with clear eloquence. The swords of the evil ones and those with enmity and oppression have been unsheathed against you. Now there is this one who has risen in Mecca, so let us go out together and we will come to the sanctuary and join this man. If he is of our opinions, we will join him in *jihād* against the enemy; if his opinions are different from ours, we will fight in defense of the sanctuary to the best of our ability and afterward consider our situation."

Consequently, they left and came to ᶜAbdallāh b. al-Zubayr, who was delighted at their coming to him, indicated to them that he shared their views, and satisfied them unhesitatingly without any cross-examination. They fought together with him until the death of Yazīd b. Muᶜāwiyah and the Syrians' departure from Mecca.

Then the Khārijīs met among themselves and said, "That which you did formerly was thoughtless and was wrong. You were fighting together with a man who perhaps does not share your views. It is not long since he and his father were fighting against you and calling out 'Vengeance for ᶜUthmān!'[408] Go to him, therefore, and ask him about ᶜUthmān. If he dissociates himself from him, then he is your friend, but if he refuses, he is your enemy."[409]

So they went to him and said, "Listen! We have fought [515] alongside you, but we did not examine you regarding your views to find out if you are with us or our enemies. Tell us what you say about ᶜUthmān!" He considered and saw that

---

407. Of the Banū Ḥanīfah (Bakr b. Wā'il), he is the eponym of the Azāriqah sect of Khārijites (on him see *EI¹*, s.v.).

408. At the Battle of the Camel, those who were to become the Khawārij fought with ᶜAlī against ᶜĀ'ishah, Ṭalḥah and al-Zubayr, who claimed to be seeking vengeance for the murdered ᶜUthmān.

409. The notion of "dissociation" or "quittance" (barā'ah) is a key concept of the Khawārij, as of the Shīᶜah. Its correlative is wilāyah, "friendship."

there were few of his supporters around him and so he said
to them, "You have come to me and met me unexpectedly
when I desired to leave. Come to me this evening so that I
can tell you about that which you wish to know." They,
therefore, went away while he sent to his supporters and said
to them, "Put on your weapons and come to me all together
this evening," and they did what he asked.

When the Khawārij came, Ibn al-Zubayr's men had positioned themselves around him in two lines wearing their
weapons, and a large group of them stood before him with
spears in their hands. Ibn al-Azraq said to his followers, "The
man is afraid of being taken unaware by you. He has decided
to resist you and has prepared for you, as you see." Then Ibn
al-Azraq approached Ibn al-Zubayr and said to him, "Oh Ibn
al-Zubayr, fear God your Lord and hate the faithless one who
claims everything for himself! Treat as an enemy he who was
the first to make error into a model for behavior [sanna al-
dalālah], introduced innovations and opposed the ordinances
of the Book. If you do that you will satisfy your Lord and
save yourself from painful punishment. But if you reject that,
you will be one of those who 'enjoyed their share'[410] and
wasted their good things in the life of this world. Oh ᶜAbīdah
b. Hilāl,[411] describe to this man and those with him the
undertaking we are engaged in and to which we are calling
the people," so ᶜAbīdah b. Hilāl came forward.

According to Hishām—Abū Mikhnaf—Abū ᶜAlqamah al-
Khathᶜamī—Qabīṣah b. ᶜAbd al-Raḥmān al-Quhāfī of Khathᶜam: By God, I saw ᶜAbīdah b. Hilāl when he came forward
and spoke. I never heard any speaker who spoke more eloquently or more appositely in what he said than he. He shared
the views of the Khawārij. He united eloquence with significance of meaning and ease of vocabulary. He praised God
and extolled Him, and then he said:

Now, God sent Muḥammad, calling people to serve
God and make pure the religion. He called people to   [516]

---

410. Cf. Qur'ān 9:70, 46:19.
411. Of the Banū Yashkur (Bakr b. Wā'il), he was one of the four men
who killed the leader of the force which had killed Abū Bilāl. On ᶜAbīdah,
see Shammākhī, Siyar, 68 bottom.

that and the Muslims responded to him, and he worked among them, following the Book of God and His ordinance until God took him unto Himself. The Muslims then made Abū Bakr caliph and Abū Bakr appointed ᶜUmar as caliph after him. Both of them followed the Book and the example [*sunnah*] of the Messenger of God in what they did. Praise be to God, the Lord of the Worlds! Then the Muslims appointed ᶜUthmān as caliph, but he created reserved areas, favored kinship, appointed youths to positions of authority, abolished the lash and laid aside the whip, destroyed the Book, shed the blood of the Muslim, beat those who rejected oppression, granted shelter to him whom the Messenger had expelled, and beat those with precedence in merit, drove them out and dispossessed them. Not content with that, he seized the spoils [*fay'*] which God had given to them and shared it out among the godless ones of Quraysh and the shameless ones of the Arabs.⁴¹² Hence a band of the Muslims whose oath God had accepted that they would obey Him, heedless in God of the censure of anybody else, came to him and killed him. We are friends to them, but dissociate ourselves from Ibn ᶜAffān and his friends. What say you, Ibn al-Zubayr?

---

412. ᶜAbīdah's list of ᶜUthmān's "crimes" can be found with some variants in different sources. In pre-Islamic Arabia, the "reserved area" (*ḥimā*) is said to have been an area of pasture land, sometimes associated with a deity or sanctuary, closed to individuals or tribes; animals grazing there could not be reclaimed by their owners. The Prophet is said to have forbidden the creation of any new ones in Islam, except by himself (see Goldziher, *Muh. Stud.*, I, 235 [= Eng. tr. I, 214 f.], *EI²*, s.v. Ḥimā; cf. Qur'ān, 5:102). The accusation of nepotism refers to ᶜUthmān's appointment of his own Umayyad relatives to positions of authority. He is further accused of refusing to carry out the statutory Islamic punishment of flogging for certain offences. The destruction of "the Book" probably refers to the charge that, in compiling the standard text of the Qur'ān, he caused variant texts to be destroyed. "Him whom the Messenger had expelled" refers to the Umayyad al-Ḥakam b. Abī al-ᶜĀṣ, whom Muḥammad had forbidden to return to Mecca. "Those with precedence in merit" presumably refers to ᶜUthmān's treatment of opponents such as Abū Dharr al-Ghifārī (q.v., in *EI²*) and Kaᶜb b. ᶜAbdah al-Nahdī. In general, see *EI¹* s.v. ᶜOthmān b. ᶜAffān.

Ibn al-Zubayr praised God and extolled Him, and then he said:

I have understood what you have said. You referred to the Prophet and he was as you have said, even more than you described. I have understood what you said about Abū Bakr and ᶜUmar. You were right and hit the mark. I understood what you said about ᶜUthmān b. ᶜAffān, may God have mercy upon him, and I do not know the whereabouts of any creature of God today who knows more about Ibn ᶜAffān and his affair than I. I was with him when the mob criticized and censured him. He neglected nothing which the mob blamed him for but rebutted it. Then they came back to him with a letter[413] of his which they claimed he had written about them, ordering in it that they should be killed. He told them, "I did not write it. If you wish, then bring proof, and if there is not any, I will swear an oath to you." By God, they never brought him proof and did not ask him to swear, but fell upon him and killed him. I have heard what you have accused him of, but it was not like that. Rather, he always acted worthily and I bear witness to you and to those here present that I am a friend of Ibn ᶜAffān in this world and in the next, and a friend of his friends and enemy of his enemies.

[517]

The Khārijīs said, "May God dissociate Himself from you, Oh enemy of God!" while Ibn al-Zubayr said, "May God dissociate Himself from you, Oh enemies of God!"

Then the group split up. Nāfiᶜ b. al-Azraq al-Ḥanẓalī,[414] ᶜAbdallāh b. Ṣaffār al-Saᶜdī of the Banū Ṣarīm b. Muqāᶜis,[415]

---

413. A reference to the letter bearing ᶜUthmān's seal, intercepted by the rebels from al-Fusṭāṭ after ᶜUthmān's initial success in pacifying them. The real authorship of the letter is disputed (see N.A. Faris, "Development in Arab historiography . . . ," in B. Lewis and P.M. Holt (eds.), *Historians of the Middle East*, London 1962).

414. The *nisbah* al-Ḥanẓalī (of Tamīm) seems to be a mistake; see Wellhausen, *Oppositionsparteien*, 27 n. 5.

415. Of Tamīm (see Caskel/Ibn Kalbī, II, 538 for the Banū Ṣarīm b. al-Ḥārith of Muqāᶜis); he is the eponym of the Ṣufriyyah sect.

ᶜAbdallāh b. Ibāḍ, also of the Banū Ṣarīm,[416] Ḥanẓalah b. Bayhās,[417] and the sons of al-Māḥūz (ᶜAbdallāh, ᶜUbaydallāh and al-Zubayr) of the Banū Salīṭ b. Yarbūᶜ[418] departed and eventually reached al-Baṣrah. Abū Ṭālūt of the Banū Zimmān b. Mālik b. Ṣaᶜb b. ᶜAlī b. Mālik b. Bakr b. Wāʾil, ᶜAbdallāh b. Thawr Abū Fudayk of the Banū Qays b. Thaᶜlabah, and ᶜAṭiyyah b. al-Aswad al-Yashkurī[419] went to the Yamāmah. There they joined Abū Ṭālūt in revolt, but afterwards agreed on Najdah b. ᶜĀmir[420] as leader. As for those of them from al-Baṣrah, they went to al-Baṣrah, sharing the ideas of Abū Bilāl.

According to Hishām—Abū Mikhnaf Lūṭ b. Yaḥyā, and Abū al-Muthannā—one of his brethren of the people of al-Baṣrah: The Khārijīs of al-Baṣrah met and most of them said, "What if a party from among us rebel in the path of God, for since our companions rebelled there has been a period in which we have not been active? Our scholars would be in the world as a light to the people summoning them to the religion, and our men of piety and struggle would go out to join the Lord; they would be martyrs given their reward with God and truly alive."

So they appointed Nāfiᶜ b. al-Azraq. He took charge of three hundred men and came out in revolt. That was the time of [518] the rising of the people of al-Baṣrah against ᶜUbaydallāh b. Ziyād and the breaking down by the Khawārij of the prison gates and their escape from them. The people of al-Baṣrah were preoccupied with the fighting between Azd, Rabīᶜah, the Banū Tamīm and Qays over the shedding of Masᶜūd b. ᶜAmr's blood and the Khawārij took advantage of their preoccupation with the fighting to prepare themselves and gather together. When Nāfiᶜ b. al-Azraq revolted, they followed him.

---

416. The eponym of the Ibāḍiyyah sect (on him, see Caskel/Ibn Kalbī, II, 113).

417. Also of Tamīm, he is possibly the eponym of the Bayhāsiyyah sect, but cf. *EI²*, s.v. Abū Bayhās.

418. Also of Tamīm (see Caskel/Ibn Kalbī, II, 508, for the Banū Salīṭ b. al-Ḥārith of the Banū Yarbūᶜ b. Ḥanẓalah).

419. All three of the Banū Bakr b. Wāʾil.

420. Of the Banū Ḥanīfah (Bakr b. Wāʾil), eponym of the Najadāt sect.

The people of al-Baṣrah made peace among themselves, appointing ᶜAbdallāh b. al-Ḥārith b. Nawfal b. al-Ḥārith b. ᶜAbd al-Muṭṭalib to lead them in prayer, and Ibn Ziyād left for Syria. The Azd and the Banū Tamīm made peace with one another, devoted themselves to the problem of the Khawārij, pursuing them and terrifying them so that those of them who remained in al-Baṣrah left and joined Ibn al-Azraq, except for a few of them of those who did not want to revolt at that time. Among these were ᶜAbdallāh b. Ṣaffār and ᶜAbdallāh b. Ibāḍ and some men with them who shared their views.

Nāfiᶜ b. al-Azraq reflected, and formed the opinion that the support of those who had not followed him was unnecessary and that there was no salvation for those who had not followed him. He said to his men, therefore, "God has honored you by your coming out in revolt. He has revealed to you what others have been blind to. Do you not know that you have come out in revolt only to seek His way [sharīᶜah] and His affairs? His affairs are a commander for you and the Book is an imām for you. You are only following His examples [sunan] and His paths." They replied, "Indeed, yes!" He said, "Is not your precept regarding your friend the precept of the Prophet regarding his friend, and your precept regarding your enemy the precept of the Prophet regarding his enemy? Your enemy today was the enemy of God and of the Prophet, just as the enemy of the Prophet was then he who is the enemy of God and of you today." They answered, "Yes." He said, "God, blessed and exalted is He, has revealed, 'An acquittal [barā'ah] from God and His Messenger to those of the polytheists with whom you have made a covenant,[421] and He has said, 'Do not marry polytheist women until they believe.'[422] Hence God has prohibited taking them as friends, living among them, allowing their witness, eating animals slaughtered by them, taking knowledge of religion from them, marrying them and inheriting from them. God has insisted that we recognize this, and it is incumbent upon us that we make this religion known to those out of the midst of whom we have separated and that

[519]

---

421. Qur'ān, 9:1.
422. Qur'ān, 2:220.

we do not hide what God has revealed. Moreover, God says, 'Those who hide what we have revealed of proofs and guidance, after we have made it clear to the people in the Book, God will curse them and the execrators will curse them.' "[423] All of his companions answered positively to this view.

Then he wrote, "From ʿAbdallāh Nāfiʿ b. al-Azraq to ʿAbdallāh b. Ṣaffār and ʿAbdallāh b. Ibāḍ and those of the people with those two. Greetings to those of the servants of God who are in obedience to God! The situation is thus. . . ," and he told the story and described the picture as above. He sent the letter to them both.

It was brought to them. ʿAbdallāh b. Ṣaffār read it, then took it and put it behind him. He did not read it out to the people out of fear that they would split and fall into dispute. ʿAbdallāh b. Ibāḍ said to him, "What is the matter? In your father's name, what is it that you should be afflicted so? Is it that our brethren have been struck down or some of them made prisoner?" Ibn Ṣaffār gave him the letter, and he read it and said, "Damn him! Whatever opinion he held, Nāfiʿ b. al-Azraq was sincere. Even if the people in general were polytheists, he was the most correct in the views and decisions according to which he gave advice, and his mode of life was like that of the Prophet among the polytheists. But now he has lied and accused us of lying when he says that the people are infidels who have rejected the divine grace and ordinances, that they (Ibn al-Azraq's party) are dissociators from polytheism, and that we must shed the blood of the 'polytheists' and act similarly with their property, something which has been forbidden to us." Ibn Ṣaffār said to him, "God is quit [barī'a] of you, for you have fallen short, and God is quit of Ibn al-Azraq, for he has gone too far. God is quit of the two of you

[520]   together." But the other said, "God is quit of you and of him."

Then the Khārijites divided into subgroups. Ibn al-Azraq's power increased and his followers multiplied. He advanced toward al-Baṣrah until he was close to the bridge, and ʿAbdallāh b. al-Ḥārith sent Muslim b. ʿUbays b. Kurayz b. Rabīʿah b.

---

423. Qur'ān, 2:154.

Ḥabīb b. ᶜAbd Shams b. ᶜAbd Manāf against him with a company of Baṣrans.[424]

Abū Jaᶜfar (al-Ṭabarī) said: In the middle of the month of Ramaḍān this year, al-Mukhtār b. Abī ᶜUbayd arrived in al-Kūfah.[425]

The Arrival of al-Mukhtār in al-Kūfah

According to Hishām b. Muḥammad al-Kalbī—Abū Mikhnaf—al-Naḍr b. Ṣāliḥ: The Shīᶜah had been criticizing and blaming al-Mukhtār for his behavior in the affair of al-Ḥasan b. ᶜAlī—on the day when al-Ḥasan had been stabbed at Muẓlim Sābāṭ and carried to the White Palace at al-Madā'in[426] and then for what he had done in the time of al-Ḥusayn, when the latter had sent Muslim b. ᶜAqīl to al-Kūfah.[427] Muslim had stayed in the house of al-Mukhtār b. Abī ᶜUbayd (today it is the house of Salm b. al-Musayyab), and al-Mukhtār had given Muslim the oath of allegiance, with those of the people of al-Kūfah who gave it to him, had acted as his adviser, and had called upon those who took his orders to join Muslim's movement. On the day when Ibn ᶜAqīl came out in revolt, al-Mukhtār was in a settlement of his at Khuṭarniyah called Laqafā.[428] At the time of the midday prayer, news came that Ibn ᶜAqīl had manifested himself in al-Kūfah, for he had not

---

424. See below, pp. 164ff.

425. Parallels and variants: *Ansāb*, V, 214ff.; Ibn Aᶜtham, VI, 53–8, 73–7; Ibn al-Athīr, IV, 139–43; Wellhausen, *Oppositionsparteien*, 74–6 (= Eng. tr. 125–7); K.A. Fariq, "The story of an Arab diplomat," 7–17.

426. In the immediate aftermath of Muᶜāwiyah's march into Iraq in 40/661, panic broke out among al-Ḥasan's supporters in al-Madā'in/Ctesiphon, and al-Ḥasan, injured, was carried to the house of the governor, al-Mukhtār's uncle; al-Mukhtār, it is alleged, has suggested to his uncle that he use Ḥasan as a bargaining counter in his own negotiations with the triumphant Muᶜāwiyah (see Ṭabarī, II, 2).

427. Before setting out for al-Kūfah in 61/680, al-Ḥusayn is reported to have sent his cousin Muslim b. ᶜAqīl to ascertain the situation there; Muslim sent Ḥusayn a message of reassurance, leading him to set out on his ill-fated journey, but meanwhile was captured and executed by the new governor of al-Kūfah, ᶜUbaydallāh b. Ziyād (see Ṭabarī, II, 227ff.).

428. For Khuṭarniyah, "one of the districts of Babylon," see Yāqūt, *Buldān*, II, 453; Abū Muslim is said to have come from there (Wellhausen, *Arab Kingdom*, 505); the reading Laqafā is uncertain.

revolted on the day he had arranged with his supporters, but only when he was told that Hāni' b. ᶜUrwah al-Murādī[429] had been beaten and imprisoned. Al-Mukhtār came with some of his mawlās and reached Bāb al-Fīl[430] after the sunset prayer. ᶜUbaydallāh b. Ziyād had given a command over all of the people to ᶜAmr b. Ḥurayth[431] to lie in wait in the mosque for the supporters of Ibn ᶜAqīl. While al-Mukhtār was waiting at Bāb al-Fīl, Hāni' b. Abī Ḥayyah al-Wadāᶜī[432] passed by and said, "Why are you waiting here? You are neither with the people nor in your camp." He said, "I was uncertain what I should do, on account of the gravity of the mishap which has befallen you."[433] Hāni' said to him, "By God, I think you are killing yourself!" Then he went into ᶜAmr b. Ḥurayth and told him what he had said to al-Mukhtār and what al-Mukhtār had replied.

[521]

Abū Mikhnaf—al-Naḍr b. Ṣāliḥ—ᶜAbd al-Raḥmān b. Abī ᶜUmayr al-Thaqafī: I was sitting with ᶜAmr b. Ḥurayth when Hāni' b. Abī Ḥayyah reported to him these words of al-Mukhtār. ᶜAmr said to me, "Go to your cousin and tell him that his companion (Muslim b. ᶜAqīl) does not know where he is and that he should not lay himself open to any action (on the part of the authorities)." I stood up to go to him, but Zā'idah b. Qudāmah b. Masᶜūd[434] rushed up to ᶜAmr and said to him, "Is he going to come to you under safe-conduct?" ᶜAmr b. Ḥurayth answered him, "As far as I am concerned he has safe-conduct from me, and, if he is brought up before the governor ᶜUbaydallāh b. Ziyād, I will stand as witness for

---

429. Muslim b. ᶜAqīl stayed in the house of this supporter of the Shīᶜah, subsequently executed together with Muslim, after leaving that of al-Mukhtār; Hāni' b. ᶜUrwah belonged to the Banū Murād of Madhḥij (on him, see Caskel/ Ibn Kalbī, II, 279).

430. For an explanation of the name of this place in al-Kūfah, see Ṭabarī, II, 27.

431. See above, n. 183.

432. On him, see Caskel/Ibn Kalbī, II, 278; the Banū Wadīᶜah b. ᶜAmr belonged to Hamdān.

433. See Gloss. s.v. rajja; I have adopted the reading khaṭb from Ansāb, V, 215⁵, in preference to the Leiden text's khaṭī'ah.

434. Like al-Mukhtār and the narrator himself, of Thaqīf. Subsequently, he is named as the one who killed Muṣᶜab b. al-Zubayr at the battle of Dayr al-Jāthalīq, shouting "Vengeance for al-Mukhtār!" (see Ansāb, V, 430).

him and intercede for him to the best of my ability." Zā'idah
b. Qudāmah said to him, "God willing, that can only be good
for him."

So I went off, with Zā'idah accompanying me, to al-Mukhtār,
and we told him what Ibn Abī Ḥayyah had said and how ᶜAmr
b. Ḥurayth had answered, and we implored him for God's
sake not to lay himself open to any action. Consequently, he
came down to Ibn Ḥurayth, greeted him, and sat beneath his
banner until morning. The people talked about al-Mukhtār's
conduct, and ᶜUmārah b. ᶜUqbah b. Abī Muᶜayṭ[435] went off to   [522]
ᶜUbaydallāh b. Ziyād and told him about it. At daybreak, the
gate of ᶜUbaydallāh b. Ziyād was opened, the people were
permitted to enter and al-Mukhtār was among those who went
in. ᶜUbaydallāh summoned him and said to him, "Are you
the one who came with the gang to help Ibn ᶜAqīl?" He
answered, "No, but I came and camped beneath ᶜAmr b.
Ḥurayth's banner and passed the night with him until morning."
And ᶜAmr said to Ibn Ziyād, "He has spoken the truth, may
God preserve you!" But Ibn Ziyād took up his baton, aimed
it at al-Mukhtār's face, and hit him in the eye and cut it.
Then he said, "That is what you deserve! Indeed, by God, if
it were not for ᶜAmr's testimony on your behalf, I would cut
off your head. Take him off to prison!" So they took him off
to prison and he was detained there. There he stayed until
al-Ḥusayn was killed.

After al-Ḥusayn's death, al-Mukhtār sent to Zā'idah b. Qudāmah asking him to go to ᶜAbdallāh b. ᶜUmar[436] in Medina
to ask him to write on his behalf to Yazīd b. Muᶜāwiyah
(requesting Yazīd) to write to ᶜUbaydallāh b. Ziyād ordering
his release. Zā'idah rode to ᶜAbdallāh b. ᶜUmar and came to
him and delivered al-Mukhtār's message to him. Ṣafiyyah, al-
Mukhtār's sister who was married to ᶜAbdallāh b. ᶜUmar, found
out about her brother's place of imprisonment and wept and
grieved. When ᶜAbdallāh b. ᶜUmar saw that, he sent a letter
with Zā'idah to Yazīd b. Muᶜāwiyah, "Now, ᶜUbaydallāh b.

---

435. An Umayyad (family of Abū ᶜAmr), son of an opponent of the Prophet
who was killed at Badr, a uterine brother of the caliph ᶜUthmān (Ansāb, IVb,
170; Rotter, Bürgerkrieg, 111).
436. See n. 276 above.

Ziyād has imprisoned my brother-in-law al-Mukhtār. I should like him pardoned and his condition improved. If you think, may God have mercy on us and on you, that you should write to Ibn Ziyād telling him to release him, I know you will. Peace be upon you!"

[523] Zā'idah went on his way with the letter and brought it to Yazīd in Syria. When he read it, Yazīd laughed and said, "Abū ᶜAbd al-Raḥmān[437] is interceding. He is the right one for that!" Then he wrote to Ibn Ziyād, "Now, release al-Mukhtār b. Abī ᶜUbayd when you have looked at my letter. Peace be upon you!" Zā'idah brought it and gave it to Ibn Ziyād, who called for al-Mukhtār and had him brought out. He told him, "I give you three days. If I find you in al-Kūfah after that, my undertaking toward you is void." Al-Mukhtār went off to get ready to leave and Ibn Ziyād said, "By God, Zā'idah risked himself against me when he went to the Commander of the Faithful to bring me a letter telling me to release a man whom I had decided to keep in prison for a long time. Fetch him to me!" But ᶜAmr b. Nāfiᶜ Abū ᶜUthmān, a secretary of Ibn Ziyād, went to him while he was being sought and told him, "Save yourself! Remember this as a favor you owe me." So Zā'idah went and hid himself on that day, and then he went with some members of his clan to al-Qaᶜqāᶜ b. Shawr al-Dhuhlī[438] and Muslim b. ᶜAmr al-Bāhilī[439] and they obtained safe-conduct from Ibn Ziyād.

Hishām—Abū Mikhnaf: And on the third day al-Mukhtār left for the Ḥijāz.

Abū Mikhnaf said that al-Ṣaqᶜab b. Zuhayr reported to him from Ibn al-ᶜIrq, a mawlā of Thaqīf: I had come from the Ḥijāz and when I reached al-Basīṭah beyond Wāqiṣah,[440] I met al-Mukhtār b. Abī ᶜUbayd who was leaving for the Ḥijāz after Ibn Ziyād had freed him. When I met him I greeted him and

---

437. Ibn ᶜUmar's *kunyah*.

438. Of Dhuhl b. Thaᶜlabah/Shaybān (on him, see Caskel/Ibn Kalbī, II, 465).

439. Father of Qutaybah b. Muslim. Bāhilah were part of Qays; for Muslim, see Crone, *Slaves*, 136–7.

440. Al-Basīṭah is mentioned at Ṭabarī, I, 2222, as the place where Saᶜd b. Abī Waqqāṣ's army gathered en route to al-Qādisiyyah; evidently it is in the Najd, on the route from the Ḥijāz to Iraq.

turned to him, but when I saw how his eye had been cut I uttered the formula that we are God's creatures and shall return to Him. After I had commiserated with him, I asked him, "What is the matter with your eye, may God turn all evil from you?" He replied, "The son of the fornicator struck it with his baton so as to cause what you see." I said, "Whatever made him do that, may his fingertips be withered?" Al-Mukhtār said, "May God kill me if I do not cut his fingertips, his veins and his limbs to pieces!" I was surprised at his words and I said to him, "How do you know you will do that, may God have mercy on you?" He replied, "Remember what I am telling you until you see it come true."

[524]

Then he began asking me about ᶜAbdallāh b. al-Zubayr, and I told him, "He has taken refuge at the sanctuary and has said, 'I am only he who takes refuge with the Lord of this building.'[441] The people are saying that he is accepting the oath of allegiance in secret, but I do not think he will make his opposition manifest unless his strength increases and he finds he has a lot of allies[442] among the men." He replied, "Yes, indeed, there is no doubt about it! Indeed, he is the man of the Arabs today. Indeed, if he follows my footsteps and listens to what I say, then I will suffice him for the affairs of the people. But if he does not do it, then by God I am not less than one of the Arabs. Oh Ibn al-ᶜIrq, the time of commotion and distress [al-fitnah] has come like thunder and lightning. It is as if it has been sent and tramples down everything like a camel led by its noseband. When you see that and hear about it in a place where I have shown myself, say that al-Mukhtār with his troops of the Muslims is seeking vengeance for the blood of he who was killed unjustly, the martyr, the one slain at al-Ṭaff,[443] the lord of the Muslims and the son of their lord, al-Ḥusayn b. ᶜAlī. Then, by your Lord, I will surely kill, in recompense for his murder, the

---

441. See n. 52 above.

442. *Add. et emend.* suggests the deletion of one of the two *illā*s ("unless"); possibly the second of them could be the accusative form of *ill*, "pact" (= "allies")?

443. I.e., al-Ḥusayn; the battle at Karbalā' is often called the battle of al-Ṭaff (see Yāqūt, *Buldān*, III, 539).

number of those who were killed in recompense for the shedding of the blood of John the Baptist."[444] I said, "Praise be to God, for these are wonders and things unheard of before!" He answered, "It is as I tell you. Remember what I have said until you see it come true." Then he urged on his mount and went on his way, and I went with him for a time asking God for his welfare and good companions.

Then he halted and made me swear an oath when I left him. I took his hand and said goodbye and wished him peace and left him, and I said to myself, "That which this man—meaning al-Mukhtār—tells me of what he claims is going to happen, is it a thing which his own prompting tells him of? By God, God does not acquaint anyone with knowledge of the hidden things. It is merely something which he wishes for and thinks is going to happen and it entails the ideas he has. But, by God, they are confused ideas. By God, not everything which a man thinks is going to happen does happen!" But, by God, I lived to see everything which he had said. By God, if that was the result of some knowledge which was vouchsafed to him, then it was confirmed; if it was an idea which he conceived and something he wished for, well it came about!

[525]

Abū Mikhnaf—al-Saqʿab b. Zuhayr—Ibn al-ʿIrq: I narrated this report to al-Ḥajjāj b. Yūsuf, who laughed and then said to me that he used also to say:

> By a woman lifting her coats
>   and calling out her woe
>   by the Tigris or around it.[445]

I asked him, "Do you think that this is something which he thought up himself and made a guess at, or is it the result of knowledge given to him?" He said, "By God, I do not know the answer; but how capable he was, whether he was

---

444. In Muslim tradition, in response to the execution of John the Baptist (Yaḥyā b. Zakariyyā') by the Jewish king, Jerusalem is sacked by Nebuchadnessar (Bukhtnaṣṣar) and 70,000 Israelites are killed (see, e.g., Ṭabarī, I, 713ff.).

445. On occasions, al-Mukhtār's dicta seem to be composed for their sound rather than their meaningfulness. Al-Ḥajjāj here seems to be laughing at al-Mukhtār's harmonious nonsense.

a man of this world,[446] a kindler of war, or a fighter against enemies!"

Abū Mikhnaf—Abū Yūsuf al-Anṣārī, of the Banū Khazraj—cAbbās b. Sahl b. Sacd: Al-Mukhtār arrived at Mecca where we were, and he went to cAbdallāh b. al-Zubayr while I was sitting with him. Al-Mukhtār greeted Ibn al-Zubayr, who returned his greetings, welcomed him, and made room for him. Then Ibn al-Zubayr asked him, "Tell me about the condition of the people in al-Kūfah, Oh Abū Isḥāq." He replied, "In public they are supporters of their authorities, but in private they are opponents of them." Ibn al-Zubayr said to him, "That describes the slaves of evil; when they see their masters they serve and obey them, but when they are away they calumniate and curse them."

He sat with us for a while and then he leaned toward[447] Ibn al-Zubayr as if he would confide a secret to him, and he said to him, "What are you waiting for? Hold out your hand. Let me give you the oath of allegiance and you give us what will please us. Seize control of the Ḥijāz, for the people of the Ḥijāz are all with you." Al-Mukhtār thereupon got up and went out. He was not seen again for a year.

[526]

Then, while I was sitting with Ibn al-Zubayr, behold, he said to me, "When did you last have news about al-Mukhtār b. Abī cUbayd?" I said to him, "I have not heard about him since I saw him with you last year." He said, "Where do you think he went off to? If he had been in Mecca, he would have been seen there afterward." I told him, "I went back to al-Madīnah a month or two after I saw him with you, and I remained there for some months. Then I came to you and I heard a group of the people of al-Ṭā'if who had come to perform the minor pilgrimage [cumra][448] claiming he had come to them in al-Ṭā'if asserting he was the lord of wrath and the extirpator of tyrants." Ibn al-Zubayr said, "God damn him! He has been sent as a liar and self-proclaimed soothsayer. If God extirpates tyrants, then al-Mukhtār is one of them."

---

446. See *Add. et emend.* for the reading *dunyā*.
447. See *Add. et emend.* for the reading *māla*.
448. The minor pilgrimage may be accomplished at any time of the year and involves fewer rituals than the *ḥajj*.

By God, it was not long after the conclusion of our talk before he appeared before us at the side of the mosque, and Ibn al-Zubayr said, "Speak of the devil![449] Where do you think he is heading for?" I said, "I think he is heading for the sanctuary." He came to the sanctuary and stood facing the (Black) Stone[450] and then he circumambulated the sanctuary seven times and then made a ritual prayer of two *rakᶜas* by the Ḥijr[451] and then sat down. Before long some men of his acquaintance, of the people of al-Ṭā'if and others of the people of the Ḥijāz, joined him and sat together with him, and Ibn al-Zubayr was kept waiting for his coming to him. Ibn al-Zubayr said, "What do you think he is up to that he does not come to us?" I said, "I do not know, but I will obtain information of him for you." He replied, "Whatever you wish." That had surprised him.[452]

[527] So I got up and passed by as if I intended to leave the mosque, but then I turned in his direction and went toward him. I greeted him, sat down and took his hand, and then I said to him, "Where have you been? Where did you get to after I met you? Were you at al-Ṭā'if?" He said to me, "I was at al-Ṭā'if and elsewhere." And he made his affair appear very mysterious to me. So I leaned toward him and, whispering, said to him, "Does someone like you keep away from someone like him to whom the people of nobility and the great families of the Arabs from Quraysh, the Anṣār and Thaqīf[453] have rallied? There is left no family or tribe whose leader or chief has not come and given the oath of allegiance to this man. It is surprising of you and your views that you should not have come to him and given him the oath of allegiance and taken

---

449. For the proverb, see Freytag, *Proverbia*, I, 505.

450. Unvocalized, the Arabic *ḥjr* in this context may refer to the Black Stone (*al-ḥajar* [*al-aswad*] or *al-rukn*) fixed in the southeast corner of the Kaᶜbah or to the semicircular area attached to the northwest side of the Kaᶜbah known as al-Ḥijr; since the circumambulation of the Kaᶜbah begins from the Black Stone, it seems that that is what is meant here, while the subsequent reference is to the Ḥijr. But there is a possible ambiguity.

451. The Ḥijr is regarded as a sacred area which at one time was a part of the Kaᶜbah; Ishmael (Ismāᶜīl) is said to have been buried there.

452. Cairo reads *ka-inna dhālik aᶜjabahu* "it was as if that had surprised him."

453. I.e., the peoples of Mecca, Medina and al-Ṭā'if.

your share in this business." He answered me, "Did you not
see me go to him last year and advise him of my views, but
he kept me out of his business? When I saw he had no need
of me, I wanted to show him I had no need of him. By God,
he needs me more than I do him!" I said to him, "You have
said to him what you have said while he was conspicuous in
the mosque. But these words should not be said unless the
curtains are lowered on them and the doors locked on them.
Meet him tonight if you wish, and I will be with you." He
answered me, "I will. After we have performed the ʿatamah
prayer[454] we will go to him and we will meet in the Ḥijr."

I got up from my place by him and went out and then
returned to Ibn al-Zubayr. I told him about the words which
had passed between us and he was pleased. And when we had
made the ʿatamah prayer, we met in the Ḥijr and then we
went off to the dwelling of Ibn al-Zubayr. Al-Mukhtār and I
asked his permission to enter and he gave it to us. I said, "I
will leave you two alone," but they said together, "We have
no secret from you," so I sat down. When Ibn al-Zubayr had
taken his hand, greeted him, welcomed him, asked him how
he and his family were, and they had remained silent for a
short while, al-Mukhtār spoke to him (and I was listening).
After he had begun on the preliminaries of his speech and
praised God and extolled Him, he said, "There is no point in
verbosity or in stopping short of what is needed. I have come   [528]
to you to give you the oath of allegiance on condition that
you will not take decisions without me and that I will be
among the first of those to whom you give access, and that
when you triumph you make use of me in the more meritorious
of your operations." Ibn al-Zubayr said to him, "I will accept
your oath of allegiance (only) on the stipulation that I will
act according to the Book of God and the exemplary practice
[sunnah] of His Prophet." He replied, "And from the worst
of my slave lads you are taking the oath of allegiance on the
Book of God and the Sunnah of His Prophet! There is no
share for me in this business which is not (also) for the farthest

---

454. The prayer of nightfall, more commonly called ṣalāt al-ʿishāʾ.

of mankind from you! No, by God, I will never give you the oath of allegiance except on these stipulations."

ᶜAbbās b. Sahl said: I obtained the ear of Ibn al-Zubayr and said to him, "Buy his obedience [dīn] from him so that you can reflect what you will do." And Ibn al-Zubayr said to him, "What you ask for is yours," and he held out his hand, and al-Mukhtār gave him the oath of allegiance. He stayed with him and was present at the first siege when al-Ḥusayn b. Numayr al-Sakūnī came to Mecca. He fought at that battle and was one of the most valiant of the people at that time and the most capable of them. After al-Mundhir b. al-Zubayr,[455] al-Miswar b. Makhramah[456] and Muṣᶜab b. ᶜAbd al-Raḥmān b. ᶜAwf al-Zuhrī[457] had been killed, al-Mukhtār cried out, "To me, Oh people of Islam, to me! I am Ibn Abī ᶜUbayd b. Masᶜūd, and I am the son of the attackers, not of the fugitives. I am the son of those who advance not those who retreat. To me, Oh defenders and zealous protectors of your honor!"[458] And he stirred up the people and was resolute and fought a good fight. Then he remained with Ibn al-Zubayr during that siege until the day when the sanctuary was set alight—that was Saturday, Rabīᶜ I 3, 64 (October 31, 683). At that time, he fought in a band of about 300 men the best fight anyone of the people put up. He fought until worn out and then he sat down with his men surrounding him. When [529] he had rested he would get up and fight again. And he never went toward a band of the Syrians without fighting them until he had defeated them.

According to Abū Mikhnaf—Abū Yūsuf Muḥammad b. Thābit—ᶜAbbās b. Sahl b. Saᶜd: In charge of the fighting against the Syrians on the day when the Kaᶜbah was set alight were

---

455. ᶜAbdallāh b. al-Zubayr's brother; other reports contradict the view that he was killed in Ḥusayn b. Numayr's siege of Mecca (see Rotter, *Bürgerkrieg*, 54).

456. Of Quraysh (the Banū Zuhrah; see Zubayrī, *Nasab Quraysh*, 263), he is reported to have been held in respect by the Khawārij; again there is doubt about whether he was in fact killed in Ibn Numayr's siege (Ibn Ḥajar, *Iṣāba*, III, 858, Yaᶜqūbī, *Ta'rīkh*, II, 282).

457. Of the Banū Zuhrah of Quraysh (Zubayrī, *Nasab Quraysh*, 267–9), son of the "elector" of the *shūrā* appointed by ᶜUmar, ᶜAbd al-Raḥmān b. ᶜAwf.

458. See *Gloss.*, s.v. *w-t-r*.

ᶜAbdallāh b. Muṭīᶜ,[459] myself and al-Mukhtār. And on that day
there was not among us any man more valiant than al-Mukhtār.
Before the Syrians learned about the death of Yazīd b. Muᶜāwiyah, he fought strenuously one day in particular. That
was Sunday, Rabīᶜ II 15, 64 (December 13, 683). The Syrians
had hoped to defeat us and had taken up positions against us
on the roads leading into Mecca.

Ibn al-Zubayr came out, and many men gave him the oath
of allegiance on the understanding that they would fight to
the death. I went out with a band who were with me fighting
on one flank, and al-Mukhtār was with another band fighting
on another flank among a group of the people of the Yamāmah.
They were Khawārij who were only fighting in defense of the
sanctuary, and they were positioned on one flank. ᶜAbdallāh
b. Muṭīᶜ was on another flank. The Syrians pressed hard against
me and pushed me back with my men until I and al-Mukhtār
with his men were gathered together in the same place. I never
did anything without him doing likewise, while he never did
anything which I did not try hard to do likewise. I never saw
anyone more resolute than he. While we were fighting, lo,
footmen and horse of the Syrian cavalry pressed against us
and forced me and him to retreat, with about seventy of those
prepared to accept hardship and suffering, to the side of one
of the houses of the Meccans. And al-Mukhtār fought against
them on that day. One man started to say to another:

The soul of a man who flees never finds refuge.

Al-Mukhtār and I sallied forth, and I said (to the Syrians),
"Send a man from among you against me." One man came
out against me and another against al-Mukhtār. I engaged my
opponent and killed him while al-Mukhtār engaged his and   [530]
killed him. Then we and our men gave a yell and pressed
against them, and, by God, we fought against them until we
had driven them out of all the roads, and then we went back
to the two opponents we had killed. Behold, the man I had
killed was very red in color like a Greek, while he whom al-
Mukhtār had killed was very black! And al-Mukhtār said to

---

459. Of the Banū ᶜAdī of Quraysh (Zubayrī, *Nasab Quraysh*, 384f.).

me, "Mark well, by God! I think that these two whom we killed were slaves. If these two had killed us, our clans and those who have expectations for us would have been distressed on our account. In my opinion, these two are no more than two dogs. After this day I will never go forth to fight a man unless he is someone I know." I replied, "And I, by God, will not go forth unless for a man I know."

Al-Mukhtār remained with Ibn al-Zubayr until Yazīd b. Muᶜāwiyah died, when the siege came to an end and the Syrians returned to Syria; the Kūfans resolved their differences by agreeing on ᶜĀmir b. Masᶜūd, after Yazīd's death, to lead them in the ritual prayer until the whole people should agree on an *imām*. It was no more than a month before ᶜĀmir sent his oath of allegiance and that of the Kūfans to Ibn al-Zubayr. Al-Mukhtār was with Ibn al-Zubayr for five months and some days after Yazīd's end.

According to Abū Mikhnaf—ᶜAbd al-Malik b. Nawfal b. Musāḥiq—Saᶜīd b. ᶜAmr b. Saᶜīd b. al-ᶜĀṣ: By God, I was with ᶜAbdallāh b. al-Zubayr, who was accompanied by ᶜAbdallāh b. Ṣafwān b. Umayyah b. Khalaf.[460] We were making the ritual circumambulation of the sanctuary when Ibn al-Zubayr looked, and there was Mukhtār! Ibn al-Zubayr said to Ibn Ṣafwān, "Look at him! By God, he is more wary than a jackal encircled by lions." He carried on his circumambulation, we accompanying him, and when we had finished and performed the ritual two *rakᶜahs*[461] of prayer after circumambulation, we joined al-Mukhtār, who asked Ibn Ṣafwān, "What did Ibn al-[531] Zubayr say about me?" But he did not reveal it and said, "He only said good of you." Al-Mukhtār responded, "Yes, indeed, by the Lord of this building! Surely I am the equal of you two!"[462] By God, either he will follow after me or I will start a blaze against him!" And he remained with him for five months, but when he saw that Ibn al-Zubayr was not giving

---

460. Of the Banū Jumaḥ of Quraysh (*ibid.*, 389–90).

461. A succession of specified ritual body movements and prayers (see *EI*[1], s.v. ṣalāt).

462. The suggested alternative reading *in kuntu āmanu sha'nakumā* with the translation "I do not trust the pair of you" is proposed in *Add. et emend.*; for the reading and translation adopted here see *Gloss.* s.v. sha'n.

him any position of authority, he started asking everybody who came from al-Kūfah the state of the people there and their condition.

According to Abū Mikhnaf—ʿAṭiyya b. al-Ḥārith Abū Rawq al-Hamdānī: Hāniʾ b. Abī Ḥayyah al-Wadāʿī came to Mecca to perform the ʿumrah of Ramaḍān. Al-Mukhtār asked him about his own state and that of the men of al-Kūfah and their condition. Hāniʾ told him about their concord and agreement to give obedience to Ibn al-Zubayr, except that there was a party of them, with the support of plenty among the people of that garrison town,[463] which, if there were somebody who would gather them for the propagation of their views, could devour the earth with them for as long as he wished.

Al-Mukhtār said to him, "I am Abū Isḥāq! By God, I am the one for them. I will unite them in the path of truth and with them I will drive out the retinue of falsehood and kill every obdurate tyrant." But Hāniʾ b. Abī Ḥayyah said to him, "Alas for you, Oh Ibn Abī ʿUbayd! If it were possible for you not to involve yourself in error, then someone else would be their leader, for the lord of the time of commotion and distress [al-fitnah] is the closest of anything to the time of death and the worst of the people in deeds." Al-Mukhtār answered him, "I will not call them to commotion and distress but only to right guidance and community."

Then he arose, went out, mounted his camels and set off toward al-Kūfah. When he reached al-Qarʿāʾ,[464] Salamah b. Marthad, the brother of Bint Marthad al-Qābiḍī of Hamdān,[465] met him. He was one of the bravest of the Arabs and was an ascetic. When they met, they clasped hands and questioned each other. Al-Mukhtār told him the news of the Ḥijāz, then said to Salamah b. Marthad, "Tell me about the people in al-Kūfah." He replied, "They are like sheep whose shepherd has gone astray." Al-Mukhtār b. Abī ʿUbayd said, "I am he who will guide them right and reach their goal." Salamah said to

[532]

---

463. Read al-miṣr.

464. See Yāqūt, Buldān, IV, 61.

465. Qābiḍ b. Zayd were a branch of Ḥāshid of Hamdān (Caskel/Ibn Kalbī, II, 454). This seems to be Ṭabarī's only reference to Salamah. Probably "Bint" should be read "Thubayth b." (see p. 126 below).

him, "Fear God, and know that you die and are resurrected, are called to account and give recompense for your deeds—if they were good you receive good, if evil you receive evil!" Then they parted and al-Mukhtār went on until he reached the lake of al-Ḥīrah on a Friday.

There he dismounted, performed his ablutions in it, annointed himself lightly with oil, changed his clothes, put on a turban and girded his sword. Then he mounted his camel and passed the mosque of the Sakūn and the *jabbānah* of Kindah.[466] At every tribal council he passed, he greeted its people and said, "Rejoice at the victory and the prizing open. What you wish for has come to you." He went on until he passed by the mosque of the Banū Dhuhl[467] and the Banū Ḥujr,[468] but found nobody there; they had gone to the community prayer. He went on until he passed the Banū Baddā',[469] where he found ᶜAbīdah b. ᶜAmr al-Baddī of Kindah. He greeted him and said, "Rejoice at the victory, the ease and the prizing open! You, Abū ᶜAmr, are holding good opinions. God will not leave any of your offenses unpardoned or any sin unforgiven." ᶜAbīdah was one of the most resolute of the people, the most perceptive and the strongest in his love for ᶜAlī, but he had not refrained from drink. When al-Mukhtār addressed these words to him, ᶜAbīdah replied, "May God give you good rejoicing, for you have wished us joy! Can you interpret things for us?" "Yes," he answered. "Come to us tonight in the camping place." Then he passed on.

Abū Mikhnaf—Fuḍayl b. Khadīj[470]—ᶜAbīdah b. ᶜAmr: Al-Mukhtār said this to me and then said, "Meet me in the

---

466. For the topography of al-Kūfah, see Massignon, "Explication du plan de Kūfa" (sketch map at p. 36 of the reprint in his *Opera minora*) and *EI²*, s.v. al-Kūfa. "The Lake of al-Ḥīrah" presumably refers to a body of water formed by the Euphrates as it empties itself into the swamps south of al-Ḥīrah. The name is not usual. The word *jabbānah* followed by the name of a tribe frequently occurs in connection with events in al-Kūfah. A *jabbānah* is a cemetery, but in al-Kūfah they seem to have been used as a sort of public square (see further *EI²*, art. cit., p. 347a).

467. The Banū Dhuhl b. Muᶜāwiyah b. al-Ḥārith al-Akbar of Kindah (Caskel/Ibn Kalbī, II, 239).

468. The Banū Ḥujr b. Wahb b. Rabīᶜah of Kindah (*ibid.*, II, 331).

469. The Banū Baddā' b. al-Ḥārith al-Akbar of Kindah (*ibid.*, I, 218).

470. See *Add. et emend.*

camping place and tell the people of your mosque this from me,[471] that they are a people upon whom God has imposed a covenant to obey Him by fighting against the violators of His law and seeking vengeance for the shed blood of the descendants of the prophets, and He will guide them to the clear light." Then he passed on, asking me the way to the Banū Hind. I told him, "Wait for me, I will guide you." I called for my horse which had been saddled for me and mounted it. I went with him to the Banū Hind.[472] Al-Mukhtār said to me, "Guide me to the abode of Ismāᶜīl b. Kathīr!"[473] So I went with him to his dwelling and asked Ismāᶜīl to come out. He saluted and greeted him, clasped his hands and wished him joy. He said to him, "You and your brother come to me tonight with Abū ᶜAmr, for I have brought you everything you wish for." Then he went on his way, and I with him, until he passed the mosque of Juhaynah of al-Bāṭinah.[474] Then he passed on to Bāb al-Fīl, where he made his camel kneel and dismounted. He entered the mosque and the people showed him respect. They said, "This is al-Mukhtār, who has come." Al-Mukhtār stood beside one of the pillars of the mosque where he prayed until the service of ritual prayer was held, when he prayed together with the people. Then he went to another pillar and offered all the prayers of the interval between Friday noontime prayer and that of the afternoon. And, when he had prayed the afternoon prayer with the people, he departed.

Abū Mikhnaf—al-Mujālid b. Saᶜīd—ᶜĀmir al-Shaᶜbī: Al-Mukhtār passed the circle of Hamdān in the mosque. He was wearing his traveling clothes and he said, "Rejoice, for I have brought to you that which will make you happy!" Then he passed on and came to his house; it is the house called the house of Salm b. al-Musayyab. And the Shīᶜah were frequently visiting it and him in it.

---

471. Read ᶜannī (see *Add. et emend.*).
472. The Banū Hind of Kindah (Caskel/Ibn Kalbī, II, 283).
473. See below, p. 182, for a report from him.
474. Apparently the Banū Juhayna b. Zayd of Quḍāᶜah (Caskel/Ibn Kalbī, II, 265, *EI² Suppl.*, s.v. Djuhayna).

Abū Mikhnaf—Fuḍayl b. Khadīj—ʿAbīdah b. ʿAmr and Ismāʿīl b. Kathīr of the Banū Hind: That night we went to him
as we had agreed. When we had entered in upon him and sat
down, he questioned us about the affairs of the people and
the condition of the Party. We told him the Party had rallied
to Sulaymān b. Ṣurad al-Khuzāʿī and that it would not be long
before he revolted. He praised God and extolled Him and
made prayers for the Prophet, and then he said, "Now, the
mahdī, son of the Legatee [*waṣī*], Muḥammad the son of ʿAlī,
sent me to you as a trustee, a helper [*wazīr*], a chosen one,
and a commander. He ordered me to fight the wicked ones
[*al-mulḥidīn*], to seek vengeance for the blood of his family
and to defend the weak."

[534]

Abū Mikhnaf—Fuḍayl b. Khadīj: ʿAbīdah b. ʿAmr and Ismāʿīl
b. Kathīr told me that they were the first of God's creatures
to respond, and they seized his hand and gave him the oath
of allegiance. Al-Mukhtār began sending to the Party who had
gathered with Sulaymān b. Ṣurad, saying to them:

> I have come to you from he who is in authority, the
> source of virtue, the legatee of the Legatee, and the
> Imām the *mahdī*, with an authority in which there is
> restoration of health, removal of the covering, fighting
> against the enemies, and fulfillment of favors. Sulay-
> mān b. Ṣurad, may God have mercy on us and upon
> him, is no more than a useless old man and a worn-
> out thing.[475] He has no experience of affairs and no
> knowledge of warfare. He only wants to get you to
> go out, and he will kill himself and you. But I only
> act following an example which was given to me and
> a command in which there was made clear to me the
> might of the one in authority over you, the killing of
> your enemies and the restoration of your spirits. Listen
> to what I say and obey my command, and then rejoice
> and spread the good news, for I am the best leader for
> the achievement of everything you hope for.

By God, he continued with these and similar words until
he had won the support of a section of the Shīʿah and they

---

475. See *Gloss.*, s.vv. ʿ-sh-m, ḥ-f-sh.

used to visit him frequently, honor him and recognize his
authority. But most of the Shīʿah at that time, and their leaders,   [535]
were with Sulaymān b. Ṣurad, who was the shaykh of the
Shīʿah and the senior one of them. They did not consider
anybody as equal with him except that al-Mukhtār had won
the support of a small section of them. Sulaymān b. Ṣurad
was the most opposed of God's creatures to al-Mukhtār. At
that time, everything was ready for Ibn Ṣurad and he wanted
to take the offensive, but al-Mukhtār did not want to move
or take any action, until[476] he should see how Sulaymān's
affair turned out, hoping that the command of the Shīʿah
would revert to himself and that they would reinforce him in
attaining what he sought.

When Sulaymān b. Ṣurad had left and gone toward Mesopotamia, ʿUmar b. Saʿd b. Abī Waqqāṣ, Shabath b. Ribʿī and
Yazīd b. al-Ḥārith b. Ruwaym said to ʿAbdallāh b. Yazīd al-
Khaṭmī and Ibrāhīm b. Muḥammad b. Ṭalḥah b. ʿUbaydallāh,
"Al-Mukhtār is a greater threat to you than Sulaymān b.
Ṣurad. Sulaymān merely went out to fight your enemies and
humiliate them for you, and he has departed from your territories. But al-Mukhtār wants to attack you in your garrison
town. Go to him, therefore, put him in irons, and keep him
in prison so that the affairs of the people may be stabilized."
They went out against him, therefore, with some men. He
was unaware until they had surrounded him and his house
and forced him to come out. When he saw the crowd he said,
"What is the matter with you? By God, you have seized the
wrong man!"[477] Ibrāhīm b. Muḥammad b. Ṭalḥah b. ʿUbaydallāh
said to ʿAbdallāh b. Yazīd, "Put him in shackles and make
him walk barefoot." But ʿAbdallāh b. Yazīd said, "Praise be
to God, I will neither make him walk nor make him go
barefoot. I will not do that with a man who has not manifested   [536]
any enmity to us or any hostility. We have only taken him
out of suspicion." Ibrāhīm b. Muḥammad said to him, "It is

---

476. Read ḥattā (see *Add. et emend.*).
477. See *Add. et emend.* for a suggested alternative reading *(bi-ghirri mā)*;
the printed text seems to give a more obvious meaning, however.

nothing to do with you.[478] Walk ahead of me! What are you and what is this we hear about you, Oh Ibn Abī ᶜUbayd?" He answered, "What you have heard about me is nothing but lies. I take refuge in God from a treachery like that of your father and grandfather."[479] Fuḍayl said: By God, I was looking at him when he was brought out and I listened to these words when he spoke to him, only I do not know whether Ibrāhīm heard him say it or not. When he had said it he was silent.

Al-Mukhtār was brought a black mule to ride. Ibrāhīm said to ᶜAbdallāh b. Yazīd, "Will you not fasten him with fetters?" but he replied, "Prison is a sufficient fetter for him."

Abū Mikhnaf: As for Yaḥyā b. Abī ᶜĪsā, he told me: I went in to him with Ḥumayd b. Muslim al-Azdī.[480] We were visiting him and looking after him, and I saw that he was in shackles. And I heard him saying, "Indeed, by the Lord of the seas, of the palms and trees, of the plains and deserts, of the godly angels, and of the goodly chosen ones, I shall slay every tyrant with every dangerous blade and sharp sword, in a band of the Helpers who are without the inclination of inexperienced ones or the dissociation of wicked ones, until, when I have erected the pillars of the religion and have repaired the scattering of the fissure of the Muslims and satisfied the thirst of the hearts of the Believers and achieved vengeance for the prophets, the continuation of this life will not be important for me and I will not mind death when it comes." Whenever we visited him while he was in prison, he used to repeat these words to us until his release. And after Ibn Ṣurad had left, al-Mukhtār showed himself as courageous before his supporters.

[537]

Abū Jaᶜfar (al-Ṭabarī) said: In this year also, Ibn al-Zubayr demolished the Kaᶜbah. Its walls had buckled as a result of the catapult stones which had been fired at it.[481]

Ibn al-Zubayr's Demolition of the Kaᶜbah

According to Muḥammad b. ᶜUmar al-Wāqidī—Ibrāhīm b. Mūsā—ᶜIkrimah b. Khālid: Ibn al-Zubayr demolished the sanc-

---

478. Literally, "it is not your nest."
479. See n. 400.
480. The authority of Abū Mikhnaf; see index, s.v.
481. Parallels and variants: *Ansāb*, IVb, 55–6; Azraqī, 143.

tuary until he had leveled it to the ground, and he dug out its foundation and made the Ḥijr a part of it. The people used to make the ritual circumambulation outside the foundations and make the prayer while facing its site. He placed the Black Cornerstone by it in an ark [tābūt] in a strip of silk, and he put the sanctuary ornaments, and the clothes and perfumes which he found inside it, in the treasury of the sanctuary in the care of the doorkeepers, replacing them when he rebuilt it.

Muḥammad b. ᶜUmar—Maᶜqil b. ᶜAbdallāh—ᶜAṭāʾ: I saw Ibn al-Zubayr demolish the whole sanctuary until he had razed it.

ᶜAbdallāh b. al-Zubayr led the people in the Pilgrimage of this year; his official over Medina was his brother ᶜUbaydah b. al-Zubayr; over al-Kūfah ᶜAbdallāh b. Yazīd al-Khaṭmī, with Saᶜd b. Nimrān in charge of the judiciary, for Shurayḥ refused to act as judge, saying, according to what is reported, "I will not judge during the time of commotion and distress"; over al-Baṣrah, ᶜUmar b. ᶜUbaydallāh b. Maᶜmar al-Taymī, with Hishām b. Hubayrah[482] in charge of the judiciary; and over Khurāsān, ᶜAbdallāh b. Khāzim.

---

482. Morony, *Iraq*, 440, says he was a Ḍabbī.

The
Events of the Year
65
(AUGUST 18, 684–AUGUST 7, 685)

*The Departure of the Penitents from al-Kūfah and
Their Destruction by the Syrian Army at the
Battle of ᶜAyn al-Wardah*[483]

According to Hishām—Abū Mikhnaf—Abū Yūsuf—ᶜAbdallāh
b. ᶜAwf al-Aḥmarī:[484] When Sulaymān b. Ṣurad wanted to set
out in the year 65 (684–5), he sent to his leading supporters
and they came to him. At the new moon of Rabīᶜ II (November
15, 684) he left with his leading supporters, having arranged
with the body of his followers to leave on that night for the
camp at al-Nukhaylah. He journeyed until he had reached his
army, and he went around among the men and his prominent
supporters, and was displeased at the number of the men. He,
therefore, sent Ḥakīm b. Munqidh al-Kindī and al-Walīd b.
Ghuḍayn al-Kinānī[485] each with a detachment of horse, telling
them, "Go and enter al-Kūfah and shout out, 'Revenge for al-

---

483. Parallel and variant accounts: Ibn al-Aᶜtham, VI, 58–73, 77–87; *Ansāb*,
V, 208ff.; Ibn al-Athīr, IV, 144–57.
484. For him, see Caskel/Ibn Kalbī, II, 108; the Banū al-Aḥmar b. Zuhayr
were of Azd.
485. Ḥakīm does not seem to be otherwise known; for al-Walīd, see Caskel/
Ibn Kalbī, II, 586.

Ḥusayn!' Go to the great mosque and shout that out." They
left and they were the first of God's creatures to give the cry,
"Revenge for al-Ḥusayn!"

Ḥakīm b. Munqidh al-Kindī with his detachment of horse
and al-Walīd b. Ghuḍayn with his, then, came and passed by
the Banū Kabīr.[486] A man of the Banū Kabīr of the Azd, called
ʿAbdallāh b. Ḥāzim,[487] with his wife Sahlah bint Sabrah b.
ʿAmr of the Banū Kabīr (she was one of the most beautiful
of them and beloved by him), heard the cry, "Revenge for al-
Ḥusayn!" He had not been among those who joined the Pen-   [539]
itents or responded to them, but now he hurriedly got his
clothes and put them on, called for his weapons and ordered
his horse to be saddled. His wife said to him, "Alas for you!
Have you gone mad?" He answered, "No, by God, but I have
heard God's summoner and I will answer him. I will seek
vengeance for the blood of this man until I die or God makes
an end of my affair, whichever is more pleasing to Him." His
wife said, "And to whom do you leave this little son of yours?"
He replied, "To God alone who has no partner! Oh my God,
I entrust to You my family and my children! Oh my God,
preserve me in them!" That son of his was called ʿAzrah and
he survived until he was subsequently killed with Muṣʿab b.
al-Zubayr.[488] Ibn Ḥāzim went out and joined the Penitents.
His wife remained at home weeping for him, and her female
relatives joined her while he went on with the company.

That night, the horsemen went around al-Kūfah and eventually came to the mosque after the ʿatamah prayer. In the
mosque there was a large number of people who had been
praying, and they shouted out, "Revenge for al-Ḥusayn!"
Among them was Abū ʿIzzah al-Qābiḍī.[489] Karib b. Nimrān
was leading the prayer, and Abū ʿIzzah said, "Revenge for al-
Ḥusayn! Where is the assembly of the people?" He was told,
"At al-Nukhaylah," and he left and went to his family, where

---

486. Leiden and Cairo both read Banū Kathīr, but Caskel/Ibn Kalbī lists
no such segment of Azd. See the note to *Ansāb*, V, 211[3,4]. Caskel/Ibn Kalbī,
II, 367, has two Banū Kabīrs of Azd.
487. Leiden and Cairo both read Khāzim. See *Ansāb*, V, loc. cit.
488. When ʿAbd al-Malik took Iraq from the Zubayrids in 692.
489. See n. 465.

he got his weapons and called for his horse to ride. His daughter al-Ruwāᶜ, who was married to Thubayth b. Marthad al-Qābiḍī, came to him and said, "Oh my father, what is happening? I see that you have girded on your sword and fastened on your weapons." He answered her, "Oh my daughter, your father is fleeing from his sin to his Lord." She began to weep and cry. His relatives by marriage and his cousins came to him, and he bade them farewell, then left and joined the company.

Before morning about the same number had joined Sulaymān b. Ṣurad as had been in his army when he came to it. Then, when morning came, he called for his register [dīwān] to see from it the number of those who had given him the oath of allegiance. He found (listed in the register as having promised [540] allegiance) 16,000, and he said, "For God's sake, only 4,000 have come to us out of 16,000."

According to Abū Mikhnaf—ᶜAṭiyyah b. al-Ḥārith—Ḥumayd b. Muslim: I said to Sulaymān b. Ṣurad, "By God, al-Mukhtār is stopping the people from joining you. I was with him three days ago and I heard a group of his followers saying, 'We are two thousand men altogether.'" Sulaymān replied, "Supposing that is so and 10,000 do not join us, are not these here Believers, do they not fear God, and do they not call to mind God and the agreements and covenants which they gave to us freely that they would indeed wage jihād and render assistance?" He remained at al-Nukhaylah for three days, sending those of his companions he trusted to those who had not joined him, to remind them of God and of what they had freely given to him, and about a thousand came out to join him. Al-Musayyab b. Najabah came to Sulaymān b. Ṣurad and said, "May God be merciful to you! Those who are reluctant will be of no avail to you, for only those whose own purpose caused them to come out will fight alongside you. Let us not wait for anyone, but seize the initiative!" He replied, "By God, your opinion is excellent."

Then Sulaymān b. Ṣurad stood up among the people, leaning on an Arab bow of his, and he said, "Oh people! Whomsoever desire for God's face and the rewards of the next world has caused to come out, he is one of us and we belong to him.

May God have mercy on him alive and dead! But whoever merely desires this world and its cultivation, by God we do not bring any spoils [*fay'*] to hand out or booty [*ghanīmah*] to distribute apart from the favor of God, the Lord of the Worlds. We have no gold or silver, and no silk or rich fabric. We have only our swords on our shoulders, our spears in our hands, and provisions enough to bring us to confront our enemy. Let he who had other intentions not accompany us!"

Ṣukhayr b. Ḥudhayfah b. Hilāl b. Mālik al-Muzanī[490] then arose and said, "God has given you right guidance and shown you your arguments. By God, and there is no other than He, there is no good for us in the fellowship of anyone whose concerns and intentions are with this world. Oh people, only repentance from our sin and seeking vengeance for the blood of the son of our Prophet's daughter have caused us to come out! We have neither dīnār nor dirham with us, we bring only the blades of our swords and the tips of our spears." And from every side the people cried out, "We do not seek this world, and it is not for it that we have come out." [541]

According to Abū Mikhnaf—Ismāʿīl b. Yazīd al-Azdī—al-Sirrī b. Kaʿb al-Azdī: We went to our companion ʿAbdallāh b. Saʿd b. Nufayl to bid him farewell.[491] He got up and we did so too; he went in to Sulaymān and we with him. Sulaymān had resolved to depart, and ʿAbdallāh b. Saʿd b. Nufayl advised him to set out against ʿUbaydallāh b. Ziyād. Sulaymān and his leading companions said, "Our opinion is that we should do what ʿAbdallāh b. Saʿd b. Nufayl advises: set out against ʿUbaydallāh b. Ziyād, the murderer of our lord and the one by whom we were destroyed." ʿAbdallāh b. Saʿd said to him, and sitting around him were the leaders of his companions, "I have conceived an idea which, if it is right, then God will make it successful, but, if it is wrong, then it is mine. I will not withhold from you and myself sincere advice, right or wrong. We have only come out seeking vengeance for the blood of al-Ḥusayn. But his killers are all in al-Kūfah! Among

---

490. One of the *quṣṣāṣ* with the Penitents (see below p. 145); the Banū Muzaynah are counted to Khindif (Caskel/Ibn Kalbī, II, 439).

491. I.e., ʿAbdallāh was getting ready to leave with the Penitents (see pp. 8off. above).

them are ᶜUmar b. Saᶜd b. Abī Waqqāṣ, the leaders of the quarters, and the tribal notables. Why should we leave here and leave unavenged the killing and the crimes of violence?"[492] Sulaymān b. Ṣurad said, "What do you think?" and they answered, "By God, he has expressed a sound opinion and things are indeed as he has said. By God, Ibn Ziyād is the only killer of al-Ḥusayn we shall encounter if we go off toward Syria. What we seek is to be found here in the garrison town itself."

[542]

But Sulaymān b. Ṣurad said, "I do not think that is right for you. He who killed your lord, made ready the armies against him, and said, 'I give him no safe conduct unless he surrenders and my jurisdiction is applied to him,' this one is the transgressor [al-fāsiq] the son of the transgressor, Ibn Marjānah, ᶜUbaydallāh b. Ziyād. So go out against your enemy in the name of God. If God grants you victory over him, we hope that those who come after him will be less powerful than he, and we hope that the people of your garrison town whom you have left behind will yield to you seeking your pardon. Then you will search for everybody who had a part in shedding the blood of al-Ḥusayn, and you will fight against him but not act unjustly. If you die as martyrs (fighting Ibn Ziyād), then you have fought against those who profane God's law [al-muḥillīn], 'What is with God is a blessing for the upright and the righteous.'[493] I desire that you will use your weapons and your strength against the first of the profaners and the unrighteous [al-muḥillīn wa-al-qāsiṭīn]. By God, if you fight tomorrow against the people of your garrison town, there will be no one who will not think that another man has killed his brother and his father and his close friends or that another man did not want to kill him. So seek guidance from God and set out." So the people prepared for departure.

When ᶜAbdallāh b. Yazīd and Ibrāhīm b. Muḥammad b. Ṭalḥah heard about Ibn Ṣurad and his men going out, they considered their position and concluded they would go to them and urge them to stay and join forces. If they insisted

---

492. See *Gloss.*, s.v. *w-t-r*.
493. Qur'ān, 3:197.

on leaving, they would ask them to wait so they could raise an army to go with them and fight against their enemy with mass and strength. ᶜAbdallāh b. Yazīd and Ibrāhīm b. Muḥammad b. Ṭalḥah sent Suwayd b. ᶜAbd al-Raḥmān[494] to Sulaymān b. Ṣurad, and he told him that ᶜAbdallāh and Ibrāhīm were saying, "We now wish to join you for something in which God may perhaps grant righteousness to us and to you." Sulaymān answered, "Tell them to come to us." And he said to Rifāᶜah b. Shaddād al-Bajalī, "You go and muster the people properly, for these two men have sent saying such-and-such." Then he called his leaders and they sat down around him.   [543]

They had been there less than an hour when ᶜAbdallāh b. Yazīd came with the Kūfan notables, the police force, and many of the soldiers, and Ibrāhīm b. Muḥammad with a group of his companions. ᶜAbdallāh b. Yazīd had said to each prominent figure who was known to have had a part in the shedding of al-Ḥusayn's blood, "Do not come with me to them," fearing they would see him and threaten him. While Sulaymān b. Ṣurad camped with his army at al-Nukhaylah, ᶜUmar b. Saᶜd slept only in the governor's residence [qaṣr al-imārah] with ᶜAbdallāh b. Yazīd, out of fear that the crowd would come to him in his dwelling place and attack him while he was unprepared and unaware, killing him. And ᶜAbdallāh b. Yazīd had told ᶜAmr b. Ḥurayth, "If I am delayed, you lead the people in the midday prayer."

When ᶜAbdallāh b. Yazīd and Ibrāhīm b. Muḥammad came to Sulaymān b. Ṣurad, they went in to him and ᶜAbdallāh b. Yazīd praised God and extolled Him. Then he said, "The Muslim is the brother of the Muslim. He neither betrays him nor deceives him. You are our brethren, the people of our land, and the best loved of the inhabitants of a garrison town which God created for us. Do not cause us distress in your persons, impose your views tyranically upon us, or decrease our numbers by leaving our community. Stay with us so we can make things easy and get ready. Then, when we learn that our enemies have approached our land, we will go out together   [544]

---

494. Apparently Suwayd b. ᶜAbd al-Raḥmān b. Bujayr al-Minqarī (of the Banū Saᶜd/Tamīm); see Crone, *Slaves,* 139.

and fight them." Ibrāhīm b. Muḥammad spoke in a similar vein.

Sulaymān b. Ṣurad praised God and extolled Him and then said to them, "I know that you two have been sincere in advice and diligent in counsel, but we are with God and belong to Him. We have come out in pursuance of a matter and we ask God for resolution in following His guidance and direction to the best attainment of it. Do you not see that we must go out if God wishes it?" ᶜAbdallāh b. Yazīd said, "Stay so that we can raise a concentration of soldiers to go with you and face your enemy en masse, united and with sharp swords." But Sulaymān said to him, "You go back and we will consider wherein we differ. Please God, our opinion will be made known to you."

According to Abū Mikhnaf—ᶜAbd al-Jabbār (i.e. Ibn ᶜAbbās al-Hamdānī)—ᶜAwn b. Abī Juḥayfah al-Suwāʾī: Then ᶜAbdallāh b. Yazīd and Ibrāhīm b. Muḥammad b. Ṭalḥah proposed to Sulaymān that he remain with them so they could confront the host of Syrians and they would make over the tax [kharāj] of Jūkhā⁴⁹⁵ for him and his men alone to the exclusion of the other men. But Sulaymān said to them, "It is not for this world that we have come out to fight." They only made that offer because of what they had heard about ᶜUbaydallāh b. Ziyād's approach toward Iraq. And Ibrāhīm b. Muḥammad and ᶜAbdallāh b. Yazīd returned to al-Kūfah, while the band of Ibn Ṣurad decided to depart and head toward Ibn Ziyād. But when they made an inspection, they suddenly realized their party (shīᶜah) from al-Baṣrah had not come to keep the rendezvous, nor those of al-Madāʾin. Some of Sulaymān b. Ṣurad's companions began criticizing those who had not turned up. But Sulaymān said, "Do not criticize them, for I am sure they would have rushed to join you if they had news of you and the time of your setting out. I am sure it is only lack of money and ill-preparedness which has kept them back and [545]   detained them. Wait so they can smooth things out and get ready and come to you in strength. Then how swift they will be in following you!"

---

495. See Le Strange, *Eastern caliphate*, 42.

Then Sulaymān b. Ṣurad stood among the people to deliver an official address. He praised God and extolled Him, then said:

> Now, Oh people, God knows what you purpose and what you have come out to seek. There are merchants of this world and merchants of the next. As for the merchant of the next world, he is rushing toward it sustained by what it requires. He will not sell it for any price. He is seen only in the attitudes of prayer— standing, sitting, bowing and prostrating. He seeks neither gold nor silver, neither things of this world nor pleasure. And as for the merchant of this world, he is addicted to it and revels in it. He does not desire anything in exchange for it. You, may God have mercy on you, in this purpose of yours, must pray long in the depths of the night and frequently make reference to God in all circumstances. Offer to God (great is His name!) every blessing you can until you confront this enemy and this unrighteous profaner of God's law (al-muḥill al-qāsiṭ) and wage *jihād* against him. For you will not attain your Lord's favor by anything which He finds more worthy of reward than *jihād* and prayer. *Jihād* is the summit of the good works. May God place us and you among those of His servants who are righteous, resolute in struggle, and patient in the face of adversity. Tonight we are leaving this abode of ours, God willing. So get ready for it!

He left on the evening of Friday, the fifth of Rabīᶜ II of the year 65 of the Hijrah (Thursday, November 17, 684).

When Sulaymān and his companions had left al-Nukhaylah, Sulaymān b. Ṣurad summoned Ḥakīm b. Munqidh, who then proclaimed among the people, "Come on! Indeed, no man of you shall pass the night before reaching Dayr al-Aᶜwar!"[496] And they passed that night at Dayr al-Aᶜwar, but many of the men stayed behind. Then he went on until he came to al-

---

496. Yāqūt, *Buldān*, II, 644.

Aqsās, Aqsās Mālik[497] on the bank of the Euphrates, where

[546] he mustered the men, but about a thousand of them were missing. Ibn Ṣurad said, "I am pleased that those who have deserted you are not with you. If they had come out with you they would only have brought disorder. God did not like their being sent and He held them back and selected you for the merit of it. Praise your Lord, therefore." He left his camp by night and next morning they came to the tomb of al-Ḥusayn. There they remained for a night and a day praying over him and asking God's pardon for him. When the people reached al-Ḥusayn's tomb, they shouted out in unison and wept. Never was a day seen when there was more weeping.

According to Abū Mikhnaf—ᶜAbd al-Raḥmān b. Jundab—ᶜAbd al-Raḥmān b. Ghaziyyah: When we came to the tomb of al-Ḥusayn (peace be upon him) the people wept together, and I heard most of the people expressing the wish that they had fallen with him. Sulaymān said, "Oh God, have mercy on al-Ḥusayn, the martyr the son of the martyr, the right-guided one (mahdī) son of the right-guided one, the righteous one the son of the righteous one. Oh God, we testify to you that we follow their religion and their path, and we are enemies of those who killed them, friends of those who love them." Then he departed and he and his companions encamped.

According to Abū Mikhnaf—al-Aᶜmash—Salamah b. Ku-hayl—Abū Ṣādiq: When Sulaymān b. Ṣurad and his companions reached the tomb of al-Ḥusayn, they cried in unison, "Oh Lord, we have betrayed the son of our Prophet's daughter! Pardon us for what we did in the past and relent toward us, for you are the relenting one and the compassionate one. Have mercy on al-Ḥusayn and his companions, the martyrs and the righteous ones. We bear witness before you, Oh Lord, that we are doing the same as what they were when they were killed. If you do not pardon us our sin and have mercy on us, then we are among those who are lost." They remained there a day and a night praying over him, weeping and abasing

[547] themselves. And from that time onwards, the people did not cease to plead for mercy on him and his companions until

---

497. *Ibid.*, I, 337.

they made the early morning prayer by his tomb on the
following day, and that increased their fury. Then they mounted
up and Sulaymān ordered the people to proceed. And no man
would pass on until he had come to the tomb of al-Ḥusayn,
stood in prayer over it, and asked for mercy on him and
pardon for him. And, by God, I saw them thronging about
the tomb of al-Ḥusayn more thickly than the people throng
around the Black Stone.

Sulaymān stood by al-Ḥusayn's tomb, and whenever a group
prayed for him and asked for mercy on him, al-Musayyab b.
Najabah and Sulaymān b. Ṣurad said to them, "Join your
brethren, may God have mercy on you!" He continued in this
manner until about thirty of his companions were left, and
then Sulaymān and his companions made a circle around the
tomb and Sulaymān said, "Praise be to God who, if He had
wished, would have honored us with martyrdom with al-
Ḥusayn. Oh my God, since you forbade us it together with
him, do not forbid us it on his account after him." And
ᶜAbdallāh b. Wāl said, "Verily, by God, I consider al-Ḥusayn
and his father and brother as the best of Muḥammad's community (who will be) imploring God's favor (on behalf of the
Muslims) on the Day of Resurrection. Are you not amazed at
the test to which this community has been subjected by its
enemies? They killed two and brought the third to the brink
of death." Al-Musayyab b. Najabah said, "I am one of those
who will kill them. I dissociate[498] myself from whoever shares
their views. Them I will treat as an enemy and fight."

All of the leaders spoke most eloquently. Al-Muthannā b.
Mukharribah[499] was a companion of one of the leaders and
notables, and it pained me when I did not hear him making
a speech with the people in a manner similar to their speeches,
but before long he delivered a speech which was not inferior
to any of the others. He said, "God made these men, whose
status you have mentioned relative to their Prophet, superior
to anyone except their Prophet. A mob to whom we are

---

498. See n. 409 above.
499. For the name, see *Add. et emend.*; of ᶜAbd al-Qays (Rabīᶜah), he
subsequently worked in al-Baṣrah on behalf of al-Mukhtār (Rotter, *Bürgerkrieg*,
217).

enemies and with whom we recognize no ties killed them.

[548]   We have left our homes, our people and our properties seeking the extirpation of those who killed them. By God, even if the fight against them is where the sun goes down or the earth ends, it is incumbent upon us to seek it until we attain it. That is our booty and it is martyrdom, the reward for which is heaven." We said to him, "You have spoken the truth, you have achieved your end, and you have been granted success." Then Sulaymān b. Ṣurad traveled on from the tomb of al-Ḥusayn and we went with him. We took the road by al-Ḥaṣṣāṣah, then al-Anbār, then al-Ṣadūd, then al-Qayyārah.[500]

According to Abū Mikhnaf—al-Ḥārith b. Ḥaṣīrah and others: Sulaymān sent Kurayb b. Yazīd al-Ḥimyarī ahead over his vanguard.

According to Abū Mikhnaf—al-Ḥusayn b. Yazīd—al-Sirrī b. Kaʿb: We set out with some men of our clan. After we had come to the tomb of al-Ḥusayn, and Sulaymān b. Ṣurad and his companions had left it and followed the road, ʿAbdallāh b. ʿAwf b. al-Aḥmar went before them on a worn-out clipped dark bay horse of medium size. He was reciting in *rajaz*:[501]

These mares set forth bearing us aloft in com-
    panies,
    like lions, carrying us as heroes.
By our setting out we want to confront our
    foes,
    the unjust ones, the perfidious ones, the
    ones in error.
We have abandoned family and property,
    our bashful, fair and pale-skinned women.
By it we will satisfy the Lord of blessings and
    beneficence.

According to Abū Mikhnaf—Saʿd b. Mujāhid al-Ṭāʾī—Mu-
[549]   ḥill b. Khalīfah al-Ṭāʾī: ʿAbdallāh b. Yazīd wrote to Sulaymān b. Ṣurad. (Muḥill said, I think:) He sent me with the letter

---

500. For Ḥaṣṣāṣah, see Yāqūt, *Buldān*, II, 274; for Anbār, see Le Strange, *Eastern Caliphate*, map II and pp. 65–6; Ṣadūd does not seem to be listed in Yāqūt; for Qayyārah, Yāqūt, IV, 211.
501. For the verses, cf. *Murūj*, V, 215.

and I caught up with him at al-Qayyārah. He had gone ahead
of his companions so it was thought he had outstripped them.
He halted and signaled to his men, and they gathered around
him. Then he read them his letter, which said:

> In the name of God, the Merciful, the Compassionate.
> From ᶜAbdallāh b. Yazīd to Sulaymān b. Ṣurad and
> those of the Muslims with him, greetings! Now, this
> letter of mine to you is the letter of a sincere adviser
> and true pastor. How often a sincere adviser is sus-
> pected of treachery, and how often a deceiver is asked
> for sincere advice and loved! I have heard that you
> wish to go few in number against the numerous host.
> But he who wishes to remove the mountains from their
> places, his picks become blunt and he desists, and he
> is blameworthy both in his intelligence and his deeds.
> Oh people of ours, do not give your enemy encour-
> agement against the inhabitants of your land! All of
> you are the pick (of our community), and when your
> enemy falls on you they will know that you are the
> most eminent of your garrison town, and that will give
> them encouragement against those you have left be-
> hind. Oh people of ours, "If they get the better of
> you, they will stone you or force you back to their
> confession and then you will never prosper!"[502] Oh
> people, today our hands are joined with yours and we
> have the same enemy. When we speak with one voice,
> we will conquer our enemy, but when we disagree,
> our power will be as nothing to those who are against
> us. Oh people of ours, do not consider as deceitful my
> sincere advice and do not oppose my authority. Come
> when my letter is read out to you! May God bring
> you to obedience to Him and turn you away from
> disobedience to Him! Peace be with you!

When the letter was read out to Ibn Ṣurad and his companions, he said to the men, "What do you think?" They said,
"What do you think? We refused you and him this when we

---

502. Qur'ān, 18:19.

were in our garrison town and among our own people. And now, when we have come out and accustomed ourselves to *jihād* and drawn close to the land of our enemy, this is no sound opinion!" Then they called to him, "Tell us what you think!" He said, "By God, I think that you have never been closer than you are today to one of the two good things, martyrdom and victory, and I do not think that you should turn away from the truth upon which God has united you and the blessings you desire. We and they are of different views. If they gain the upper hand, they will summon us to *jihād* alongside Ibn al-Zubayr, but I consider *jihād* alongside Ibn al-Zubayr as error. If we are victorious, we will return this authority to its rightful possessors; if we are struck down, then we are holding to our intentions to repent from our sins. We have one outlook and Ibn al-Zubayr another. We and they are, as the brother of the Banū Kinānah said:

I see, woman, that your outlook is different from
  mine, so refrain
  from censure, for you have been changed and
  the outlook is different.

The people departed with him and they came to Hīt[503] where Sulaymān wrote:

In the name of God, the Merciful, the Compassionate. To the governor ʿAbdallāh b. Yazīd from Sulaymān b. Ṣurad and those of the believers with him, greetings! We have read your letter and understood what you have proposed. By God, what an excellent prefect you are, what an excellent governor, and what an excellent clan brother! By God, in whom we trust while absent, to whom we turn for counsel and advice, and whom we praise in every circumstance, we have heard Him say in His Book, "God has purchased from the believers their own selves and their property in exchange for the promise of heaven. . ." as far as His words ". . . so tell the believers the good news!"[504] The people have

[550]

---

503. See Le Strange, *Eastern Caliphate,* map II, and p. 65.
504. Qur'ān, 9:112–3.

rejoiced at the oath of allegiance which they have
sworn. They have turned away in repentance from their
great sin and toward God, they have depended on Him
and accepted what God has decreed. "Our Lord, we
rely on you, turn to you in repentance and come to
you."[505] Peace be with you!

[551]

When he received this letter, Ibn Yazīd said, "The people
are seeking death. The first you will hear of them will be the
news of their death. I swear by God they will be killed nobly
as Muslims! But, by He who is their Lord, before their enemy
kills them their strength will have become great and those
slain in their quarrel many."

According to Abū Mikhnaf—Yūsuf b. Yazīd—ᶜAbdallāh b.
ᶜAwf b. al-Aḥmar and ᶜAbd al-Raḥmān b. Jundab—ᶜAbd al-
Raḥmān b. Ghaziyyah: We left Hīt and came to Qarqīsiyā.[506]
When we drew close, Sulaymān b. Ṣurad halted and mustered
us in good order until we had passed alongside Qarqīsiyā and
camped close by it. Zufar b. al-Ḥārith al-Kilābī had fortified
himself inside the town against our people and did not come
out against them. Sulaymān called al-Musayyab b. Najabah
and said, "Go to this cousin[507] of yours and tell him to send
out a market for us. It is not him we want, we go only against
these profaners of God's law." Al-Musayyab b. Najabah went
to the gate of Qarqīsiyā and said, "Open up! Against whom
do you fortify yourselves?" They asked, "Who is that?" He
replied, "Al-Musayyab b. Najabah!" Al-Hudhayl b. Zufar went
to his father and told him, "There is a man of good appearance
who is asking to be allowed to enter to you. We asked him
who he was and he said al-Musayyab b. Najabah."

Al-Hudhayl b. Zufar said: At that time I had no knowledge
of the people and did not know who of them he was. Zufar
said, "Do you not know, Oh my son, who this is? This is the
champion of the whole of Muḍar al-Ḥamrā'.[508] If the number

---

505. Qur'ān, 60:4.
506. See Le Strange, *Eastern Caliphate*, map II and index (see also pp. 63ff.
above).
507. Zufar and Musayyab both belong to Qays.
508. The meaning of Muḍar al-Ḥamrā' is obscure (see Caskel/Ibn Kalbī, II,
417).

of its notables was only ten, he would be one of them. In addition to that, he is an ascetic and pious man. Let him enter!" So I gave him permission to enter and my father seated him beside himself and questioned him courteously. Al-Musayyab b. Najabah asked, "Against whom do you fortify yourself? By God, it is not you we desire. All we require is that you help us against that unjust and profaning mob. Send out to us a market and we will only remain in your land for a day or so." Zufar b. al-Ḥārith said to him, "We only closed the gates of this town so that we might know whether it was for us that you came or somebody else. By God, we are not short of strength against your people so long as no trick takes us unawares. We do not want to be put to the test of fighting against you, for we have heard that you are righteous and of good and handsome conduct."

Then he called his son and told him to set up a market for them, and he ordered that al-Musayyab be given a thousand dirhams and a horse. But al-Musayyab said, "As for the money, I have no need of it. By God, it is not for money that we came out and it is not money which we seek. As for the horse, I will accept it, for perhaps I will have need of it if my horse goes lame or falls beneath me." And he took it away with him and returned to his companions. The market was sent out to them and they traded for their needs. After sending out the market, fodder and much food, Zufar b. al-Ḥārith sent to al-Musayyab twenty camels for slaughter, and to Sulaymān b. Ṣurad similarly. Zufar had told his son to ask about the prominent men in the army, and there were named to him ᶜAbdallāh b. Saᶜd b. Nufayl, ᶜAbdallāh b. Wāl and Rifāᶜah b. Shaddād. The commanders of the quarters were named too. He sent to those three commanders ten camels for slaughter each and plenty of fodder and food, and he sent out for the soldiers a large train (of animals) and a quantity of barley. The slave lads of Zufar then said, "Take and slaughter from this train (of animals) as much as you want, carry away as much barley as you wish, and provision yourselves with as much flour as you can." All day long the people continued stocking up. They did not need to buy anything from the markets which had been set up, for they were given enough in the way of meat, barley and flour, except that someone might buy a garment or a whip.

On the next morning, they set out again, and Zufar sent word to them, "I am coming out to you and will accompany you," and he came to them. They left in good order. Zufar went along with them and said to Sulaymān, "Five commanders have been sent out against you and have left al-Raqqah. Among them are al-Ḥusayn b. Numayr al-Sakūnī, Shuraḥbīl b. Dhī al-Kalāᶜ, Adham b. Muḥriz al-Bāhilī (the father of Mālik b. Adham),[509] Rabīᶜah b. al-Mukhāriq al-Ghanawī,[510] and Jabalah b. ᶜAbdallāh al-Khathᶜamī.[511] They have come against you like thorns and trees and there has come against you a great number and blades of iron. I swear by God that I have seen few men who are better prepared or equipped or more ready for every kind of good work than those I have seen with you. But I have heard that a number beyond all computation has been sent against you." Ibn Ṣurad answered, "We rely on God. Let those who place their trust place it in Him." Then Zufar said to him, "May I ask your opinion on a suggestion which I will put before you, by means of which God will perhaps achieve something good for us both? If you wish, we will open up our town to you so that you can come in and then we will act together for the same end. Alternatively, if you wish, you will encamp at the gates of our town and we and our army will come out alongside you. Then, when this enemy comes against us, we will fight them together." Sulaymān answered Zufar, "The people of our garrison town wanted us to act in a similar way to what you want, and they spoke like you and they wrote to us about it after we had left. But it was never agreeable to us and we will not do it."

[554]

---

509. Of Qays; see Crone, *Slaves*, 168–9. The Leiden text here reads "Adham b. Muḥriz al-Bāhilī and Abū Mālik b. Adham." Since Adham's son was Mālik and not Abū Mālik it seems that a gloss has been interpolated and the *wa-abū* should be amended to *huwa abū*. In that case, there would be no implication that Mālik was present with his father. Cf. *Ansāb*, V, 209–10, where there is no mention of Mālik with Adham.

510. Of Qays; see Rotter, *Bürgerkrieg*, 191.

511. Counted to Yemen (Caskel/Ibn Kalbī, II, 345, s.v. Hatᶜam b. Anmar), but also to ᶜAdnān ("northerners"); see *EI*², s.v. Khathᶜam.

Zufar said, "Consider the advice I have given you and accept it and take it. I am an enemy of that mob and I want God to give the victory to you. I am friendly toward you and I want God to encompass you with success. The enemy has left al-Raqqah. If you rush to ᶜAyn al-Wardah[512] ahead of them and put the town at your back, then the *rustāq*,[513] the water and the food will be in your hands, and you will have security in the region between your town and ours. By God, if I had as many horses as I have men, I would give you reinforcements. Move your camp this instant to ᶜAyn al-Wardah. The enemy is marching as an army, but you have horses, and, by God, I have rarely seen a group of horses more noble than they. Get them ready immediately and I hope you will get there before them and beat them to ᶜAyn al-Wardah. Do not fight them, firing and thrusting at them, in an open space, for they outnumber you and you will have no security if they can surround you. Do not stand still firing at them and thrusting at them, for you have nothing like their manpower, and if you leave yourselves open to them it will not be long before they rush on you. And do not form a line when they confront you, for I see no footsoldiers with you but see that you are all horsemen, while the enemy is coming against you with foot and horse. Their cavalry will protect their infantry and their infantry their cavalry, but you have no footmen to defend your cavalry. So meet them with squadrons and detachments of cavalry and distribute them between the right and left wings of the enemy. Place a cavalry squadron alongside another and then, if one of the two is attacked, the other can dismount and both the men and the horses can be re-supplied from it. Whenever a detachment wishes to be increased, it can be, and, if it wishes to be decreased, it can be. But, if you fight in one line and the enemy's men advance on you so you are forced out of the line, it will be broken and that means defeat."

[555]

Then he stood and took his leave of the men and asked God to accompany them and grant them victory. The men

---

512. Identified as Ra's al-ᶜAyn, for which see Le Strange, *Eastern Caliphate*, map III, and index.

513. Sasanid administrative term for a sub-district (see Morony, *Iraq*, 534, s.v. rōstāk).

praised him and called on God on his behalf, and Sulaymān b. Ṣurad said to him, "How good it was to stay with you! You showed generosity to us in our stay, were the best of hosts and gave us sincere advice in consultation." Then the people pressed on in their journey and began to double the distance between halts.

(ᶜAbd al-Raḥmān b. Ghaziyyah continued:) We passed by towns until we reached Sāᶜ,[514] and then Sulaymān b. Ṣurad organized the cavalry detachments as Zufar had advised. Then he pushed on to ᶜAyn al-Wardah, to the west of which he pitched camp. He got there before the enemy, and he and his men made their camp. He remained there for five days without moving, and they took their rest, relaxed and refreshed their horses.

Hishām—Abū Mikhnaf—ᶜAṭiyyah b. al-Ḥārith—ᶜAbdallāh b. Ghaziyyah:[515] The Syrians advanced with their host until they were a day and a night's journey from ᶜAyn al-Wardah.

ᶜAbdallāh b. Ghaziyyah: Sulaymān stood among us and praised God lengthily and extolled him lavishly. Then he mentioned the heavens and the earth, the mountains and the seas, and the signs of God they contain. He mentioned the favors and blessings of God; this world, from which he urged abstention; and the next, for which he excited desire. He mentioned more of this than I could keep track of or remember. Then he said, "Now, God has brought you your enemy toward whom you have persevered in journeying all night and all day seeking that in which you will display your sincere repentance and meet God seeking forgiveness. They have come to you, or rather you have come to them on their own ground and domain. When you meet them, show your righteousness and be patient, for God is with those who are patient. Let no man turn his back unless it be turning to fight or joining another band.[516] Do not kill the straggler, do not finish off a wounded

[556]

----

514. On the river Khābūr (see the note to *Ansāb*, V, 210[7]; Ṭabarī's text seems to deny the possibility of Goitein's suggested alternative reading).

515. Is this the same authority as the previously named ᶜAbd al-Raḥmān b. Ghaziyyah (pp. 132, 141)? Subsequently, the name ᶜAbdallāh appears consistently (see especially p. 155 below).

516. Cf. Qur'ān, 8:16.

man and do not kill a prisoner of your confession unless he
fights against you after you have captured him or he is one
of those who slew our brethren at al-Ṭaff (may God have
mercy on them!). This was the practice of the Commander of
the Faithful, ᶜAlī b. Abī Ṭālib, regarding the people of this
confession." Then Sulaymān said, "If I am killed, the commander of the people is al-Musayyab b. Najabah. If al-Musayyab falls, the commander of the people is ᶜAbdallāh b. Saᶜd
b. Nufayl. If ᶜAbdallāh b. Saᶜd is killed, the commander of
the people is ᶜAbdallāh b. Wāl. If ᶜAbdallāh b. Wāl is killed,
the commander of the people is Rifāᶜah b. Shaddād. May God
have mercy on the man who fulfills the compact which God
has made with him!" Then he sent for al-Musayyab b. Najabah
with four hundred horsemen and he said to him, "Go off until
you meet the first of their troops and raid them. If you observe
a favorable result, carry on, but otherwise, come back to me
with your men. And be sure not to dismount or allow any
one of your men to dismount or go beyond that unless it is
absolutely necessary."

According to Abū Mikhnaf—his father—Ḥumayd b. Muslim: I was with those horsemen of al-Musayyab b. Najabah.
We proceeded, traveling for the rest of that day and night.
Just before dawn we camped and fastened the nosebags on
our mounts. We snatched a brief doze, enough for them to
chew just a little, and then we mounted them and rode on
until, when the dawn appeared to us, we dismounted and
performed the prayer, and then al-Musayyab went on with
us. He sent off Abū al-Juwayriyyah b. al-Aḥmar[517] with 100
men, ᶜAbdallāh b. ᶜAwf b. al-Aḥmar with 120, and Ḥanash b.
Rabīᶜah Abū al-Muᶜtamir al-Kinānī with a similar number,
remaining himself with 100. He said, "See whom you meet
first and bring him to me." The first person we met was a
bedouin herding donkeys (aḥmirah), and he was saying:

> Oh my property, do not hurry to my companions,
>   but graze freely, for you are the peaceful one
>   of the herd.

[557]

---

517. For the Banū al-Aḥmar, see n. 484 above.

Ibn Aḥmar said, "He means ᶜAbdallāh b. ᶜAwf b. al-Aḥmar. Oh Ḥumayd b. Muslim, rejoice at glad tidings, by the Lord of the Kaᶜbah!" Ibn ᶜAwf b. al-Aḥmar said to him, "What people do you belong to, Oh bedouin?" He answered, "I am from the Banū Taghlib." Ibn ᶜAwf said, "Please God, 'you will conquer' (ghalabtum), by the Lord of the Kaᶜbah."

Al-Musayyab b. Najabah reached us and we told him what we had heard from the bedouin. We brought the bedouin to him, and al-Musayyab b. Najabah said, "Indeed, I am pleased at your saying 'rejoice' and at your words 'Oh Ḥumayd b. Muslim!' for I hope that you will rejoice at what pleases you and it will only please you that you 'praise' (taḥmadū) your affair and 'achieve safety' (taslamū) from your enemies. This omen[518] is a good one, and the Prophet used to be pleased when he saw an omen." Then al-Musayyab b. Najabah said to the bedouin, "How far is there between us and the nearest to us of this enemy of ours?" He replied, "The nearest of their soldiers to you are those of Ibn Dhī al-Kalāᶜ. There is a dispute between him and al-Ḥusayn. Al-Ḥusayn claims command of the body of their forces, but Ibn Dhī al-Kalāᶜ told him he had no power over him. They have both sent letters to ᶜUbaydallāh b. Ziyād and they are awaiting his command. This force of Ibn Dhī al-Kalāᶜ is a mile away from you."

We left the man and hurried toward them. By God, they [558] were completely unaware until we were on them and they were taken by surprise. We attacked the flank of their camp and, by God, we did not fight long before they were put to flight. We caused losses among their men, caused many wounds, and got possession of some of their mounts. They deserted their camp and left us free to plunder it. We took from it that which pleased us. Then al-Musayyab gave the call to us to go back, "You have won the victory, taken booty and are unharmed. Go back, therefore!" So we went back and came to Sulaymān.

ᶜUbaydallāh b. Ziyād received news of what had happened, and he dispatched al-Ḥusayn b. Numayr quickly against us.

---

518. I.e., the omen derived from the correspondence between the names of those involved and nouns or verbs derived from the same stems; Aḥmar/ aḥmira, Taghlib/ghalabtum, Ḥumayd/taḥmadū, and Muslim/taslamū.

He came with 12,000 men and we went out to meet them on Wednesday, the twenty-second of Jumādā I (January 4, 685). Sulaymān b. Ṣurad put ʿAbdallāh b. Saʿd b. Nufayl over his right wing, al-Musayyab b. Najabah over his left, while he stood fast in the centre. Ḥusayn b. Numayr came, having organized his army to meet us. He put Jabalah b. ʿAbdallāh over his right wing and Rabīʿah b. al-Mukhāriq al-Ghanawī over his left. Then they advanced against us, and when they drew near they summoned us to make common cause with them in accepting ʿAbd al-Malik b. Marwān and to accept obedience unto him. We called upon them to hand over ʿUbaydallāh b. Ziyād to us so tht we could kill him in recompense for one of our brethren who had been killed, that they should cast off their allegiance to ʿAbd al-Malik b. Marwān, and that those of the family of Ibn al-Zubayr who were in our land should be expelled. Then we would restore this authority to the family of our Prophet from among whom God brought us blessing and honor. The enemy refused our summons and we refused theirs.

[559]   Ḥumayd b. Muslim: Our right wing attacked their left and defeated them, while our left wing attacked their right. Sulaymān in the center attacked the body of them, and we put them to flight and forced them back to their camp. We continued to have the upper hand over them until night fell and cut us off from them. Then we retired, having driven them back to their camp.[519] Next morning, Ibn Dhī al-Kalāʿ came to them with 8,000 men ʿUbaydallāh b. Ziyād had sent to reinforce them. Ibn Ziyād abused Ibn Dhī al-Kalāʿ and disparaged him, saying, "You acted like a novice, losing your camp and your weapons. Go to al-Ḥusayn b. Numayr. He is in charge of the men." So he joined him. Then they fell on us and we fell on them, and all day we fought against them such a fight as neither the white-haired old man nor the beardless youth had ever seen. Only the times of prayer caused us to break off fighting. When evening came and we separated, by God, they had caused us many wounded and we had inflicted wounds on them, too.

---

519. See *Add. et emend.* and *Gloss.*, s.v. *ajhara*.

With us were three *quṣṣāṣ*,[520] Rifāʿah b. Shaddād al-Bajalī, Ṣukhayr b. Ḥudhayfah b. Hilāl b. Mālik al-Muzanī, and Abū al-Juwayriyyah al-ʿAbdī. Rifāʿah was delivering stirring orations and urging on the men of the right wing unceasingly. Abū al-Juwayriyyah was wounded early on the second day and remained with the supplies. Ṣukhayr went around among us all night long saying, "Rejoice, servants of God, in His generosity and pleasure. All that is required from someone who is kept from meeting those he loves, entering heaven, and obtaining rest from the toils and injuries of this world, merely by the need for separation from this essence which is constantly urging him to evil, is that separation from it should be given generously and that he should meet his Lord joyfully."

We remained thus until next morning when Ibn Numayr and Adham b. Muḥriz al-Bāhilī appeared with about 10,000 men. They came out against us and we fought fiercely for the third day, Friday, until noon. Then the Syrians outnumbered us and pressed down upon us from every side. Sulaymān b. Ṣurad saw what was happening to his men, and he dismounted and cried, "Oh servants of God! Whoever desires to come early to his Lord, repentance from his sin, and fulfillment of his undertaking, to me!" He broke the sheath of his sword and a large number of men dismounted with him, breaking their sword sheaths too. They went forward with him on foot and the enemy's horsemen sprang forward too so that they were intermingled with the foot soldiers. They fought against them until the men on foot attacked fiercely with drawn swords—they had broken the sheaths of their swords—and the cavalry attacked the enemy's horsemen, and they did not stand firm. They fought against them and killed a large number of the Syrians and wounded many.

When al-Ḥusayn b. Numayr saw the fortitude of our men and their bravery, he sent the foot soldiers to fire arrows at them while the horse and infantry surrounded them. Sulaymān b. Ṣurad was killed (may God have mercy on him). Yazīd b. al-Ḥusayn hit him with an arrow and he fell. He rose up again

[560]

---

520. Literally, "storytellers," here they seem to be orators whose task it is to incite the men (see *EI²*, s.v. Ḳāṣṣ).

but then fell once more. After he was killed, al-Musayyab b. Najabah took the banner. He said to Sulaymān b. Ṣurad, "Oh my brother, may God have mercy on you! You spoke the truth and fulfilled your duty. Our's remains still." Then he took the banner, pressed forward with it, fought for a while and then retired. Then he pressed forward again, fought and retired. He did that repeatedly, pressing forward and retiring, and then he was killed. May God have mercy on him!

According to Abū Mikhnaf—Farwah b. Laqīṭ: At al-Madā'in I met a mawlā of al-Musayyab b. Najabah al-Fazārī with Shabīb b. Yazīd the Khārijite.[521] He told me the story as far as the report of the people of ʿAyn al-Wardah.

According to Hishām—Abū Mikhnaf: This Shaykh told me regarding al-Musayyab b. Najabah: By God, I never saw any man braver than he or than any of the band to which he belonged. I saw him on the day of ʿAyn al-Wardah fighting fiercely, and I did not think any one man could be tested as he was tested or cause so much damage to his enemy as he did. He killed many men. I heard him saying before he was killed and while he was fighting them:

[561]

She of the tumbling locks,
    pure of heart and breast, knows
That I, on the morning of fear and struggle,
    was braver than a pouncing lion,
A cutter down of my opponents, feared in all
    quarters.

According to Abū Mikhnaf—his father and maternal uncle—Ḥumayd b. Muslim and ʿAbdallāh b. Ghaziyyah, and according to Abū Mikhnaf—Yūsuf b. Yazīd—ʿAbdallāh b. ʿAwf: When al-Musayyab b. Najabah was killed, ʿAbdallāh b. Saʿd b. Nufayl took the banner. He said (may God have mercy on him!), "My two brothers[522] are among those who 'some of them have fulfilled their vow and some of them wait (for its fulfillment), and they have not made changes (in their insistence on fulfilling

---

521. For Shabīb, see Wellhausen, *Oppositionsparteien*, 42ff. (Eng. tr. 70ff.); *EI¹*, s.v.; Caskel/Ibn Kalbī, II, 522.
522. I.e., Sulaymān b. Ṣurad and al-Musayyab b. Najabah.

it).' "[523] He advanced with those of Azd who were with him surrounding his banner, and, by God, that is how we were when three horsemen came to us, ʿAbdallāh b. al-Khaḍal al-Ṭāʾī, Kathīr b. ʿAmr al-Muzanī, and Siʿr b. Abī Siʿr al-Ḥanafī.[524] They had left with Saʿd b. Ḥudhayfah b. al-Yamān and 170 men of al-Madāʾin. Saʿd, on the day when he set out, had sent them ahead on spritely swift horses to follow in our tracks. He had told them, "Cover the ground quickly and join with our brethren. Tell them the good news about our joining them so they may be more resolute, and tell them also about the coming of the Baṣrans." (Al-Muthannā b. Mukharribah al-ʿAbdī had set out with 300 Baṣrans and, five days after Saʿd b. Ḥudhayfah had left al-Madāʾin, had advanced as far as the town of Bahurasīr.[525] His departure from al-Baṣrah previously had become known to Saʿd b. Ḥudhayfah before the latter left al-Madāʾin.)

[562]

When these three reached us they said, "Good news! Your brethren from al-Madāʾin and al-Baṣrah have come to join you." ʿAbdallāh b. Saʿd b. Nufayl replied, "Now, if only they had come while we were still alive." Then they looked at us. When they saw the desolate state of their brethren and how many of us were wounded, they all wept and said, "We can see how much you have suffered. 'To God we belong and to Him we return!'"[526] By God, what they saw afflicted their eyes. ʿAbdallāh b. Nufayl said to them, "It was this for which we came."

Then we joined battle, and we only fought for a short while before the Muzanī was killed and the Ḥanafī stabbed. He fell among the slain but was then pulled out and saved. The Ṭāʾī, too, was stabbed and his nose cut off short, but he fought fiercely. He was a warrior and poet, and he began saying:

---

523. Qurʾān, 33:23.

524. For Siʿr's role in support of al-Mukhtār, see below pp. 189ff.; the other two do not seem to be known elsewhere.

525. On the west bank of the Tigris, slightly north of Ctesiphon (al-Madāʾin); see Le Strange, *Eastern Caliphate*, map II and pp. 34–5.

526. A common formula acknowledging dependence on God, known as the *istirjāʿ.*

She of the sweet figure knows
    that I am not with the weak ones[527] or
    the cowardly
On a day, nor with the timid who stand
    aside.

Rabīʿah b. al-Mukhāriq attacked us viciously and we fought fiercely. Then he and ʿAbdallāh b. Saʿd b. Nufayl exchanged blows, but their swords had no effect and they seized each other about the neck and fell to the ground. They got up and swapped blows again, and the nephew of Rabīʿah b. al-Mukhāriq attacked ʿAbdallāh b. Saʿd, stabbed him in his gullet [*thughrat naḥrihi*] and killed him. ʿAbdallāh b. ʿAwf b. al-Aḥmar then attacked Rabīʿah b. al-Mukhāriq, stabbed him and felled him. But he was not fatally hit and got up and assailed ʿAbdallāh again while his companions stabbed ʿAbdallāh and downed him. However, ʿAbdallāh b. ʿAwf's men rescued him and Khālid b. Saʿd b. Nufayl said, "Show me who killed my brother!" We pointed out Rabīʿah b. al-Mukhāriq's nephew to him, and Khālid attacked him and got his sword from him, but his opponent seized him around the neck and he fell to the ground. Rabīʿah's men attacked and so did we, but they outnumbered us and rescued their man and killed ours. There was nobody standing by our banner.

[563]

We called out to ʿAbdallāh b. Wāl after they had killed our champions. He had been surrounded alongside of us in a band of his followers, but Rifāʿah b. Shaddād attacked and relieved him. He made toward his banner, which ʿAbdallāh b. Ḥāzim al-Kabīrī[528] had hold of. Ibn Ḥāzim asked him to take the banner from him, but Ibn Wāl answered, "You take it for me, for I am in the same situation as you." Ibn Ḥāzim insisted, "Take your banner from me, for I wish to join in the *jihād*," but Ibn Wāl said, "What you are doing now is *jihād* and brings its rewards." We shouted out, "Oh Abū ʿIzzah,[529] obey your commander, may God have mercy on you!" He continued to hold it for a short time, and then Ibn Wāl took it from him.

---

527. Read *al-wanī* (see *Add. et emend.*).

528. See nn. 486, 487 above (cf. *Add. et emend.*).

529. In view of the report on p. 125 above about ʿAbdallāh b. Ḥāzim's son ʿAzrah, it may be that the *kunyah* should be read as Abū ʿAzrah.

According to Abū Mikhnaf—Abū al-Ṣalt al-Taymī al-Aᶜwar (the one eyed)—a shaykh of the clan, who was with him on that day: Ibn Wāl said to us, "Whoever desires the life after which there is no death, the ease after which there is no exertion, and the joy after which there is no sadness, let him seek his Lord's favor by waging *jihād* against these profaners of God's law and by going[530] to Paradise, may God have mercy on him!" That was at the time of the afternoon prayer. He pressed hard against them, we with him, and, by God, we killed a number of men and pushed them back for a long while. But they redoubled their effort against us from all sides and pushed us back until they had us where we had started from. We were in a place where they could only come against us from one direction. Around evening, Adham b. Muḥriz al-Bāhilī directed the fighting against us. He pressed hard against us with his cavalry and foot soldiers, and ᶜAbdallāh b. Wāl al-Taymī was killed. [564]

Abū Mikhnaf—Farwah b. Laqīṭ: During the time when al-Ḥajjāj b. Yūsuf was governor, I heard Adham b. Muḥriz al-Bāhilī telling the tale to some of the Syrians. He said: I made my way toward one of the commanders of the Iraqis, a man whom they called ᶜAbdallāh b. Wāl, and he was saying, " 'Do not count those as dead who are killed in the path of God. No, they are alive with their Lord, sustained (by Him). Rejoicing. . .' " to the end of the three verses.[531] That angered me, and I said to myself, "These people assign to us the status of polytheists, thinking that those among them whom we kill are martyrs." I then attacked him, and I was hitting at his left hand and I quickly cut it off. I drew close and said to him, "Indeed, I think you would like to be with your family now." He answered, "How wrong you are! Indeed, by God, I am glad that it was not your hand just now, unless there were in it for me a reward like there is for my hand." I said to him, "Why?" and he replied, "So that God would lay the responsibility for it on you and grant me the honor of the reward for it." That angered me so I gathered my cavalry and

---

530. Following the Cairo reading *wa('l-rawwāḥ)*.
531. Qur'ān, 3:163–5.

footsoldiers and attacked him and his companions. I fought
my way to him and stabbed and killed him as he unceasingly
came at me. Afterward they claimed he had been one of the
religious scholar [fuqahā'] among the Iraqis, frequently engag-
ing in fasting and prayer, and giving legal rulings to the people.

According to Abū Mikhnaf—someone I trust—Ḥumayd b.
Muslim and ʿAbdallāh b. Ghaziyyah:[532] After the death of
ʿAbdallāh b. Wāl, we looked and there was ʿAbdallāh b. Ḥāzim
fallen alongside him, but we thought it was Rifāʿah b. Shaddād
al-Bajalī. A man of the Banū Kinānah, called al-Walīd b.
Ghuḍayn, said, "Hold your banner," but he (Rifāʿah) replied,
"I do not want it." I said to him, "We all belong to God!
What is the matter with you?" He answered, "Let us go back,
and perhaps God will gather us together again for a day which
will be evil for them!" ʿAbdallāh b. ʿAwf b. al-Aḥmar rushed
up to him and said, "You have ruined us! By God, if you give
up and go back they will indeed be on our heels and we will
not make even a farsakh before we are destroyed from behind,
and, if any one of us does escape, the bedouin and the villagers
will seize him and give him up to the enemy so that he will
suffer death as a captive [ṣabran]. I implore you by God not
to do it! Here the sun has set on us and night has enveloped
us. Let us fight them on these horses of ours, for we now
have some protection. When it becomes dark, we will mount
our horses in the first part of the night and charge off with
them. We will do thus, so when morning comes we will be
journeying without haste. Each one of us will take with him
a wounded man and wait for a companion, and groups of ten
and twenty will travel together. The men will know the route
they are taking and they will follow one another in it. But if
we do what you say, no mother will see her son again nor
any man know where he is going, where he falls and where
he dies, and before next day we will be either dead or taken
captive." Rifāʿah b. Shaddād said, "Your opinion is most excellent!"

Then he went up to the Kinānī and said, "Will you hold it
or shall I take it from you?" The Kinānī answered, "I do not

[565]

---

532. The start of the following report seems to be corrupt; see *Add. et
emend.*, and cf. *Ansāb*, V, 210–1.

injured man who could not help himself and handed him over to his own group. Then he led the people on the way during the whole of that night until next morning he had reached al-Tunaynir,[537] where he crossed the Khābūr river and cut the bridges, and he continued on his way cutting every bridge he came to. Next day, al-Ḥusayn b. Numayr sent out and found they had left, but he did not send anyone in pursuit of them. Rifāʿah led the people, hurrying on, and he made Abū al-Juwayriyyah al-ʿAbdī take up the rear with seventy horsemen to give cover. Whenever they came on someone who had fallen off, he picked him up, or, if they came on any equipment and goods which had fallen off, he took possession until he knew whose it was. If it was being sought or needed, he sent to Rifāʿah and informed him.

[568]

They continued in this way until they came to Qarqīsiyā from the open land side, where Zufar sent them food and fodder as he had done on the first occasion. He also sent them physicians and told them, "Stay here with us as long as you like, and you will find generosity and liberality." They stayed for three days and then each man of them provisioned himself with as much food and fodder as he liked.

Saʿd b. Ḥudhayfah b. al-Yamān continued on his way until he reached Hīt, where the bedouin came to him and told him what had happened to Ibn Ṣurad's men. Thereupon he turned back. At Ṣandūdā'[538] he met al-Muthannā b. Mukharribah al-ʿAbdī and told him the news. They waited there until they heard the news that Rifāʿah was approaching, and, when he drew near the place, they went out to receive him. The men greeted each other and wept for each other, and they told one another of their brethren's death. For a day and a night they remained there, and then the men of al-Madā'in returned to al-Madā'in, the Baṣrans to al-Baṣrah, and the Kūfans proceeded to al-Kūfah where they found al-Mukhtār imprisoned.

According to Hishām—Abū Mikhnaf: ʿAbd al-Raḥmān b. Yazīd b. Jābir b. Adham b. Muḥriz al-Bāhilī told us that he brought tidings of victory to ʿAbd al-Malik b. Marwān, who

---

537. Yāqūt, *Buldān*, I, 887.
538. *Ibid.*, III, 420.

went up on the *minbar*, praised God and extolled Him, and then said:

[569]   God has destroyed the spreader of disorder and commotion [*fitnah*] and the head of error among the leaders of the Iraqis, Sulaymān b. Ṣurad; Oh, the swords have left the head of al-Musayyab b. Najabah spinning like a top; Oh, God has killed two great heads among their leaders who wandered in error and led others into error, ᶜAbdallāh b. Saᶜd, brother of the Azd, and ᶜAbdallāh b. Wāl, brother of Bakr b. Wā'il. After these there is none left with power or strength.

According to Hishām—Abū Mikhnaf: I was told that al-Mukhtār waited about a fortnight and then said to his supporters, "Count the days for this warrior lord of yours, more than ten but less than a month. Then there will come to you false news of a forceful attack and a cutting blow and much killing and stoning. Whoever is for it, I shall be for it! Do not be deceived, I shall be for it!"

According to Abū Mikhnaf—al-Ḥusayn b. Yazīd—Abān b. al-Walīd: While he was still in prison, al-Mukhtār wrote to Rifāᶜah b. Shaddād after he came from ᶜAyn al-Wardah:

Now, welcome to the bands whose reward God made great when they set out and whose coming back He was pleased with when they returned. Verily, by the Lord of the building which He built, no one of you has taken a step or made a move but that God's reward for him is greater than sovereignty over this world. Sulaymān fulfilled his duty, and God took him and placed his spirit with those of the prophets, the righteous ones, the martyrs, and the upright. But he was never your lord, he with whom you would be rendered victorious! I myself am the designated leader, the trusted one, the commander of the army, the fighter against the tyrants, the taker of vengeance from the enemies of the religion, and the securer of the vital places. Make ready and stand prepared, rejoice and be glad! I call you to the Book of God and the Sunnah of His

Prophet, to the seeking of vengeance for the blood of
the family, to the defense of the weak, and *jihād* against
the profaners of God's law. Peace be with you!   [570]

According to Abū Mikhnaf—Abū Zuhayr al-ᶜAbsī: The people were talking about this business of al-Mukhtār, and
ᶜAbdallāh b. Yazīd and Ibrāhīm b. Muḥammad heard about it.
They came out with the troops, went to al-Mukhtār and seized
him.

According to Abū Mikhnaf—Sulaymān b. Abī Rāshid—Ḥumayd b. Muslim: When we were ready to go back, ᶜAbdallāh
b. Ghaziyyah said, standing over the fallen, "May God have
mercy on you! You have been true and borne your suffering
patiently. We have been false and fled." And when we had
set out next day, there was ᶜAbdallāh b. Ghaziyyah with about
twenty men wanting to go back and meet the enemy. Rifāᶜah,
ᶜAbdallāh b. ᶜAwf b. al-Aḥmar and a group of the leading men
went and said to them, "We implore you by God not to make
our flight more desolate or to weaken us further! We shall
not cease to do good so long as there remain among us men
with a firm purpose like you." They kept on at them imploring
them in that way until they had caused them to change their
minds, except for a man of Muzaynah called ᶜUbaydah b.
Sufyān, who rode along with them until, when their attention
was distracted, turned back and met the Syrians, threatening
them with his sword and striking at them until he was killed.

According to Abū Mikhnaf—al-Ḥusayn b. Yazīd al-Azdī—
Ḥumayd b. Muslim al-Azdī: That man of Muzaynah was a
friend of mine. When he went off I implored him by God,
but he said, "You have never asked me for anything of this
world when I have not recognized that I had a duty toward
you to give it to you. But I am seeking God by that which
you are asking of me now." He separated from me and met
the enemy and was killed. By God, I wanted nothing more
than to meet someone who could tell me about him and how
he had fared when he met the enemy.   [571]

In Mecca I met ᶜAbd al-Malik b. Juz' b. al-Ḥidrijān al-Azdī.
A conversation developed between us in which a reference to
that day occurred, and he said, "I marveled at what I saw on

the day of ʿAyn al-Wardah after the destruction of the army—
a man came and threatened me with his sword and we set
out toward him." When he reached the man he saw that he
was wounded and was saying:

I am from God and to God I flee;
  Oh my God, I proclaim your favor and I make
  glad!

"We said to him, 'Who are your people?' and he answered,
'The descendants of Adam.' We said, 'Who?' and he answered,
'I do not want to know you or you to know me, Oh destroyers
of the sacred sanctuary.' Sulaymān b. ʿAmr b. Muḥsin al-Azdī
of the Banū al-Khiyār[539] engaged him. At that time he was
one of the bravest of our men. They wore each other down.
Then the men came down on him from all sides and killed
him. By God, I have never seen anyone more valiant than
he." When he told me this, I being so anxious to find out
about him, tears came to my eyes, and he asked me, "Was
there any tie of relationship between you and him?" "No," I
replied. "That was a man of Muḍar who was a friend and
brother to me." He said to me, "May God cause your tears
to continue! Do you weep for a man of Muḍar who was killed
in pursuit of error!" I answered, "No, by God, he was not
killed in pursuit of error but of a clear sign from his Lord
and following divine guidance." He said to me, "May God
thrust you into the same place as him!" I said, "Amen! And
may He thrust you into the place where He has thrust al-
Ḥusayn b. Numayr! And may He cause you to continue weeping for him!" Then we both stood up.

Among the poetry recited on that subject are the words of
Aʿshā Hamdān,[540] and this is one of the underground[541] poems
which were composed at that time:[542]

---

539. See Caskel/Ibn Kalbī, II, 347, s.v. Ḥiyar b. Saʿd.
540. See *EI²*, s.v.
541. See *Add. et emend.*
542. See R. Geyer (ed.), *Gedichte von 'Abû Baṣîr Maimûn ibn Qais al-
Aʿshâ*, London, 1928, 315 (among the poems of Aʿshā Hamdān), *Murūj*, V,
220 (begins at l. 30).

An image of you has drawn near, Oh Umm Ghālib,   [572]
    and you are given our greeting from a distant
    loved one.
You are still for me an object of distress and I am
    still pining
    on account of a grief which has assailed me
    from being separated from you.
Whatever I forget, I will never forget your turning
    in the morning,
    to us with the fair and comely maidens.
There showed herself to us, slim, narrow of waist,
    graceful of hips, full in the bottom,
Elegant and beautiful, a young girl whose youth
    is like the morning sun smiling between the
    clouds.
When the clouds and their shadows cover her,
    a small part of her still shows and she jealously
    guards what still shows.
This passion is for me craving and desire.
    Love with it a beloved who is not near.
May God not disdain youth and its remembrance,
    or the powerful love of full-breasted women!
Our sweet rebukes increase
    just as my desire and my abundant tears for the
    dear friend who is near.
If I do not forget them, I will recall
    the pain of loss of a hidden treasure of noble   [573]
    origin.
He made entreaties to God truthfully,
    and fear of God achieves the best of rewards.
And he abstained from this world and did not get
    involved in it,
    but turned in repentance to God, the Lofty, the
    Most High.
He abandoned this world and said, "I have cast it
    away,
    and, so long as I live, I will not return to it.
I am not concerned with that, the loss of which
    people think important,
    and strive to obtain it with all their effort."

It caused him to set out on the signposted roads,
    against Ibn Ziyād leading troops who put all to
    flight,
With a throng who were people of divine fear and
    understanding,
    one who was active in courage and noble of
    lineage.
They passed on, leaving Ibn Ṭalḥah to his own
    thoughts,
    and answering not the governor who addressed
    them.
They journeyed on together with the seeker after
    piety,
    and another one repenting what he had done in
    the past.
[574]   At ʿAyn al-Wardah, they met the army which was
    setting out
    against them, and they slaughtered them with
    cutting swords
Of Yemen, smashing the fist, and sometimes
    with noble horses, well-bred and long in the
    body.
There came against them a host from Syria, and
    after it
    hosts from every side, like the breakers of the
    sea.
They did not cease until their noble ones were
    destroyed,
    and none of them escaped there except for a
    few.
The steadfast ones were abandoned, fallen,
    and the wind from the east and from all sides
    came to buffet them.
The Khuzāʿī chief[543] was pierced with a lance,
    as if he had never once fought or made war.
The chief of the Banū Shamkh[544] the hero of his
    people

---

543. I.e., Sulaymān b. Ṣurad.

544. Subtribe of Fazārah (Caskel/Ibn Kalbī, I, 525), i.e., al-Musayyab b.
Najabah.

of Shanū'ah,[545] the Taymī,[546] the leader of the
  detachments,
ᶜAmr b. Bishr, al-Walīd,[547] Khālid,
  Zayd b. Bakr, al-Ḥulays b. Ghālib,
And from Hamdān a striker from every segment,
  the noblest of those acquiring divine reward did
  not shrink when he pressed forward.
The leader of every clan has been struck down,
  and the one of noble descent in the piercing
  peak of glory.
They rejected everything apart from a blow, the fall
  of which would cleave the head asunder
  and a thrust with the piercing tips of the spears.
Saᶜīd,[548] on the day when he perished, full of vigor,
  was braver than a pouncing lion of Durnā.
Oh best of armies, for Iraq and its people,
  you have been given drink out of water skins
  pouring forth blood.
Our champions and our defenders did not withdraw
  when the war became vehement.
If they were killed, then that is the most noble of
  deaths,
    and one day every young man will be one of
    the dead.
They were not slain before they had hurled themselves in fury at a group
    of those who violate God's law, like the charg-
    ing of billy goats.

Sulaymān b. Ṣurad and those of the Penitents who were
killed with him at ᶜAyn al-Wardah were slain in the month
of Rabīᶜ II.

In this year also, Marwān b. al-Ḥakam ordered the Syrians
to give the oath of allegiance to his two sons ᶜAbd al-Malik

---

545. Azd Shanū'ah are one of the four branches of Azd, i.e., ᶜAbdallāh b.
ᶜAwf b. al-Aḥmar (?).
546. ᶜAbdallāh b. Wāl.
547. Al-Walīd b. Ghuḍayn (?).
548. Saᶜīd b. Munqidh al-Hamdānī (?).

and ᶜAbd al-ᶜAzīz in succession to himself, and he appointed the two of them as his heirs apparent.[549]

Marwān's Designation of His Two Sons ᶜAbd al-Malik and ᶜAbd al-ᶜAzīz as His Heirs Apparent

According to Hishām—ᶜAwānah: After ᶜAmr b. Saᶜīd b. al-ᶜĀṣ al-Ashdaq had defeated Musᶜab b. al-Zubayr, when the latter's brother ᶜAbdallāh sent him to Palestine,[550] he turned back to return to Marwān. At that time, Marwān was in Damascus, having won control over all Syria and Egypt. He heard that ᶜAmr was saying the rule would pass to him after Marwān and that he was claiming Marwān had made him a promise. Marwān, therefore, called Ḥassān b. Mālik b. Baḥdal and told him that he wanted to take the oath of allegiance for his two sons ᶜAbd al-Malik and ᶜAbd al-ᶜAzīz in succession to himself and he told him what he had heard about ᶜAmr b. Saᶜīd. Ḥassān said, "I will deal with ᶜAmr for you!" When the people had gathered in front of Marwān in the evening, Ibn Baḥdal stood and said, "We have heard that there are some men who have fanciful desires. Stand and give the oath of allegiance to ᶜAbd al-Malik and to ᶜAbd al-ᶜAzīz after him!" So the people stood and gave the oath of allegiance down to the last man.

In this year too, Marwān b. al-Ḥakam died in Damascus at the beginning of the month of Ramaḍān (April 10, 685).[551]

[577] *The Death of Marwān*

According to Al-Ḥārith—Ibn Saᶜd—Muḥammad b. ᶜUmar—Mūsā b. Yaᶜqūb—Abū al-Ḥuwayrith: When death came to Muᶜāwiyah b. Yazīd Abū Laylā, he refused to appoint anyone as caliph after him. Ḥassān b. Baḥdal desired that the authority after Muᶜāwiyah b. Yazīd should be made over to the latter's

---

549. For the following account, cf. *Ansāb*, V, 149–50.
550. See above, p. 64.
551. For what follows, cf. *Ansāb*, V, 159–60.

brother, Khālid b. Yazīd b. Mucāwiyah.[552] Khālid was a minor, and Ḥassān b. Mālik was the maternal uncle of his father, Yazīd b. Mucāwiyah.[553] Ḥassān gave the oath of allegiance to Marwān, but he wanted authority after him to be made over to Khālid b. Yazīd. When he and the Syrians gave the oath of allegiance to Marwān, it was suggested to Marwān, "Marry Khālid's mother (his mother was Umm Khālid, the daughter of Abū Hāshim b. cUtbah)[554] so you can diminish his importance and he will not seek the caliphate." So he married her.

One day, Khālid went in to Marwān, with whom there was a large group of people. Khālid was walking between the lines of people and Marwān said, "By God, I do not know anyone more stupid than he! Come up here, you son of a whore [yā 'bna al-raṭbati 'l-ist]." He was abrupt with him in order to diminish him in the eyes of the Syrians. Khālid returned to his mother and told her. She said to him, "You must not let this become known. Keep it quiet and I will deal with him for you." Marwān went to her and asked her, "Did Khālid say anything about me to you?" She answered, "Khālid say anything about you! Khālid has too much respect for you to say anything about you," and he believed her. She waited some days and then, when Marwān was sleeping with her, she suffocated him with a pillow and killed him.

Abū Jacfar said: Marwān's death was in the month of Ramaḍān (April–May 685) in Damascus, and he was 63 years old, according to al-Wāqidī. Hishām b. Muḥammad al-Kalbī, however, said that on the day of his death he was 61. It is also said that when he died he was 71, also 81. His *kunyah* was Abū cAbd al-Malik, and he was Marwān b. al-Ḥakam b. Abī al-cĀṣ b. Umayyah b. cAbd Shams. His mother was Āminah bint cAlqamah b. Ṣafwān b. Umayyah al-Kinānī. After the oath of allegiance was given to him as caliph, he lived for 9 months, and it is also said for 10 months, but 3 days.

Before his death, he had dispatched two expeditions, one of them to Medina under Ḥubaysh b. Duljah al-Qaynī,[555] the

[578]

---

552. See above, n. 253.
553. See above, n. 274.
554. See above, p. 65 and n. 307.
555. On him, see Crone, *Slaves*, 96–7; Rotter, *Bürgerkrieg*, index; the Banū al-Qayn (or Bal-Qayn) b. Jasr of Quḍācah (see *EI²*, s.v. al-Ḳayn).

other to Iraq under ᶜUbaydallāh b. Ziyād. ᶜUbaydallāh b. Ziyād had got as far as al-Jazīrah when the news of Marwān's death reached him. The Penitents among the people of al-Kūfah had gone out against him seeking vengeance for the blood of al-Ḥusayn, and what happened to them has already been mentioned.[556] Please God, we shall report the remainder of the information about ᶜUbaydallāh until he was killed.

The Failure of the Syrian Expedition
against Medina

In this year too, Ḥubaysh b. Duljah was killed.[557] According to what is reported from Hishām—ᶜAwānah b. al-Ḥakam, Ḥubaysh b. Duljah had got as far as Medina, where Jābir b. al-Aswad b. ᶜAwf,[558] the nephew of ᶜAbd al-Raḥmān b. ᶜAwf, had been given authority by ᶜAbdallāh b. al-Zubayr. Jābir fled from Ḥubaysh, but then al-Ḥārith b. ᶜAbdallāh b. Abī Rabī-ᶜah,[559] the brother of ᶜUmar b. ᶜAbdallāh b. Abī Rabīᶜah, sent an army from al-Baṣrah to fight Ḥubaysh b. Duljah. ᶜAbdallāh b. al-Zubayr had made al-Ḥārith prefect of al-Baṣrah. Commanding the army was al-Ḥantaf b. al-Sijf al-Tamīmī.[560] When Ḥubaysh b. Duljah heard about them, he left Medina to go out against them, and ᶜAbdallāh b. al-Zubayr sent ᶜAbbās b. Sahl b. Saᶜd al-Anṣārī[561] to govern Medina with orders to pursue Ḥubaysh b. Duljah until the army of al-Baṣrah under al-Ḥantaf, which had come to help Ibn al-Zubayr, should arrive. ᶜAbbās hurriedly set off following them and caught up with them at al-Rabadhah.[562] Ibn Duljah's men had advised him, "Leave

[579]

---

556. See above, pp. 124–59.

557. For what follows, cf. *Ansāb*, V, 150–9.

558. On him, see Zubayrī, *Nasab Quraysh*, 273 (and see n. 92 above).

559. His brother's name indicates that the Leiden text is lacking *ibn ᶜAbdallāh* after the name al-Ḥārith, and see p. 43 and n. 211 above.

560. Text reads al-Ḥunayf b. al-Sijf, but see the note to *Ansāb*, V, 151¹², and Caskel/Ibn Kalbī, II, 297.

561. See *Add. et emend.* for the name and cf. pp. 111ff. above for a report from him; he was of the Banū Sāᶜidah/Khazraj (Caskel/Ibn Kalbī, II, 103).

562. See Yāqūt, *Buldān*, II, 748f: a settlement of Medina, 3 *amyāl* from Dhāt ᶜIrq, on the Ḥijāz road coming from Fayd toward Mecca.

them alone, do not rush into an engagement with them." He,
however, said, "I shall not rest until I have eaten some of
their *muqannad*" (meaning *sawīq* sweetened with *qand*).[563] He
was killed by an arrow fired by an unknown man.[564] Also
killed were al-Mundhir b. Qays al-Judhāmī and Abū ʿUqāb,[565]
the mawlā of Abū Sufyān. Also with him on that day were
Yūsuf b. al-Ḥakam and al-Ḥajjāj b. Yūsuf,[566] and the two of
them only managed to escape on the same camel. About five
hundred of them were held in custody in the prison tent[567]
of Medina. ʿAbbās said to them, "Throw yourselves on my
judgment!" They did so and he cut off their heads. The fugitives from Ḥubaysh's army returned to Syria.

According to Aḥmad b. Zuhayr—ʿAlī b. Muḥammad: He
who killed Ḥubaysh b. Duljah the day of al-Rabadhah was
Yazīd b. Siyāh al-Uswārī;[568] he shot him with an arrow and
killed him. When they entered Medina, Yazīd b. Siyāh was
sitting on a grey nag and wearing white clothes, but it was
not long before his clothes became black, as I saw, from that
which the people anointed him with and the perfumes they
poured over him.

The Plague of al-Jārif in al-Baṣrah

Abū Jaʿfar said: In this year too there broke out in al-Baṣrah
the plague known as the plague of al-Jārif. A great number
of Baṣrans perished in it.

According to ʿUmar b. Shabbah—Zuhayr b. Ḥarb—Wahb   [580]
b. Jarīr: My father told me on the authority of al-Muṣʿab b.
Zayd that al-Jārif broke out while ʿUbaydallāh b. ʿUbaydallāh

---

563. The gloss on *al-muqannad* is in the text. *Sawīq* is a sort of broth made
with barley or other flour (see *EI¹*, s.v. sawīḳ), *qand* is the solidified extract
of sugar cane (cf. Eng. "candy").

564. Ar. *sahmu gharb* (see Lane, *Lexicon*, s.v. gharb).

565. Cairo reads Abū ʿAttāb; he is missing from the parallel passage, *Ansāb*,
V, 155–6.

566. The future important governor of Iraq, al-Ḥajjāj (see *EI²*, s.v. al-
Ḥadjdjādj), and his father.

567. See Dozy, *Suppl.*, s.v. ʿamūd, for the suggestion "prison tent." *Ansāb*,
V, 156, has ʿamūd al-Rabadhah, and cf. the note *ad loc.* for the suggestion
that it should be understood as the name of a place.

568. A descendant of the Persian cavalry troops which had gone over to
the Arabs during the period of conquest (see n. 149 above).

b. Maᶜmar had authority over al-Baṣrah. His mother died in it and no one could be found to carry her bier, so they had to hire four non-Arabs. They carried her to her grave, and he was the governor at that time![569]

In this year also, the strength of the Khawārij in al-Baṣrah increased and Nāfiᶜ b. Azraq was killed.[570]

The Threat to al-Baṣrah from Nāfiᶜ b. al-Azraq and the Khārijites and al-Muhallab b. Abī Ṣufrah's Victory over Them

According to ᶜUmar b. Shabbah—Zuhayr b. Ḥarb—Wahb b. Jarīr—his father—Muḥammad b. Zubayr: ᶜUbaydallāh b. ᶜUbaydallāh b. Maᶜmar sent his brother ᶜUthmān b. ᶜUbaydallāh[571] with an army against Nāfiᶜ b. al-Azraq. He came up against them at Dūlāb,[572] where ᶜUthmān was killed and his army routed.

According to ᶜUmar—Zuhayr—Wahb—Muḥammad b. Abī ᶜUyaynah—Sabrah b. Nakhf: Ibn Maᶜmar ᶜUbaydallāh sent his brother ᶜUthmān against Ibn al-Azraq, but his army was routed and he was killed.

According to Wahb: My father told me the Baṣrans sent an army under Ḥārithah b. Badr.[573] When he met the Khawārij he said to his men:

Feed your guest with *karnib* and get water from a *dūlāb*,
but depart wherever you wish.[574]

---

569. For ᶜUbaydallah b. ᶜUbaydallāh, see p. 45 and n. 224 above. Cf. p. 46 above, where this story is related of ᶜAbdallāh b. al-Ḥārith Babbah and the authority for it is named as al-Ṣaᶜb b. Zayd.

570. See pp. 97–105 above for Nāfiᶜ b. al-Azraq's previous history. For the following, cf. Wellhausen, *Oppositionsparteien* 32ff. (Eng. tr. 45ff); Rotter, *Bürgerkrieg*, 80ff. Variants and parallels: *Aghānī*, VI, 3–7; *Ansāb*, IVb, 115, XI, 78–109; Mubarrad, *Kāmil*, 616–20, 623ff.

571. Ibn Maᶜmar al-Taymī (Quraysh). See p. 45 above for his brothers, but cf. Zubayrī, *Nasab Quraysh*, 288, which, although mentioning ᶜUthmān b. ᶜUbaydallāh who was killed by the Harūriyyah, does not refer to ᶜUbaydallāh b. ᶜUbaydallāh (ᶜUmar b. ᶜUbaydallāh is referred to in *ibid.*, 189).

572. In the vicinity of Ahwāz (Yāqūt, *Buldān*, II, 622).

573. Of the Banū Ghudāna b. Yarbūᶜ b. Ḥanẓalah of Tamīm (Caskel/Ibn Kalbī, II, 316).

574. *Karnib* is a dish of dates mixed with milk; a *dūlāb* is a water wheel. Cf. p. 169 below.

According to ʿUmar—Zuhayr—Wahb—his father and Muḥammad b. Abī ʿUyaynah—Muʿāwiyah b. Qurrah: We went   [581]
with Ibn ʿUbays to fight.[575] When we met the Khawārij in
battle, Ibn al-Azraq was killed as well as two or three sons
of al-Māḥūz, and Ibn ʿUbays was killed.

Abū Jaʿfar (al-Ṭabarī): As for Hishām b. Muḥammad, he
reported a narrative about Ibn al-Azraq and the sons of al-
Māḥūz from Abū Mikhnaf on the authority of Abū al-Mukhāriq al-Rāsibī which is different from the narrative of ʿUmar
b. Shabbah from Zuhayr b. Ḥarb on the authority of Wahb
b. Jarīr.

According to Hishām b. Muḥammad's report: Because the
Baṣrans were involved with the dispute between the Azd,
Rabīʿah and Tamīm which arose from Masʿūd b. ʿAmr's killing,
the power of Nāfiʿ b. al-Azraq increased and his followers
became more numerous. He set out toward al-Baṣrah and,
when he approached the bridge, ʿAbdallāh b. al-Ḥārith sent
Muslim b. ʿUbays b. Kurayz b. Rabīʿah b. Ḥabīb b. ʿAbd Shams
b. ʿAbd Manāf with the Baṣrans against him. He went out to
meet Nāfiʿ b. al-Azraq and began pushing him away from al-
Baṣrah, keeping him out of its territory. Eventually he came
to a place in the territory of al-Ahwāz called Dūlāb.

The men prepared to face one another and marched against
each other. Muslim b. ʿUbays put al-Ḥajjāj b. Bāb al-Ḥimyarī[576]
over his right wing and Ḥārithah b. Badr al-Tamīmī, al-Ghudānī, over his left. Ibn Azraq had over his right wing ʿAbīdah
b. Hilāl al-Yashkurī[577] and over his left al-Zubayr b. al-Māḥūz
al-Tamīmī. They met in battle and clashed and the men fought
more fiercely than had ever been seen. Muslim b. ʿUbays, the
commander of the Baṣrans, and Nāfiʿ b. al-Azraq, the chief of
the Khawārij, were killed. The Baṣrans gave al-Ḥajjāj b. Bāb
al-Ḥimyarī the command over them, while the Azāriqah appointed ʿAbdallāh b. al-Māḥūz.

Then they began fighting again more fiercely. Al-Ḥajjāj b.
Bāb al-Ḥimyarī, the commander of the Baṣrans, was killed,   [582]

---

575. See pp. 104f. above and Caskel/Ibn Kalbī, II, 437.
576. I am unable to identify him further.
577. See pp. 99f. above.

and so was ᶜAbdallāh b. al-Māḥūz, the commander of the Azāriqah. The Baṣrans made Rabīᶜah al-Ajdham al-Tamīmī[578] their commander, while the Khawārij made ᶜUbaydallāh b. al-Māḥūz theirs. They began fighting again and continued until evening. Some of them had experienced a reaction against this mutual hostility and a revulsion against the fighting, and were desisting and holding back from the others, when there joined the Khawārij a large detachment of theirs which had not taken part in the battle. They attacked in the sector of ᶜAbd al-Qays and the Baṣrans were defeated. Rabīᶜah al-Ajdham, the commander of the Baṣrans, fought and was killed, and Ḥārithah b. Badr took hold of the Baṣrans' banner. He fought for a time after his men had withdrawn, protecting their rear with the more resolute and steadfast of the men. Then he went off with the men and made camp with them at al-Ahwāz. Referring to that, the poet of the Khawārij[579] said:

Oh heart without hunger or thirst!
    and Oh my heart which loves Umm Ḥakīm!
If she had been with me on the day of Dūlāb, she
    would have seen
    the thrusting in battle of a man not base.
In the morning (the slain of) Bakr b. Wā'il floated
    in the water,
    and we set the heads of the horses against
    Tamīm.
The first of our swords were directed against ᶜAbd
    al-Qays,
    and the shaykhs of the Azd ignominiously swam!

The Baṣrans heard about that and it terrified and frightened them. In view of the crisis, Ibn al-Zubayr sent al-Ḥārith b. ᶜAbdallāh b. Abī Rabīᶜah al-Qurashī, and he came and removed ᶜAbdallāh b. al-Ḥārith from office. The Khawārij advanced toward al-Baṣrah, and then, when the Baṣrans were in this

[583]

---

578. Al-Mubarrad, *Kāmil*, 616, and *Ansāb*, XI, 86, call him Rabīᶜ b. ᶜAmr al-Ajdham al-Ghudānī (the Banū Ghudāna b. Yarbūᶜ of Tamīm).

579. Elsewhere, this poet is variously named: Qaṭarī b. al-Fujāᶜah (al-Mubarrad, *Kāmil*, 214, 618f.); Ibn Sahm al-Tamīmī (*Ansāb*, XI, 84); and Ṣāliḥ b. ᶜAbdallāh al-ᶜAbshamī (ibid., 88–9).

When Ḥārithah b. Badr al-Ghudānī heard that al-Muhallab had been given command of the fighting against the Azāriqah, he said to those of his men with him:

Feed your guest with *karnib* and get water from a *dūlāb*,
    but depart wherever you wish, for the *amīr* is al-Muhallab.

Those who were with him then set off in the direction of al-Baṣrah but al-Ḥārith b. ᶜAbdallāh b. Abī Rabīᶜah diverted them toward al-Muhallab. When al-Muhallab camped with his men, he dug a ditch around himself, posted lookouts, sent out spies and placed sentries. His army continued in its battle lines, with the soldiers organized according to their banners and fifths, and men were entrusted with watching the entrances to the ditch. And whenever the Khawārij wished to make a night attack on al-Muhallab, they found the issue was already decided and withdrew. They never fought anyone who was more resolute against them or more angry against their hearts than al-Muhallab.

According to Abū Mikhnaf—Yūsuf b. Yazīd—ᶜAbdallāh b. ᶜAwf b. al-Aḥmar: One of those Khārijīs told him that the Khawārij sent ᶜAbīdah b. Hilāl and al-Zubayr b. al-Māḥūz by night with two large troops of horse against al-Muhallab's camp. Al-Zubayr came from his right flank and ᶜAbīdah from his left; they proclaimed the battle cry "God is most great!" and shouted out at the men, but found they were in good order and in their battle lines, on the watch and ready, and they could not fall on the army unaware or obtain any ad- [586] vantage over them. When they had withdrawn in order to go back, ᶜUbaydallāh b. Ziyād b. Ẓabyān called out to them saying:

"You have found us holding firm and standing steady,
    not treacherously opened up nor tottering feebly.

Far from it! When we are shouted at we refuse to comply. Oh people of Hell, indeed, hurry to it soon, for it is your resting place and your abode!" They answered, "Oh wicked one, is Hell kept for anyone but you and your kind? It was prepared for the unbelievers and you are one of them!" He said, "Are you listening? I would emancipate every slave I possess if you entered Paradise and there remained between

Safawān and the furthest boulder of land of Khurāsān any
Magian, who marries his mother, his daughter and his sister,
who would not enter it also!"[585] ᶜAbīdah answered him, "Be
silent, Oh wicked one! You are merely a slave of the contu-
macious tyrant [al-jabbār al-ᶜanīd] and a wazīr of the iniquitous
unbeliever [al-ẓālim al-kafūr]." Ibn Ẓabyān said, "Oh wicked
one, you are the enemy of the Godfearing believer and the
wazīr of the accursed Satan."[586] The men said to Ibn Ẓabyān,
"God has given you success, Oh Ibn Ẓabyān. By God, you
have given the wicked one the right answer and you have
spoken the truth!"

Next morning, al-Muhallab brought out the men arraigned
in their formations and fifths. Their positions were: the Azd
and Tamīm on the right, Bakr b. Wā'il and ᶜAbd al-Qays on
the left, and the Ahl al-ᶜĀliyah[587] in the middle, the center of
the army. The Khawārij came out with ᶜAbīdah b. Hilāl al-
Yashkurī over their right, and al-Zubayr b. al-Māḥūz over their
left. They were better equipped and had more noble horses
and more weapons than the Baṣrans because they had gone
[587] through the land, stripping it bare and devouring everything
between Kirmān and al-Ahwāz. They came wearing helmets
which weighed down their heads, suits of armor which they
trailed behind, and thigh pieces of chain mail which they
fastened by iron hooks to their belts. The men met and fought
a battle of the fiercest sort. For most of the day, they withstood
one another, and then the Khawārij as a whole bore down on
the Baṣrans in a way not to be stood. The Baṣrans panicked
and turned tail in that flight in which a mother does not heed
her child, until the fugitives reached al-Baṣrah, fearing they
would be taken captive.

---

585. For Safawān, see Yāqūt, *Buldān*, III, 97f. (presumably the place meant
here is the spring "one stage from the Mirbad gate of al-Baṣrah"). The
Zoroastrian practice of endogamy frequently figures in Muslim polemic against
the "Magians."

586. For the epithet "accursed" (al-rajīm), see Jeffery, *Foreign vocabulary*,
s.v.

587. The name for one of the fifths of al-Baṣrah, consisting of various tribal
groups, including Quraysh, sometimes explained (convincingly?) by reference
to the connection between the tribes of which it was formed and the high
ground of the Ḥijāz.

Al-Muhallab hastened and got before them to an elevated
spot at the side away from the paths taken by the fugitives.
Then he called out to the men, "To me, to me, Oh servants
of God!" and a group of his own people rejoined him and a
detachment of ʿUmān.[588] About 3,000 of them joined him.
When he saw those who had joined him, he was pleased with
their company, and he praised God and extolled Him and then
said:

> Now, many a time God assigns the larger number to
> their own devices and they are defeated, while He
> sends down His help upon the smaller number and
> they achieve the victory. By my life, now you are not
> few in number. I am pleased with your company. You
> are men of resolution and patience in the face of
> hardships and you are the true warriors of your garrison
> town. I do not want any of those who were put to
> flight to be with you, for they, if they were among
> you, would only cause you more confusion. I have
> decided that each one of you should pick up ten stones.
> Then go with us toward their camp, for just now they
> feel secure and their horsemen have gone off searching
> for your brethren. By God, I hope their horse will not
> return before you have sacked their camp and killed
> their commander!

They did what he asked, and then he headed back with
them, and, by God, the Khawārij knew nothing until al-Muhallab attacked them with the Muslims on the edge of their
camp. Then ʿUbaydallāh b. al-Māḥūz and his men advanced   [588]
to meet them clad in full armor and fully armed. Each man
of al-Muhallab's made for one of the enemy and took aim at
his face with the stone he carried, so that he could stun him
and afterward stab him with his spear or hack at him with
his sword. Before they had fought for very long, ʿUbaydallāh
b. al-Māḥūz had been slain, God had smote the leaders of his
men, and al-Muhallab had seized the enemy's camp with everything in it and inflicted a devastating slaughter on the Azāriqah.

---

588. The division of Azd known as Azd ʿUmān (al-Muhallab's tribe).

Those who had gone off in pursuit of the Baṣrans now came returning to their camp, but al-Muhallab had put horsemen and footmen on the road to seize and kill them. They fell back in retreat, defeated, slain, fought against and vanquished, and went away to Kirmān and the outskirts of Iṣfahān, while al-Muhallab remained in al-Ahwāz. Al-Ṣalatān al-ʿAbdī[589] said with reference to that day:

At Sillā wa-Sillabrā was the destruction of youths,
    who were noble and slaughtered ones whose cheeks were
    never comforted.[590]

When the Khawārij withdrew, indeed, men who had formerly been around five or six different campfires now gathered around a single one as a result of the rout and the paucity of their numbers until reinforcements joined them from al-Baḥrayn.

They retreated, then, in the direction of Kirmān and Iṣfahān while al-Muhallab remained in al-Ahwāz, and he continued there until Muṣʿab[591] came to al-Baṣrah and removed al-Ḥārith b. ʿAbdallāh b. Abī Rabīʿah from office as governor. When al-Muhallab had achieved his victory over the Azāriqah, he wrote:

> In the name of God, the Merciful and Compassionate. To the governor al-Ḥārith b. ʿAbdallāh from al-Muhallab b. Abī Ṣufrah, greetings! I give praise, hoping that He will favor you, to God, other than whom there is no god. Now, praise be to God who granted victory to the Commander of the Faithful, vanquished the transgressors, sent down His punishment upon them, slaughtered them in every way and drove them away completely. I wish to inform the governor, may God favor him, that we met the Azāriqah at a place in the territory of al-Ahwāz called Sillā wa-Sillabrā. We marched against them and then struggled with them and fought a battle of the hardest sort for a long time

[589]

---

589. Quthām b. Khabīʿah al-Ṣalatān of ʿAbd al-Qays/Rabīʿa (Caskel, II, 473, *Aghānī*, XXI, 28).
590. I.e., they were not properly buried.
591. Muṣʿab b. al-Zubayr, sent by his brother to al-Baṣrah to be governor.

during the day. But then detachments of the Azāriqah gathered together and made attacks on parties of the Muslims and defeated them. Among the Muslims there was confusion, which I feared would become a real flight.[592] When I saw that, I repaired to an elevated place and went upon it. Then I called out, "To me, my clan in particular and the Muslims in general!" A number of groups willing to sell themselves in their desire for the favor of God, men of religion, fortitude and patience in the face of hardship, uprightness and fidelity, rejoined me. With them I headed for the enemy's camp, in which was the mass of their men, their keen blades, and their commander with, gathered around him, those of them possessed of merit and a firm purpose. We fought for a while, firing arrows and thrusting with spears, and then the two sides had recourse to swords, the fight with which was for an hour of the day hand-to-hand on foot. But then God sent down his aid to the Believers and smote the faces of the unbelievers. Their tyrant [ṭāghiyah] fell, together with many of their defenders and the purposeful ones among them, and God killed them in the battle. Then I sent the cavalry after their flight, and they were slain on the road and in the camping place and settlement. Praise be to God, the Lord of the Universe, and peace be with you, may God have mercy on you!

When al-Ḥārith b. ᶜAbdallāh b. Abī Rabīᶜah received this letter, he sent it to Ibn al-Zubayr and it was read out to the people in Mecca. And al-Ḥārith Ibn Abī Rabīᶜah wrote to al-Muhallab, "Now, I have received your letter in which you mention the assistance which God gave you and the victory of the Muslims. I wish for you, Oh brother of Azd, the honor and glory of this world and the rewards and merits of the next. Peace be with you and may God have mercy on you." When al-Muhallab read his letter, he laughed and said, "Did you think he would acknowledge me as anything other than [590]

---

592. See *Gloss.*, s.v. *ṣarra.*

'brother of Azd'? The people of Mecca are no more than bedouins."

According to Abū Mikhnaf—Abū al-Mukhāriq al-Rāsibī: Abū ᶜAlqamah al-Yaḥmadī[593] fought on the day of Sillā wa-Sillabrā in a manner unsurpassed by anyone else, and he began to call out to the young men of Azd and the youths of Yaḥmad, "Lend us your skulls for an hour of the day!" Some of them started to charge and fight and then go back to him, laughing and saying, "Oh Abū ᶜAlqamah, the cooking pots are loaned!" When al-Muhallab had triumphed and he learned of Abū ᶜAlqamah's resolution, he gave him 100,000 dirhams.

It is said that the Baṣrans had asked al-Aḥnaf, before al-Muhallab was chosen, to fight against the Azāriqah but that he advised them in favor of al-Muhallab saying, "He will be stronger than me in fighting them." And it is said that when al-Muhallab responded to their request to fight against them, he laid a condition on the Baṣrans that whatever land he conquered would be for him and those who went out to fight with him, his tribesmen or others, for three years, but that there would be nothing from him for those who deserted him. The Baṣrans agreed to that and he wrote a contract with them about that. They sent a delegation to Ibn al-Zubayr about the
[591]   matter, and he endorsed all those conditions in favor of al-Muhallab and authorized them. When a favorable response was received, al-Muhallab sent his son Ḥabīb with 600 horsemen against ᶜAmr al-Qanā[594] who was encamped with 600 horsemen behind the smaller bridge. Al-Muhallab gave orders that the smaller bridge be secured. Ḥabīb prevented ᶜAmr and his men from taking the bridge, and fought them and expelled them from the area between the two bridges. They were put to flight and evacuated the region of the Euphrates.

Al-Muhallab with those of his tribe who went to fight with him—12,000 men—and with 70 of the rest of the men, made ready and set out and stopped at the larger bridge. ᶜAmr al-Qanā was opposite him with 600 men. Al-Muhallab sent his

---

593. The Banū Yaḥmad b. ᶜAbdallāh are a subtribe of Azd (Caskel/Ibn Kalbī, I, table 216).
594. ᶜAmr al-Qanā Abū al-Musaddī of the Banū Saᶜd b. Zayd Manāt of Tamīm (al-Mubarrad, *Kāmil*, 682 and *passim*).

son al-Mughīrah with horsemen and footsoldiers. The footmen
put them to flight with their arrows while the horsemen gave
chase. Al-Muhallab gave orders regarding the bridge, and it
was made secure and he and his men crossed. At that time,
ᶜAmr al-Qanā joined Ibn al-Māḥūz and his men who were at
al-Maftaḥ.[595] He told them the news, and they set out and
formed camp eight farsakhs from al-Ahwāz. For the remainder
of the year, al-Muhallab remained where he was, levying dues
from the districts of the Tigris and paying his men. When
they heard that, reinforcements came from the people of al-
Baṣrah and al-Muhallab entered them in the register and gave
them pay, with the result that they increased to 30,000.

Abū Jaᶜfar said: According to the reports of these authorities,
the battle in which the Azāriqah were routed and which caused
their departure from the environs of al-Baṣrah and al-Ahwāz
for those of Iṣfahān and Kirmān was in the year 66 (685–86),
and it is said that when they departed from al-Ahwāz they
numbered 3,000 and that in the battle between them and al-
Muhallab at Sillā wa-Sillabrā 7,000 of them were killed.

Abū Jaᶜfar said: In this year too, Marwān b. al-Ḥakam, before   [592]
his death, sent his son Muḥammad[596] to Mesopotamia,[597] that
being before he himself set out for Egypt.

Ibn al-Zubayr's Dismissal and Appointment of Governors in al-Kūfah and Medina

In this year, ᶜAbdallāh b. al-Zubayr deposed ᶜAbdallāh b. Yazīd
from al-Kūfah and gave ᶜAbdallāh b. Muṭīᶜ authority over it.
He also removed his brother ᶜUbaydah b. al-Zubayr from
Medina and gave authority over it to his brother Muṣᶜab b.
al-Zubayr. He removed from office his brother ᶜUbaydah, according to the report of al-Wāqidī, because the latter had

---

595. See Yāqūt, *Buldān*, IV, 586 (presumably Maftaḥ Dujayl on the river
Kārūn in Ahwāz is meant, rather than the village between al-Baṣrah and
Wāsiṭ).

596. See *EI¹*, s.v. Muḥammad b. Marwān.

597. Ar. al-Jazīrah, i.e., the region between the upper reaches of the Tigris
and Euphrates, with al-Mawṣil as its chief center, and expanding with conquest
into Ādharbayjān, Armenia and the Caucasus.

delivered an official address to the people and had said to them, "You have seen what was done with a people concerning a she-camel, the value of which was 500 dirhams." He because known as "the valuer of the she-camel." Ibn al-Zubayr heard about that and said, "This is sheer affectation of speech."[598]

In this year also, ᶜAbdallāh b. al-Zubayr rebuilt the sacred sanctuary [al-bayt al-ḥarām], incorporating the Ḥijr within it.

Ibn al-Zubayr's Rebuilding of the Kaᶜbah

According to Isḥāq b. Abī Isrā'īl—ᶜAbd al-ᶜAzīz b. Khālid b. Rustam al-Ṣanᶜānī Abū Muḥammad: Ziyād b. Jiyal[599] told me he was in Mecca on the day when Ibn al-Zubayr was overcome, and he heard him say, "My mother Asmā' bint Abī Bakr told me that the Messenger of God said to ᶜĀ'ishah: 'If it were not that your people had only recently been in a state of unbelief, I would restore the Kaᶜbah on the foundations of Abraham and I would add to the Kaᶜbah part of the Ḥijr.' "[600] Ibn al-Zubayr gave the order for it and it was excavated, and they found rocks as big as a camel. They moved a boulder of them and a bright light flashed out. They re-established it on its foundation and Ibn al-Zubayr rebuilt it, giving it two doors, from one of which it was entered and from the other vacated.[601]

[593]   Abū Jaᶜfar said: In this year ᶜAbdallāh b. al-Zubayr led the pilgrimage; over Medina was his brother Muṣᶜab b. al-Zubayr; ᶜAbdallāh b. Muṭīᶜ was over al-Kūfah at the end of the year; al-Ḥārith b. ᶜAbdallāh b. Abī Rabīᶜah al-Makhzūmī, called al-Qubāᶜ, was over al-Baṣrah, with Hishām b. Hubayrah in charge of its judiciary; and ᶜAbdallāh b. Khāzim was over Khurāsān.

---

598. Cf. *Ansāb*, V, 155, where this story is applied to the governor of Medina for Ibn al-Zubayr, ᶜAbdallāh b. ᶜUbaydallāh b. Abī Thawr. Presumably the reference is to the she-camel [al-nāqah] in the story of the people of Thamūd (Qur'ān, passim).

599. See n. 3 above.

600. For versions of the ḥadīth, see A.J. Wensinck, *Concordance et indices de la tradition musulmane*, s.vv. *kufr, asas*.

601. Cf. Azraqī, *Akhbār Makkah*, 143; ᶜAbd al-Razzāq, *Muṣannaf*, V, 9157.

In this year too, those of the Banū Tamīm who were in Khurāsān opposed ᶜAbdallāh b. Khāzim and warfare broke out between them.[602]

The Continuation of Tribal Warfare in Khurāsān under ᶜAbdallāh b. Khāzim

The cause, it is reported, was that those of the Banū Tamīm in Khurāsān had aided ᶜAbdallāh b. Khāzim against those of Rabīᶜah who were there and in the fighting against Aws b. Thaᶜlabah, and a number of them had been killed. Ibn Khāzim had defeated Aws b. Thaᶜlabah and Khurāsān had completely submitted to him. When it had done so and no one disputed it with him, Ibn Khāzim treated Tamīm harshly. He had assigned Herat to his son Muḥammad, appointed him over it, made Bukayr b. Wishāḥ commander of his police force, and attached Shammās b. Dithār al-ᶜUṭāridī to him. The mother of his son Muḥammad was a woman of Tamīm called Ṣafiyyah.

When Ibn Khāzim treated the Banū Tamīm harshly, they went to his son Muḥammad in Herat. But Ibn Khāzim wrote to Bukayr and Shammās, telling them to prevent the Banū Tamīm from entering Herat. Shammās b. Dithār, however, refused, and he left Herat and joined the Banū Tamīm. Bukayr, on the other hand, did prevent them from entering.

According to ᶜAlī b. Muḥammad—Zuhayr b. al-Hunayd—shaykhs of his tribe: When Bukayr b. Wishāḥ prevented the Banū Tamīm from entering Herat, they remained in the district of Herat, and Shammās b. Dithār went out to join them. Bukayr sent, telling Shammās, "I will give you 30,000 dirhams and I will give every man of Tamīm 1,000 on condition they go away." They, however, refused, entered the town and killed Muḥammad b. ᶜAbdallāh b. Khāzim.

According to ᶜAlī—al-Ḥasan b. Rushayd—Muḥammad b. ᶜAzīz[603] al-Kindī: Muḥammad b. ᶜAbdallāh b. Khāzim went hunting at Herat after he had prevented the Banū Tamīm from

[594]

---

602. See pp. 70–9 above and nn. 324–5.
603. See *Add. et emend.*

entering the town. They ambushed him, seized him and put him in chains. They drank all night and every time one of them wanted to urinate he did so over Muḥammad Ibn Khāzim. Shammās b. Dithār said to them, "Since you have gone this far with him, why not kill him in retaliation for your two companions he killed by flogging?" (Shortly before that Muḥammad Ibn Khāzim had seized two men of the Banū Tamīm and flogged them to death.) So they killed him. Someone alleged to us, on the authority of one of their shaykhs who witnessed the killing of Muḥammad Ibn Khāzim, that Jayhān b. Mashjaᶜah al-Ḍabbī tried to stop them killing him and threw himself over him. ᶜAbdallāh b. Khāzim was grateful to him for that and did not kill him with those whom he killed on the Day of Fartanā.[604] ᶜĀmir b. Abī ᶜUmar claimed he heard the shaykhs of the Banū Tamīm alleging that it was two men of the Banū Mālik b. Saᶜd called ᶜAjalah and Kusayb who carried out the killing. Ibn Khāzim said, "How evil is that

[595] which Kusayb has acquired [iktasaba] for his people, and ᶜAjalah has hastened [ᶜajjala] a calamity on his people!"

According to ᶜAlī—Abū al-Dhayyāl Zuhayr b. Hunayd al-ᶜAdawī: When the Banū Tamīm had killed Muḥammad b. ᶜAbdallāh b. Khāzim, they returned to Marw. Bukayr b. Wishāḥ went in pursuit of them and caught up with and killed a man of the Banū ᶜUṭārid called Shumaykh. Shammās and his companions reached Marw, where they said to the Banū Saᶜd, "We have taken your revenge for you. We have killed Muḥammad b. ᶜAbdallāh b. Khāzim for the man of the Banū Jusham[605] who was struck down at Marw." Then they agreed to fight Ibn Khāzim and appointed al-Ḥarīsh b. Hilāl al-Qurayᶜī to lead them.

(Zuhayr): Abū al-Fawāris told me from Ṭufayl b. Mirdās: Most of the Banū Tamīm agreed to fight against ᶜAbdallāh b. Khāzim.

(Zuhayr b. Hunayd): With al-Ḥarīsh there were warriors never surpassed; each of them a detachment on his own.

---

604. See p. 179 below, and Ṭabarī, II, 695–700, for the siege of Fartanā (Yāqūt, Buldān, III, 868).
605. See p. 72 above.

Among them were Shammās b. Dithār, Baḥīr b. Warqā' al-Ṣarīmī, Shuʿba b. Ẓahīr al-Nahshalī, Ward b. al-Falaq al-ʿAnbarī, al-Ḥajjāj b. Nāshib al-ʿAdawī, who was one of the best marksmen among them, and ʿĀṣim b. Ḥabīb al-ʿAdawī.[606] Al-Ḥarīsh b. Hilāl fought against ʿAbdallāh b. Khāzim for two years.

When the fighting and the enmity had dragged on between them, they became vexed. Al-Ḥarīsh went out and called to Ibn Khāzim, and the latter went out to him. Al-Ḥarīsh said, "The war has dragged on between us. What is the point of my people and yours being killed? Come out against me in single combat and, whichever one of us slays the other, the land is his." Ibn Khāzim answered, "By your father, you have offered me a fair deal!" He came out against him and they skirmished with one another like a pair of stallions, neither of them managing to achieve what he wanted, but Ibn Khāzim showed a lapse of concentration and al-Ḥarīsh hit at his head and butted him in the face with the top of his head. The stirrups of al-Ḥarīsh snapped and he drew his sword. Ibn Khāzim clung on to the neck of his horse, heading back to his men with a blow inflicted by the head of al-Ḥarīsh. Next day, the fighting between the two sides began again and continued for some days after the blow (received by Ibn Khāzim). Then the two sides grew weary and split into three factions. [596]

Baḥīr b. Warqā' went to Abrashahr[607] with a band (of followers), Shammās b. Dithār al-ʿUṭāridī headed for another district (it is said that he went to Sijistān), and ʿUthmān b. Bishr b. al-Muḥtafiz[608] betook himself to Fartanā and took up residence in a fortress there. Al-Ḥarīsh went to the district of Marw al-Rūdh, where Ibn Khāzim pursued him. He caught up with him at one of its settlements called Qaryat al-Malḥama or Qaṣr al-Malḥama.[609] Al-Ḥarīsh b. Hilāl had twelve men with him, for his followers had left him, and they were

---

606. These are all champions of Tamīm; for Baḥīr b. Warqā' al-Ṣarīmī (which seems more likely than the text's Ṣuraymī), see Wellhausen, *Arab Kingdom*, 420–3; for the groups Ṣarīm, Nahshal, ʿAnbar and ʿAdawiyah of Tamīm, see Caskel/Ibn Kalbī, I, tables 76, 60, 81 and 68, 59.

607. I.e., Nīshāpūr (see Le Strange, *Eastern caliphate*, 383f.).

608. Of the Banū Muzaynah (see Caskel/Ibn Kalbī, I, table 88).

609. See *Add. et emend.*, which suggest the subsequent verses point to the name Qaṣr al-Milḥ.

in a ruined place where he had erected spears which he had with him and shields. Ibn Khāzim reached him and al-Harīsh went out to him with his companions.

With Ibn Khāzim there was a mawlā of his who was very brave. He attacked al-Harīsh and struck him, but al-Harīsh did nothing. A man of the Banū Dabbah said to al-Harīsh, "Do you not see what the slave is doing?" but al-Harīsh [597] answered, "He is very well armed and my sword will be of no avail against his weapons, but find me a heavy piece of wood." So the man cut a heavy staff for him from a jujube tree (it is also said that he found it in the fortress) and gave it to him. With it, he then attacked and struck at the mawlā of Ibn Khāzim, who fell mortally wounded.

Next he went toward Ibn Khāzim and said, "What is it you want with me, when I have left the province to you?" He replied, "But you will return to it." Al-Harīsh said, "I will not return." Then he made peace with him on condition that al-Harīsh would leave Khurāsān for him and would not resume fighting against him, and Ibn Khāzim gave him 40,000 dirhams. Al-Harīsh opened the gate of the fortress to him, and Ibn Khāzim entered and gave him gifts and undertook to clear his debts, and they talked together for a long time. The cotton cloth which was fixed on the head wound given Ibn Khāzim by al-Harīsh flew off. Al-Harīsh got up, picked it up, and put it back on his head. Ibn Khāzim said to him, "Your touch today is more gentle than your touch yesterday, Oh Abū Qudāmah!" He answered, "I excuse myself to God and to you. By God, if my stirrups had not snapped, the sword would have made a fine mess of your molars!" Ibn Khāzim laughed and departed from him, and the band of Tamīm broke up.

One of the poets of Tamīm said about that:

If you had been like al-Harīsh, you would have been
    resolute,
       and you would have been the best of the warriors
       in the fortress of al-Milh;
Then you would have given Ibn Khāzim to drink with
    lamentations
       a bowl of blood which would have left long evil
       thoughts for him.

Al-Ashᶜath b. Dhu'ayb, brother of Zuhayr b. Dhu'ayb,[610] was killed in this war, and his brother Zuhayr said to him while still a spark of life remained, "Who killed you?" He answered, "I do not know. A man on a light brown nag stabbed me." Zuhayr then attacked every man whom he saw on a light brown nag. Some of them he killed, some of them fled. The men of the army shunned the light brown nags and they were left free in the army; no one would ride them.

Concerning the fighting against Ibn Khāzim, al-Ḥarīsh said:

Carrying the spear all night and all day   [598]
    has kept the bone of my right hand out of joint.
For two years my eyes have not closed at any resting place,
    unless my fist made a pillow for me upon a stone.
My coat is of iron, and when night brings sleep,
    my covering is the saddle[611] of a full-grown stallion.

---

610. See p. 73 above.

611. See, however, *Gloss.*, s.v. *mijall*, suggesting the reading *maḥal*, "vertebrae, dorsum."

The
Events of the Year
66
(AUGUST 8, 685–JULY 27, 686)

Among the events of this year was the rising of al-Mukhtār b. Abī ᶜUbayd in al-Kūfah seeking vengeance for the blood of al-Ḥusayn b. ᶜAlī b. Abī Ṭālib, and his expulsion of Ibn al-Zubayr's governor, ᶜAbdallāh b. Muṭīᶜ al-ᶜAdawī, from the town.

Al-Mukhtār's Revolutionary Movement in al-Kūfah and His Appeal to the Shīᶜah There

According to Hishām b. Muḥammad—Abū Mikhnaf—Fuḍayl b. Khadīj—ᶜAbīdah b. ᶜAmr and Ismāᶜīl b. Kathīr of the Banū Hind:612 When Sulaymān b. Ṣurad's followers arrived back in al-Kūfah, al-Mukhtār wrote to them:

> Now, may God increase your reward and lighten your burden in exchange for your separation from the unrighteous [al-qāsiṭīn] and your jihād against the profaners of His law [al-muḥillīn]! There was no expense

[599]

---

612. See pp. 105ff. above and n. 425; for the following, cf. Wellhausen, *Oppositionsparteien*, 74ff; Rotter, *Bürgerkrieg*, 98–102; cf. the account of J.O. Blichfeldt, *Early Mahdism*, 122ff.

in which you shared, no difficult path which you followed, and no step which you took, but that God has given you a higher place in the hereafter in reward for it and inscribed for you in recompense blessings which only God can number because they are so many. Rejoice! If I had come out to you, I would, with God's permission, have unsheathed my sword against your enemies everywhere from the rising to the setting of the sun, and I would, with God's permission, have made a pile of them, and I would have slain them as individuals and pairs. May God welcome those of you who have drawn near to Him and been rightly guided, and may He only dismiss those who disobey and reject His commands! Peace be with you, Oh people of right guidance!

Sīḥān b. ʿAmr of the Banū Layth of the Banū ʿAbd al-Qays[613] brought them this letter, which he had put in the lining of his cap.[614] He brought the letter to Rifāʿah b. Shaddād, al-Muthannā b. Mukharribah al-ʿAbdī, Saʿd b. Ḥudhayfah b. al-Yamān, Yazīd b. Anas,[615] Aḥmar b. Shumayṭ al-Aḥmasī,[616] ʿAbdallāh b. Shaddād al-Bajalī and ʿAbdallāh b. Kāmil.[617] He read it to them, and in reply they sent Ibn Kāmil to al-Mukhtār, telling him to say, "We have read your letter and our position is whatever pleases you. If you want us to come to you and get you out, we will do so." Ibn Kāmil went to him, entered upon him in the prison, and reported to him what he had been sent to say to him. Al-Mukhtār was pleased with the assent of the Shīʿah to him and he answered them, "You do not want to do this. I will get out in a few days."

Al-Mukhtār had sent a slave lad of his called Zirbiyyā to ʿAbdallāh b. ʿUmar b. al-Khaṭṭāb and had written to him, "I   [600]

---

613. This seems to be the only reference to him (for the Banū Layth b. Ḥudād of ʿAbd al-Qays, see Caskel/Ibn Kalbī, I, table 170).

614. Ar. *qalansūwa*, a tall Persian headpiece (Dozy, *Vêtements*, s.v.).

615. On him, see Caskel/Ibn Kalbī, II, 593, Rotter, *Bürgerkrieg*, 190–1 (of Asad b. Khuzaymah of Khindif).

616. For the Banū Aḥmas b. Ghawth of the Banū Bajīlah, see Caskel/Ibn Kalbī, I, table 223.

617. On him, see Caskel/Ibn Kalbī, II, 113; he belonged to the Banū Shākir b. Rabīʿah of Jusham/Hamdān (ibid., I, table 230).

have been unjustly imprisoned and the authorities hold false suspicions of me. Write on my behalf, may God have mercy on you, a courteous letter to these two evil doers.[618] Perhaps God will deliver me from their hands through your good will, your blessedness, and your favor. Peace be with you!" In response, ʿAbdallāh b. ʿUmar wrote to the two of them, "Now, you know the marriage ties which exist between me and al-Mukhtār b. Abī ʿUbayd and you know the love which there is between me and the two of you. I implore you, by the ties of obligation which bind me and you two, that you release him when you have looked into this letter of mine. Peace be with you and may God have mercy on you!" When ʿAbdallāh b. ʿUmar's letter reached ʿAbdallāh b. Yazīd and Ibrāhīm b. Muḥammad b. Ṭalḥah, they called for guarantors for al-Mukhtār who would stand surety for his person. Many of his supporters came to him, and Yazīd b. al-Ḥārith b. Yazīd b. Ruwaym said to ʿAbdallāh b. Yazīd, "What are you doing with all of these as guarantors? Let ten of them who are well-known notables guarantee him, and let the rest of them go." And he did so.

After they had stood surety for him, ʿAbdallāh b. Yazīd and Ibrāhīm b. Muḥammad b. Ṭalḥah summoned him and made him swear before God, other than whom there is no god, He who knows what is hidden and what is seen, the Merciful and the Compassionate, that he had no intention of any mischief against them and that he would not rebel against them so long as they had authority. If he did, he would have to sacrifice 1,000 head of livestock before the door of the Kaʿbah and all of his slaves, male and female, would be emancipated. He swore to them on those terms and then departed, went to his house and abode there.

According to Abū Mikhnaf—Yaḥyā b. Abī ʿĪsā—Ḥumayd b. Muslim: Afterward, I heard al-Mukhtār saying, "God damn them! How stupid they are if they think I will fulfill these vows of theirs. As for my swearing to them before God, if I have taken an oath and I see a greater good, then I must abandon what I have sworn and bring about the greater good,

[601]

---

618. I.e., ʿAbdallāh b. Yazīd and Ibrāhīm b. Muḥammad b. Ṭalḥah.

and expiate my oath. That I should rebel against them is a greater good than that I should desist from it, and I will expiate my oath. As for offering a thousand head of livestock, it is easier for me than spitting. Should the cost of a thousand head of livestock worry me? As for the freeing of my slaves, I wish it would give me success in my affair and then I would never own a slave again!"

When al-Mukhtār took up residence in his house at the time of his coming out of prison, the Shīʿah frequently visited him, were unanimous in accepting him and were satisfied with him. Those who took the oath of allegiance for him while he was in prison were five men, al-Sāʾib b. Mālik al-Ashʿarī,[619] Yazīd b. Anas, Aḥmar b. Shumayṭ, Rifāʿah b. Shaddād al-Fityānī and ʿAbdallāh b. Shaddād al-Jushamī. The number of his supporters continued to increase and his authority to strengthen and grow stronger until Ibn al-Zubayr removed ʿAbdallāh b. Yazīd and Ibrāhīm b. Muḥammad b. Ṭalḥah from office and sent ʿAbdallāh b. Muṭīʿ to al-Kūfah to take over their function.

According to Abū Mikhnaf—al-Ṣaqʿab b. Zuhayr—ʿUmar b. ʿAbd al-Raḥmān b. al-Ḥārith b. Hishām: Ibn al-Zubayr summoned ʿAbdallāh b. Muṭīʿ, the brother of the Banū ʿAdī b. Kaʿb,[620] and al-Ḥārith b. ʿAbdallāh b. Abī Rabīʿah al-Makhzūmī. He sent ʿAbdallāh b. Muṭīʿ over al-Kūfah and al-Ḥārith b. ʿAbdallāh b. Abī Rabīʿah over al-Baṣrah. News of that reached Baḥīr b. Raysān al-Ḥimyarī,[621] who met them and said, "Oh you two, tonight the moon is in al-Nāṭiḥ,[622] so do not go." As for Ibn Abī Rabīʿah, he complied with his advice, remained a short while, then left to take up his office and had no trouble. As for ʿAbdallāh b. Muṭīʿ, he answered him, "Do we seek anything but thrusting [al-naṭḥ]?" And, by God, he met thrusting and being laid low [naṭḥᵃⁿ wa-baṭḥᵃⁿ]. ʿUmar (b. ʿAbd al-Raḥmān b. al-Ḥārith b. Hishām) said, "Misfortune matches words."

[602]

---

619. On him, see Caskel/Ibn Kalbī, II, 499, and, for the Banū Ashʿar b. Udad (of Yemen), ibid., I, table 273.

620. For the Banū ʿAdī b. Kaʿb of Quraysh, see Zubayrī, *Nasab Quraysh*, 346ff.

621. Apparently a former governor of the Yemen for Yazīd (Ṭabarī, II, 277).

622. I.e., star β in the second horn of Aries (the Ram), a bad omen.

ᶜUmar b. ᶜAbd al-Raḥmān b. al-Ḥārith b. Hishām: ᶜAbd al-Malik b. Marwān heard that Ibn al-Zubayr had sent officials out over his dominions, and he asked whom he had sent over al-Baṣrah. He was told, "He has sent al-Ḥārith b. ᶜAbdallāh b. Abī Rabīᶜah over it," and ᶜAbd al-Malik said, "There is no freeman in the wādī of ᶜAwf. He has sent ᶜAwf and he has sat down."[623] Then he said, "And whom did he send over al-Kūfah?" and they said, "ᶜAbdallāh b. Muṭīᶜ." ᶜAbd al-Malik said, "A brave man who has fallen many a time, and a valiant one, how he hates fleeing!" Then he asked, "Whom has he sent over Medina?" and was told, "He has sent his brother Muṣᶜab b. al-Zubayr." He said, "That is the raging lion. He is the real man of his family."

According to Hishām—Abū Mikhnaf: ᶜAbdallāh b. Muṭīᶜ arrived in al-Kūfah in Ramaḍān of the year 65, on a Thursday when five days were left of the month of Ramaḍān (i.e. Thursday, May 4, 685). He said to ᶜAbdallāh b. Yazīd, "If you want to stay here with me, I shall value your companionship and treat you generously. But if you join the Commander of the Faithful ᶜAbdallāh b. al-Zubayr, then he and those of the Muslims who accept him owe you a favor." To Ibrāhīm b. Muḥammad b. Ṭalḥah he said, "Get yourself to the Commander of the Faithful!" Ibrāhīm departed and arrived in Medina, and he failed to deliver the full amount of the tax [kharāj] to Ibn al-Zubayr saying, "It was no more than a state of turmoil and disorder [fitnah]." But Ibn al-Zubayr took no action against him.

Ibn Muṭīᶜ remained governing al-Kūfah, controlling both prayer and taxation. He dispatched Iyās b. Muḍārib al-ᶜIjlī[624] to command his troop of police, ordering him to act in an exemplary manner and to come down hard on any suspicious behavior.

[603]

According to Abū Mikhnaf: Ḥaṣīrah b. ᶜAbdallāh b. al-Ḥārith b. Durayd al-Azdī, who lived at that time and witnessed the

---

623. See Freytag, *Proverbia*, II, 531, 831, for variant explanations of the first part of the proverb (only the first part is given in *Ansāb*, V, 277). The significance of ᶜAbd al-Malik's use of it here, however, is not clear to me.

624. ᶜIjl are a subgroup of Bakr. See *Add. et emend.* for variant readings of Iyās's patronym.

killing of Muṣᶜab b. al-Zubayr, told me: I was present in the mosque where ᶜAbdallāh b. Muṭīᶜ arrived. He went up on the *minbar*, praised God and extolled Him, and said:

Now, the Commander of the Faithful, ᶜAbdallāh b. al-Zubayr, has sent me to govern your garrison town and your border regions. He has ordered me to levy the income due to you from the lands which you have conquered [*fay'akum*] and not to remove the surplus of that income away from you without your approval, (and to comply with) the dispositions which ᶜUmar b. al-Khaṭṭāb made at the time of his death and the manner of conduct which ᶜUthmān b. ᶜAffān pursued regarding the Muslims. Fear God and stand upright, and do not fall into dispute or rely on the aid of the ignorant ones among you. Otherwise, blame yourselves and do not blame me! By God, I will surely come down hard on the rebellious miscreant and I will make straight the aversion of the doubting sneerer!

Al-Sā'ib b. Mālik al-Ashᶜarī arose before him and said:

As for Ibn al-Zubayr's command to you not to take away the surplus of our income from our conquests without our approval, we bear witness before you that we do not consent to your taking the surplus of it away from us or to its being shared out other than among us; and we do not consent to any manner of conduct being followed among us other than that of ᶜAlī b. Abī Ṭālib, who provided us with an exemplary mode of doing things [*sīrah*] in this land of ours until his death, may God have mercy upon him! We have no need for ᶜUthmān's mode of conduct [*sīrah*] regarding our income from the conquered lands (*fay'*) or our selves, for it was only arbitrary and willful; and we have no need for the mode of conduct of ᶜUmar b. al-Khaṭṭāb regarding our income from the conquered lands even if it was less injurious to us (than ᶜUthmān's) and he did not fail to achieve some good for the people.

[604]   Yazīd b. Anas said, "Al-Sā'ib b. Mālik has spoken truly and honestly. Our view is like his and we say the same as he!" Ibn Muṭīᶜ answered, "We will act among you with any mode of conduct you wish or incline to." Then he stood down. Yazīd b. Anas al-Asadī said, "You have brought to an end the (loss of our) surplus, Oh Sā'ib, may the Muslims never have to do without you! By God, I got to my feet and wanted to stand and speak to him in a similar vein, for I did not want God to entrust the refutation of him to any man of our garrison town who is not one of our party [shīᶜah]."

Iyās b. Muḍārib went to Ibn Muṭīᶜ and said, "Al-Sā'ib b. Mālik is one of the leaders of al-Mukhtār's supporters, and I do not trust al-Mukhtār. Send for him and let him come to you. When he does, confine him in your prison until the people's affairs are straightened out. My sources have come and told me that his enterprise is all set up for him and he has virtually come out in revolt in the garrison town." Ibn Muṭīᶜ sent to him, therefore, Zā'idah b. Qudāmah and Ḥusayn b. ᶜAbdallāh al-Bursumī of Hamdān,[625] who entered in upon him and said, "Give answer to the governor!" He called for his robes, ordered that his mount be saddled and made a lot of fuss about getting ready to go with them. When Zā'idah b. Qudāmah saw that, he recited God's words, "When those who disbelieve plot against you to hold you fast, kill you or drive you out, they plot; but God plots too, and God is the best of plotters!"[626] Al-Mukhtār understood and he sat down and cast off his clothes and then said, "Throw a rug over me. I think I must be ill, for I am shivering violently." Then he cited the saying of ᶜAbd al-ᶜUzzā b. Ṣuhal al-Azdī:[627]

"When a group of people reject a call made to them,
    and do not go to a misfortune, they are not afraid.

You two go back to Ibn Muṭīᶜ and tell him of the state I am in." Zā'idah b. Qudāmah said to him, "As for me, I will do

---

625. See Ṭabarī, II, 117: he was a member of Ziyād's shurṭah and was sent to summon Ḥujr b. ᶜAdī.
626. Qur'ān, 8:30.
627. Caskel/Ibn Kalbī, II, 133.

so. You, Oh brother of Hamdān, ask pardon for me when we come to him, for that would be better for you."   [605]

Abū Mikhnaf—Ismā'īl b. Nu'aym al-Hamdānī—Ḥusayn b. 'Abdallāh: I said to myself, "By God, if I do not give an account of this which is satisfactory to him, I will have no security that he will not triumph tomorrow and kill me!" So I said to Zā'idah, "Yes, I will beg pardon for you from Ibn Muṭī' and I will tell him what you desire." Then we left al-Mukhtār's presence, and there we found his supporters waiting at his door and a great crowd of them in his house. We went towards Ibn Muṭī' and I said to Zā'idah b. Qudāmah, "Indeed, I understood what you were saying when you recited that verse (of scripture) and I knew what you meant by it. I knew it was to stop him from leaving with us after he had put on his clothes and saddled his mount, and I knew when he cited that verse of poetry that he merely wanted to let you know that he had understood what you wanted him to understand and that he would not go to him." He denied that he had intended any of that, but I said to him, "Do not swear! By God, I am not going to report anything about you or him which the two of you would find offensive. I know that you feel concern for al-Mukhtār, feeling for him what a man feels for his cousin." So we came to Ibn Muṭī' and told him about his illness and what he complained of. He believed us and what we said.

Al-Mukhtār sent for his supporters and began to gather them in the houses round about him, intending to revolt in al-Kūfah in Muḥarram (August, 685). One of his supporters of Shibām[628] came, a great noble called 'Abd al-Raḥmān b. Shurayḥ,[629] and he met Sa'īd b. Munqidh al-Thawrī,[630] Si'r b. Abī Si'r al-Ḥanafī, al-Aswad b. Jarād al-Kindī[631] and Qudāmah b. Mālik al-Jushamī.[632] They met together in the dwelling of

---

628. Shibām b. As'ad of Hamdān (ibid., II, 529).

629. A man with a history of support for 'Alid movements (Ṭabarī, I, 3411, II, 253, 257).

630. Of the Banū Hamdān.

631. Does not seem to be otherwise known.

632. This is Ṭabarī's only reference to him; from the Banū Jusham of Hamdān.

[606] Si‘r al-Ḥanafī and Ibn Shurayḥ praised God and extolled Him, and then he said:

> Now, al-Mukhtār wishes to revolt and we have given him the oath of allegiance, but we do not know whether Ibn al-Ḥanafiyyah sent him to us or not. Let us go to Ibn al-Ḥanafiyyah and inform him of what al-Mukhtār has come to us with, of what he is summoning us to. If he says it is permissible to follow al-Mukhtār, we will do so, but, if he forbids it, we will keep away from him. By God, nothing of this world must be preferred by us to the safety of our religion.

They answered him, "God has guided you. You are right and correct. Lead us off if you wish." And they all agreed to set out on that day and did so, joining Ibn al-Ḥanafiyyah, with ‘Abd al-Raḥmān b. Shurayḥ as their leader [imām]. When they came to him, Ibn al-Ḥanafiyyah asked them about the circumstances of the people, and they told him about their state and what they were doing.

According to Abū Mikhnaf—Khalīfah b. Warqā'—al-Aswad b. Jarād al-Kindī: We said to Ibn al-Ḥanafiyyah, "We need to ask you something." "Is it a secret or a public thing?" he asked. "Indeed, no, it is a secret" we said. He replied, "Do not rush, then." We waited a short while and then he moved off to one side and called us, and we stood before him. ‘Abd al-Raḥmān b. Shurayḥ began and spoke. He praised God and extolled Him, and then he said:

> Now, you are a family which God has singled out for virtue and ennobled with prophethood. He has made recognition of your legitimacy as leaders of this community a grave matter, and only those whose reason has been duped and whose share (in the hereafter) has been diminished are ignorant of your rights. You have been afflicted by (the killing of) Ḥusayn, may God have mercy on him, an affliction most sore, by which He has singled you out and by which the Muslims were enveloped.[633] Al-Mukhtār b. Abī ‘Ubayd has come to

---

633. Cf. the reading of the Cairo text.

us claiming he has come from you, and has summoned us to the Book of God and the Sunnah of His Prophet, seeking vengeance for the blood of the Family, and protection of the weak. We have given him the oath of allegiance on those terms. But then we considered that we should come to you and tell you what he has summoned us to and charged us with. If you tell us to follow him, we will do so, and, if you forbid us to join him, we will keep clear of him.

[607]

Then we all spoke one by one as our companion had spoken, and Ibn al-Ḥanafiyyah listened to us until, when we had finished, he praised God and extolled Him, prayed for the Prophet, and then said:

Now, concerning what you have said about the way God has singled us out in merit, "God imparts it to whomever He wishes, for God is possessed of great merit."[634] God be praised! And as for what you said about our affliction with the killing of Ḥusayn, that was ordained by Divine Wisdom;[635] it was an apocalyptic catastrophe [malḥamah] foreordained for him, it was an honor which God granted him by which the standing in the hereafter of a people who were with him has been exalted while others have been cast down. "God's command is carried out and God's command is preordained!"[636] Regarding what you have mentioned about the summons of he who has summoned you to seek vengeance for our blood, by God, I want God to aid us against our enemies by means of any of His creatures He wishes. This is what I say and I ask God's forgiveness for me and for you.

We left him, and we were saying, "He has given us permission. He has said, 'I want God to aid us against our enemies by means of any of His creatures He wishes.' If he had disapproved, he would have said, 'Do not do it!' "

---

634. Cf. Qur'ān, 3:66–7, 57:21, 29, 62:4.
635. Ar. al-dhikr al-ḥakīm, often an epithet for the Qur'ān.
636. Cf. Qur'ān, 33:37–8.

We went back and some of the Party, those of our brethren we had told of our departure and apprised of our feelings and who shared our views, were awaiting our return. Al-Mukhtār had heard about our departure and it troubled him, for he feared that we would bring him an order which would cause [608] the Party to abandon him. He had wanted to bring them out in revolt before we got back, but that was not possible for him. He had been saying, "A few of you have wavered, vacillated and been disappointed. If they get what they want, they will draw near and repent, but, if they fail, are afraid, hinder and are dispelled, they will perish and fail."

Within a month or so, the party arrived back on their camels and went in to al-Mukhtār before going in to their stopping place. He asked them, "What is the news where you have come from? You have been tested and you have wavered." They answered, "We were told to help you!" Al-Mukhtār said, "God is most great! I am Abū Isḥāq! Assemble the Party before me!" Those who were at hand were assembled and he said, "Oh people of the Party, a group of you wanted to learn confirmation of what I have brought. They went to the *imām* of guidance, the acceptable noble one, the son of a better than Ṭashy and Mashy[637] except for the Prophet, the chosen one. They asked him about that with which I came to you and he told them that I am his *wazīr* and his helper, his messenger and his friend, and he ordered you to follow and obey me in that to which I summon you concerning fighting against the profaners of God's law and seeking vengeance for the blood of the chosen ones of the family of your Prophet."

ᶜAbd al-Raḥmān b. Shurayḥ then rose to his feet, praised God and extolled Him, and said, "Now, Oh people of the Party, we wanted to obtain verification for ourselves in particular and for all of our brethren in general. We went to the rightly guided one [*al-mahdī*],[638] the son of ᶜAlī, and we questioned him about this war of ours and about that to which al-Mukhtār summons us, and he told us to help him and assist

---

637. The meaning of this phrase, if it has one, is very obscure (see *Gloss.* s.v. *ṭashy*).
638. See above, n. 395.

him and to respond to that to which he summoned us. We
have returned with light spirits and glad hearts, from which
God has driven all doubt, distaste and vacillation, and our
minds are settled on fighting against our enemies. Let those   [609]
of you who are here tell those of you who are absent about
that! And prepare and make ready!"

He sat down while we got to our feet one after the other
and spoke in the same vein. And the Party united around al-
Mukhtār and was favorably disposed to him.

According to Abū Mikhnaf—Numayr b. Waᶜlah and (al-
Ḍaḥḥāk b. ᶜAbdallāh) al-Mashriqī—ᶜĀmir al-Shaᶜbī:[639] My father and I were the first to respond to al-Mukhtār.

When his plans had been laid and the time for his revolt
drew near, Aḥmar b. Shumayṭ, Yazīd b. Anas, ᶜAbdallāh b.
Kāmil and ᶜAbdallāh b. Shaddād said to him, "The notables
[ashrāf] of al-Kūfah have decided to side with Ibn Muṭīᶜ in
opposing you, but, if we agree that Ibrāhīm Ibn al-Ashtar[640]
should have our command, we might hope, with God's permission, for more strength against our enemies and that those
who oppose us will not harm us. He is a valiant young man
and the son of a noble and renowned man, and his clan is
mighty and numerous." Al-Mukhtār answered them, "Go to
him and summon him, and tell him what we are commanded
in seeking vengeance for the blood of al-Ḥusayn and his
family."

Al-Shaᶜbī: They went off to Ibn al-Ashtar, and my father
and I with them. Yazīd b. Anas spoke for them and said, "We
have come to you about something we wish to put before
you and call you to. If you accept it, it will be beneficial for
you; if you reject it, then we have brought you sincere advice
about it and we should like you to keep it secret." Ibrāhīm
Ibn al-Ashtar answered them, "For someone like me, there
cannot worry him either evil aimed at him, or slander directed
at him, or calumny against him by the people seeking favor
with those in authority over him. Those are only little things

---

639. A famous Kūfan traditionist and jurist (d. *ca.* 104/722); see *EI¹*, s.v.
640. Son of a leading supporter of ᶜAlī, and leader of Madhḥij in al-Kūfah
(see *EI²*, s.v. Ibrāhīm b. Mālik).

of insubstantial importance." Yazīd said to him, "All we are summoning you to is the undertaking upon which the opinions of the assembly of the Party have agreed: to the Book of God and the Sunnah of His Prophet, and to seeking vengeance for the blood of the Family, fighting against the violators of God's law, and defense of the weak."

[610]

Then Aḥmar b. Shumayṭ spoke, saying to him, "I am a sincere adviser to you and desirous of your prosperity. Your father, who was a sayyid, has died, but in you there is a successor to him, if you protect the rights of God. We have summoned you to an undertaking and, if you respond to us, the position of your father among the people will revert to you and you will restore something of it which has passed away. Only a small effort is enough for someone like you to reach the utmost goal. The foundations have already been laid for you." Aḥmar strove in his arguments, and all of the group approached Ibn al-Ashtar, appealing to him to join their undertaking and inciting him to it.

He said to them, "I have decided to respond to that to which you summon me regarding seeking vengeance for the blood of al-Ḥusayn and his family, on the condition that you give me charge over the business." They answered, "You are worthy of that, but there is no way we can agree to it, for this al-Mukhtār has come to us from the *mahdī*, and he is his messenger and charged with commanding the fighting. We have been told to obey him." Ibn al-Ashtar remained silent and did not answer them, and we left him and went back to al-Mukhtār, whom we told about the answer Ibn al-Ashtar had made to us.

Three days passed and then al-Mukhtār summoned about ten of the foremost of his supporters. (Al-Shaʿbī said that he and his father were among them.) He set off with us, going ahead of us and passing between the houses of al-Kūfah with us so that we did not know where he was aiming for, until finally he stopped at the door of Ibrāhīm Ibn al-Ashtar. We asked if we could enter upon him and Ibn al-Ashtar gave us permission. Cushions were thrown down for us and we sat on them, while al-Mukhtār sat with him on his couch.

Al-Mukhtār said:

Praise be to God, and I testify that there is no god but God! May He bless Muḥammad and grant him salvation! Now, this is a letter to you from the *mahdī*, Muḥammad the son of the Commander of the Faithful, the Legatee. Today he is the best of the people on earth and the son of the best of the people on the whole of the earth previously, apart from God's prophets and messengers. He asks you to help and support us. If you do, you will be happy; if you do not, then this letter will be a testimony against you and God will suffice the *mahdī* Muḥammad and his friends without any help from you.

Al-Shaᶜbī: Al-Mukhtār had handed the letter to me when he left his house, and when he had finished speaking now he said to me, "Give him the letter!" and I gave it to him. Ibn al-Ashtar called for a lamp, broke the seal and read it. This is what it said:

In the name of God, the Merciful and Compassionate. From Muḥammad the *mahdī* to Ibrāhīm b. Mālik al-Ashtar, greetings! I praise God, other than whom there is no god, before you. Now, I have sent to you my *wazīr*, my trustee, my choice one, with whom I am pleased for myself. I have ordered him to fight my enemies and seek vengeance for the blood of my family. With him arouse yourself, your clan and those who obey you. If you help me, respond to my call, and assist my *wazīr*, you will obtain merit with me in recompense as well as the reins of the horses and every raiding army and every garrison town, *minbar* and border land which you conquer between al-Kūfah and the farthest part of the land of the Syrians on fulfilling that in the covenant of God. If you do that, you will obtain by it the highest mark of honor with God; but, if you refuse, you will experience a destruction from which you can never ask to be released. Peace be with you!

When Ibrāhīm had finished reading the letter, he said, "Ibn al-Ḥanafiyyah has written to me, but whenever I wrote to him

[612]   previously he only wrote to me using his personal name and his patronym." Al-Mukhtār said to him, "Well, that was then but now is now." Ibrāhīm asked, "Who knows that this is a letter from Ibn al-Ḥanafiyyah to me?" and al-Mukhtār said, "Yazīd b. Anas and Aḥmar b. Shumayṭ and ʿAbdallāh b. Kāmil and a whole group of them." (Al-Shaʿbī said: But not my father and me!) And they said, "We testify that this is the letter of Muḥammad b. al-Ḥanafiyyah to you." At that, Ibrāhīm moved away from the center of the couch and caused al-Mukhtār to sit on it, saying to him, "Hold out your hand and I will give you the oath of allegiance and then he called for fruit, which we took, and he called for honeyed beverage which we drank. Afterward, we rose and Ibn al-Ashtar departed with us, riding with al-Mukhtār until he went in to his dwelling. Then when Ibrāhīm returned to his own dwelling, he took my hand and said, "Come back with me, Oh Shaʿbī."

I went back with him and we went on until we entered his dwelling, when he said, "Oh Shaʿbī, I have observed that neither you nor your father testified with the others. Do you think that they testified truthfully?" I answered him, "They testified as you saw, and they are the lords of the *qurrā*',[641] the elders of the garrison town and the champions of the Arabs. I do not think that men like them would speak other than truthfully." I said these words to him even though, by God, I was suspicious of their testimony. Nevertheless, the revolt was pleasing to me and I shared the view of the people and wished for the carrying through of that business, so I did not reveal to him what was in my mind. Then Ibn al-Ashtar said to me, "Write down for me their names for I do not know all of them." And he called for a sheet to write on and an inkwell and wrote on it:

> In the name of God, the Merciful and Compassionate, this is what there bore witness to al-Sā'ib b. Mālik al-Ashʿarī, Yazīd b. Anas al-Asadī, Aḥmar b. Shumayṭ al-

---

641. The derivation and meaning of this term have been debated. Traditionally it has been understood as referring to pietists among the early Muslims who memorized the text of the Qur'ān; but see *EI²*, s.v. Ḳurrā', and cf. J. Wansbrough, *The Sectarian Milieu*, 69.

Aḥmasī, Mālik b. ᶜAmr al-Nahdī[642] . . . until he had   [613]
completed the names of the whole group, and then he
wrote: They have testified that Muḥammad b. ᶜAlī b.
al-Ḥanafiyyah wrote to Ibrāhīm Ibn al-Ashtar asking
him to aid al-Mukhtār and assist him in fighting against
the profaners of God's law and in seeking vengeance
for the blood of the family. And there testified in favor
of these men who bore this witness Sharāḥīl b. ᶜAbd,
who is Abū ᶜĀmir al-Shaᶜbī the jurisprudent [al-fa-
qīh],[643] ᶜAbd al-Raḥmān b. ᶜAbdallāh al-Nakhaᶜī,[644] and
ᶜĀmir b. Sharāḥīl al-Shaᶜbī.

I said to him, "What will you do with this, may God have
mercy on you?" but he said, "Leave it be!" Then he summoned
his clan, his brethren and those who obeyed him, and he began
to visit al-Mukhtār frequently.

According to Hishām b. Muḥammad—Abū Mikhnaf—
Yaḥyā b. Abī ᶜĪsā al-Azdī: Ḥumayd b. Muslim al-Azdī[645] was
a confidant of Ibrāhīm Ibn al-Ashtar, who used to visit him
frequently and go around with him. Ibrāhīm used to go off
every evening at dusk, visit al-Mukhtār and stay with him
until the stars were out. They remained like that, organizing
their affairs until they had agreed they would revolt on Thursday night, the fourteenth of Rabīᶜ I, 66,[646] and they got their
party (shīᶜah) and those who responded to them ready for
that.

---

642. For the Banū Nahd b. Zayd, a Yemenī clan, see Caskel/Ibn Kalbī, II,
443.
643. The father of al-Shaᶜbī the narrator.
644. This seems to be the uterine brother of Ibrāhīm b. al-Ashtar, whose
clan within Madhḥij was the Banū Nakhaᶜ (see Ṭabarī, II, 709).
645. Text has al-Asadī, but presumably this is the same Ḥumayd b. Muslim
al-Azdī who is often cited as a source by Abū Mikhnaf.
646. Since much of the subsequent action takes place at night, the provision
of equivalent A.D. dates presents a problem. The day according to the Hijrī
(Muslim) calendar lasts for 24 hours from sunset to sunset. Hence expressions
such as laylat al-khamīs, which, translated literally, would mean "Thursday
night," may in fact indicate the previous night, in this case Wednesday–Thursday according to the A.D. calendar. Thursday 14 Rabīᶜ I 66 =
Thursday, October 19, 685, but, since the night is specified, it may be that
we should envisage the night of Wednesday, October 18.

About sunset, Ibrāhīm Ibn al-Ashtar arose and had the call to prayer made. Then he went forward and led us in the sunset prayer and afterward, after sunset, went out with us when you say, "Your brother or the wolf?"[647] He was heading for [614] al-Mukhtār and we proceeded, bearing our weapons. But Iyās b. Muḍārib had gone to ʿAbdallāh b. Muṭīʿ and told him, "Al-Mukhtār is going to come out against you tonight or tomorrow night." So Iyās came out with the men of the police force and sent his son Rashīd to al-Kunāsah[648] while he himself began to go around the market with the police force. Then Iyās b. Muḍārib went in to Ibn Muṭīʿ and said to him, "I have sent my son to al-Kunāsah, and if I had sent one of your men into every jabbānah in al-Kūfah, together with a band of loyal men, the mischief makers would fear to come out against you."

Ibn Muṭīʿ sent ʿAbd al-Raḥmān b. Saʿīd b. Qays[649] to the jabbānah of al-Sabīʿ,[650] and said to him, "Guard me against your people. I shall not be approached from your direction. Direct the affairs of the jabbānah to which I have sent you. Indeed, nothing untoward shall occur there. They are weak and feeble."

He sent Kaʿb b. Abī Kaʿb b. al-Khathʿamī[651] to the jabbānah of Bishr, Zaḥr b. Qays[652] to the jabbānah of Kindah, Shamir b. Dhī Jawshan[653] to the jabbānah of Sālim, ʿAbd al-Raḥmān b. Mikhnaf b. Sulaym[654] to the jabbānah of al-Sāʿidiyyīn, and Yazīd b. al-Ḥārith b. Ruwaym Abū Ḥawshab to the jabbānah

---

647. See p. 16 above.

648. Originally the rubbish heap, west of the town, it had become a district with an important market, (EI², s.v. al-Kūfa, 347a).

649. Of Hamdān (Rotter, Bürgerkrieg, index).

650. The jabbānahs are prominent features in the topography of al-Kūfah. Possibly originally tribal cemeteries (cf. the Jabbān of al-Baṣrah, n. 142 above), they became focuses of tribal life and may perhaps be envisaged as public squares (see EI², s.v. al-Kūfah, loc. cit.)

651. For the Banū Khathʿam, see EI², s.v.

652. Zaḥr b. Qays al-Juʿfī of Madhḥij (Rotter, Bürgerkrieg, index) is said to have carried the head of al-Ḥusayn to Yazīd for ʿUbaydallāh b. Ziyād (Ṭabarī, II, 374).

653. Of the Banū Kilāb (Qays), he was one of the leaders of the forces which killed al-Ḥusayn at Karbalā' (see Jafri, Shīʿa Islam, 187, 189–91).

654. One of the leaders of Azd in al-Kūfah.

of Murād. He charged each of them to supervise his own people for him, that he should not be approached from that direction, and that he control the affairs of the area he was sending him to. He also sent Shabath b. Ribʿī to al-Sabakhah,[655] telling him, "When you hear the shouts of the rebels, head towards them."

Those people had gone off on the Monday and occupied those *jabbānah*s. Ibrāhīm Ibn al-Ashtar left his halting place after sunset, intending to go to al-Mukhtār. He had heard that the *jabbānah*s were full of men and that the men of the police force had surrounded the market and the governor's residence. [615]

According to Abū Mikhnaf—Yaḥyā b. Abī ʿĪsā—Ḥumayd b. Muslim: On Tuesday (i.e. the night of Monday–Tuesday) night after sunset, I went out with Ibrāhīm from his residence and we passed ʿAmr b. Ḥurayth's house. With Ibn al-Ashtar, we were a detachment of about a hundred. We were wearing mail covered by *qabāʾ*s[656] and our swords. We had no weapons other than the swords on our shoulders and we had concealed the mail beneath our *qabāʾ*s. When we had gone by the house [*dār*] of Saʿīd b. Qays,[657] and we had passed it going toward the house of Usāmah,[658] we said, "Lead us to the house of Khālid b. ʿUrfuṭah,[659] then go on with us to Bajīlah, and let us go through their houses so we eventually emerge at the house of al-Mukhtār."

Ibrāhīm was a valiant and raw young man and had no objection to a confrontation with Ibn Muṭīʿ's men, and he said, "By God, I will go past the house of ʿAmr b. Ḥurayth toward the side of the governor's residence in the middle of the market. I will frighten our enemy by it and I will show them how insignificant we consider them." We took the di-

---

655. On the northeastern side of the town: see the map of Massignon, "Kūfa," *Opera minora*, III, 36.

656. For the *qabāʾ*, see n. 162 above.

657. Saʿīd b. Qays al-Hamdānī al-Sabīʿī took part in the conquest of Iraq and was one of the first settlers at al-Kūfah. Here and subsequently, *dār* may mean some sort of residential complex rather than merely "house."

658. Presumably the Companion of the Prophet, Usāmah b. Zayd b. Ḥārithah, to whom ʿUthmān is said to have granted estates near al-Kūfah.

659. Khālid b. ʿUrfuṭah al-ʿUdhrī, another participant in the conquest of Iraq who was given estates near al-Kūfah.

rection of Bāb al-Fīl by the house of Habbār.[660] Then he took the left-hand side of the house of ᶜAmr b. Ḥurayth so that, when we had passed it, we found Iyās b. Muḍārib with his police with weapons displayed. He said to us, "Who are you and what are you?" and Ibrāhīm answered him, "I am Ibrāhīm Ibn al-Ashtar." Ibn Muḍārib said to him, "What is this troop with you and what do you want? By God, you are intent on mischief and I have heard that you come this way every evening. I will not let you pass before I have been with you to the governor and he makes up his mind about you." But Ibrāhīm said, "Damned bastard![661] Get out of our way!" He replied, "Never! By God, I will not."

[616]   With Iyās b. Muḍārib there was a man of Hamdān called Abū Qaṭan, who had had authority in the police force and they respected him and liked him. He was a confidant of Ibn al-Ashtar, who said to him, "Oh Abū Qaṭan, draw close to me." Abū Qaṭan had a long spear of his with him, and he came close with the spear, thinking that Ibn al-Ashtar wanted him to intercede for him with Ibn al-Muḍārib so that he would let them go on. But Ibrāhīm said, seizing the spear from him, "This spear of yours is very long!" and he attacked Ibn Muḍārib with it, stabbing him in the gullet [fī thughrat naḥrihi] and bringing him to the ground. He said to one of his men, "Get down and cut off his head!" He did so and Ibn Muḍārib's men scattered and fled back to Ibn Muṭīᶜ. Then Ibn Muṭīᶜ sent Iyās b. Muḍārib's son, Rāshid b. Iyās, to command the police force in place of his father, and he sent Suwayd b. ᶜAbd al-Raḥmān al-Minqarī, the father of Qaᶜqāᶜ b. Suwayd,[662] to al-Kunāsah in place of Rāshid b. Iyās on that night.

Ibrāhīm Ibn al-Ashtar came to al-Mukhtār on Wednesday night (i.e. the night of Tuesday–Wednesday) and went in to him. He said to al-Mukhtār, "We have prepared the revolt for tomorrow, Thursday night (i.e. the night of Wednesday–Thursday), but something has happened which makes it

---

660. Read "the house of Ibn Habbār"; Ibn Habbār was also given estates by ᶜUthmān (Ṭabarī, I, 2376).

661. See Gloss., s.v. ghayr for the form of this curse.

662. Crone, Slaves, 139.

inevitable that we begin the revolt tonight." Al-Mukhtār asked, "What is it?" and Ibn al-Ashtar said, "Iyās b. Muḍārib intercepted me on the road, aiming to detain me, or so he claimed. But I killed him and that is his head with my men at the gate." Al-Mukhtār said, "God has proclaimed good news to you! This is a propitious omen and, God willing, the first of our conquests." Then he said, "Arise, Oh Saʿīd b. Munqidh, and kindle the fires among the brush piles and show them to the Muslims. And you, Oh ʿAbdallāh b. Shaddād, arise and call out, 'Oh Manṣūr! Deal death!'[663] And you, Oh Sufyān b. Layl,[664] and you, Oh Qudāmah b. Mālik, arise and cry, 'Vengeance for al-Ḥusayn!' " Then he said, "Bring me my armor and my weapons!" They were brought and he began to don his weapons, saying:

A fair woman, a beauty at the camp's remains,   [617]
With cheeks that are lucid and a firm backside, knows
    that on the day of fear, I shall be a bold champion!

Then Ibrāhīm Ibn al-Ashtar said to al-Mukhtār, "Those leaders whom Ibn Muṭīʿ stationed in the *jabbānah*s are preventing our brethren from joining us and are harassing them. If I were to go out with those of my men who are with me so I could reach my people, and all of my people who have given me the oath of allegiance could join me; and if I went with them around the districts of al-Kūfah proclaiming our slogan and those who wanted to join our revolt came out to me, and those of the people who could get to you; and if you kept those who got to you with those who are already with you and did not disperse them; then, if you are taken by surprise and attacked, you would have with you people who could defend you whilst I, if I had finished this task, could hasten to join you with horse and footsoldiers." Al-Mukhtār

---

663. This battle cry, subsequently used by the Hāshimiyyah, was allegedly used by the Prophet, (M. Sharon, *Black Banners from the East*, 176, n. 70); Lewis, "The regnal titles of the early ʿAbbāsids," 16ff., argues that the messianic title al-Manṣūr (designating the forerunner rather than the Messiah himself) generally had a South Arabian connotation; see too, Goldziher, "Pinehas–Manṣûr," *ZDMG*, LVI (1902), 411–2.

664. This seems to be the only reference to him in Ṭabarī's *History*.

said, "In that case, hurry and make sure that you do not go to their governor to fight him, and do not fight anybody so long as you are able to avoid it. Remember what I have charged you with, unless anyone attacks you first."

Ibrāhīm b. al-Ashtar, with the detachment with which he had come, left al-Mukhtār and went to his own people. Most of those who had given him the oath of allegiance and responded to him joined him. Then he went with them about the lanes of al-Kūfah for a large part of the night, all the time keeping clear of the lanes where the enemy commanders were, and going toward those who had with them the groups which Ibn Muṭīᶜ had stationed in the *jabbānah*s and the debouchments of important roads, until he came to the mosque of the Sakūn. Some of the horsemen of Zahr b. Qays al-Juᶜfī, who had no commander and no one in authority over them, rushed at him, and Ibrāhīm Ibn al-Ashtar and his men fought hard against them and defeated them until they entered the *jabbānah* of Kindah. Ibrāhīm said, "Who is in charge of the horsemen in the *jabbānah* of Kindah?" (He and his men pressed them hard, saying while doing so, "Oh God, you know that we are zealous for the family of your Prophet and seek vengeance for them. Give us aid against them and fulfill for us everything we ask for," until he and his men reached them, got in among them and defeated them.) He was told, "Zahr b. Qays," and he said, "Let us withdraw from them!" and they rode off in confusion. Whenever they came to an alley, a group of them went in and (the rest of them) left, continuing on.[665]

[618]

Then Ibrāhīm went off, continuing until he came to the *jabbānah* of Uthayr where he halted for a long time and called to his men with their battle cry. Suwayd b. ᶜAbd al-Raḥmān al-Minqarī heard where they were, and hoped he would fall on them and thus win the favor of Ibn Muṭīᶜ. Ibn al-Ashtar knew nothing until they were there in the *jabbānah* with him, but when he saw that, he called to his men, "Oh cohort [*shurṭah*] of God, dismount! You are more deserving of God's help than these evil doers who have waded in the blood of

---

665. I suspect the text is disordered here.

the family of the Messenger of God." They dismounted, and Ibrāhīm fought hard against them and attacked them until he had driven them from the ṣaḥrā'.[666]

Suwayd's men turned in flight, jostling one another in confusion and blaming each other, and one of them said, "This is indeed something intended. They do not send any group to us but (Ibn al-Ashtar's men) defeat them."

They continued routing them until they had driven them into al-Kunāsah. Ibrāhīm's men said to him, "Pursue them and take advantage of the fear which has infected them. God knows whom we are calling the people to support and what we seek, and He knows whom they are calling the people to support and what they seek." But Ibrāhīm refused and said, "Come with me to our master so that God may give him security through us against his being left alone, that we may be apprised of his affairs and he too may know of our concern, and that he and his men may add strength and ardor to that which they have already. Furthermore, I do not feel sure he may not have been attacked."

[619]

Ibrāhīm and his men proceeded, and came to the mosque of al-Ashᶜath,[667] where he halted for a short time. Then he went on until he came to the house of al-Mukhtār, where he found raised voices and the men engaged in battle. Shabath b. Ribᶜī had come from al-Sabakhah and al-Mukhtār had detailed Yazīd b. Anas to withstand him, and Ḥajjār b. Abjar al-ᶜIjlī[668] had come and al-Mukhtār had stationed Aḥmar b. Shumayṭ against him. The people were fighting when Ibrāhīm came from the direction of the governor's residence [al-qaṣr]. Ḥajjār and his men heard that Ibrāhīm had come against them from their rear, and they scattered before he could reach them and fled into the lanes and alleys.

Qays b. Ṭahfah[669] came with about a hundred men of the Banū Nahd of those who supported al-Mukhtār and attacked

---

666. A number of ṣaḥrā's feature in the topography of al-Kūfah; their function and relationship to the jabbānahs is not clear (see EI², s.v. Kūfa).

667. Al-Ashᶜath b. Qays had been the chief of Kindah in al-Kūfah (see EI², s.v. al-Ashᶜath).

668. This notable of Bakr b. Wā'il had been among those who testified against Ḥujr b. ᶜAdī (Ṭabarī, II, 133).

669. According to the list in Ansāb, V, 219, this Qays had been one of the guarantors demanded for al-Mukhtār by ᶜAbdallāh b. Yazīd and Ibrāhīm b. Muḥammad b. Ṭalḥah. For the Banū Nahd, see n. 642 above.

Shabath b. Rib°ī, who was fighting against Yazīd b. Anas. (Yazīd) cleared the road for (Qays and his men) so they were able to join forces, and then Shabath b. Rib°ī abandoned the lane to them and went off and joined Ibn Muṭī°.

He said to Ibn Muṭī°, "Send for the commanders of the squares and tell them to come to you, and assemble all your men and then rush upon this mob and fight them. Send somebody you trust against them, and may fighting them be enough, for their movement has strengthened and al-Mukhtār has come out in revolt and shown himself and their movement has been entrusted to him." When al-Mukhtār heard of the advice which Shabath b. Rib°ī had given to Ibn Muṭī°, he went forth with a group of his men and halted behind Dayr Hind in the vicinity of the garden of Zā'idah[670] in al-Sabakhah.

Abū °Uthmān al-Nahdī[671] went forth and gave the call among Shākir,[672] who were gathered together in their houses for fear of showing themselves in the *maydān* because of Ka°b b. Abī Ka°b al-Khath°amī's proximity to them. Ka°b was in the *jab-* [620] *bānah* of Bishr. When he heard Shākir were coming out, he came forward and established himself in the *maydān*, barring the lanes and roads against them.

When Abū °Uthmān al-Nahdī came against (Ka°b and his men) with a group of his companions, he called out, "Revenge for al-Ḥusayn! Oh Manṣūr, deal death! Oh you clan of the rightly-guided, verily, the one given authority by the family of Muḥammad, and their *wazīr*, has come forth and stopped at Dayr Hind. He has sent me to you as a summoner and bringer of good tidings. Come out to join him, may God have mercy on you!" They came out of the houses, calling to one another, "Revenge for al-Ḥusayn!" and then attacked Ka°b b. Abī Ka°b until he opened the road for them, and they went to al-Mukhtār and waited with him in his camp.

°Abdallāh b. Qurād al-Khath°amī came forth with a group of about two hundred of Khath°am and joined al-Mukhtār and waited with him in his camp. Ka°b b. Abī Ka°b had opposed

---

670. Bustān Zā'idah is mentioned at II, 960, in connection with the entry of Shabīb into al-Kūfah.
671. This man is often cited as a traditionist; see the general index.
672. The Banū Shākir b. Rabī°ah of Hamdān (Caskel/Ibn Kalbī, II, 524).

him and drawn up battle lines against him, but when he recognized them and saw they were people of his own tribe, he let them pass and did not fight them.

Shibām came forth in the latter part of the night and they agreed to go to the *jabbānah* of Murād. When ᶜAbd al-Raḥmān b. Saᶜīd b. Qays heard that, he sent to them, saying, "If you wish to join al-Mukhtār, do not pass over the *jabbānah* of al-Sabīᶜ," and they joined al-Mukhtār. Of the 12,000 who had given him the oath of allegiance, 3,800 came to al-Mukhtār and joined with him before dawn broke. By morning, he had completed his preparations.

According to Abū Mikhnaf—(al-Ḥārith b. Kaᶜb) al-Wālibī: I and Ḥumayd b. Muslim and al-Nuᶜmān b. Abī al-Jaᶜd[673] went out to join al-Mukhtār on the night he began his revolt. We came to him in his house and went out with him where his army was. And, by God, dawn had not broken before he had completed his preparations. He came forward next morning [621] and led us in the prayer of daybreak while it was still dark. Then he recited (the Koranic surahs) "Those who draw out" and "He frowned and turned around,"[674] and we never heard an *imām* leading a people in prayer with a clearer tone than he.

According to Abū Mikhnaf—Ḥaṣīrah b. ᶜAbdallāh: Ibn Muṭīᶜ sent to the men of the *jabbānah*s and told them to gather in the mosque, and he said to Rāshid b. Iyās b. Muḍārib, "Call to the men and let them go to the mosque!" The crier proclaimed, "Anybody who is not present in the mosque tonight will be held liable," and the men all went to the mosque. When they had gathered, Ibn Muṭīᶜ sent Shabath b. Ribᶜī with about 3,000 men against al-Mukhtār, and he sent Rāshid b. Iyās with 4,000 of the men of the police force.

According to Abū Mikhnaf—Abū al-Ṣalt al-Taymī—Abū Saᶜīd al-Ṣayqal:[675] When al-Mukhtār had conducted the morn-

---

673. I am unable to identify al-Nuᶜman, cf. p. 210 below; for identification of al-Wālibī, see p. 208 below.

674. Qur'ān, sūrahs 79, 80 (both deal with eschatology and divine punishment of evil-doers in forceful and martial language).

675. Previously (I, 3423, 3429), this narrator has appeared as Abū Saᶜīd al-ᶜUqaylī; see pp. 207f. below for his status as a mawlā.

ing prayer and turned away, we heard voices raised somewhere between the Banū Sulaym and the lane of the Barīd.[676] Al-Mukhtār said, "Who will get us information about those; what are they?" and I said to him, "I will, may God preserve you!" Al-Mukhtār said, "In that case, throw down your sword and hurry so you can get in among them as if you were an onlooker, and then bring me news about them."

So I did that, and when I drew near them I saw that their muezzin was summoning to prayer. I came and drew nearer to them and I saw Shabath b. Ribᶜī. With him was a powerful troop of horse commanded by Shaybān b. Ḥurayth al-Ḍabbī,[677] while Shabath himself was among the footmen, of whom there was a large number. When their muezzin had called to prayer, Shabath went forward and conducted his men in the ritual prayer, reciting, "When the earth trembles with her quaking!"[678] I said to myself, "Indeed, by God, I hope that God will cause you to tremble!" And he recited, "By the chargers snorting!"[679] Some of his companions said to him, "If only you would recite two sūrahs longer than these two!" but Shabath replied, "You see the Daylamī's have pitched camp in your courtyard and yet you say, 'If only you would read sūrat al-Baqarah and Āl ᶜImrān!'"[680] There were three thousand of them.

[622]

I went on quickly and got back to al-Mukhtār and gave him the news about Shabath and his men. At the time I came to him, there came with me Siᶜr b. Abī Siᶜr al-Ḥanafī galloping from the direction of the Banū Murād. He was one of those who had given the oath of allegiance to al-Mukhtār, but had not been able to join him on the night when he began his revolt for fear of the guard. But in the morning he came on his horse and passed the square of Murād where Rāshid b. Iyās was. They said to him, "Stop, you![681] Who are you?" but

---

676. Massignon, "Kūfa," does not refer to this *sikkah*.
677. This seems to be the only appearance of this al-Ḍabbī.
678. Qur'ān, sūrah 99.
679. Qur'ān, sūrah 100.
680. "Daylamīs" (literally, men from Daylām, the province southwest of the Caspian) is often metaphoric for "fiends" (cf. "Turks," "Abyssinians"). Sūrat al-Baqarah and sūrat Āl ᶜImrān are the two longest sūrahs in the Qur'ān.
681. See, for this sense of *kamā anta*, *Gloss.*, s.v. *ka*.

he outpaced them and got to Mukhtār, to whom he reported on Rāshid while I reported on Shabath.

Al-Mukhtār dispatched Ibrāhīm Ibn al-Ashtar toward Rāshid b. Iyās with 900 men (it is also said: 600 horsemen and 600 footmen), and he sent Nuʿaym b. Hubayrah,[682] the brother of Maṣqalah b. Hubayrah, with 300 horsemen and 600 footmen. He told them both, "Push on until you confront your enemy. When you meet them, dismount among the footmen, force the issue and attack them on foot, but do not leave yourselves open to them for they outnumber you, and do not come back to me until you have won the victory or been slain." Ibrāhīm set forth to meet Rāshid while al-Mukhtār sent Yazīd b. Anas forward ahead of him to the place of Shabath's mosque with 900 men. Nuʿaym b. Hubayrah set off toward Shabath.

According to Abū Mikhnaf—Abū Saʿīd al-Ṣayqal: I was one of those who set out with Nuʿaym b. Hubayrah against Sha-bath, and Siʿr b. Abī Siʿr al-Ḥanafī was with me. When we came against him, we attacked fiercely. Nuʿaym b. Hubayrah put Siʿr b. Abī Siʿr al-Ḥanafī in charge of the cavalry while he himself marched with the footsoldiers, and he fought them until the sun had risen and it was light. We fought them until we had driven them into their houses, and then Shabath b. Ribʿī called out to them, "Oh warriors of wickedness! Wretched fighters for the truth are you! Do you flee from your slaves!" A group of them rallied to him and fought hard against us, and we were scattered and put to flight. Nuʿaym b. Hubayrah stood resolute and patient and was killed, and Siʿr stood with him and was made captive. I too was taken captive together with Khulayd the mawlā of Ḥassān b. Maḥdūj.[683]

Shabath said to Khulayd, who was comely and physically huge, "Who are you?" and he replied, "Khulayd the mawlā of Ḥassān b. Maḥdūj al-Dhuhlī." Shabath said to him, "Oh son of a fishwife! You have given up the selling of fish at al-Kunāsah, and the recompense for him who freed you is that

[623]

---

682. Of the Banū Shaybān (Bakr b. Wā'il), he has a reputation as a "Shīʿī" (Ṭabarī, I, 3441) while his brother, Maṣqalah, who had been governor for ʿAlī over Ardashīr Khurrah, was one of the witnesses against Ḥujr b. ʿAdī (ibid., I, 3439ff., II, 133).
683. For the name, see *Add. et emend.*

you assail him with your sword to flail at his shoulders! Cut off his head!" And he was slain. He saw Siʿr al-Ḥanafī and recognized him, and he said to him, "(Are you a) brother of the Banū Ḥanīfah?" Siʿr replied, "Yes!" Shabath said to him, "Woe unto you! What did you want in following this Saba'iyyah?[684] God has abhorred your point of view! Leave that one alone, men!"

I said to myself, "He killed the mawlā but left the Arab. By God, if he knows I am a mawlā, he will kill me!" When I was arraigned before him, therefore, he said, "Who are you?" and I answered, "I am from the Banū Taym Allāh." "Are you an Arab or a mawlā?" he asked. I replied, "Indeed no, I am an Arab from the family of Ziyād b. Khaṣafah."[685] "Good, good," he said, "you have mentioned the worthy noble man. Go and join your people." So I went on my way until I reached the Ḥamrā',[686] and I had shown ardor in the fighting against the enemy.

[624]

Then I came to al-Mukhtār and said to myself, "By God, surely I will go to my companions and assist them myself. May God consider a life apart from them as base!" I went to them, Siʿr al-Ḥanafī having already reached them before me. The horsemen of Shabath advanced against Mukhtār and news of the killing of Nuʿaym b. Hubayrah reached him, resulting in great concern among al-Mukhtār's men. I drew close to al-Mukhtār and informed him of what had happened to me, but he said, "Hush! This is not the place for talk."

Shabath came on until he had encircled al-Mukhtār and Yazīd b. Anas, and Ibn Muṭīʿ sent Yazīd b. al-Ḥārith b. Ruwaym with two thousand men from the direction of the lane of the butcher Jarīr, and they waited at the entrances to these lanes. Al-Mukhtār put Yazīd b. Anas in charge of his cavalry while he himself went out in the infantry.

According to Abū Mikhnaf—al-Ḥārith b. Kaʿb al-Wālibī (Wālibah of the Azd): The horsemen of Shabath b. Ribʿī at-

---

684. A polemical name for the supporters of ʿAlī (see *EI²*, s.v. ʿAbd Allāh b. Saba').

685. Or Ziyādah b. Khaṣafah al-Taymī; see Caskel/Ibn al-Kalbī, II, 608.

686. Descendants of the Persian infantry who had joined the Arabs at the time of the conquest of Iraq.

tacked us twice, but no man of us moved from where he was. Yazīd b. Anas addressed us:

> Oh group of the Party [yā maʿshar al-shīʿah], you have been put to the slaughter, your hands and feet have been cut off, your eyes have been gouged out, and you have been hung on the trunks of palm trees in your love for the family of your Prophet. But you were remaining in your houses and in submission to your enemies. What do you think these people will do if they defeat you today? In that case, by God, they will not leave of you an eye to squint and, indeed, they will slaughter you patiently enduring. Indeed, you may expect of them a fate worse than death insofar as your offspring, your wives and your properties are concerned. By God, the only things which will save you from it will be uprighteousness, patience and endurance, accurate thrusting in their eyes, and effective blows[687] on their heads. Make ready to fight and prepare to attack. When I wave my banner twice, attack!

So we prepared and made ready, we rested on our knees and   [625]
awaited his order.

According to Abū Mikhnaf—Fuḍayl b. Khadīj al-Kindī: When Ibrāhīm b. al-Ashtar approached Rāshid b. Iyās, he went forward and came upon him in (the jabbānah of) Murād. He was surprised to see Rāshid had 4,000 men with him, but Ibrāhīm said to his men, "Do not let their number alarm you! By God, many a time one man is better than ten 'and many a time a band small in number has defeated a more numerous band with God's permission, and God is with the patiently enduring.' "[688] Then he said, "Oh Khuzaymah b. Naṣr,[689] go against them with the cavalry!" He dismounted and went on foot with the foot soldiers. His banner was with Muzāḥim b. Ṭufayl and Ibrāhīm started saying to him, "Go forward with your banner! Straight ahead, straight ahead!" The men did

---

687. See *Add. et emend.* and *Gloss.*, s.v. *dirāk.*
688. Qurʾān, 2:250.
689. Of the Banū ʿAbs b. Baghid of Ghaṭafān/Qays (Caskel/Ibn al-Kalbī, II, 135).

battle together and their fighting was fierce. Khuzaymah b. Naṣr al-ᶜAbsī caught sight of Rāshid b. Iyās, attacked and killed him. Then he called out, "I have killed Rāshid, by the Lord of the Kaᶜbah!" and Rāshid's men were put to flight.

After the killing of Rāshid, Ibrāhīm b. al-Ashtar, Khuzaymah b. Naṣr and those with them went toward al-Mukhtār, and Ibrāhīm sent al-Nuᶜmān b. Abī al-Jaᶜd to announce the good news of the success granted him and the killing of Rāshid. When the messenger informed al-Mukhtār's men they called out, "God is most great!" and they took heart, while Ibn Muṭīᶜ's men became discouraged.

Ibn Muṭīᶜ sent Ḥassān b. Fā'id b. Bukayr al-ᶜAbsī[690] with a powerful force of about 2,000 men, and he came on Ibrāhīm Ibn al-Ashtar a little above the (quarter of the) Ḥamrā', attempting to divert him from those of Ibn Muṭīᶜ's men in al-Sabakhah. Ibrāhīm sent Khuzaymah b. Naṣr forward against Ḥassān b. Fā'id with the cavalry, while he himself went on foot towards him wtih the infantry. He said, "By God, no sooner have we stabbed with a spear or struck with a sword then they have been put to flight."

[626]   Ḥassān b. Fā'id stayed behind in the rear guard to protect his men and Khuzaymah b. Naṣr attacked him. When he saw him, he recognized him and said to him, "Oh Ḥassān b. Fā'id, indeed, by God, if it were not for kinship, I know that I would seek with all my effort to kill you, but (now) flee!" But Ḥassān's horse stumbled with him and he fell. Khuzaymah said to him, "Bad luck, Oh Abū ᶜAbdallāh!" and the men rushed on him and surrounded him. He fought against them with his sword for a while, and Khuzaymah b. Naṣr called out to him, saying, "You have a safe conduct, Oh Abū ᶜAbdallāh. Do not kill yourself!" He went and stood over him and the men held back. Ibrāhīm came up and Khuzaymah b. Naṣr said to him, "This is my cousin, and I have given him safe conduct." Ibrāhīm said to him, "You have done well!" and Khuzaymah ordered that Ḥassān's horse be sought, and it was brought and he was mounted upon it. Khuzaymah then said, "Go and join your people!"

---

690. I.e., of the same tribe as Khuzaymah.

Ibrāhīm went forward toward al-Mukhtār, while Shabath surrounded al-Mukhtār and Yazīd b. Anas. When Yazīd b. al-Ḥārith (b. Ruwaym), who was guarding the lanes of al-Kūfah in the vicinity of al-Sabakhah, saw Ibrāhīm advancing against Shabath, he himself moved forward to prevent Ibrāhīm from attacking Shabath and his men. Ibrāhīm then dispatched a party of his men with Khuzaymah b. Naṣr, saying to him, "Protect us from Yazīd b. al-Ḥārith," while he went on with the rest of his men against Shabath b. Ribʿī.

According to Abū Mikhnaf—al-Ḥārith b. Kaʿb: When Ibrāhīm approached us, we saw Shabath and his men slowly drawing back behind them, and, when Ibrāhīm got close to Shabath and his men, he attacked them and Yazīd b. Anas ordered us to attack them too. We did so, and they were thrown into disorder and had to withdraw into the houses of al-Kūfah. Khuzaymah b. Naṣr attacked Yazīd b. al-Ḥārith b. Ruwaym and defeated him, and they crowded together in the openings of the lanes. Yazīd b. al-Ḥārith had stationed bowmen at the openings of the lanes in front of the houses. Al-Mukhtār advanced against Yazīd b. al-Ḥārith in a body of men, and when al-Mukhtār's men reached the mouths of the lanes, these bowmen fired arrows at them and prevented them from entering al-Kūfah from that direction. Ibn Muṭīʿ's men then withdrew to him in defeat from al-Sabakhah, and he heard about the killing of Rāshid b. Iyās and his spirit was broken.[691]

According to Abū Mikhnaf—Yaḥyā b. Hāniʾ: ʿAmr b. al-Ḥajjāj al-Zubaydī[692] said to Ibn Muṭīʿ, "Do not lose heart and do not throw in your hand! Go out to the people, assign them against your enemy and attack them. Our people are numerous and all of them are with you, apart from this leader of error [ṭāghiyah], who has rebelled against the people, by God, shaming and destroying them. (I volunteer to be) the first to be assigned; detail a party to go with me and a party with someone else." So Ibn Muṭīʿ went out and stood among the people, praised God and extolled Him, and then said:

[627]

---

691. See *Gloss.*, s.v. *saqaṭa*.
692. One of those who bore witness against Ḥujr b. ʿAdī (Ṭabarī, II, 133; Caskel/Ibn al-Kalbī, II, 174); for the Banū Zubayd of Madhḥij, see Caskel/Ibn al-Kalbī, II, 608.

> Oh people, one of the most surprising things is your lack of resolution before a gang fewer in number than you, wicked in religion, misguided and misguiding. Go out against them, defend your women against them, fight them to protect your garrison town, and defend your income from the conquered lands [fay'akum] against them. If you do not, by God, those who have no right to it will surely share in your fay'. By God, I have heard that there are among them 500 of your manumitted slaves under a commander who is one of them. If they increase in number it can only mean the passing away of your power and authority and the alteration of your religion.

Then he got down. Yazīd b. al-Ḥārith prevented them from entering al-Kūfah.[693] Al-Mukhtār went on from al-Sabakhah and won control over the *jabbānah*, and then he went up to the houses of Muzaynah,[694] and instilled zeal and fire in them. He rested by their mosque and their houses, which were detached and separate from the houses of the (other) Kūfans, and they brought water for him and provided drink for his men. Al-Mukhtār, however, refused to drink. His men thought [628] he was fasting, and Aḥmar b. Hudayj of Hamdān[695] said to Ibn Kāmil, "Do you think the commander is fasting?" He replied, "Yes, he is fasting." Aḥmar said to him, "If he broke his fast today, it would make him stronger." Ibn Kāmil answered, "He is immune from error [maᶜṣūm],[696] and he knows best what he is doing." Aḥmar said, "What you say is true, and I ask for God's pardon."

Al-Mukhtār said, "This is an excellent place for fighting." Ibrāhīm b. al-Ashtar said to him, "God has defeated them and broken them, and instilled fear into their hearts. You dismount here and lead us forward. By God, there is nobody outside

---

693. Presumably this refers to the central area, the fighting so far having been in outlying areas.

694. On the north of the town; Massignon, "Kūfa," in *Opera Minora*, III, 36.

695. One of the Fā'ishiyyūn of Hamdān (Ṭabarī, II, 666).

696. On this concept, see *EI²*, s.v. ᶜIṣma, but cf. *Gloss.*, s.v., which suggests the more neutral *sanctus* ("blameless?").

the governor's residence [al-qaṣr] to resist and there will be almost no opposition."697 Al-Mukhtār said, "Let every shaykh who lacks strength and every sick man rest here. Put down your burdens and your equipment so you can set out against our enemy." The did that, and al-Mukhtār appointed Abū ᶜUthmān al-Nahdī to remain behind in charge of them. Ibrāhīm Ibn al-Ashtar went on ahead of him and he got his men ready in the condition in which they had been in al-Sabakhah.

ᶜAbdallāh b. Muṭīᶜ sent ᶜAmr b. al-Ḥajjāj with 2,000 men, and he came out against Ibrāhīm b. al-Ashtar from the lane of the Thawriyyūn.698 Al-Mukhtār sent to Ibrāhīm, "Contain him but do not remain with him!" So Ibrāhīm closed him up, and al-Mukhtār summoned Yazīd b. Anas and told him to move out against ᶜAmr b. al-Ḥajjāj. Yazīd headed towards him while al-Mukhtār himself went off following Ibrāhīm. They proceeded together until al-Mukhtār came to the place of the oratory of Khālid b. ᶜAbdallāh,699 where he halted and ordered Ibrāhīm to go ahead until he entered al-Kūfah from the direction of al-Kunāsah. Ibrāhīm went on and came out to it from the lane of Ibn Muḥriz.700 Shamir b. Dhī al-Jawshan advanced with 2,000 men and al-Mukhtār sent against him Saᶜīd b. Munqidh al-Hamdānī, who engaged him in battle. Al-Mukhtār sent to Ibrāhīm, telling him, "Contain him and carry on ahead!" He proceeded until he came to the lane of Shabath, where he found Nawfal b. Musāḥiq b. ᶜAbdallāh b. Makhramah701 with about 2,000 men (or it is said 5,000, which is correct). Ibn Muṭīᶜ had ordered Suwayd b. ᶜAbd al-Raḥmān (to give the command) and (the latter) gave the summons, "Join Ibn Musāḥiq!" Ibn Muṭīᶜ himself left Shabath b. Ribᶜī behind in control of the governor's residence [al-qaṣr] and went out and halted at al-Kunāsah.

[629]

---

697. See *Gloss.*, s.v. *aḥad.*

698. For the Thawriyyūn of the Banū Hamdān, see Ṭabarī, I, 3348 (N.B. *not* the Banū Thawr who were part of the confederation of Ribāb).

699. Apparently a reference to the later governor of Iraq, Khālid b. ᶜAbdallāh al-Qasrī (724–38).

700. The index to the Cairo edition identifies him as al-ᶜAlā' b. ᶜAbd al-Raḥmān b. Muḥriz.

701. Of Quraysh (see Zubayrī, *Nasab Quraysh*, 427; Ibn Saᶜd, *Ṭabaqāt*, V, 179–80), Ibn Muṭīᶜ was his maternal uncle.

According to Abū Mikhnaf—Ḥaṣīrah b. ʿAbdallāh: I saw Ibn al-Ashtar when he went forward with his men. When he drew close to the enemy, he said to his men, "Dismount!" and they dismounted. He said, "Tether your horses close together and then advance against them on foot with sword drawn. Do not let it alarm you that it is said, 'Shabath b. Ribʿī has come against you, and the people of ʿUtaybah b. al-Nahhās,[702] and the people of al-Ashʿath, and the people of so-and-so, and the people of Yazīd b. al-Ḥārith!' " He named several of the leading families of the Kūfans and then he said, "If they (once) experience the heat of the swords, they will abandon Ibn Muṭīʿ like goats fleeing from a wolf."

I saw Ibn al-Ashtar and his men when they tethered their horses close together and when Ibn al-Ashtar took the hem of his *qabāʾ*, lifted it up and pushed it into a red belt made from the borders of *burdah* materials[703] which he had put on over his *qabāʾ*. He had covered up his armor with the *qabāʾ*. Then he said to his men, "Attack them, may my paternal and maternal uncles be a ransom for you!" And by God, it was not long before he had defeated them and they jostled one another in the mouth of the lane and crowded together. Ibn al-Ashtar reached Ibn Musāḥiq, seized the bridle of his mount, and lifted his sword against him. Ibn Musāḥiq said to him, "Oh Ibn al-Ashtar, I implore you by God! Do you seek vengeance from me? Is there any hatred between us?" And Ibn al-Ashtar let him go, and said to him, "Remember it!" Subsequently, Ibn Musāḥiq remembered what he owed to Ibn al-Ashtar. They started to advance until they reached al-Kunāsah on the enemy's heels. They penetrated the market and the mosque, and besieged Ibn Muṭīʿ for three days.

According to Abū Mikhnaf—al-Naḍr b. Ṣāliḥ: Ibn Muṭīʿ remained three days distributing meal to his men in the governor's residence where he was besieged. With him were the notables of the population, except for ʿAmr b. Ḥurayth, who

[630]

---

702. Of the Banū ʿIjl (Bakr b. Wāʾil), he had participated in the conquest of Iraq and governed Ḥulwān under ʿUthmān.

703. A *burdah* is a type of mantle; here the word seems to refer to a type of material rather than a garment (see *Gloss.*, s.v. and *EI²*, s.v. Libās, 734a).

went to his house and did not think it necessary to submit
to the siege. Then ᶜAmr betook himself off and settled outside
the town.

Al-Mukhtār came and pitched camp at the side of the market
and entrusted the siege of the governor's residence to Ibrāhīm
Ibn al-Ashtar, Yazīd b. Anas, and Aḥmar b. Shumayṭ. Ibn al-
Ashtar was next to the mosque and the gate of the governor's
residence [al-qaṣr], Yazīd b. Anas adjoined (the houses of) the
Banū Ḥudhayfah[704] and the lane of Dār al-Rumiyyīn,[705] while
Aḥmar b. Shumayṭ abutted the house of ᶜUmārah[706] and the
house of Abū Mūsā.[707]

When the siege became oppressive to Ibn Muṭīᶜ and his
companions, the notables put their arguments to him. Shabath
arose and said, "May God preserve the governor! Consider
your position and that of those with you. By God, they have
neither enough for you nor for themselves." Ibn Muṭīᶜ said,
"Come, all of you, and advise me of your views." Shabath
said, "We think you should obtain a safe-conduct from this
man for yourself and for us, and that you should leave and
not destroy yourself and those with you." Ibn Muṭīᶜ said, "By
God, I am reluctant to obtain a safe-conduct from him while
the authority of the Commander of the Faithful[708] is accepted
in the whole of the Ḥijāz and in the territory of al-Baṣrah."
Shabath said, "Then, leave and no one will know, and take   [631]
shelter in a dwelling in al-Kūfah with someone from whom
you can ask advice and in whom you trust. (Al-Mukhtār) will
not know where you are before you leave and join your lord."
Ibn Muṭīᶜ said to Asmā' b. Khārijah,[709] ᶜAbd al-Raḥmān b.
Mikhnaf, ᶜAbd al-Raḥmān b. Saᶜīd b. Qays, and the notables
of the Kūfans, "What do you think about this view which
Shabath has put to me?" They said, "We have no view other

---

704. I.e., Hudhayfah b. al-Yamān al-ᶜAbsī (?).
705. See Morony, *Iraq*, 267.
706. ᶜUmārah b. ᶜUqbah b. Abī Muᶜayṭ (of Quraysh) (*nazala 'l-Kūfah:* Zubayrī, *Nasab Quraysh*, 140) or ᶜUmārah b. Ruwaybah al-Tamīmī (Morony,
Iraq, 241)?
707. Abū Mūsā al-Ashᶜarī, a former governor of al-Kūfah.
708. I.e., Ibn al-Zubayr.
709. Of the Banū Fazārah (Qays), he was one of the witnesses against Ḥujr
b. ᶜAdī (Ṭabarī, II, 133).

than that which he has put to you." He replied, "Wait, then, until evening."

According to Abū Mikhnaf—Abū al-Mughallas al-Laythī: ᶜAbdallāh b. ᶜAbdallāh al-Laythī[710] was looking down on al-Mukhtār's men from the governor's residence in the evening, shouting insults at them. Mālik b. ᶜAmr Abū Nimrān al-Nahdī[711] fired an arrow at him and it scraped his throat, cutting a piece oḷ skin, so that he stumbled and fell. But then he got up and recovered. When he hit him, the Nahdī said, "Take that from Mālik, whoever acts thus!"

According to Abū Mikhnaf—al-Naḍr b. Ṣāliḥ—Ḥassān b. Fā'id b. Bukayr: When we got to the evening of the third day in the governor's residence, Ibn Muṭīᶜ called us, spoke of God as befits Him, prayed for His Prophet and said:

> Now, I know who they are, those of you who have done this, and I know they are merely the base ones among you, the ignorant, the lowly, and the mean, apart from one or two. The noble ones among you, and those of worth, have never stopped hearing, obeying, and profering sincere advice. I shall inform my lord of that and let him know of your obedience and your struggle [jihād] against his enemies until God took control of his affair. You know what the view was which you put to me. I think I should go forth now.

[632]

Shabath said to him, "May God bless you for a governor! You have refrained from taking our wealth, you have been generous to the noble ones among us, you have given good advice to your lord, and you have fulfilled your duties. By God, we would never part from you were it not that we have permission from you." He said, "May God bless you! A man takes the road wherever he wishes." Then he went in the direction of the road of the Rūmiyyūn until he reached the house of Abū Mūsā. He vacated the governor's residence, and his men opened the gate and said, "Oh Ibn al-Ashtar, do we

---

710. The Banū Layth of Kinānah; this seems to be Ṭabarī's only reference to him.

711. For the form of the name, see *Add. et emend.*, and see n. 642 above.

have safe-conduct?" He replied, "You have safe-conduct," and they came out and gave the oath of allegiance to al-Mukhtār.

According to Abū Mikhnaf—Mūsā b. ᶜĀmir al-ᶜAdawī (of ᶜAdī Juhaynah; he was Abū al-Ashᶜar): Al-Mukhtār entered the governor's residence where he passed the night. Next morning, the notables among the people were in the mosque and at the gate of the governor's residence. Al-Mukhtār went forth and ascended the *minbar*. He praised God and extolled him, saying:

> Praise be to God who has promised assistance to His friend and damage to His enemy, and He has made it for him until the end of time a promise carried out and a decree achieved, and he who fabricated a slander has failed! Oh people, a banner has been raised for us and an objective set before us. Regarding the banner we have been told, "Raise it up and do not put it down!" and regarding the objective, "Pursue it and do not abandon it!" We have heard the call of the caller and what was said by the memorizer, and how many are the men and women who wail for those slain in the memorable event! Away with he who tyrannizes, turns his back, disobeys (God), lies, and faces away! Verily, Oh people, enter in and give an oath of allegiance which is rightly guided. By He Who created the Heavens as a vault held back, and the earth as broad paths, after the one to ᶜAlī b. Abī Ṭālib and the family of ᶜAlī, you have not taken any oath of allegiance more rightly guided than it!

Then he went in, and we and the notables went in to him [633] and clasped his hand (in allegiance). The people rushed to him and gave him the oath of allegiance, and he began, saying, "You are giving me the oath of allegiance on (the understanding that we will follow) the Book of God and the Sunnah of His Prophet, that we will seek vengeance for the blood of the family, pursue *jihād* against those who violate God's law, protect the weak, fight against those who fight us and give peace to those who seek it from us, and fulfill the oath of allegiance which you have given to us. We will not release

you from it nor ask you to cancel it." When each man said,
"Yes," he took the oath of allegiance from him.

By God, it is as if I can see now al-Mundhir b. Ḥassān b.
Ḍirār[712] as he came to him and greeted him as the holder of
authority. Then he gave him the oath of allegiance and left
him. But, as he came out of the residence, he drew near Saʿīd
b. Munqidh al-Thawrī in a group of the Shīʿah waiting by the
maṣṭaba.[713] When they saw him, and with him he had his son
Ḥayyān b. al-Mundhir, one of the stupid ones of them said,
"By God, this is one of the leaders of the tyrants [al-jabbārīn]!"
They attacked him and his son and killed them. Saʿīd b.
Munqidh called out to them, "Wait! Wait until we see what
your commander [amīr] thinks about him!" Al-Mukhtār heard
about that and was so angry about it that it could be seen in
his face; and he began to arouse the hopes of the people and
to win their love and that of the notables, and to follow a
righteous way of life as much as he could.

Ibn Kāmil came to him and said to al-Mukhtār, "Are you
aware that Ibn Muṭīʿ is in the house of Abū Mūsā?" He
answered him not a word. Ibn Kāmil repeated it three times,
but he did not answer. Then he repeated it again, but he still
did not answer, and Ibn Kāmil suspected it must be unwelcome
news to him, for previously Ibn Muṭīʿ had been a friend to
al-Mukhtār. In the evening, al-Mukhtār sent 100,000 dirhams
to Ibn Muṭīʿ and said to him, "Use this to make ready and
go. I have discovered where you are and I think the only thing
[634]   preventing your departure must be that you do not possess
enough to encourage you to leave."

Al-Mukhtār won possession of 9,000,000 dirhams in the
treasury of al-Kūfah. He gave to every one of his men with
whom he had fought when he besieged Ibn Muṭīʿ in the
residence—3,800 of them—500 dirhams. And he gave to 6,000
of his men who had joined him after he had encircled the
residence, and who had remained with him for that night and
those three days until he entered the residence, 200 dirhams

---

712. One of the leaders of the Banū Ḍabbah who had taken part in the
conquest of Iraq (Donner, Conquests, index).
713. A stone bench built into a wall.

each. He showed kindness to the people and led them to expect justice and righteousness of conduct. He attracted the notables to him, and they were his companions in his councils and discussions. Over the police troop he appointed ᶜAbdallāh b. Kāmil al-Shākirī, and over his (personal) guard Kaysān Abū ᶜAmrah, a mawlā of ᶜUraynah.[714]

One day, the latter stood guarding him and saw the notables talking with him and he saw him tête-à-tête with them in his conversation. Some of his mawlā companions said to Abū ᶜAmrah, "Do you not see how Abū Isḥāq has drawn close to the Arabs and does not regard us?" Al-Mukhtār summoned Abū ᶜAmrah and said to him, "What were those men I saw saying to you?" He said to him, whispering, "It troubled them, may God preserve you, that you have turned your face from them to the Arabs." Al-Mukhtār said to him, "Tell them, 'Indeed do not let that trouble you, for you are of me and I am of you!'" Then he was silent for a considerable time before reciting, 'We shall surely take vengeance on the sinners.'[715]

(According to Abū Mikhnaf)—Ḥaṣīrah b. ᶜAbdallāh al-Azdī, Fuḍayl b. Khadīj al-Kindī, and al-Naḍr b. Ṣāliḥ al-ᶜAbsī: The first man to whom al-Mukhtār gave a banner was ᶜAbdallāh b. al-Ḥārith, the brother of al-Ashtar; he gave him authority over Armenia. And he sent Muḥammad b. ᶜUmayr b. ᶜUṭārid[716] over Ādharbayjān, ᶜAbd al-Raḥmān b. Saᶜīd b. Qays over al-Mawṣil, Isḥāq b. Masᶜūd[717] over al-Madā'in and the region of Jūkhā, Qudāmah b. Abī ᶜĪsā b. Rabīᶜah al-Naṣrī, an ally of Thaqīf,[718] over upper Bihqubādh,[719] Muḥammad b. Kaᶜb b. Qaraẓah[720] over central Bihqubādh, Ḥabīb b. Munqidh al-Thawrī[721] over lower Bihqubādh, and Saᶜd b. Ḥudhayfah b. al-

[635]

---

714. See *EI²*, s.v. Kaysān.

715. Qur'ān, 32:22.

716. Of Tamīm, he had been one of the witnesses against Ḥujr (Ṭabarī, II, 133).

717. This seems to be the only reference to him, and I have not been able to identify him from independent sources.

718. Apparently, Ṭabarī's only reference to him.

719. For Upper, Middle and Lower Bihqubadh, see Le Strange, *Eastern Caliphate*, 81.

720. Presumably the same man as the often-cited traditionist Muḥammad b. Kaᶜb al-Quraẓī (of the Banū Qurayẓah/Anṣār) (?).

721. Brother of the above mentioned Saᶜīd b. Munqidh.

Yamān over Ḥulwān. With Saʿd b. Ḥudhayfah there were a thousand horsemen at Ḥulwān. Each month, al-Mukhtār paid him 1,000 dirhams, and he ordered him to fight the Kurds and keep the roads open. He wrote to his (financial) officials who had authority in the Jibāl,[722] telling them to bring the revenue from their districts to Saʿd b. Ḥudhayfah at Ḥulwān.[723]

ʿAbdallāh b. al-Zubayr had sent Muḥammad b. al-Ashʿath b. Qays over al-Mawṣil telling him to exchange correspondence with Ibn Muṭīʿ and to listen to him and obey him, except that Ibn Muṭīʿ would have no power to remove him from office, unless on the orders of Ibn al-Zubayr. Previously, under the governorate of ʿAbdallāh b. Yazīd and Ibrāhīm b. Muḥammad, Muḥammad b. al-Ashʿath had been independent in the governorate of al-Mawṣil, communicating with no one but Ibn al-Zubayr. When ʿAbd al-Raḥmān b. Saʿīd b. Qays came upon him as governor from al-Mukhtār, he fell back from al-Mawṣil before him and took up residence in Takrīt where he remained with some of the notables of his tribe and others. He was withdrawn [muʿtazil] from the conflict, waiting to see what the people would do and how their affairs would turn out. Then he departed, went to al-Mukhtār, gave him the oath of allegiance and entered into what the people of his land had entered into.

[636]	According to Abū Mikhnaf—Ṣilah b. Zuhayr al-Nahdī—Muslim b. ʿAbdallāh al-Ḍabbābī: When al-Mukhtār had triumphed and seized power, Ibn Muṭīʿ had fled, and he had sent out his officials, he began to hold sessions for the people morning and evening and to judge between those in dispute. Then he said, "By God, with what I am striving and endeavoring for I am too preoccupied to judge between the people." And he caused Shurayḥ[724] to hold sessions for the people and he gave judgment for them. But then Shurayḥ feared them and pretended to be sick. They used to say that he was an ʿUthmānī,[725] that he was one of those who had borne witness

---

722. See Le Strange, *Eastern Caliphate*, map II.
723. Concerning the above list, cf. Rotter, *Bürgerkrieg*, 103.
724. Shurayḥ b. al-Ḥārith al-Kindī, a famous *qāḍī* who is supposed to have been first appointed by the caliph ʿUmar.
725. I.e., a supporter of the views of the murdered caliph ʿUthmān.

against Ḥujr b. ᶜAdī,[726] that he had not reported from Hāni'
b. ᶜUrwah the information which Hāni' had sent to him, and
that ᶜAlī b. Abī Ṭālib had removed him from his office as
judge. When Shurayḥ heard that and saw them blaming him
and applying such opinions to him, he feigned illness and al-
Mukhtār appointed in his place ᶜAbdallāh b. ᶜUtbah b. Masᶜūd.
But then ᶜAbdallāh fell sick, and al-Mukhtār made ᶜAbdallāh
b. Mālik al-Ṭā'ī judge in his stead.

Muslim b. ᶜAbdallāh said: ᶜAbdallāh b. Hammām[727] had
heard Abū ᶜAmrah[728] referring to the Shīᶜah and decrying
ᶜUthmān b. ᶜAffān, and he had obtained satisfaction from him
with the whip. When al-Mukhtār achieved the victory Ibn
Hammām remained neutral, and eventually ᶜAbdallāh b. Shaddād sought a safe conduct for him. One day, Ibn Hammām
came to al-Mukhtār and said:[729]

Indeed, Umm Sarīᶜ has turned away from you with her love
　　and turned her back
　　openly forsaking ties of affection.
A slanderer who spread lies without stopping short beset
　　her,
　　and you have returned full of grief in your heart.
But do not take the matter so seriously. Let not passion
　　destroy you;
　　the passing of a need is not anything marvellous.
One night al-Mukhtār, distracting the young man　　　　　[637]
　　and making him forget the playful freshness of youth,
Proclaimed, "Revenge for al-Ḥusayn!" and there came
　　detachments from Hamdān after a third part of the
　　night.
And the chief Ibn Mālik came from Madhḥij,
　　leading bands arranged for battle in units.
And from Asad, Yazīd came to his aid,
　　with every young man protecting and defending those
　　things which it is his duty to.

---

726. See Ṭabarī, II, 134.
727. ᶜAbd Allāh b. Hammām al-Salūlī, the poet (see *EI²*, s.v.).
728. Abū ᶜAmrah Kaysān, the leader of al-Mukhtār's bodyguard.
729. Cf. Dīnawārī, *al-Akhbār al-ṭiwāl*, 291.

And Nuᶜaym, the best man of the whole of Shaybān, brought
    something which, at the time of fighting, is sharper by
    far.
And Ibn Shumayṭ, when he incited his clansmen,
    was there neither left without help nor neglected,
Nor was Qays of Nahd, indeed, nor Ibn Hawāzin;
    everyone was a brother in humility and submissiveness.
And Abū al-Nuᶜmān set out, may his hastening be for God,
    against Ibn Iyās, going out to the fighting,
With horsemen wearing armor on the day of battle
    and others uncovered, without armor.
The horsemen made an attack which overtook the enemy,
    and at the start of it assailed Ibn Muṭīᶜ.

[638]   He turned in flight with a blow, the fall of which would
    split open the head,
    and a painful thrust of the spear on the "Day of the
    Two Lanes."
He was besieged in the government house, returning to it
    with disgrace, humiliation and submissiveness.
But the *wazīr* of the son of the Legatee was gracious to
    them
    and was the best intercessor for them among the people.
Right guidance indeed returned to its seat,
    most rightly returning and coming back
To the Hāshimī, the rightly guiding and the rightly guided;
    him we hear and obey.

When he had recited it to al-Mukhtār, al-Mukhtār said to
his men, "He has praised you as you heard, and he has been
generous in his praising you. Be generous in rewarding him,
therefore!" Then al-Mukhtār arose and went in, saying to his
men, "Do not depart until I come out to you!"

ᶜAbdallāh b. Shaddād al-Jushamī said, "Oh Ibn Hammām, I
have a horse and shawl for you." And Qays b. Ṭahfah al-
Nahdī, who was married to al-Ribāb bint al-Ashᶜath, said,
"And I have a horse and shawl for you." Each of them was
[639]   embarrassed that the other might give him something and he
not give the same. Qays said to Yazīd b. Anas, "What will
you give him?" and Yazīd replied, "If he was aiming at a

reward from God by saying what he did, then what is with God is a benefit for him. But if he only wanted to get his hands on our property by making this speech, by God, there is nothing in our property which will suffice him—what was left over out of my pay has gone to strengthen my brethren." Aḥmar b. Shumayṭ, getting in ahead of them before they addressed Ibn Hammām, said, "Oh Ibn Hammām, if you desired the face of God in saying what you did, then seek your reward from God; but if you merely aimed at the approval of the people and the seeking of their property, then you will not achieve anything! By God, he who makes a speech to someone other than God, and concerning something other than what God possesses, is not fitting to be made presents to or donated to."

Ibn Hammām said to him, "May you bite the penis of your father!" and Yazīd b. Anas raised his whip and said to Ibn Hammām, "Do you say that, Oh wicked one!" and he said to Ibn Shumayṭ, "Strike him with your sword!" Ibn Shumayṭ lifted his sword against him and sprang at him, and the companions of Yazīd b. Anas and Ibn Shumayṭ sprang at him too, to escape Ibn Hammām's tongue. However, Ibrāhīm Ibn al-Ashtar took him by the hand, placed him behind himself, and said, "I grant him protection. Why do you behave toward him as I see? By God, he is attaching himself to our ties of friendship, approving of what we are doing, and generous in his praise. Even if you will not reward him for the generosity of his praise, at least do not abuse his honor and shed his blood." Madhḥij sprang up and interposed themselves in front of him, saying, "Ibn al-Ashtar has given him protection! No, by God, he shall not be reached!"

Al-Mukhtār heard their clamor, went out to them and signaled to them with his hand, "Sit down!" They sat and he said to them, "When something good is said to you, accept [640] it. And if you have the ability to reward it, then do so. If you cannot give a reward, then withdraw. And fear the tongue of the poet; his ill will is long-lasting, what he says causes damage, his slander is fertile and he deceives you in future times." They said, "And shall we not slay him?" He replied, "No! We have given him safe-conduct and protection, and

your brother Ibrāhīm Ibn al-Ashtar has given him protection."
Then Ibn Hammām sat with the people.

Ibrāhīm arose and returned to his abode, and he gave 1,000
dirhams and a horse and shawl to Ibn Hammām who went
back with it and said, "No, by God, I shall never take more
than these!" Hawāzin came and waxed furious and gathered
in the mosque to defend Ibn Hammām, but al-Mukhtār sent
to them, asking them to forgive the offense, and they did so.
Ibn Hammām said to Ibn al-Ashtar, eulogizing him:

The master of generous deeds, Ibn Mālik, put out for me
the fire of two dogs,
who incited the dogs against me.
(He is) a young man who, when he confronts the horsemen,
disperses them
with an effective spear thrust or a speedy blow.
A group of Hawāzin defended me,
(a group) mighty and powerful.
When Ibn Shumayṭ or Yazīd opposed it,
those two fell into deadly confusion.
Oh mawlās of Ṭayyi', you attacked us suddenly
with Ibn Shumayṭ, the most evil man who walked or
moved,
And the most slanderous turncoat against God.
But no slandering heretic can be compared with a pious
ascetic.
[641]   How surprising then that an Aḥmasī,[730] son of an Aḥmasī,
attacked me with spears and lances,
As if your strength compared with that of Qays and Khathᶜam;
but are you any more than the shameful things of
menstruating women?

On the following day ᶜAbdallāh b. Shaddād came and sat in
the mosque, saying, "The Banū Asad and the Aḥmas attacked
us. By God, we shall never find that acceptable." Al-Mukhtār
heard of it and sent for him, and summoned Yazīd b. Anas
and Ibn Shumayṭ. He praised God and extolled Him and then

---

730. I.e., Aḥmar b. Shumayṭ al-Aḥmasī.

said, "Oh Ibn Shaddād, what you have done is one of the
promptings of Satan. Turn to God in repentance!" He said,
"I have repented." Al-Mukhtār said, "These two are your
brethren. Turn to them and submit to them, and give me this
thing!" He replied, "It is yours."

Ibn Hammām had meanwhile composed another *qaṣīdah*
about the affair of al-Mukhtār. He said:

Sulaymā appeared after a long period of rebuke
     and the ending and passing away of the irritability of
     youth.
She had decided on leaving me and avoiding me,
     and after she had done this she went to extremes in an
     attempt to conciliate me.
When I saw the governor's residence, its door locked,
     and Hamdān in charge of the ropes;   [642]
And when I saw the men of no substance, as if
     they were bees around the dens of foxes;
And when I saw the gates of the lanes around us
     closed off with every sort of stick and sword tip;
I knew for sure that the horsemen of the rightly guided party,
     not even a fly's penis would survive them.

Bibliography of Cited Works

ʿAbd al-Razzāq, Abū Bakr al-Ṣanʿānī. *al-Muṣannaf.* 11 vols. Beirut, 1970 ff. (cited by vol. no. and tradition no.).

al-Aʿshā, Maymūn b. Qays, *Dīwān.* ,Edited by R. Geyer in *Gedichte von 'Abû Basîr Maimûn ibn Qais al-'Aʿshâ.* London, 1928.

al-Azraqī, Abū al-Walīd. *Akhbār Makkah.* F. Wüstenfeld *Die Chroniken der Stadt Mekka.* 4 vols. Leipzig 1857–61.

al-Balādhurī, Aḥmad b. Yaḥyā. *Kitāb futūḥ al-buldān.* Edited by M. J. de Goeje under the title *Liber expugnationis regionum.* Leiden, 1866.

————. *Ansāb al-ashrāf.* Vol. IVb. Edited by M. Schloessinger, Jerusalem, 1938. Vol. V. Edited by S. D. F. Goitein, Jerusalem, 1936. Vol. XI. Edited by W. Ahlwardt under the title *Anonyme arabische Chronik . . . vermuthlich das Buch . . . von elbalādorī.* Greifswald, 1883.

Becker, C. H. *Islamstudien.* 2 vols. Leipzig, 1924–32.

Blichfeldt, J. O. *Early Mahdism.* Leiden, 1985.

Bosworth, C. E. *Sistan under the Arabs.* Rome, 1968.

Buhl, F. "Zur Krisis der Umajjadenherrschaft im Jahre 684." *ZA* XXVII (1912): 50–64.

al-Bukhārī, Abū ʿAbdallāh Muḥammad. *al-Jāmiʿ al-ṣaḥīḥ.* 4 vols. Edited by L. Krehl and Th. W. Juynboll. Leiden, 1862–1908 (cited by reference to *kitāb* and *bāb*).

Caskel, W., and Strenziok, G. See Ibn al-Kalbī.

Crone, P. *Slaves on Horses.* Cambridge, 1980.

al-Dhahabī, Muḥammad b. Aḥmad. *al-Mushtabih.* Edited by P. de Jong. Leiden, 1881.

al-Dīnawarī, Abū Ḥanīfah Aḥmad b. Dāwūd. *al-Akhbār al-ṭiwāl.* Cairo, 1960.

Dixon, ᶜAbd al-Ameer ᶜAbd. *The Umayyad Caliphate, 65–86/684–705.* London, 1971.

Donner, F. M. *The Early Islamic Conquests.* Princeton, 1981.

Dozy, R. *Supplément aux dictionnaires arabes.* 2 vols. Leiden, 1881–1927.

——— . *Dictionnaire détaillé des noms des vêtements chez les arabes.* Amsterdam, 1845.

Fariq, K. A. "The story of an Arab diplomat." *Studies in Islam* III–IV (1966–67): 119–42.

Freytag, G. W. See al-Maydānī.

Goitein, S. D. *Studies in Islamic History and Institutions.* Leiden, 1966.

Goldziher, I. *Muhammedanische Studien.* 2 vols. Halle, 1889–90. Translated by C. R. Barber and S. M. Stern and edited by Stern under the title *Muslim Studies.* 2 vols. London, 1867–71.

——— . "Pinehas–Manṣûr." *ZDMG* LVI (1902): 411–12.

Ibn ᶜAbd Rabbihi, Aḥmad b. Muḥammad al-Andalusī. *al-ᶜIqd al-farīd.* 7 vols. Cairo, 1940–65.

Ibn ᶜAsākir. *Tahdhīb Taʾrīkh Dimashq.* 7 vols. Damascus, 1911ff.

Ibn Aᶜtham, Abū Muḥammad al-Kūfī. *Kitāb al-futūḥ.* 8 vols. Hyderabad, 1968–75.

Ibn al-Athīr, ᶜIzz al-Dīn. *al-Kāmil fiʾl-taʾrīkh.* Edited by C. J. Tornberg under the title *Chronicon quod perfectissimum inscribitur.* 14 vols. Leiden, 1851–76.

Ibn Ḥajar, Aḥmad b. ᶜAlī al-ᶜAsqalānī. *al-Iṣāba.* 4 vols. Calcutta 1856–73.

Ibn Hishām, ᶜAbd al-Malik. *Sīrat al-nabī.* 2 vols. Cairo, 1955. Translated by A. Guillaume under the title *The Life of Muhammad.* Oxford, 1955.

Ibn al-Kalbī, Hishām b. Muḥammad. *Jamharat al-nasab.* Rearranged and translated by W. Caskel and G. Strenziok under the title *Ğamharat an-nasab. Das genealogische Werk des Hišām b. Muḥammad al-Kalbī.* 2 vols. Leiden, 1966.

Ibn Manẓūr. *Lisān al-ᶜarab.* 15 vols. Beirut, 1955ff.

Ibn Saᶜd, Muḥammad. *Kitāb al-ṭabaqāt al-kabīr.* 9 vols. Edited by E. Sachau et al. Leiden, 1905–28.

al-Iṣfahānī, Abū al-Faraj. *Kitāb al-aghānī.* 20 vols. Būlāq, 1868–69.

Jafri, S. H. M. *The Origins and Early Development of Shiᶜa Islam.* London, 1979.

al-Jāḥiẓ. ᶜAmr b. Baḥr. *al-Bayān wa ʾl-tabyīn.* 4 vols. Cairo, 1960–61.

Jeffery, A. *The Foreign Vocabulary of the Qurʾān.* Baroda, 1938.

Khalīfah b. Khayyāṭ, *Taʾrīkh.* 2 vols. Damascus, 1967–68.

Lammens, H. *L'avènement des Marwānides et le califat de Marwān 1er*. Beirut, 1927. Originally in *Mélanges de l'Université Saint-Joseph* XII/2 (1927): 43–147.

————. "Moᶜâwia II ou le dernier des Sofiânides." *RSO* VII (1916–18): 37–38.

Lane, E. W. *An Arab-English Lexicon*. 8 vols. London, 1863–93.

Le Strange, G. *The Lands of the Eastern Caliphate*. Cambridge, 1905.

Lewis, B. "The regnal titles of the early ᶜAbbāsids." In his *Studies in Classical and Ottoman Islam*, London, 1976, no. II.

Lewis, B., and Holt, P. M. (eds.). *Historians of the Middle East*. London, 1962.

Madelung, W. "ᶜAbd Allāh b. al-Zubayr and the Mahdī." *JNES*, XL, (1981): 291–305.

Massignon, L. "Explication du plan de Baṣra." In his *Opera Minora* III. Beirut, 1963, 61–87.

————. "Explication du plan de Kūfa." In ibid., 35–60.

al-Masᶜūdī, Abū al-Ḥasan, *Murūj al-dhahab*. Edited and translated by C. Barbier de Meynard and Pavet de Courteille under the title *Les prairies d'or*. 9 vols. Paris, 1861–77.

al-Maydānī, Aḥmad b. Muḥammad. *Majmaᶜ al-amthāl*. Cairo, 1959. Translated by G. W. Freytag under the title *Arabum proverbia*. 3 vols. Bonn, 1838–43.

Morony, M. *Iraq after the Muslim Conquest*. Princeton, 1984.

al-Mubarrad, Abū al-ᶜAbbās. *al-Kāmil*. Edited by W. Wright. Leipzig, 1864–92.

Naqā'iḍ (Jarīr wa-) al-Akhṭal. Edited by A. Ṣālḥānī under the title *Naqā'iḍ de Ǧarīr et de Aḫṭal*. Beirut, 1922.

Naqā'iḍ (Jarīr wa-) al-Farazdaq. Edited by A. A. Bevan under the title *The Naḳā'iḍ of Jarīr and al-Farazdaḳ*. 3 vols. Leiden, 1905–12.

al-Narshakhī. *Ta'rīkh-i Bukhārā*. Translated by R. N. Frye under the title *The History of Bukhara*. Cambridge, Mass., 1954.

Noth, A. *Quellenkritische Studien zu Themen, Formen und Tendenzen frühislamischer Geschichtsüberlieferung*. Bonn, 1973.

Robertson Smith, W. *Kinship and Marriage in Early Arabia*. 2nd edition. London, 1903.

Rotter, G. *Die Umayyaden und der zweite Bürgerkrieg (680–692)*. Wiesbaden, 1982.

————. "Zur Überlieferung einiger historischer Werke Madā'inīs in Ṭabarī's Annalen." *Oriens* XXIII–XXIV (1974): 103–33.

Sauvaget, J. *La mosquée omeyyade de Médine*. Paris, 1947.

Sayed, R. *Die Revolte des Ibn al-Ašᶜaṯ und die Koranleser*. Freiburg, 1977.

Sezgin, F. *Geschichte des arabischen Schrifttums.* Vol. I. *Qur'anwissenschaften, Ḥadīt, Geschichte, Fiqh, Dogmatik, Mystik bis ca. 430 H.* Leiden, 1975.

al-Shammākhī, Aḥmad b. Saʿīd. *Kitāb al-siyar.* Lithograph Cairo, 1301/1884.

Sharon, M. *Black Banners from the East. The Establishment of the ʿAbbasid State.* Jerusalem, 1983.

al-Ṭabarī, Abū Jaʿfar Muḥammad b. Jarīr. *Ta'rikh al-Rusul wa-al-mulūk.* Edited by M. J. de Goeje et al. 16 vols. Leiden, 1879–1901. Vol. 16 including *Glossarium* and *Addenda et emendanda.* Edited by Muḥammad Abū al-Faḍl Ibrāhīm. 10 vols. Cairo, 1960–69.

Wansbrough, J. E. *The Sectarian Milieu.* London, 1978.

Wellhausen, J. "Prolegomena zur ältesten Geschichte des Islams." In his *Skizzen und Vorarbeiten.* Vol. VI, Berlin, 1899, 1–160.

———. *Die religiös-politischen Oppositionsparteien im alten Islam.* Berlin, 1901. Translated by R. Ostle and S. M. Walzer under the title *The Religio-Political Factions in Early Islam.* Amsterdam, 1975.

———. *Das arabische Reich und sein Sturz.* Berlin, 1902. Translated by M. G. Weir under the title *The Arab Kingdom and Its Fall.* Calcutta, 1927. (Cited here in the translation.)

Wensinck, A. J., et al. *Concordances et indices de la tradition musulmane.* 6 vols. Leiden, 1933 ff.

Wieder, N. *The Judaean Scrolls and Karaism.* London, 1962.

Wright, W. *A Grammar of the Arabic Language.* 2 vols. 3rd edition. Cambridge, 1896–98.

al-Yaʿqūbī, Aḥmad b. Abī Yaʿqūb. *Ta'rīkh.* 2 vols. Beirut, 1970.

Yāqūt, Abū ʿAbdallāh, *Irshād al-arīb.* 7 vols. Edited by D. S. Margoliouth. Leiden and London, 1907–27.

———. *Muʿjam al-buldān.* 6 vols. Edited by F. Wüstenfeld. Leipzig, 1866–70.

al-Zabīdī, Abū al-Fayḍ Muḥammad. *Tāj al-ʿarūs.* 10 vols. Benghazi, n.d.

al-Zubayrī, al-Muṣʿab b. ʿAbdallāh. *Kitāb Nasab Quraysh.* Edited by E. Lévi-Provençal. Cairo, 1953.

Index

A

Abān b. al-Walīd 154

ʿAbbād b. al-Ḥusayn b. Yazīd 31–32

al-ʿAbbās b. al-Aswad b. al-ʿAwf 20

al-ʿAbbās b. Sahl b. Saʿd 111, 114, 162–63

ʿAbd al-ʿAzīz b. Khālid b. Rustam al-Ṣanʿānī, *rāwī* 2, 176

ʿAbd al-ʿAzīz b. Marwān 62, 159–60

ʿAbd al-Ghāfir b. Masʿūd b. ʿAmr 18

ʿAbd al-Jabbār b. al-ʿAbbās al-Hamdānī 130

ʿAbd al-Malik b. ʿAbdallāh b. ʿĀmir b. Kurayz 43, 44

ʿAbd al-Malik b. Juz' b. al-Ḥidrijān al-Azdī 155–56

ʿAbd al-Malik b. Marwān 48, 144, 153–54, 159–60, 186

ʿAbd al-Malik b. Nawfal b. Musāḥiq 62, 116

(Banū) ʿAbd al-Qays (Rabīʿah) 89 n. 388, 133 n. 499, 166, 170, 172

ʿAbd al-Raḥmān b. ʿAbdallāh al-Nakhaʿī 197

ʿAbd al-Raḥmān b. Abī Bakrah 12–13, 36

ʿAbd al-Raḥmān b. Abī ʿUmayr al-Thaqafī 106

ʿAbd al-Raḥmān b. al-Ḍaḥḥāk b. Qays 55

ʿAbd al-Raḥmān b. Ghaziyyah 132, 137, 141. See also ʿAbdallāh b. Ghaziyyah

ʿAbd al-Raḥmān b. al-Ḥakam, brother of Marwān I 68

ʿAbd al-Raḥmān b. al-Ḥārith b. Hishām 45

ʿAbd al-Raḥmān b. Jahdam al-Fihrī 48, 64

ʿAbd al-Raḥmān b. Jawshan 12–13

ʿAbd al-Raḥmān b. Jundab 132, 137

ʿAbd al-Raḥmān b. Mikhnaf b. Sulaym 198, 215

ʿAbd al-Raḥmān b. Saʿīd b. Qays al-Hamdānī 198, 205, 215, 219, 220

ʿAbd al-Raḥmān b. Shurayḥ 189, 190, 192

ʿAbd al-Raḥmān b. Yazīd al-Bāhilī 153

(Banū) ʿAbd Shams (Quraysh) 43 n. 209

ʿAbd al-ʿUzzā b. Ṣuhal al-Azdī, poet 188

(Banū) ʿAbd Wadd 61, 63

ʿAbdallāh b. ʿAbdallāh al-Laythī 216

ᶜAbdallāh b. ᶜĀmir b. Kurayz al-Qurashī 24

ᶜAbdallāh b. al-Aswad al-Zuhrī 20 n. 92, 23

ᶜAbdallāh b. ᶜAwf b. al-Aḥmar al-Azdī, *rāwī* 80, 125, 134, 137, 142, 143, 146, 148, 150, 151, 155, 169

ᶜAbdallāh b. ᶜAzīz (ᶜUzayr?) al-Kindī 151

ᶜAbdallāh b. Ḍamḍam b. Yazīd al-Ḥanafī 75

ᶜAbdallāh b. Ghaziyyah 141, 146, 150, 155. See also ᶜAbd al-Raḥmān b. Ghaziyyah

ᶜAbdallāh b. Hammām al-Salūlī, poet 47, 92, 221–25

ᶜAbdallāh b. al-Ḥārith, brother of al-Ashtar 219

ᶜAbdallāh b. al-Ḥārith b. Nawfal (Babbah) 20–24, 29, 43–46, 103, 104, 165–66

ᶜAbdallāh b. al-Ḥāzim al-Kabīrī 125, 148, 150

ᶜAbdallāh b. Ḥiṣn 10

ᶜAbdallāh b. Ibāḍ 102–4

ᶜAbdallāh al-Iṣbahānī, gate of, in al-Baṣrah 244

ᶜAbdallāh b. Jarīr al-Māzinī, *rāwī* 19

ᶜAbdallāh b. Kāmil al-Shākirī 183, 193, 196, 212, 218, 219

ᶜAbdallāh b. Khaḍal al-Ṭāʾī 147

ᶜAbdallāh b. Khāzim xiii, 24, 70–79, 123, 176, 177–81

ᶜAbdallāh b. al-Māḥūz al-Tamīmī 165–66

ᶜAbdallāh b. Mālik al-Ṭāʾī al-Ḥizmirī 87–88, 221

ᶜAbdallāh b. Muṭīᶜ al-ᶜAdawī 115, 175, 176, 182–225

ᶜAbdallāh b. Nāfiᶜ, uterine brother of Ziyād 10

ᶜAbdallāh b. Qurād al-Khathᶜamī 204

ᶜAbdallāh b. Saᶜd b. Nufayl al-Azdī 80, 82, 89, 127, 138, 142–48, 154

ᶜAbdallāh b. Ṣaffār al-Saᶜdī 101, 103, 104

ᶜAbdallāh b. Ṣafwān b. Umayyah al-Jumaḥī 116

ᶜAbdallāh b. Shaddād al-Bajalī 183, 185, 193, 201, 221, 222, 224, 225

ᶜAbdallāh b. Thawr, Abū Fudayk 102

ᶜAbdallāh b. ᶜUbaydallāh b. Abī Thawr 176 n. 598

ᶜAbdallāh b. ᶜUmar b. al-Khaṭṭāb 57, 107–8, 183–84

ᶜAbdallāh b. ᶜUthmān al-Thaqafī 36

ᶜAbdallāh b. Wāl al-Taymī 82, 84, 96, 133, 138, 142, 148–50, 154, 159 n. 546

ᶜAbdallāh b. Yazīd al-Khaṭmī 47, 92–97, 121–23, 128–30, 134–37, 155, 158, 175, 184–86, 220

ᶜAbdallāh b. Yazīd b. Muᶜāwiyah 51, 52

ᶜAbdallāh b. Ziyād, brother of ᶜUbaydallāh 15, 19, 22, 27

ᶜAbdallāh b. al-Zubayr xi–xiii, 12, 43, 45, 47, 92, 136, 144, 160, 162, 175–76; besieged in Mecca 1–6; his supporters in Syria 47–69; with the Khawārij in Mecca 97–105; with Mukhtār in Mecca 109, 111–17; his demolition and rebuilding of the Kaᶜbah 122–23, 176; appoints al-Muhallab to fight the Khawārij 166–67, 173–74

(Banū) Abī ᶜAmr (Banū Umayyah) 107 n. 435

(Banū) Abī al-ᶜĀṣ (Banū Umayyah) 47 n. 235

(Banū) Abī Sufyān (Banū Umayyah) 49 n. 246, 52 n. 255

ᶜAbīd b. Naqīd 78

ᶜAbīdah b. ᶜAmr al-Baddī 118, 119, 120, 182

ᶜAbīdah b. Hilāl al-Yashkurī 99–100, 165, 169, 170

Abraham, "foundations of" 176
Abrashahr, see Nīsābūr
(Banū) ᶜAbs b. Baghid 209 n. 689
ᶜAbs b. Ṭalq b. Rabīᶜah al-Ṣarīmī 31–32
al-Abṭaḥ, at Mecca 3 n. 9
Abū ᶜAlqamah al-Khathᶜamī 99
Abū ᶜAlqamah al-Yaḥmadī 174
Abū ᶜAmrah, see Kaysān
Abū ᶜĀṣim al-Nabīl 35
Abū Bakr, caliph 49, 100–1
Abū Bakr b. al-Faḍl, rāwī 18
Abū Bilāl 97, 102
Abū Dharr al-Ghifārī 100 n. 412
Abū al-Fawāris, rāwī 178
Abū Ḥafṣ al-Azdī, rāwī 71
Abū Ḥammād al-Sulamī, rāwī 77
Abū al-Ḥuwayrith 54, 160
Abū ᶜIzzah al-Qābiḍī 125
Abū al-Juwayriyyah al-ᶜAbdī, qāṣṣ 145, 153
Abū al-Juwayriyyah b. al-Aḥmar 142
Abū al-Khansā' Kusayb al-ᶜAnbarī, rāwī 33
Abū Labīd al-Jahḍamī, rāwī 17, 20
Abū Mikhnaf Lūṭ b. Yaḥyā, akhbārī, 16–17, 61–69(?), 80–97, 97–105, 105–22, 124–59, 165–75, 182–225
Abū al-Mughallas al-Laythī, rāwī 216
Abū al-Mukhāriq al-Rāsibī 97, 165, 174
Abū Muqarrin ᶜUbaydallāh al-Duhnī, rāwī 44–45
Abū Mūsā al-Ashᶜarī, house of, in al-Kūfah 215, 216, 218
Abū al-Muᶜtamir Ḥanash b. Rabīᶜah al-Kinānī 84
Abū al-Muthannā, rāwī 102
Abū Naᶜāmah al-ᶜAdawī, rāwī 30, 72, 78
Abū Qaṭan al-Hamdānī 200
Abū Rayḥānah al-ᶜUraynī 32
Abū Saᶜdān, rāwī 21
Abū Ṣādiq, rāwī 132

Abū Saᶜīd al-Ṣayqal (al-ᶜUqaylī?), rāwī 205, 207
Abū al-Ṣalt al-Taymī, rāwī 149, 205
Abū al-Sarī al-Khurāsānī, rāwī 73, 77 n. 358
Abū Ṭālūt 102
Abū ᶜUbaydah Maᶜmar b. Muthannā 9–17, 21–34
Abū ᶜUbaydah b. Ziyād, brother of ᶜUbaydallāh 70
Abū ᶜUqāb, mawlā of Abū Sufyān 163
Abū ᶜUthmān al-Nahdī 204, 213
Abū Yūsuf Muḥammad b. Thābit al-Anṣārī, rāwī 111, 114, 125
Abū Zuhayr al-ᶜAbsī, rāwī 155
(Banū) al-ᶜAdawiyyah (Tamīm) 34, 179 n. 606; lane of, in al-Baṣrah 29, 31
Adham b. Muḥriz al-Bāhilī 139, 145, 149
Ādharbayjān 219
(Banū) ᶜAdī (Tamīm) 78
(Banū) ᶜAdī b. Kaᶜb (Quraysh) 115, 185
Ahl al-ᶜĀliyah 170
Aḥmad b. Zuhayr, rāwī 163
Aḥmar b. Shumayṭ al-Aḥmasī 183, 185, 193, 194, 196–97, 203, 215, 222, 223, 224
(Banū) al-Aḥmar b. Zuhayr (Azd) 124 n. 484
(Banū) Aḥmas b. Ghawth (Bajīlah) 183 n. 616, 224
al-Aḥnaf b. al-Ashhab al-Ḍabbī, rāwī 74
al-Aḥnaf b. Qays al-Tamīmī 11, 13, 27–28, 30–31, 40–47, 167, 168, 174
Ahwāz 46, 165, 166, 168, 170, 172, 175
ᶜĀ'ishah, wife of the Prophet 176
ᶜAjalah 178
ᶜAlī b. Abī Ṭālib 142, 187, 217
ᶜAlī b. al-Ḥusayn, Zayn al-ᶜĀbidīn 4–5

ᶜAlī b. Muḥammad Abū al-Ḥasan al-Madā'inī 5, 14, 21, 35, 44–46, 70–79, 163, 177–81
ᶜAlī b. Zayd, *rāwī* 6
al-Aᶜmash, *rāwī* 132
Āminah bt. ᶜAlqamah, mother of Marwān I 161
(Banū) ᶜĀmir (Qays) 67
ᶜĀmir b. ᶜAbdallāh, *rāwī* 55
ᶜĀmir b. Abī ᶜUmar, *rāwī* 178
ᶜĀmir b. Masᶜūd al-Jumaḥī, Duḥrūjat al-Juᶜal 37, 40, 46–47, 92, 116
ᶜĀmir b. Sharāḥīl al-Shaᶜbī 119, 193–97
ᶜAmr b. Bishr 159
ᶜAmr b. al-Ḥajjāj al-Zubaydī 211, 213
ᶜAmr b. Ḥurayth al-Makhzūmī 37–40, 89–90, 92, 106–7, 129, 214–15; house of, in al-Kūfah 199, 200
ᶜAmr b. ᶜĪsā, *rāwī* 24
ᶜAmr b. al-Khālī 63
ᶜAmr b. Marthad 73, 79
ᶜAmr b. al-Mikhlāt al-Kalbī, poet 67
ᶜAmr (or ᶜĀmir) b. Mismaᶜ al-Shaybānī 39
ᶜAmr b. Nāfiᶜ Abū ᶜUthmān 108
ᶜAmr al-Qanā Abū al-Musaddī 174–75
ᶜAmr b. Saᶜīd al-Ashdaq 58, 59, 64, 65, 160
ᶜAmr b. Yazīd al-Ḥakamī 52
ᶜAmr b. al-Zubayr 35
Anas b. Mālik 45
(Banū) ᶜAnazah 26
al-Anbār, place 134
(Banū) ᶜAnbar (Tamīm) 179 n. 606
Anṣār (of Medina) 112
Aqsās, place 132
ᶜArham b. ᶜAbdallāh b. Qays, poet 34
Armenia 219
Arqam b. Muṭarrif al-Ḥanafī 75
(Banū) al-ᶜĀṣ (Umayyah) 59
(Banū) Asad (Quraysh) 48 n. 237

(Banū) Asad b. Khuzaymah 183 n. 615, 221, 224
Asāwirah 30 n. 149, 32, 45, 163 n. 568; "river of," in al-Baṣrah 40
Aᶜshā Hamdān, poet 156–59
al-Ashᶜath b. Dhu'ayb 181
al-Ashᶜath b. Qays, mosque of, in al-Kūfah 203; "people of" 214
Ashyam b. Shaqīq b. Thawr al-Sadūsī 25–26, 33, 44
ᶜĀṣim b. Ḥabīb al-ᶜAdawī 179
ᶜĀṣim b. al-Ṣalt al-Ḥanafī 75
Asmā' bt. Abī Bakr 58, 176
Asmā' b. Khārijah 215
astrology 185
al-Aswad b. Jarād al-Kindī 189, 190
al-Aswad b. Shaybān, *rāwī* 8, 19
ᶜAṭā' b. Abī Rabāḥ 123
ᶜAṭiyyah b. al-Ḥārith Abū Rawq al-Hamdānī, *rāwī* 117, 126, 141
ᶜAwānah b. al-Ḥakam al-Kalbī 1 n. 2, cited 1–6, 39–43, 46–47, 48–54, 56–61(?), 160, 162–63
(Banū) ᶜAwdh b. Sūd 27 n. 133
ᶜAwn b. Abī Juḥayfah al-Suwā'ī, *rāwī* 130
(Banū) Aws (Anṣār) 47 n. 231
Aws b. Thaᶜlabah b. Zufar 71–79, 177
ᶜAyn al-Wardah, battle 124, 140, 141, 143–59
Ayyūb, mawlā of Shaqīq b. Thawr 8–9
Ayyūb b. Ḥumrān, mawlā 10
Azāriqah, Khawārij 45, 164–75
(Banū) Azd xv, xvi; in al-Baṣrah 18, 26, 27, 29, 35, 40–47, 165, 166, 170, 173–74; in Khurāsān 71–72; in al-Kūfah 125, 147, 154, 198 n. 654; Azd Mazūn 72; Azd Shanū'ah 159 n. 545; Azd ᶜUmān 171
ᶜAzrah 125

B

Babbah. See ᶜAbdallāh b. al-Ḥārith
(Banū) Baddā' b. al-Ḥārith al-Akbar 118

(Banū) Bāhilah 108 n. 439
Baḥīr b. Raysān 185
Baḥīr b. Warqā' al-Ṣarīmī 179
al-Baḥrayn 172
Bahurasīr, place 147
(Banū) Bajīlah 80 n. 371, 199
(Banū) Bakr b. Wā'il xvi, 26, 154,
    166, 168, 170; in al-Baṣrah 8–9,
    21, 24–28, 40–47; in Khurāsān
    71–79; in al-Kūfah 38–40
al-Balādhurī, Aḥmad b. Yaḥyā xviii
Balqā', place 69, 152
barā'ah. See dissociation
Barīd, lane of, in al-Kūfah 206
al-Basīṭah, place 108
al-Baṣrah 38, 123, 162–63, 176;
    events following the death of
    Yazīd 6–37, 39–47; Penitents
    from there 130, 147, 153;
    return of Khawārij from Mecca
    102, 104; afflicted by plague
    163–64; threatened by Azāriqah
    164–75
al-Bāṭinah (in al-Baṣrah) 24
al-Bayḍā', palace 36
Bayhāsiyyah, Khawārij 102 n. 417
Bihqubādh, place 219
Bishr b. Marwān b. al-Ḥakam 62
Black Stone, of the Kaʿbah 112,
    123, 133
blood money 42, 43, 45
Book of God, the, in propaganda of
    Ibn al-Zubayr 113; in
    propaganda of Khawārij 98, 99,
    100, 103; in propaganda of al-
    Mukhtār 154, 191, 194, 217; in
    propaganda of the Penitents 92,
    136
Bukayr b. Wishāḥ 78, 79, 177, 178
Bukhāriyyah, armed force 14, 18,
    44

C

Camel, "day of the" 58
Civil war, second xi–xiii

D

(Banū) Ḍabbah b. Udd 25, 180
al-Ḍaḥḥāk b. ʿAbdallāh al-Mashriqī,
    rāwī 193
al-Ḍaḥḥāk b. Khaytham, rāwī 30
al-Ḍaḥḥāk b. Qays al-Fihrī 6, 47–69
Damascus 6 n. 24, 48, 49, 50, 53,
    56, 58, 59, 64, 65
Ḍamḍam b. Yazīd al-Ḥanafī 75
Daylamīs 206
Dayr al-Aʿwar, place 131
Dayr Hind, place 204
(Banū) Dhubyān (Qays) 67
(Banū) Dhuhl (of Banū Ḍabbah b.
    Udd) 74
(Banū) Dhuhl b. Muʿāwiyah
    (Kindah) 118
(Banū) Dhuhl b. Shaybān 26
(Banū) Dhuhl b. Thaʿlabah 26, 28,
    108 n. 438
dihqāns 36
dissociation 98, 100, 101, 103, 133
(Banū) Dithār 77
(Banū) Ḍubayʿah b. Rabīʿah 26
Dūlāb, battle 164, 165, 166
Durnā, lions of 159

E

Egypt 48, 64, 175, 160
Euphrates, river 132, 174

F

Fākhitah bt. Abī Hāshim, mother of
    Khālid b. Yazīd 65, 161
fanjaqān, tactic 32
al-Farazdaq, Hammām b. Ghālib,
    poet 24, 33
Farṭanā, day of 178, 179
Farwah b. Laqīṭ, rāwī 146, 149
al-Faryāb, place 71
fay' 14, 38, 100, 127, 187, 212

(Banū) Fazārah b. Dhubyān 80 n.
369, 85 n. 382
fifths, of al-Baṣrah 168, 169, 170
(Banū) Fihr (Quraysh) 6 n. 24, 48 n.
238, 55 n. 268, 64
al-Fīl, gate at al-Kūfah 106, 119,
200
al-Fīl, mawlā 40 n. 197, 44
fitnah 6 n. 21, 109, 117, 123, 154,
186
Fuḍayl b. Khadīj al-Kindī, rāwī 118,
120, 122, 152, 182, 209, 219

G

genealogy, of Arabs xiv–xvi
(Banū) Ghassān 52 n. 256, 53 n.
261, 59, 61
Ghaṭafān b. Unayf al-Kaᶜbī 32, 34,
35 n. 173
Ghaylān b. Muḥammad, rāwī 12
(Banū) Ghudānah b. Yarbūᶜ 164 n.
573, 166 n. 578
Golden Calf, the, in the ideology of
the Penitents 83–84

H

Ḥabīb b. al-Muhallab 174
Ḥabīb b. Munqidh al-Thawrī 219
Ḥabīb b. Qurrah, rāwī 62
ḥajj 123, 176
al-Ḥajjāj b. Bāb al-Ḥimyarī 165
al-Ḥajjāj b. Nāshib al-ᶜAdawī 179
al-Ḥajjāj b. Yūsuf 63, 110, 149, 163
Ḥajjār b. Abjar al-ᶜIjlī 203
al-Ḥakam b. Abī al-ᶜĀṣ 100 n. 412
Ḥakīm b. Munqidh al-Kindī 124,
125, 131
(Banū) Hamdān xv; in al-Kūfah 39,
119, 189, 198, 200, 221, 225;
at ᶜAyn al-Wardah 152, 159
Ḥammād b. Salamah, rāwī 6
Hammām b. Ghālib, see al-Farazdaq
Hammām b. Qabīṣah al-Numayrī 66

Ḥamrā', 208, 210
Ḥanash b. Rabīᶜah Abū al-Muᶜtamir
al-Kinānī 142
Hāni' b. Abī Ḥayyah al-Wadāᶜī 106,
107, 117
Hāni' b. ᶜUrwah al-Murādī 106
(Banū) Ḥanīfah (Bakr b. Wa'il) 26,
75, 78, 98, 102 n. 420, 208
al-Ḥantaf b. al-Sijf al-Tamīmī 162
(Banū) Ḥanẓalah (Tamīm) 29 n. 143
Ḥanẓalah b. Bayhās 102
al-Ḥarīsh b. Hilāl al-Saᶜdī al-Qurayᶜī
168, 178–81
al-Ḥārith, rāwī 47, 160
al-Ḥārith b. ᶜAbdallāh b. Abī
Rabīᶜah al-Makhzūmī, al-Qubāᶜ
43, 162, 166, 167–75, 176,
185, 186
al-Ḥārith b. Ḥaṣīrah, rāwī 89
al-Ḥārith b. Kaᶜb al-Wālibī 205,
208, 211
al-Ḥārith b. Qays al-Jahḍamī 15–17,
17–18, 21–22
Ḥārithah b. Badr al-Ghudānī, poet
26; military commander
164–66, 169
al-Ḥārithiyyūn, at al-Baṣrah 12 n.
54
al-Ḥarrah, battle 3 n. 10, 50
Ḥarūriyyah 16, 164 n. 571; see also
Khārijites
al-Ḥasan b. ᶜAlī 105
al-Ḥasan al-Baṣrī 6, 33
al-Ḥasan b. Rashīd al-Juzajānī, rāwī
72, 177
(Banū) Hāshim (Quraysh) xvi, 20,
23
Ḥaṣīrah b. ᶜAbdallāh b. al-Ḥārith b.
Durayd al-Azdī, rāwī 186, 205,
214, 219
Ḥassān b. Fā'id b. Bukayr al-ᶜAbsī
216
Ḥassān b. Mālik b. Baḥdal al-Kalbī
49–53, 56, 58, 59, 66, 68, 160,
161
al-Ḥaṣṣāṣah, place 134
(Banū) Hawāzin 224

al-Haytham b. ᶜAdī 38–39
al-Haytham b. al-Aswad, poet
    42–43
Ḥayyān b. al-Mundhir b. Ḥassān b.
    Ḍirar al-Ḍabbī 218
Herat 71, 73, 74, 76, 77, 79, 177
al-Ḥijr, at the sanctuary in Mecca
    112, 113, 123, 176
Hilāl al-Ḍabbī 74–75
Ḥimṣ 49, 56, 58, 63
Himyān b. ᶜAdī al-Sadūsī 21, 24, 44
(Banū) Ḥimyar 152
(Banū) Hind (Kindah) 119, 120, 182
Hind bt. Abī Sufyān, mother of
    Babbah 23, 29
al-Ḥīrah, lake of 118
Hishām b. Hubayrah 123, 176
Hishām b. al-Mughīrah al-
    Makhzūmī 45 n. 219
Hishām b. Muḥammad al-Kalbī xvi,
    1–6, 39–43, 46–47, 48–54,
    56–61, 61–68(?), 80–97,
    97–105, 105–22, 124–59, 160,
    161, 162–63, 165–75, 181–225
Hishām b. ᶜUrwah b. al-Zubayr 54
(Banū) Ḥiṣn b. Ḍamḍam b. Janāb 67
Hīt, place 137, 153
(Banū) Ḥizmir b. Akhzam 88 n. 387
House, "day of the" 58
Hubayrah b. Ḥudayr, rāwī 27, 28,
    30, 32
Ḥubaysh b. Duljah al-Qaynī 161–63
al-Ḥuḍayn b. al-Mundhir al-
    Shaybānī 8–9
(Banū) Ḥudhayfah, houses of, in al-
    Kūfah 215
al-Hudhayl b. Zufar b. al-Ḥārith al-
    Kilābī 137
Ḥujr b. ᶜAdī 81, 86
(Banū) Ḥujr b. Wahb (Kindah),
    mosque of, in al-Kūfah 118
al-Ḥulays b. Ghālib 159
Ḥulwān, place 220
Ḥumayd b. Bahdal 69
Ḥumayd b. Hilāl, rāwī 30
Ḥumayd b. Muslim al-Azdī 82, 85,
    122, 126, 142, 143, 144, 146,
    150, 155, 184, 197, 199, 205

(Banū) Humaym 26
Ḥumrān, mawlā 10
al-Ḥusayn b. ᶜAbdallāh al-Bursumī
    188, 189
al-Ḥusayn b. ᶜAlī 35–36, 39, 105;
    in the ideology of al-Mukhtār
    109, 182, 190–94, 197, 201–3,
    217, 221; in the ideology of the
    Penitents 80–97, 124–28,
    132–34, 162. See also Karbalā',
    al-Ṭaff
al-Ḥusayn b. Numayr al-Sakūnī xiii;
    siege of Mecca 1–6, 114–16;
    supporting Marwān in Syria 48,
    56–57, 68–69; at ᶜAyn al-
    Wardah 139, 143–45, 153, 156
al-Ḥusayn b. Yazīd Ibn Nufayl 85,
    90, 134, 154–55
Huwwārīn, place 70

I

Ibāḍiyyah, Khārijites 102 n. 416
Ibn Abī al-Zinād, rāwī 54, 55
Ibn ᶜArādah, poet 70
Ibn ᶜAyyāsh, rāwī 38–39
Ibn Habbār, house of, in al-Kūfah
    200
Ibn al-Ḥanafiyya, see Muḥammad b.
    ᶜAlī
Ibn al-ᶜIrq 108, 110
Ibn Muḥriz, lane of, in al-Kūfah
    213
Ibn (Abū?) Rajā' al-ᶜAwdhī 27
Ibn Ruwaym, see Yazīd b. al-Ḥārith
Ibn Saᶜd, see Muḥammad b. Saᶜd
Ibn Sahm al-Tamīmī, poet 166 n.
    579
Ibrāhīm b. Mālik Ibn al-Ashtar
    193–203, 207, 209–16, 221,
    223–24
Ibrāhīm b. Muḥammad b. Ṭalḥah
    al-Taymī, al-Aᶜraj 47, 92–97,
    121–22, 128–30, 155, 158,
    184–86, 220
Ibrāhīm b. Mūsā, rāwī 122

(Banū) ᶜIjl 26, 186 n. 624, 214 n. 702
ᶜIkrimah b. Khālid 122
ᶜImrān b. ᶜIṣām al-ᶜAnazī 26
ᶜirāfah 95
Iṣfahān 172, 175
Isḥāq b. Abī Isrā'īl 2, 176
Isḥāq b. Masᶜūd 219
Isḥāq b. Suwayd al-ᶜAdawī 28, 30, 32, 33
Ismāᶜīl b. Kathīr 119, 120, 182
Ismāᶜīl b. Nuᶜaym al-Hamdānī, rāwī 189
Ismāᶜīl b. Yazīd al-Azdī 127
ᶜIyāḍ al-Jurashī 63
Iyās b. Muḍārib al-ᶜIjlī 186, 188, 189, 200, 201
Iyās b. Qatādah 41
Iyās b. Zuhayr b. Ḥayyān 78

J

Jabalah b. ᶜAbdallāh al-Khathᶜamī 139, 144
al-Jabbān, al-Baṣrah 29, 31
Jabbānahs, al-Kūfah 118 n. 466, 198; of Bishr 198, 204; of Kindah 198, 202; of Murād 199, 205; of al-Sabīᶜ 198, 205; of al-Ṣāᶜidiyyīn 198; of Sālim 198; of Uthayr 202
Jābir b. al-Aswad b. al-ᶜAwf 20 n. 92, 162
al-Jābiyah, place 53, 55, 56, 59
(Banū) Jahḍam b. Jadhīmah (al-Jahāḍimah) 15 n. 61, 16, 17 n. 76
(Banū) Jaḥdar (Shaybān) 24, 74
Jāhiliyyah, tribal alliances in the 26, 28
al-Jārif 46, 163–64
Jarīr, rāwī 17 n. 76, 46, 163, 164, 165
al-Jārūd al-Hudhalī 13
Jawwās b. Qaᶜṭal, poet 67
Jayhān b. Mashjaᶜah al-Ḍabbī 178

Jayrūn, "first day of" 53
al-Jazīrah 162, 175 n. 597
al-Jibāl 220
Jisr Manbij, place 95
jizyah 96
John the Baptist 110
Jordan, military district 47, 49 n. 248, 50, 53, 59
(Banū) Judhām 49
(Banū) Juhaynah b. Zayd, mosque of 119
Jūkhā, place 130, 219
(Banū) Jumaḥ (Quraysh) 116 n. 460
jund 49 n. 243
Junzah, place 70
(Banū) Jurash (Ḥimyar) 63
(Banū) Jusham (Hamdān) 189 n. 632
(Banū) Jusham b. Saᶜd (Tamīm) 72, 178
Juzjān 71

K

Kaᶜb, slave 76
Kaᶜb b. ᶜAbdah al-Nahdī 100 n. 412
Kaᶜb b. Abī Kaᶜb al-Khathᶜamī 198, 204
Kaᶜb b. Maᶜdān al-Ashqarī, poet 76
(Banū) Kaᶜb b. Mālik b. Ḥanẓalah 30 n. 148
Kaᶜbah, 112 nn. 450 and 451, 184; damaged by fire xiii, 114; demolished and rebuilt 122–23, 176; in oaths 143, 210
(Banū) Kabīr (Azd) 125
Kābul 70
(Banū) al-Kalāᶜ (Ḥimyar) 63
(Banū) Kalb xv, 47–69
Karbalā' 109 n. 443. See also al-Ḥusayn b. ᶜAlī; al-Ṭaff
Karib b. Nimrān 125
Kārūn, river 175
Kathīr b. ᶜAmr al-Muzanī 147
Kaysān, Abū ᶜAmrah 219, 221
Khābūr, river 153

Khālid b. ᶜAbdallāh (al-Qasrī?),
    oratory of 213
Khālid b. Saᶜd b. Nufayl 84, 85,
    148, 159
Khālid b. Sumayr, *rāwī* 8
Khālid b. ᶜUrfuṭah, house of 199
Khālid b. Yazīd b. Muᶜāwiyah
    51–59, 65, 68, 69, 161
Khalīfah b. Warqā' 190
Khallād b. Yazīd al-Bāhilī, *rāwī* 35
kharāj 36 n. 180, 47 n. 233, 92,
    96, 130, 186
Khārijites (Khawārij) xii, 35–37, 38,
    40–45, 97–105, 114 n. 456,
    115, 164–75
(Banū) Khathᶜam 139 n. 511, 198 n.
    651, 204, 224
(Banū) Khaṭmah (Anṣār) 47 n. 231
Khayrah bt. Khufāf b. ᶜAmr 18
(Banū) Khindif 75
(Banū) al-Khiyār (Azd) 156
Khulayd, mawlā 207
Khurāsān 69, 167, 170, 176; and
    Ibn Khāzim 70–79, 123,
    177–81
Khuṭarniyah, place 105
(Banū) Khuzāᶜah 80 n. 368
Khuzaymah b. Naṣr al-ᶜAbsī 209,
    210, 211
Khwārazm 70
(Banū) Kilāb 198 n. 653
(Banū) Kinānah 84, 136, 150
(Banū) Kindah xv, 28, 38–40, 56,
    59 n. 283, 69, 118, 151
Kirmān 170, 172, 175
al-Kūfah, its governors 38–40,
    46–47, 123, 175, 176; the
    movement of the Penitents
    79–97, 124–31; and al-Mukhtār
    105–22, 182–225
al-Kunāsah, al-Kūfah 198, 200, 203,
    207, 213, 214
kunyah 5 n. 18
Kurayb b. Yazīd al-Ḥimyarī 134,
    152
Kurds 220
Kusayb 178

L

Lahāzim 25–26
(Banū) Lakhm 49
Laqafā (?), place 105
(Banū) Layth (Kinānah) 216

M

Maᶜadd xv
al-Madā' in 85, 87, 105, 130, 146,
    147, 153, 219
al-Madā'inī, see ᶜAlī b. Muḥammad
(Banū) Madhḥij 42 n. 203, 43 n.
    207, 193 n. 640, 198 n. 652,
    221, 223
al-Maftaḥ, place 175
Magians 170
Māh Afrīdhūn 30, 32
mahdī 93 n. 395, 120, 132, 192,
    194, 195
Maḥmiyah al-Ḥanafī 78
al-Māḥūz, sons of 102, 165
al-Malḥama (?), village or fortified
    place 179
Mālik b. Adham b. Muḥriz al-Bāhilī
    139
Mālik b. ᶜAmr al-Nahdī 197, 216
Mālik b. Dīnār 30
Mālik b. Hubayrah al-Sakūnī 56,
    57, 62, 68–69
Mālik b. Mismaᶜ al-Shaybānī 8–9,
    19, 24–28, 31, 34, 38 n. 187,
    39 n. 195, 41–45, 168
(Banū) Mālik b. Saᶜd 178
Mālik b. Yazīd b. Mālik b. Kaᶜb 60
(Banū) Maᶜn b. Mālik b. Fihr (Azd)
    28 n. 136
manṣūr, in battle cry 201, 204
Maᶜqil b. ᶜAbdallāh 123
maqṣūrah 32 n. 157
Marj Rāhiṭ, battle xi, 55–69
Marjānah, mother of ᶜUbaydallāh b.
    Ziyād 15; "son of," as
    derogatory name 8, 10, 11, 16,
    17, 40, 128

Marw al-Rūdh 71–74, 79, 178–79

Marwān b. al-Ḥakam, establishment of his caliphate 47–69; fears that his family will be too powerful 57; takes oath of allegiance for his sons 159; his death 160–61; sends expeditions 161–62, 175

Maslamah b. Muḥārib b. Salm b. Ziyād, *rāwī* 21, 28, 34, 70–71

Maṣqalah b. Hubayrah 207

Masʿūd b. ʿAmr al-Azdī 14, 16–22, 26–35, 40–45, 165

maʿṣūm 212

mawlā 8 n. 38, 46, 208, 219

al-Mawṣil, place 219

(Banū) Māzin b. Mālik (Tamīm) 38

Mecca 63, 155, 173, 174, 176; Umayyad siege of 1–6; Ibn al-Zubayr and the Khārijites 97–105; Ibn al-Zubayr and al-Mukhtār 109–17

Medina 50, 55; attacked from Syria xiii, 161–63; Ibn al-Zubayr's governors 48, 123, 175–76, 186; Umayyad army in 4–5

al-Milḥ, castle 179 n. 609, 180

minbar 11 n. 48

al-Miswar b. Makhramah 114

Muʿāwiyah b. Qurrah, *rāwī* 165

Muʿāwiyah II b. Yazīd, his caliphate 1–6; illness and death 5; succession arrangements 48–49, 160

Mudallij (or Mudlij) b. al-Miqdam (Miqdād?) al-Jurashī 60

(Banū) Muḍar 20, 24, 25, 27, 42, 44, 45, 156; quarrel with Rabīʿah in Khurāsān 71–79; Muḍar al-Ḥamrā' 137

al-Mufaḍḍal b. Muḥammad al-Ḍabbī, *rāwī* 72

al-Mughīrah b. Ḥabnā', poet 79

al-Mughīrah b. al-Muhallab b. Abī Ṣufrah 175

muhājir 6 n. 28

al-Muhallab b. Abī Ṣufrah xii, xv, 15 n. 61, 71–72, 164; his defeat of the Khārijites 167–75

Muḥammad b. ʿAbdallāh, the Prophet, *ḥadīth* of 176; see also *sunnah*

Muḥammad b. ʿAbdallāh b. Khāzim 79, 177, 178

Muḥammad b. ʿAbdallāh al-Kindī 151

Muḥammad b. Abī ʿUyaynah, *rāwī* 6, 16, 164, 165

Muḥammad b. ʿAlī, Ibn al-Ḥanafiyyah 93, 120, 190–92, 195–97

Muḥammad b. al-Ashʿath al-Kindī 38–40

Muḥammad b. ʿAzīz al-Kindī 177

Muḥammad b. Ḥafṣ, *rāwī* 27

Muḥammad b. Ḥurayth b. Sulaym 64

Muḥammad b. Kaʿb b. Qaraẓah 219

Muḥammad b. Marwān b. al-Ḥakam 175

Muḥammad b. Saʿd, 47–48, 54–55, 160–62

Muḥammad b. ʿUmar al-Wāqidī, 47–48, 54–55, 122–23, 160–62, 175–76

Muḥammad b. ʿUmayr b. ʿUṭārid 219

Muḥammad b. al-Zubayr 46, 164

(Banū) Muḥārib b. Khaṣafah 62

Muhill b. Khalīfah al-Ṭā'ī 134

al-Mujālid b. Saʿīd, *rāwī* 119

al-Mukhtār b. Abī ʿUbayd al-Thaqafī xii, 92–94, 105–22, 126, 153–55, 182–225

munāfiq, Ibn al-Zubayr, called 50, 51, 58

al-Mundhir b. Ḥassān b. Ḍirar al-Ḍabbī 218

al-Mundhir b. Qays al-Judhāmī 163

al-Mundhir b. al-Zubayr 114

Muqātil b. Mismaʿ al-Shaybānī 38

(Banū) Murād (Madhḥij) 106 n. 429, 206

Mūsā b. ᶜAbdallāh b. Khāzim 74
Mūsā b. ᶜĀmir al-ᶜAdawī, *rāwī* 217
Mūsā b. Ismāᶜīl, *rāwī* 6
Mūsā b. Yaᶜqūb, *rāwī* 54, 160
Muṣᶜab b. ᶜAbd al-Raḥmān b. ᶜAwf al-Zuhrī 114
Muṣᶜab b. Thābit 55
Muṣᶜab b. al-Zubayr, 64, 125, 160, 172, 175–76, 186, 187
al-Musayyab b. Najabah al-Fazārī 81–82, 95–96, 126, 133, 137–38, 142–46, 154
Muslim, name of a non-Arab 41
Muslim b. ᶜAbdallāh al-Ḍabbābī, *rāwī* 220–21
Muslim b. ᶜAmr al-Bāhilī 108
Muslim b. ᶜAqīl 105–7
Muslim b. Ubays 104–5, 165
Muslim b. ᶜUqbah al-Murrī xiii
Muslim b. Zaḥr al-Khawlānī, *rāwī* 152
al-Muthannā b. Mukharribah al-ᶜAbdī 89, 133, 147, 153, 183
Muzāḥim b. Ṭufayl 209
(Banū) Muzaynah 90, 127 n. 490, 152, 155, 179 n. 608; their houses in al-Kūfah 212
Muẓlim Sābāṭ 105

N

al-Naḍr b. Ṣāliḥ al-ᶜAbsī 105, 106, 214, 216, 219
Nāfiᶜ b. al-Azraq 45 n. 218, 46, 97–105, 164–65
Nāghiḍah 51, 52
(Banū) Nahd b. Zayd 197 n. 642, 203
(Banū) Nahshal (Tamīm) 179 n. 606
Nā'ilah bt. ᶜUmārah al-Kalbiyyah 63
Najadāt, Khārijites 102
Najdah b. ᶜĀmir 102
(Banū) Nājiyah b. Jarm 15, 16, 17
(Banū) Nakhaᶜ (Madhḥij) 42 n. 203, 197 n. 644
Nāshib b. al-Ḥashḥās, *rāwī* 30

Nātil b. Qays 50, 56, 63
Nawfal b. Musāḥiq b. ᶜAbdallāh b. Makhramah 213, 214
Nīsābūr 72, 179 n. 607
Nizār xv, 71–79
Nuᶜaym b. Hubayrah 207, 208, 222
Nūḥ b. Ḥabīb, transmitter of Ibn al-Kalbī 56
al-Nukhaylah, place 80, 86, 124, 125, 126, 129, 131
al-Nuᶜmān b. Abī Jaᶜd 205, 210
al-Nuᶜmān b. Bashīr al-Anṣārī 49, 56, 63
al-Nuᶜmān b. Ṣuhbān al-Rāsibī 20–23
Numayr b. Waᶜlah, *rāwī* 193

P

Palestine, military district 49, 50, 56, 64, 160
Palmyra 64–65
Penitents, see Tawwābūn
pilgrimage, see *ḥajj*, ᶜumrah
plague, see al-Jārif

Q

qabā', garment 33, 199, 214
(Banū) Qābiḍ b. Zayd 117 n. 465
Qabīṣah b. ᶜAbd al-Raḥmān al-Quḥāfī, *rāwī* 99
Qabīṣah b. Marwān, *rāwī* 18
al-Qadīm, street in al-Baṣrah 32
al-Qaflānī, *rāwī* 46
al-Qaᶜqāᶜ b. Shawr al-Dhuhlī 108
al-Qaᶜqāᶜ b. Suwayd al-Minqarī 200
al-Qarᶜā', place 117
Qarqīsiyā, place 63, 65, 137, 153
Qaṣr Asfād, place 76
Qaṣr Aws, in al-Baṣrah 71
qāṣṣ, quṣṣāṣ 145
Qaṭarī b. Fujāᶜah 166 n. 579
(Banū) Qayn b. Jasr 61, 161 n. 555

(Banū) Qays 29, 72 n. 338, 137 n.
    507, 139 nn. 509 and 510, 224;
    in al-Baṣrah after flight of Ibn
    Ziyād 40–47; support Ibn al-
    Zubayr in Syria 47–69
Qays b. al-Haytham al-Sulamī 6, 12,
    20–23
Qays b. Ṭahfah al-Nahdī 203, 204,
    222
(Banū) Qays b. Thaᶜlabah 25, 28 n.
    137, 44, 71, 73, 102
al-Qayyārah, place 134, 135
Qinnasrīn, place 49, 56, 63
al-Qubāᶜ, see al-Ḥārith b. ᶜAbdallāh
(Banū) Quḍāᶜah xv, 49 n. 246, 60,
    68–69
Qudāmah b. Abī ᶜĪsā b. Rabīᶜah al-
    Naṣrī 219
Qudāmah b. Mālik al-Jushamī 189,
    201
Qur'ān 42
(Banū) Quraysh xvi, 14, 15 n. 67,
    17, 24, 75 n. 350, 112; in Syria
    before Marj Rāhiṭ 47–69
qurrā' 196
Qurrah b. ᶜAmr b. Qays 35

R

al-Rabadhah, place 162–63
(Banū) Rabīᶜah xv–xvi, 165, 177;
    quarrel with Muḍar in al-Baṣrah
    24, 25; alliance with Azd in al-
    Baṣrah 27, 29; quarrel with
    Muḍar in Khurāsān 71–79
Rabīᶜah al-Ajdham al-Tamīmī 166
(Banū) Rabīᶜah b. Ḥanẓalah (Tamīm)
    79
Rabīᶜah b. al-Mukhāriq al-Ghanawī
    139, 144, 148
al-Raqqah, place 139, 140
Rāshid b. Iyās b. Muḍārib 198, 200,
    205–11, 222
Rawḥ b. Zinbāᶜ al-Judhāmī 49, 50,
    57
Rawwād al-Kaᶜbī, rāwī 34

al-Ribāb bt. al-Ashᶜath 222
Rifāᶜah b. Shaddād al-Bajalī 82, 129,
    138, 142, 145, 148, 150–55,
    183, 185
rug, indication of rank 60
al-Rūmiyyīn, lane in al-Kūfah 215,
    216
Ruwāᶜ bt. Abī ᶜIzzah al-Qābiḍī 126

S

Sāᶜ, place 141
al-Ṣaᶜb b. Zayd 46, 163, 164 n. 569
Saba'iyyah 208
al-Sabakhah, in al-Kūfah 199,
    203–4, 210–13
Sabrah b. Jārūd al-Hudhalī, rāwī 13
Sabrah b. Nakhf, rāwī 164
Saᶜd b. Ḥudhayfah b. al-Yamān
    85–89, 147, 153, 183, 219–20
Saᶜd b. Mujāhid al-Ṭā'ī, rāwī 134
Saᶜd b. Nimrān 123
Saᶜd (or Saᶜīd) b. Qarḥā al-Tamīmī
    38–40
(Banū) Saᶜd b. Zayd Manāt 72, 79,
    89, 129, 174 n. 594, 178
al-Sadūd, place 134
(Banū) Sadūs (Shaybān) 8–9
Safawān, in al-Baṣrah 170
Ṣafiyyah, mother of Ibn Khāzim 79,
    177
Ṣafiyyah, sister of al-Mukhtār 107
Sahlah bt. Sabrah b. ᶜAmr 125
Ṣaḥrā', of al-Kūfah 203
al-Sā'ib b. Mālik al-Ashᶜarī 185,
    187, 188, 196
Saᶜīd b. ᶜAmr b. Saᶜīd b. al-ᶜĀṣ 3,
    116
Saᶜīd b. Munqidh al-Hamdānī 159
    n. 548, 189, 201, 213, 218
Saᶜīd b. Qays al-Hamdānī, house of
    199
(Banū) Sāᶜidah (Khazraj) 162 n. 561
(Banū) Ṣakhr b. Minqar 34
(Banū) Saksak 59, 61
(Banū) Sakūn 56, 59, 118, 202

Salamah b. Dhu'ayb al-Riyāḥī 12,
     13, 30, 45
Salamah b. Kuhayl, *rāwī* 132
Salamah b. Marthad al-Qābiḍī 117
al-Ṣalatān al-ᶜAbdī, poet 172
Ṣāliḥ b. ᶜAbdallāh al-ᶜAbshamī, poet
     166 n. 579
(Banū) Salīṭ b. Yarbūᶜ 102
Sallām b. Abī Khayrah, *rāwī* 33
Salm b. al-Musayyab, house of, at
     al-Kūfah 105, 119
Salm b. Ziyād 69–72
al-Ṣalt b. Ḥurayth b. Jābir al-Ḥanafī
     27, 75 n. 349
Samarqand 70
sanctuary, the 2, 98, 109, 112, 115,
     122–23, 156, 176
Ṣandūdā', place 153
al-Ṣaqᶜab b. Zuhayr, *rāwī* 108, 110,
     185
Sarakhs, place 71
(Banū) Ṣarīm b. Muqāᶜis 101, 102,
     179 n. 606
Shabath b. Ribᶜī al-Tamīmī 97, 121,
     199, 203–8, 211–16
al-Shaᶜbī, see ᶜĀmir b. Sharāḥīl
Shabīb b. Yazīd, Khārijite 146
Shahrak, *rāwī* 6
(Banū) Shākir b. Rabīᶜah 183 n.
     617, 204 n. 672
Shamir b. Dhī Jawshan 198, 213
(Banū) Shamkh 158
Shammās b. Dithār al-ᶜUṭāridī 78,
     79, 177–79
Shaqīq b. Thawr al-Sadūsī 8–9, 19
Sharāḥīl b. ᶜAbd, father of al-Shaᶜbī
     197
Shaybān b. Ḥurayth al-Ḍabbī 206
Shīᶜah 79 n. 365; the Tawwābūn
     and al-Mukhtār 79–97; al-
     Mukhtār's arrival in al-Kūfah
     105–22; the events leading to
     ᶜAyn al-Wardah 124–59; al-
     Mukhtār's revolt in al-Kūfah
     182–225
(Banū) Shibām b. Asᶜad 189 n. 628,
     205

Shuᶜbah b. Ẓahir al-Nahshalī 179
Shumaykh al-ᶜUṭāridī 178
Shuraḥbīl b. Dhī al-Kalāᶜ 56, 139,
     143, 144, 152
Shurayḥ, *qāḍī* 123, 220–21
shurṭah 21 n. 97, 202
Ṣīhān b. ᶜAmr 183
Sijistān 70, 79, 179
Ṣilah b. Zuhayr al-Nahdī 220
Sillā wa-Sillabrā 168, 172, 175
Siᶜr b. Abī Siᶜr al-Ḥanafī 147,
     189–90, 206–8
sīrah (=*sunnah*) 187
al-Sirrī b. Kaᶜb al-Azdī 127, 134
Ṣufriyyah, Khārijites 101 n. 415
Sufyān b. al-Abrad al-Kalbī 52
Sufyān b. Layl 201
(Banū) Ṣuhayb, mawlās of Banū
     Jaḥdar 74–75
Ṣukhayr b. Ḥudhayfah al-Muzanī,
     qāṣṣ 127, 145, 152
(Banū) Sulaym (Qays) 16–17, 44,
     65–67, 206
Sulaymā, poetic ideal 225
Sulaymān b. ᶜAbdallāh b. al-Ḥārith
     23
Sulaymān b. Abī Rāshid, *rāwī* 82,
     85, 155
Sulaymān b. ᶜAmr b. Muḥṣin al-
     Azdī 156
Sulaymān b. Marthad 71–73, 79
Sulaymān b. Mujālid al-Ḍabbī 76
Sulaymān b. Ṣurad al-Khuzāᶜī and
     the beginning of the Tawwābūn
     80–97; in al-Kūfah when al-
     Mukhtār arrives 120–22; revolt
     of the Tawwābūn and his death
     124–46
Sumayyah, "son of," used
     derogatively of Ziyād 38
sunnah 33 n. 163, 99, 103; Sunnah
     of the Prophet 92, 100, 113,
     154, 191, 194, 217
Suwayd b. ᶜAbd al-Raḥmān al-
     Minqarī 129, 200, 202, 203,
     213

244   Index

Suwayd b. Manjūf b. Thawr al-
Sadūsī 19
Suwwār b. ᶜAbdallāh b. Saᶜīd al-
Jarmī 22
Syria 47–69, 160

T

al-Ṭabarī, Muḥammad b. Jarīr
xvi–xviii
al-Ṭaff 109, 142. See also al-Ḥusayn
b. ᶜAlī; Karbalā'
(Banū) Taghlib 143
al-Ṭā'if 111, 112
Takrīt 220
al-Ṭāliqān 71, 73
(Banū) Tamīm xv, xvi; in al-Baṣrah
25–37, 40–47, 165, 166, 168,
170; in al-Kūfah 38–40; in
Khurāsān 72–79, 177–81;
wolves of 30
(Banū) Tanūkh 61, 67
Tawwābūn xii, 80–97, 124–59, 162,
182–89
taxes, see *jizyah, kharāj*
(Banū) Taym (Quraysh) 43 n. 210,
45, 47 n. 232, 96, 164 n. 571
(Banū) Taym al-Lāt (Bakr) 26, 80 n.
370, 84
(Banū) Taym al-Lāt (Kalb) 67
(Banū) Ṭayyi' b. Udad 28 n. 137,
61, 67, 224
Thābit b. Qays b. al-Munqaᶜ al-
Nakhaᶜī 3
Thābit Quṭnah, poet 77
(Banū) Thaᶜlabah b. Yarbūᶜ 10
(Banū) Thaqīf 106 n. 434, 112
Thawr b. Maᶜn b. Yazīd al-Akhnas
al-Sulamī 53, 60, 66
al-Thawriyyūn, lane of, in al-Kūfah
213
(Banū) Thuᶜal (Ṭayyi') 28
Thubayth b. Marthad al-Qābiḍī 117,
126
Tihāmah 57, 69
al-Ṭufāwah, in al-Baṣrah 9

Ṭufayl b. Mirdās 178
al-Tunaynir, place 153
Turks 76–77

U

ᶜUbaydah b. Sufyān al-Muzanī 155
ᶜUbaydah b. al-Zubayr 123, 175–76
ᶜUbaydallāh b. ᶜAbdallāh al-Murrī
90
ᶜUbaydallāh b. al-Ḥurr, poet 43
ᶜUbaydallāh b. al-Māḥūz 166, 168,
171, 175
ᶜUbaydallāh b. ᶜUbaydallāh b.
Maᶜmar al-Taymī 45, 163–64
ᶜUbaydallāh b. Ziyād 89, 102;
attempts to maintain his
authority in Iraq 5–40; flees to
Syria 40, 42 n. 206; advises
Marwān 48–49, 54, 64–66; at
Marj Rāhiṭ 59, 62; at ᶜAyn al-
Wardah 127, 128, 130, 143,
144, 158, 162
ᶜUbaydallāh b. Ziyād b. Ẓabyān
168–70
(Banū) ᶜUdhrah (Quḍāᶜah) 64
(Banū) ᶜUlaym (Kalb) 60
ᶜUlayyah bt. Nājiyah al-Riyāḥī 31
ᶜUmar b. ᶜAbd al-Raḥmān b. al-
Ḥārith b. Hishām 185, 186
ᶜUmar b. ᶜAbdallāh b. Abī Rabīᶜah
162
ᶜUmar b. al-Khaṭṭāb 49, 100–1, 187
ᶜUmar b. Saᶜd b. Abī Waqqāṣ 39,
121, 128, 129
ᶜUmar b. Shabbah 5–9, 17–21,
35–37, 44–46, 70–79, 163–65
ᶜUmar b. ᶜUbaydallāh b. Maᶜmar al-
Taymī 43, 45, 46
ᶜUmārah, house of, in al-Kūfah 215
ᶜUmārah b. ᶜUqbah b. Abī Muᶜayṭ
107
ᶜUmayr b. Maᶜn al-Kātib, *rāwī*
10–11
(Banū) Umayyah, leaves Medina 5,
48, 50, 64; support for, in al-

Baṣrah 20, 23; in Syria with Marwān 47–69
Umm Abān 63
Umm Bisṭām 22
Umm Ghālib, poetic ideal 157
Umm Ḥakīm, poetic ideal 166
Umm Hāshim bt. Abī Hāshim b. ᶜUtbah b. Rabīᶜah 5
ᶜumrah, minor pilgrimage 45, 111; of Ramaḍān 117
(Banū) ᶜUqayl (Qays) 18
Usāmah b. Zayd b. Ḥārithah, house of, in al-Kūfah 199
(Banū) ᶜUṭārid b. ᶜAwf 78 n. 359, 178
ᶜUtaybah b. al-Nahhās 214
ᶜUthmān b. ᶜAffān 98–101, 187, 221
ᶜUthmān al-Battī 12
ᶜUthmān b. Bishr b. al-Muḥtafiz al-Muzanī 179
ᶜUthmān b. ᶜUbaydallāh b. Maᶜmar al-Taymī 164
ᶜUwayj al-Ṭā'ī, poet 69

W

(Banū) Wadīᶜah b. ᶜAmr 106 n. 432
Wāfid b. Khalīfah b. Asmā', poet 34
Wahb b. Ḥammād, rāwī 6, 8
Wahb b. Jarīr, rāwī 17, 18, 20, 35, 46, 163, 164, 165
(Banū) Wālibah (Azd) 208
al-Walīd b. Ghuḍayn al-Kinānī 124, 125, 150, 159 n. 547
al-Walīd b. ᶜUtbah b. Abī Sufyān 52
al-Wāqidī, see Muḥammad b. ᶜAlī
Wāqiṣah, place 108
Ward b. al-Falaq b. al-ᶜAnbarī 179
wazīr 93 n. 396, 120, 170, 192, 195, 204, 222

Y

(Banū) Yaḥmad b. ᶜAbdallāh 174
Yaḥyā b. Abī ᶜĪsā al-Azdī, rāwī 122, 184, 197, 199

Yaḥyā b. Hāni', rāwī 211
al-Yamāmah 102, 115
Yasāf b. Shurayḥ al-Yashkurī, rāwī 35
(Banū) Yashkur (Bakr) 25–26
Yazīd b. ᶜAbdallāh b. al-Shikhkhīr 46
Yazīd b. Abī al-Nims al-Ghassānī 52, 59
Yazīd b. Anas al-Asadī 183–224 passim
Yazīd b. Fahdah 32
Yazīd b. al-Ḥārith b. Yazīd al-Shaybānī Ibn Ruwaym, opposes ᶜUbaydallāh b. Ziyād in al-Kūfah 38–40; advises al-Khaṭmī 93, 97, 121, 184; fights against al-Mukhtār 198, 208, 211, 212, 214
Yazīd b. Ḥuṣayn b. Numayr 145
Yazīd I b. Muᶜāwiyah 53, 107–8, 161; death date 11, 89; news of death reaches Khurāsān and Mecca 70–71, 115–16; his dīn and his shīᶜah 50; succession arrangements 5; relationship with Ibn Ziyād 9–10
Yazīd b. Siyāh al-Uswārī 163
Yazīd b. Sumayr al-Jarmī 22
Yazīd b. Ziyād 70
Yemen (tribal group) xv, 20; support Umayyads in Syria 47–69; in Khurāsān 71
Yūnus b. Ḥabīb, rāwī 9–10, 14, 27
Yūsuf b. al-Ḥakam 163
Yūsuf b. Yazīd, rāwī 80, 137, 146, 169

Z

Zabrā', slave girl 31
Ẓabyān b. ᶜUmārah al-Tamīmī 89
Zadhān Farrūkh 36
Zahr b. Qays al-Juᶜfī 198, 202
Zā'idah, garden of, in al-Kūfah 204

Zā'idah b. Qudāmah b. Mas[c]ūd 106–8, 188, 189
al-Zard b. [c]Abdallāh al-Sa[c]dī 32
Zayd b. Bakr 159
(Banū) Zimmān b. Mālik 102
Zirbiyyā, slave 183
Ziyād b. [c]Amr al-[c]Atakī 41–42
Ziyād b. [c]Amr b. Mu[c]āwiyah al-[c]Uqaylī 59, 66
Ziyād b. Jiyal al-Abnawī, *rāwī* 2, 176
Ziyād (or Ziyādah) b. Khaṣafah al-Taymī 208
Zoroastrians, see Magians
(Banū) Zubayd (Madhḥij) 211
al-Zubayr b. al-[c]Awwām 58
al-Zubayr b. Khirrīt, *rāwī* 17, 20, 35
al-Zubayr b. al-Māḥūz 165, 169, 170

Zufar b. [c]Aqīl al-Fihrī 55
Zufar b. al-Ḥārith al-Kilābī, opposed to Marwān 49, 56, 63, 65, 67, 68; and the Penitents 137–41, 153
Zuhayr b. Dhu'ayb al-[c]Adawī 73, 76, 181
Zuhayr b. Ḥarb, *rāwī* 6, 8, 17–20, 35, 46, 163–65
Zuhayr b. Ḥayyān, see Zuhayr b. Dhu'ayb
Zuhayr b. Hunayd Abū al-Dhayyāl al-[c]Adawī, *rāwī*, cited by Abū [c]Ubaydah 24, 27, 30, 32; cited by al-Madā'inī 72, 74, 78, 79, 177, 178
Zuḥnah b. [c]Abdallāh 61–62
(Banū) Zuhrah (Quraysh) 39 n. 193, 114 nn. 456 and 457